LIFE
STORIES
OF THE
NICARAGUAN
REVOLUTION

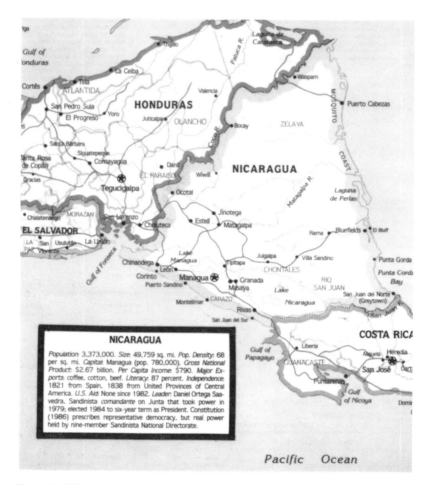

Gulf of
Honduras

Trujillo

Laguna de
Caratasca

Patuca R.

La Ceiba

Waspam

Cortés
Tela
ATLANTIDA

Valencia

MOSQUITO

Puerto Cabezas

San Pedro Sula
El Progreso
Yoro

HONDURAS

Juticalpa
OLANCHO

Bocay

ZELAYA

Santa Bárbara

Coco R.

Siguatepeque

Santa Rosa
de Copán
Comayagua

Danlí

NICARAGUA

COAST

Gracias

EL PARAISO
Wiwilí

Matagalpa R.

Laguna
de Perlas

Tegucigalpa

Ocotal

Jinotega

Chalatenango
MORAZAN
San Lorenzo

Estelí
Matagalpa

Rama
Bluefields
El Bluff

EL SALVADOR

Choluteca

LA
San
Usulután
La Unión

PAZ
Vincente

Juigalpa
Villa Sandino

Punta Gorda

Lake
Managua

Tipitapa

CHONTALES

Punta Gorda
Bay

Chinandega
León

Gulf of Fonseca

Corinto
Managua

Granada

RIO
SAN JUAN

Puerto Sandino

Masaya
Lake

San Juan del Norte
(Greytown)

Montelimar
CARAZO

Nicaragua

Rivas

San Juan R.

San Juan del Sur

COSTA RICA

NICARAGUA

Population: 3,373,000. *Size:* 49,759 sq. mi. *Pop. Density:* 68 per sq. mi. *Capital:* Managua (pop. 780,000). *Gross National Product:* $2.67 billion. *Per Capita Income:* $790. *Major Exports:* coffee, cotton, beef. *Literacy:* 87 percent. *Independence:* 1821 from Spain, 1838 from United Provinces of Central America. *U.S. Aid:* None since 1982. *Leader:* Daniel Ortega Saavedra, Sandinista *comandante* on Junta that took power in 1979; elected 1984 to six-year term as President. Constitution (1986) prescribes representative democracy, but real power held by nine-member Sandinista National Directorate.

Gulf of
Papagayo
Liberia

GUANACASTE

Alajuela
Heredia

San José
Cartago

Puntarenas

Gulf
of Nicoya

Domi

Pacific   Ocean

From the Wilson Quarterly, New Year's 1988. Copyright 1988
by The Woodrow Wilson International Center for Scholars.

LIFE STORIES

OF THE

NICARAGUAN REVOLUTION

Denis Lynn Daly Heyck

ROUTLEDGE
New York • London

Published in 1990 by

Routledge
An imprint of Routledge, Chapman and Hall, Inc.
29 West 35th Street
New York, NY 10001

Published in Great Britain by

Routledge
11 New Fetter Lane
London EC4P 4EE

Library of Congress Cataloging in Publication Data

Life stories of the Nicaraguan revolution / [edited by] Denis Lynn
    Daly Heyck.   p.   cm.
    ISBN 0-415-90210-X.—ISBN 0-415-90211-8 (pbk.)
    1. Nicaragua—History—Revolution, 1979—Personal narratives.
2. Nicaragua—Politics and government—1979– 3. Nicaragua—Social
conditions—1979– 4. Nicaragua—Economic conditions—1979–
5. Nicaragua—Biography. I. Heyck, Denis Lynn Daly.
F1528.L52   1989
972.8505′3—dc20   89-10319

British Library Cataloguing in Publication Data also available

Contents

III. Survivors' Lives

Acknowledgments

Life Stories is the work of a great many people, both here and in Nicaragua, to whom I am deeply grateful. First, I would like to thank everyone whose biography appears in this work for being so open and forthcoming. I owe a tremendous debt of thanks to those individuals in Nicaragua, some of them very good friends, who extended special courtesies to me in arranging introductions: Reinaldo and Gloria Téfel, Miriam Lazo, Comandante Leticia Herrera, Sr. JoEllen McCarthy, BVM, doña Violeta Chamorro, Msgr. Oswaldo Mondragón, Luis Flores and Luz Marina Flores.

In the U.S., first thanks go to my good friend Ted Copland who helped me understand Nicaragua and who encouraged me by his interest and example. For additional assistance, I am indebted to Carlos Tünnermann, Frank Safford, Jon Pattee, Mercedes Knight, Walter Urroz, Carol Pazera, Joan Costa, and to various members of the Ecumenical Refugee Council of Milwaukee, expecially Sallie and Bob Pettit.

For his most helpful reading of the manuscript, I am deeply grateful to Alexandrino Severino. My colleagues Kateri O'Shea and Sr. Mary Murphy, BVM, each contributed to this undertaking in important ways and deserve much recognition. Special thanks go to my editor, Jay Wilson, for his initiative and interest, and to Karen Sullivan and Michael Esposito, also of Routledge, for their careful and conscientious handling of the manuscript during the publication process.

Thanks to Hunter and Shannon Heyck, my children, for their interest in my work and their enthusiastic support throughout this project. My most profound thanks, however, must go to Bill Heyck who believed in the value of *Life Stories* at every step of the way. His numerous, insightful readings, and his consistently sound, objective advice kept me on course, and his vision enabled me always to keep sight of ultimate goals.

The inevitable errors, including those in translation, are my own.

Preface

The purpose of this work is to illuminate the experience of the Nicaraguan people during the Sandinista Revolution. This book is not an analysis of the clash of social or political forces, nor is it an apology for, or a denunciation of, the Sandinista government. Rather, it is a portrayal of the *human* dimension of the current conflict, of what it is like to be alive in Nicaragua today.

The United States, for better or worse, has chosen to intrude in the Nicaraguan revolutionary process. It follows from this fact that we North Americans ought to do what we can to understand the situation more fully, for the assertion of power carries heavy responsibility. Yet polls as late as August 1988 indicated that the majority of U. S. citizens surveyed thought that their government was supporting a democratic regime in Nicaragua against communist rebels.[1] Human lives hang in the balance of our ignorance.

There are many aspects to the Nicaraguan problem, some of which already have been widely discussed in books and articles, the global or strategic; the ideological; the economic; the historical; the military and the combat experience; the social and cultural, including the role of religion, the status of women, the place of poetry and the promotion of the arts, for example. This book seeks to communicate the *human* dimension; hence it allows the Nicaraguan people to tell their own story in a collective autobiography, a mosaic of hope and fear, triumph and tragedy.

Most of these life stories were collected in a series of conversations in Nicaragua during the summer and fall of 1987, while a few were gathered in the United States as early as 1986 and as late as 1988. Everyone with whom I spoke expressed him or herself freely. As will be obvious, no one felt any hesitation about talking candidly to me, just as they speak openly and with great animation to each other. Nicaragua is known as a nation of poets. Certainly nearly everyone I spoke with was highly verbal and articulate, whether they were formally educated or not.

I have chosen to group the stories that follow into three categories, political lives, religious lives, and survivors' lives, according to what emerged as the most basic value in each person's life, the wellspring of their thoughts and actions. Every life story has many themes. But the one that has strongest claim to authenticity is a person's *own* perception. What is presented here is each individual's sense of his or her story as it has unfolded during the Somoza regime and the Sandinista Revolution.

It was sometimes difficult to classify people as *either* religious *or* political, rather than *both/and*, for in Nicaragua today these categories are by no means mutually exclusive. On the contrary, they are overlapping designations that reflect the fluid and complex reality of life. What was *not* difficult was to recognize the power of these two overarching values for the majority of the people with whom I came into contact.

As for the third category, survivors, it is intended to suggest the large number of people for whom the entire revolutionary experience has meant principally dealing with a new situation not of their making, like it or not. Some are coping by leaving; others, by staying; some, by criticizing; some, by supporting; others, by accommodating themselves to the new order. The people in this group are, above all, realists. For them, political and religious considerations, though very important, take a back seat to practical matters.

Any revolution is the conjunction of thousands upon thousands of individual biographies. This was never more the case than in the Sandinista Revolution, because although not everyone was involved in the revolutionary effort or in the later opposition to it, everyone in Nicaragua *has* been deeply affected by it. Further, everyone is coping with this revolution and the factors, internal and external, that are complicating and altering it.

This process does not impinge upon the lives of politicians and soliders alone. Far from it. Rather, the Revolution affects daily the lives of grandmothers and schoolchildren, comandantes and campesinos, business professionals and woodcutters, poets and cleaning women, clergy and bartenders. This complex, hamstrung revolution forceably intrudes into every home, demanding adjustments to existing world views, raising questions about individual and collective identity, and complicating the everyday chores of family maintenance so they become almost impossible to complete. The biographies here included, like those of the Nicaraguan people as a whole, form a kind of multi-layered collage intended to convey the powerful impact of such a dramatically altered reality.

The strategy underlying this book is very simple: to let as many people as possible, high and low, rich and poor, young and old, powerful and powerless, tell their own story in their own words. What readers will find here is a diverse collection of autobiographies that together reflect the Nicaraguan experience from the inside, as it has been lived and felt. These histories express vividly the bitter divisions within families; the intense heat of the political and religious controversies now raging; the constant uprooting of the people as they move like bedouins from one place to another; the crushing psychological stress of living under conditions of great danger and scarcity. Yet, the stories also tell of the deep and abiding religious faith of the people; their astonishing courage and forbearance; their inventiveness in adversity; their generosity in sharing meager resources; and, above all, their overwhelming manifestations of the power of love and hope.

Introduction

These Nicaraguan experiences of revolution, like all others, have occurred in a specific cultural setting and in a particular historical moment. The individuals whose stories follow naturally refer to people and events that are part of their everyday consciousness but are foreign to us. Some remarks about this context are necessary to understand and appreciate more fully the biographies that follow.

Land and People

The renowned poet Ernesto Cardenal recently described Nicaragua in these idealized terms:

> Now we can already see the Masaya Volcano
> and its smoke
> rising from the crater, and the Masaya Lagoon, green,
> further on, the Apoyo Lagoon, very blue,
> the Sierra Mountains and the mountain ranges, sky-blue
> out to the distance, the truth is
> that our land is sky-blue,
> still further on, you see it? The Pacific,
> almost pure blue under the sky,
> the truth is that we're in heaven and don't know it. . . .

In fact, Nicaragua is a hot, wet, extremely poor and beautiful tropical country about the size of North Carolina. It is the largest (57,000 sq. mi.) and the most sparsely populated (2.9 million) of the Central American republics. Nicaragua is separated from Honduras to the north by the Río Coco and from Costa Rica to the south by the Río San Juan. It is a land of unpredictable natural phenomena that have periodically rained destruction in the form of earthquakes, volcanic eruptions, droughts, floods, and, in 1988, hurricanes. The varied topography of the country boasts lush tropical jungles, steamy coastal lowlands, high rugged mountains, majestic volcanoes, and brilliant blue lakes, the latter suggested by the indigenous name Nicaragua, meaning "place of much water." However, unrestrained use of pesticides and heedless deforestation have created serious environmental problems in what was once a natural tropical paradise.

Traditionally, Nicaragua has produced raw materials for export to Europe and the United States. Major industries are the cultivation of coffee, cotton, bananas, and sugarcane in the fertile western and northwestern portions, or Pacific region; cattle-raising and more coffee production in most of the central region; and gold mining, shellfish production, and the cutting of mahogany, ebony and other precious woods from the forests along the eastern, or Atlantic, coast. Lobstering and the extraction of coconut oil are the economic mainstays of the tiny Corn Islands in the Caribbean. The coastal economy typically has had no linkage with the rest of the country. Its forests and gold were exported to foreign markets in Europe and the United States. In fact, the isolation of the east coast is such that it is easier to get to the coastal city of Bluefields from New Orleans than from Managua.

The ethnic composition of the population is roughly 69 percent mestizo, or mixed Indian and Spanish descent; 17 percent Caucasian, made up mostly of pure Spanish and some European immigrant families, especially German; 9 percent black; and 5 percent Indian. As in most Latin American countries, the Spanish and other Europeans have long formed the upper classes. Of the ethnic minorities, the Miskitu are the largest (67,000), followed by the Afro-Caribbeans (26,000), the Sumu (5,000), the Afro-Amerindian Garífuna (1,500), and the Rama Indians (600).[2] These minority groups traditionally have had more to do with the English and North Americans than with other Nicaraguans, and they have held on to their ethnic traditions and sense of separateness. The mestizo side of the country, for its part, has evolved in ignorance of the Caribbean peoples and their ways. The demographics of Nicaragua's ethnic groups are noticeably skewed. About 90 percent of the population, the mestizos and Caucasians, live on the Pacific side of the country, while only about 10 percent, the blacks and the Indians, spread themselves very thinly along the Atlantic Coast.

Spanish is the official language of Nicaragua, but English is widely spoken among the black population on the Caribbean side, as is Garífuna, the dialect of the Black Caribs, while the dominant Indian dialects are Miskitu, Sumu, and Rama.

The vast majority of Nicaraguans are Roman Catholic, about 90 percent, although evangelical Protestant groups are rapidly gaining converts throughout the country. Along the Atlantic Coast, the Moravian and the Anglican churches have historically been very strong. Wherever they live, however, Nicaraguans are a profoundly religious people. It is not an exaggeration to say that nearly everyone, at some time in their lives, has had an important engagement with religion. Some have fallen away because of a negative encounter, while others have become religious revolutionaries, and still others have become defenders of the traditional church; but hardly anyone has escaped the experience.

This observation may seem unusual to many North Americans, because while we can readily appreciate economic, historical, and cultural particularities, we cannot so easily identify with a spiritual difference that goes beyond these structures to define basic world views. The fact is that in Nicaragua religion is an integral part of people's daily lives, from church-sponsored social activities to the sacraments themselves, and not just something that happens in church on Sunday. Nicaraguans enjoy a remarkably intimate, personal relationship with Jesus, the Virgin Mary, and all the saints, whom the faithful address with great familiarity and affection in their festivals and prayers.

Nearly every day some village in Nicaragua holds a procession in honor of its patron saint. Such religious festivals focus the social life for the entire village. It is here that people meet, celebrate, forget their troubles, renew relationships, and feel one with their community. It is not for nothing that the church occupies a central spot in the town square. The largest and most festive celebration of the year is La Purísima, the feast of the Immaculate Conception of Mary. It is celebrated with fireworks, flares, explosions, floats, dancing in the streets, and gift-giving as costumed youngsters go in search of treats and candy. The veneration of Mary, mother of Christ, is an integral part of the Nicaraguans' popular Catholicism. Theirs is a belief system rooted in the experience of the campesino, for whom Mary is the one who understands all pain, having endured the loss of her son. The strength of their religious beliefs has been a principal source of the stoic persistence and the victory over despair that have characterized the Nicaraguan people in their long history of struggle.

Officially, the population of Nicaragua is classified as about 60 percent urban, though constant migration both to and from urban areas, and recent massive government relocation efforts have made any authoritative "urban" designation impossible. In any event, *culturally* Nicaragua is a country of campesinos, wherever they may at present reside. The capital city of Managua and the traditional rivals León and Granada are the main centers of political and cultural leadership in the country.

Managua, home now to roughly one-third of the country's population, has swelled to bursting, as unplanned for and unwelcome migrants, nearly all of them poor, continue to arrive in droves. The city is grossly incapable of accommodating its burgeoning population, now about one million, as is clearly seen in the hastily erected, ephemeral and ever-present wooden shanties, and in the pirated power lines, whose overload accounts for frequent blackouts. Most of the newer residents are campesinos who were either evicted during the land-grabbing of the Somoza elite beginning in the 1950s, uprooted by the earthquake in 1972, or made homeless by the upheavals of the 1979 revolution and the subsequent contra war. The city itself is a bizarre monument to the forces of natural and human destruction. With its gutted buildings, vacant lots, and piles of rubble, Managua is a silent reminder of the earthquake and of Tachito Somoza's corruption in siphoning off international funds intended for rebuilding and relief.

Nicaraguan History to 1936

Beginning in 1520 when the Spanish pushed south from Mexico to conquer Central America and to found in 1524 the colonial cities of León and Granada, Nicaragua's history has been one of exploitation of people and natural resources by imperial powers, Spain, England, the United States, and by local elites. The other side of the coin has been the story of the Nicaraguans' recurring struggle to regain or establish local autonomy. Nicaragua's importance on the world stage may be measured by the value to others of its strategic location and natural treasures. The most attractive feature has been the country's potential as a site for a transoceanic waterway, which was for most of the nineteenth century the focus of U.S. interest. Even after Panama was selected as the canal site, the U.S. jealously guarded Nicaragua from other powers eager to carve out a canal of their own. As for strategic considerations, these became more important as the U.S. had more commercial interests to protect in the area, including the Panama Canal, and as the cold war and rivalry between the superpowers has intensified in recent years.

A member of the Central American Federation, which declared independence from Spain in 1821, Nicaragua did not become an autonomous republic until 1838. This autonomy was short-lived however, for in 1855 the filibusterer William Walker, a North American adventurer invited to Nicaragua to defend the liberals of León against the conservatives of Granada, declared himself president of Nicaragua, reintroduced slavery, decreed English as the national language, and managed to hold on for two full years before being deposed. Meanwhile, what little economic development occurred was directed by entrepreneur Cornelius Vanderbilt, who operated a lucrative steamship line for transporting California-bound goods and people across the Nicaraguan short-cut, and who envisioned a Nicaraguan paradise for private capitalists investing in transportation and extractive industries.

As the roles of Walker and Vanderbilt demonstrate, Nicaragua's history from the 1820s on can hardly be considered without frequent reference to the United States. Beginning with the Monroe Doctrine in 1823, the U.S. challenged British preeminence in the region and, by 1900, effectively controlled Nicaraguan political and economic life. Thus, Walker and Vanderbilt represent not isolated examples but the dominant pattern of U.S.-Nicaraguan relations—the combination of the stick and the dollar to secure the strategic and commercial interests of the "natural protector" of Central America.

Such a policy was not to go unchallenged, however, for many Nicaraguan leaders have resisted the roughshod treatment by their neighbors to the north. The first of these was the strongly nationalist dictator José Santos Zelaya, who came to power in 1893 determined to develop his backward country by whatever means necessary and to promote a Central American Federation with himself at its head. Ruthless and shrewd in his drive to modernize Nicaragua, Zelaya's ambition and nationalism ran head on into North American dreams of manifest destiny, and U.S. troops were sent to overthrow him in 1909. This was the first occupation of Nicaragua by U.S. Marines, who returned in 1912 to quell an uprising by the liberal Benjamin Zeledón against a U.S.-backed conservative government, and who remained until 1925 to keep order.

Order was fleeting, however, and the marines returned again in 1926 to "mediate" in a civil war between the United States' friend Emiliano Chamorro and deposed Vice-President Juan B. Sacasa, who was supported by the army under General José María Moncada. This time the marines stayed until 1933, training a native National Guard as a more efficient, less costly , and less unpopular (in the U.S.) way to maintain calm than sending U.S. forces, and to serve as a bulwark against the "bolshevik" influence from Nicaragua's revolutionary neighbor to the north, Mexico. Twenty years of military occupation were enough to install baseball as the national sport of Nicaragua, but not enough to extinguish completely the embers of nationalist sentiment, for one of Gen. Moncada's officers refused to lay down his arms, Augusto César Sandino.[3]

Though Moncada became president in 1928, followed by Juan Sacasa in 1932 in U.S.-sponsored elections, both men faded in importance beside the diminutive guerrilla leader Sandino, who swore never to cease fighting until the last marine had left his homeland. His rallying cry, "*Patria libre o morir*," "Free homeland or death," is still the motto of the Sandinistas today. In 1927, the U.S. found itself involved in the first guerrilla war in Latin America. Sandino took to the rugged mountains with a band of about 400 followers, where despite the 4,000 marines that President Coolidge sent after him, and despite savage aerial bombings, he fought the marines *and* the National Guard to a standstill. Sandino eluded and confounded his pursuers for six years, earning for himself the status of hero in the eyes of Latin Americans from Mexico to Argentina. Though the marines could never find *him*, Sandino knew *their* locations; he took pride in getting close enough to enemy encampments to take photographs, which he then sent on to marine headquarters with mocking messages.

Sandino was no campesino. He was raised in a wealthy home in an environment of books and classical music. As a young man, he worked for Standard Fruit and U.S. mining companies in various Central American countries and developed an anti-imperialist spirit as a result of the experience. He saw himself as the agent of a new Nicaragua, free of foreign domination, which he vowed to achieve. He was adored by the peasant population, who composed songs and poems in his honor, and who warmly received his troops, generously offering them food, lodging, and protection. Sandino seems genuinely to have respected the rights of the common people and required his followers to do likewise.

In contrast, the local populations offered no help at all to the marines, partly because the ordinary Nicaraguans were loyal to Sandino, partly because the overwhelming presence of so many invaders increased anti-Yankee resentment, and partly because of the contempt with which the marines regarded the campesinos. Repeated reports of marine atrocities, torture, rape, maiming and unchecked depredations upon the civilian population began to filter back to the U.S. public. Though perhaps exaggerated, these reports reflected a basic truth.

These reports could neither be ignored nor explained away, and the U.S. war against Sandino became very unpopular at home, spurring President Hoover to speed up the replacement of U.S. Marines with a native National Guard. The right kind of National Guard would take the heat off the U.S. while also protecting its interests. The careful selection of the enthusiastically pro-U.S. Anastasio (Tacho) Somoza to head the Guard, and the naming of officers from elite families partial to the status quo, assured that the Guard, while appearing to be merely a national peace-keeping institution, would actually function as the military guarantor of U.S. interests in Nicaragua, a kind of wolf in another wolf's clothing.[4]

While this process was occurring, Sandino continued fighting until the last marine left in 1933. Then, as he had promised, he put down his arms, entered Managua to a hero's welcome, and began to work amicably with the government of Sacasa. Somoza, however, was the real power, and he wanted Sandino out of the way. Sandino was promised amnesty, but he was the victim of a double-cross. Somoza's men picked him up as he left a dinner at the National Palace, took him to an empty field, and machine-gunned him to death.

The Somoza Dynasty (1936-1979)

Sandino was murdered in 1934, less than a year after the inauguration of President Franklin D. Roosevelt and his Good Neighbor Policy. When F.D.R. was informed by his advisors that Somoza was a "sonofabitch," the president reportedly responded, "Yes, but he's *our* sonofabitch," reaffirming once more U.S. priorities in Nicaragua. Somoza became president in name as well as in fact in 1936 after a coup against Sacasa, thereby ushering in the longest and most corrupt tyranny, 43 years, in Latin American history.

A former used-car salesman in Philadelphia who often preferred American slang to Spanish, Anastasio "Tacho" Somoza García, also known as "El Yanqui" for his admiration of the United States, secured entry into his country's elite through marriage to the niece of President Sacasa. But it was his blessing by the U.S. that granted him undisputed control of the National Guard, the indispensable pillar of his reign. The highest offices of the Guard were always kept within the family. This total control allowed

Somoza to run the country like a medieval fief, enriching himself beyond the dreams of avarice, *"Nicaragua es mi finca,"* "Nicaragua is my farm," he was fond of saying.

The Somoza dynasty's power depended on the support of the U.S. and the unwavering loyalty of the National Guard. Members were recruited, not drafted, from poor rural areas where opportunities were few, the illiteracy rate among the rank-and-file was over 50 percent, while the officers tended to come from the middle and lower-middle strata. Commissions were often passed from father to son, for membership brought bountiful benefits if one demonstrated loyalty to the Somozas: rapid advancement and a share in the institutionalized graft. In addition, separate schools, medical facilities, shopping and residential areas numbered among the perquisites set aside for Guard members and their families.

The Guard was universally despised by the populace for its corruption and cruelty. Despite the best efforts of U.S. advisors and many years of training, the Guard never developed a professional attitude. Rather, it always remained the personal instrument of the Somozas' will. Through a twisted code of loyalty expressed in acts of intimidation, extortion, torture, and murder, the Guard provided the muscle to back up the complex network of relationships and favors that extended into the farthest reaches of the commercial and political arenas as well. A combination of obligations and rewards made key elements in the military, civilian, business, and government sectors completely beholden to the Somozas, to the extent that not only their well-being but their very *fate* depended on the family's fortunes. And these fortunes, for a surprising number of years, soared.

When the first Somoza took power in 1936 he owned one dilapidated coffee plantation. By 1978 however, through the systematic elimination of competition and the use of government funds and foreign loans as sources of personal enrichment, the family's wealth rose to an estimated $500 million. Foreign holdings included shares in U.S. Steel and real estate in Florida and California, among other places. In Nicaragua and other Central American countries, the Somozas owned vast agricultural estates, including roughly 30 percent of the arable land in Nicaragua; industrial enterprises, such as cement production and textiles; construction materials; processing industries in dairy, meatpacking, fishing, and refining; communications enterprises, such as newspapers, radio stations, and the country's only TV station; transportation industries, including airlines, shipping, and ports; these were only some of the items that swelled the family's bank accounts.[5]

From 1936 until his assassination in 1956 by the poet Rigoberto Pérez López, Anastasio Somoza ruled supreme because the Guard was available to crush revolts, the U.S. unreservedly backed his regime, the bourgeois opposition was either silenced, bought off, or coopted by sham elections, and the populace was unorganized and intimidated. On the old man's death, the elder, more clever son Luis assumed the presidency (1956-67), and the younger, more ruthless son Anastasio (Tachito) became head of the Guard. After the assassination, thousands of suspected dissidents were summarily rounded up, jailed, and tortured. During the next several years, numerous plots against the dictator were brutally squashed, and the ill-fated invasion of Olama y Mollejones led by rebel patriots in 1959 was defeated as easily as swatting a *zancudo*, or mosquito, Somoza's name for minor political annoyances.

Upon Luis's death from a heart attack in 1967, brother Tachito, a West Point graduate, assumed the presidency. He had less interest than the two Somozas before him in retaining the fiction of elections and opposition parties. Thus, repression under Tachito was brutal from the start. Illegal financial transactions including extortion, racketeering, prostitution, drug dealing, and other corrupt activities of the Guard also increased markedly under Tachito. He ruled Nicaragua like a Mafia "family" godfather.

The dictator's disregard for the populace as a whole was absolute and abundantly clear. While Tachito and his North American mistress dined on imported wines and gave elegant parties for the 1 percent of the population that controlled over 50 percent of the country's land, the vast majority of Nicaraguans lived in conditions of abject poverty and disease. Illiteracy among the rural population stood at about 90 percent, the leading cause of death was intestinal parasites, over 50 percent of the children were malnour-ished, and Nicaragua had the lowest life expectancy of any Central American country.[6] It is no surprise that during Tachito's tenure, Nicaragua was, after Haiti, the poorest country in the Western Hemisphere.

Meanwhile, significant economic changes with consequences beyond even Somoza's control were making life more miserable for the average person, creating tensions between the government and the middle sectors, and beginning to erode the caudillo's personal power base.

During the 1960s and 1970s, the agricultural population declined seri-ously, accelerating a pattern begun in the mid 1950s with the increasing concentration of coffee and cotton estates in the hands of a few oligarchs, and with the rapid mechanization of agriculture. Displaced peasants moved to towns and cities, but they could not find places in Nicaragua's industries, which were nascent at best. During the 1960s the Alliance for Progress granted over $50 million in loans to diversify agriculture, and the Inter-American Development Bank did likewise. These loans, however, went to benefit the agricultural enterprises of the oligarchy, who were evicting farmers from their fields and purchasing mechanical cotton-pickers in a drive to build up cotton production for export. Unfortunately, this short-sighted move continued the old problem of putting too many eggs in one basket; it made the economy *less* diversified and *more* dependent on fluctuations in world prices, which entered a period of decline in the 1960s and 1970s.

Further, the environmental consequences of this shift in agricultural emphasis have been disastrous. Deforestation and the abuse of pesticides are the gravest ecological problems caused by Somoza's arrangements with multinational corporations. Deforestation has caused widespread soil erosion, dust storms, mudslides and flooding, particularly along the northeastern coast where, for a small fee to the Somozas, North American timber companies for many years were allowed to strip the area of coastal pines without having to reforest at all. Meanwhile, in the central portion, cattle-raising began to encroach upon neighboring rain forests, until by the 1970s Nicaragua had lost 30 percent of this delicate ecosystem, leaving people to ponder how so much could be destroyed so fast.

The expansion of cotton production in the 1950s and the growth of the cattle industry in the 1960s pushed peasants from lands they had tilled for years. Displaced persons moved to the rain forests, which they would clear in order to farm, soon causing erosion and exhausting the poor soil, at which point families would pull up stakes again, move further into the forest and repeat the cycle.

Meanwhile, in a drive to modernize, mechanize and increase cotton production, Somoza gave incentives to companies to experiment with pesticides in Nicaragua. Unable to resist such an invitation, the German company Bayer tried deadly pesticides, over twelve million pounds of methyl parathion in 1951 alone, resulting in death and illness among field workers in the area of León. The indiscriminate use of toxic substances continued for over two decades. As these entered the water table and the food chain, they caused more illnesses, but still their use was encouraged. By the 1970s, Nicaragua was a world leader in the use of DDT, a substance banned for years in many countries, including the United States. A study carried out in León in 1977 determined that the breast milk of mothers there contained 45 times the danger levels of DDT as set by the World Health Organization.[7]

Tachito's economic and ecological policies, disastrous and inhuman though they were, paled beside his response to the most significant event of his tenure, the earthquake of 1972. The quake devastated the center of Managua, leaving up to 20,000 dead and 120,000 homeless, destroying 75 percent of the city's housing and 90 percent of its commercial base. Tachito's contempt for human suffering and his insatiable greed soon became all too clear. Millions of viewers worldwide watched their TV screens in dismay as the dictator's cronies and Guard officers sold desperately-needed relief supplies, such as blankets, cots, and medicines from the Red Cross, on the black market. Guard members looted freely, abandoning their duty to keep order in the face of the disaster. The U.S. dispatched

600 marines to Managua to restore calm and control pillaging, and began its unsuccessful search for a substitute for Somoza.

Tachito personally exploited the earthquake to expand his already bloated financial kingdom, profiteering through his construction companies from the $78 million in Agency for International Development (AID) funds and the $54 million from the Inter-American Development Bank (IDB) that were earmarked for reconstruction. Further, Somoza's flagrant monopoly of funds came on the heels of a two-year drought, increased inflation, and unemployment for urban workers. Class tensions heightened sharply as workers and their families felt viscerally the combination of these factors, and as the depth of corruption of the system was exposed for all to see. Even those members of the bourgeoisie who had heretofore preferred to close their eyes and do business as usual now had to stand up and be counted. This pivotal opportunity was not lost on the tiny band of Sandinista revolutionaries out in the wilderness, struggling to overcome their isolation and to gain recognition as a force to be reckoned with. The Sandinista National Liberation Front, or FSLN, began in earnest to cultivate contacts with urban workers, students, health personnel, teachers, and parish groups in order to establish bases among the populace.

The Church in the Crucible

An important factor that came into play in a significant way at about the same time was the growing separation of the Catholic church from the regime. As a result of the emphasis on social justice set by the Second Vatican Council (1962–65), and of the "preferential option for the poor" sanctioned by the Latin American Episcopal Conference of 1968 in Medellín, the Catholic church in Nicaragua began gradually to dissociate itself from its previous support of the dictatorship. By 1968, Christian base communities, local study groups whose members seek to relate the Gospel message to their own lives, began forming in parish communities. Clergy also began training lay "delegates of the word," to read Scripture and lead Bible study sessions in the absence of religious personnel. Throughout 1972, the Catholic church began seriously to address itself to the needs of the people, sending pastoral teams of priests, nuns, and lay persons to the remotest corners of the country in an effort to learn the needs of the people and to make the church more responsive to them.

Such bold steps led to the creation of the so-called "popular church" favored by advocates of liberation theology. The social direction taken by many priests and nuns grew into a religious and political consciousness-raising on their part and on the part of the poor. This orientation was harshly criticized by conservative elements in the church and in Nicaraguan society as subversive and even communistic. Many members of the

Catholic church hierarchy and of the middle sectors of society claimed that the popular church undermined the discipline and authority of the traditional church and of traditional social arrangements as well. After the earthquake, the Catholic churches not only became distribution centers for food and medicine, but also grass-roots organizations of political resistance and close collaborators of the FSLN. It is important to understand then, that from the early 1970s, the FSLN and the socially oriented wing of the Nicaraguan Catholic church worked together in a broad revolutionary movement.

The Opposition Grows

In the wake of widespread unrest following the earthquake, the government cracked down on criticism, whether it came from unemployed laborers, displaced farmers now reduced to squatter status, increasingly vocal student groups, opposition leader Pedro Joaquín Chamorro's newspaper *La Prensa*, or the fledgling guerrilla band of the Sandinistas. Though things looked bad for the regime, both Tachito and his CIA advisors regarded these various groups as no match for the intensely loyal 7,500-man National Guard, well-armed and well-drilled as they were in the latest antiriot techniques.

Meanwhile, political opposition became more organized. The Democratic Union of Liberation (UDEL) was formed in 1974 by Pedro Joaquín Chamorro as a democratic opposition party that included both conservatives and socialists in its ranks. It was a last-ditch effort to arrive at a political rather than a violent solution for the country. No one knows if UDEL might have gained in strength, because another more dramatic event stole the spotlight and provoked draconian measures of repression from the government.

On December 27, 1974, an FSLN commando group carried out a daring raid on a Christmas party at the house of "Chema" Castillo Quant, a leading Somocista, and took a dozen members of Somoza's inner circle prisoner. The commandos demanded and received ransom money, publication of their communique, and release of 14 FSLN prisoners, including Daniel Ortega, who had been in jail since 1967. After the raid, Somoza created the EEBI, an elite counterinsurgency unit composed of youths trained to kill on command, and he hired mercenaries with experience in guerrilla warfare. He declared martial law and "trial" by military tribunals in a reign of terror that resulted in the death of several thousand peasants, and, inevitably, further radicalized the people in support of the FSLN.

Somoza's Guard now had to put down student riots, labor union protests, work stoppages, general strikes supported by prominent businessmen, mothers' demonstrations, and marches by religious and neighborhood groups. Still, the unrest grew.

In October 1977, the opposition "group of twelve" formed. These were not Sandinistas but highly respected intellectuals and business and professional leaders who were the most radical elements of the bourgeoisie. They had come to accept that armed struggle was the only way to remove Somoza, and they believed that the FSLN was the only group with the military organization to succeed. They threw their support behind the so-called "tercerista" faction of the FSLN, a faction that espoused political pluralism and a democratic constitution.

The Sandinistas

The Sandinista National Liberation Front had been founded in 1961 by Carlos Fonseca, Silvio Mayorga, and Tomás Borge, who is today the sole surviving founder. The FSLN was created as an anti-imperialist, pro-nationalist guerrilla group. It was inspired by Sandino and by the example of Cuba, as well as by the charismatic figure of "Che" Guevara, and dedicated to the recovery of the national patrimony.

The principal Sandinista theme was, and is, autonomy. This theme has strong marxist, nationalist, and Christian components that are sometimes in conflict, but that on the whole are seen as contributing to the objective of national self-determination. From its inception, the FSLN was radical and revolutionary; its founding members foresaw a refashioned society in which the wealth was equitably redistributed and in which social justice reigned. The founders of the FSLN were convinced, like their mentor Sandino, that armed struggle was the only way to achieve their goal.

Their first task, therefore, was the formation of a guerrilla army composed of campesinos. Between 1962 and 1967, the FSLN worked toward that end. They suffered a number of military setbacks along the way, including the serious military defeat but important moral victory at Pancasán in 1967. A series of losses in these early years caused FSLN members to take stock of their situation and to recognize the need to build a political base in the cities and a long-range strategy for the country as a whole.

Two groups emerged from the post-1967 self-study but, unfortunately, they became bitter rival factions: the Protracted People's War (GPP), and the Proletarian Tendency. The former stressed the strategic significance of the countryside and the military importance of the peasant army, while the latter maintained the primacy of political work among the urban proletariat as the way to attain a broader base of support and eventual victory.

By 1976, the split threatened the very existence of the FSLN. Carlos Fonseca, the acknowledged hero of the FSLN, and Eduardo Contreras, a fellow member of the National Directorate, returned to Nicaragua from their base of operations in Honduras to try to resolve the division. However, both were killed in combat with the Guard, and Tomás Borge, a representative of the GPP, was taken prisoner.

At this point, a third element in the Sandinista movement, the terceristas, acknowledged the importance of both factions and put forward their own strategy. The terceristas were pragmatists. They called for a series of coordinated military attacks which would then, they hoped, spark a popular insurrection. This was a critical juncture for the FSLN, because by 1976, the end of Somoza's Operation Aguila VI against the insurgents, the FSLN was reduced to only a few dozen members. By 1977, all three tendencies amounted to no more than 200 people. Though there were thousands of sympathizers, there were very few members. Thus, not only did the terceristas unify the Front, healing the life-threatening split, but they also won the support of "the twelve," whose adherence was crucial in attracting a broader political base and wider acceptability for the FSLN among the middle and professional sectors.

The Final Assault

The event that precipitated the final assault was the assassination on January 19, 1978, of Pedro Joaquín Chamorro, murdered on the orders of Anastasio Somoza Portocarrero, Tachito's son. Chamorro had long been much more than a mere *zancudo* to Somoza, and it was beginning to look as though opposition would unite behind him. Further, Chamorro's recent exposé in *La Prensa* of the Somozas' shocking profiteering from a blood plasma center, called the house of vampires by the people, had angered the dictator. Chamorro had been a principal hope for a democratic future, and he was by far the most popular of all Somoza's opponents. His assassination sparked the largest mass protest in Nicaraguan history. An estimated 120,000 people spilled onto the streets of Managua during his funeral procession, which was followed by a massive *paro cívico*, or work stoppage. This was the first mobilization of the urban population in which both workers and the bourgeoisie participated jointly, lasting from January 24 to February 6.

FSLN uprisings followed in Rivas and Granada, and reached their most dramatic point in the insurrection of the Monimbó Indian community of Masaya, which claimed, among many others, the life of Camilo Ortega, Daniel Ortega's younger brother. The rebels, armed with rifles, homemade knives, rocks, and pots of boiling water, held out against the Guards' artillery, armored cars, tanks, and aerial bombings for nearly a week before succumbing in a bloody defeat.

Still, other opposition leaders continued to seek a political solution. In

March 1978, millionaire industrialist Alfonso Robelo formed the National Democratic Movement (MDN), which was replaced in May 1978 by the Broad Opposition Front (FAO), with a wider base of support. However, the time for political efforts was past, and the guerrilla band that at its lowest ebb had only a handful of members now embodied the hopes of nearly 3 million people. In July 1978, Somoza, still confident that he would remain supreme, bowed to international pressure and allowed the twelve to return from exile. He must have had second thoughts when tens of thousands of cheering Nicaraguans greeted the patriots at the airport.

On August 22, 1978, the terceristas carried out the dramatic takeover of the National Palace, capturing more than 500 members of the elite, including many of Somoza's relatives. The commandos, led by the charismatic Edén Pastora, demanded 5 million dollars, publication of a FSLN communique, and the release of Tomás Borge and 82 other FSLN members. They left for Panama with a hero's send-off.

In September 1978, FSLN attacks in Managua, León, Estelí, Chinandega, Masaya, and other towns sparked a generalized uprising of the people, as the terceristas had anticipated. Somoza retaliated by ordering bombing attacks on his own cities. This bloody tactic apparently was adopted by Somoza as a way to spare the Guard, who surrounded the cities, called in the airstrikes, and then entered in search of survivors. The Frente's forces were compelled to withdraw from the towns, with long columns of civilians fleeing with them, for staying behind meant certain torture and death. The Guard were told to take no prisoners, and they systematically murdered all boys over the age of 12 whom they could capture. The Catholic church, represented by Bishop Miguel Obando y Bravo, vigorously protested the murder of over 6,000 peasants, and, finally, publically broke with the dictatorship.

The FSLN continued working through popular organizations, 22 of which were under the umbrella structure of the United People's Movement (MPU), formed in July 1978. In February 1979, the National Patriotic Front (FPN) was created to bring together the MPU, the "group of twelve," the trade unions, and all other opposition groups. In addition to being the most effective of all the political organizations, the FSLN was also, in a sense, the army of the FPN. This was the final political front, and it included virtually everyone except the Guard. Thus, Somoza was reduced to total dependence on his National Guard.[8]

The final offensive by the FSLN was launched in May and June 1979, in a number of areas at once: in El Jícaro, Estelí and Jinotega to the north; El Naranjo, Peñas Blanca, Sapoa to the south; Masaya, Granada, and Carazo to the west. The numerous coordinated attacks forced the Guard, now swollen to 25,000 members, to spread itself thinly, and, at that point, the end was in sight.

In early June, a nationwide strike paralyzed all activity in the country; less than two weeks later a provisional government was set up in San José, Costa Rica. It included Sergio Ramírez from the twelve; Violeta Chamorro, widow of the late editor; Alfonso Robelo of the MDN; Moisés Hassan of the MPU; and Daniel Ortega of the FSLN. By mid-July, most major towns were under FSLN control; and on July 17, Somoza fled to Paraguay, (where in 1980 he and his armor-plated Mercedes were blown to bits). The Guard disintegrated. On July 19, the Sandinistas entered Managua in triumph, after 18 years of struggle, and at the cost of some 50,000 lives, most of them campesino civilians who fell victim to the savage reprisals of Somoza's Guard.

The basic units of the popular struggle all along were the campesino army of the FSLN; the neighborhood Defense Committees, which during the period were renamed Sandinista Defense Committees (CDS); the Christian base communities; the trade unions, which represented varied groups such as teachers and factory workers; and village or town FSLN headquarters. These organizations provided the military backbone and the essential political structure for coordinating logistical and supply efforts, for effective communication, and for carrying out all mobilization and resistance efforts.

Nicaragua Since 1979

It was clear from the beginning that the revolutionary movement as a whole and the FSLN in particular was committed to much more than overthrowing Somoza. They uttered repeated warnings about the dire consequences of continuing Somicismo without Somoza. The socialist direction of some junta members caused the two more conservative members, Violeta Chamorro and Alfonso Robelo, to resign in May 1980. By 1981, there was a three man governing junta and a nine person directorate in charge of the country. Discussions became polarized by disagreements between pragmatists and hard-line Marxists, a division intensified by the consequences of the U.S. decision that same year to cut off all assistance to Nicaragua.

With some exceptions, the pragmatists have tended to dominate. This is rather a remarkable feat, for the U.S. embargo, in effect since May 1985, and the contra war have placed great and constant stresses on the government. For example, the exodus of some 20,000 middle-class professional people to Costa Rica, Miami, and elsewhere has deprived the government of badly needed talent. The latest emigrés are campesinos, families and young men fleeing the violence, the draft, and conditions of extreme hardship.

The FSLN had included national elections as part of their program even before the fall of Somoza. The elections of 1984, in which Daniel Ortega was elected president, were the subject of tremendous international scrutiny and publicity. This was the first time most Nicaraguans had ever voted, and it was the first presidential election since 1928 that the United States had not supervised or otherwise arranged. These elections were really a referendum on the FSLN's record during their first five years in power.

Six opposition parties participated in the contest. However, other than the FSLN, the group that received most of the attention was the party that did not participate: the extremely conservative and pro-U.S. Democratic Coordinating Committee and their candidate Arturo Cruz. The Coordinadora, as it is known, boycotted the elections, claiming that conditions did not exist for a fair contest. Most international observers disagreed, judging the 1984 contest a clean one, and determining that a meaningful internal political opposition does in fact exist. The FSLN won 67 percent of the vote, while 29 percent was divided among the three groups to the right, and the remaining 3 percent was taken by the three political parties to the left of the FSLN. Further, the opposition parties combined won 36.5 percent of the seats in the National Assembly.[9]

In 1979, when the revolutionaries came down from the mountains and assumed power, they were faced with the overwhelming task of rebuilding a bankrupt and spent country. The U.S., for its part, was confronted with a successful revolution that it had resisted until, quite literally, the last days of Somoza's rule. The Carter administration grew critical of the Somoza regime in 1979, but became uneasy with the provisional government in 1980, and all along sent mixed messages that misled some Sandinistas into a too-hopeful estimate of the effect that the administration's human rights advocacy would have in Nicaragua.

The mutual mistrust between the two governments increased exponentially after the election of Ronald Reagan in 1980, and beginning in 1981, his passionate support of the counterrevolutionary army, or contra, whose goal has been the overthrow by force of the Sandinistas. The Reagan administration viewed Nicaragua in the context of its global struggle with Soviet communism. It feared that the Sandinistas would export their revolution to other Central American countries, and that the Soviet Union would establish military and naval bases there. Therefore, U.S. policy was based on force or the threat of force, as it has been since the 1820s in Nicaragua and Central America as a whole.

Meanwhile, in the face of U.S. disapproval, the Sandinistas set about putting into practice their social and economic goals. First, the vast landed holdings of the Somozas and their friends were turned into state farms, which account for about one fifth of the nation's agricultural land. Under the Agrarian Reform Law of 1981, the private property rights of all those who farmed efficiently were protected. However, abandoned or neglected fields were likely to be expropriated and turned over to cooperatives (CAS) or to small private farmers. Cooperatives are generally made up of around 15 or 20 farmers who together request title and land. They own the land and can pass it on to their children, but they cannot sell it. In the past few years, the government has distributed more land to individual farmers than before, recognizing the reluctance of many to make the leap to a cooperative arrangement. In addition, tenant farmers are protected by state regulation of rent.

The Nicaraguan agrarian reform program has provided the majority of campesinos either with new land or with titles to land they had already been working. On the other hand, agricultural production has not met government targets and by most accounts is seriously down from pre-1979 levels. In theory, all produce in rice, beans, coffee, and other staples is sold to the government, and many farmers resent this regulation. But the biggest difficulties facing the rural poor today are not lack of land, but the dislocations of war and contra depredations against local cooperatives, which have resulted in loss of life, intimidation of farmers, and loss of productivity.[10]

The government's environmental recovery efforts have followed a pattern similar to the agricultural plans. The greatest threat to the environment now is the war, while the greatest previous threat was the Somoza dictatorship. Since the revolution, the government has moved quickly to control or ban the use of pesticides and has embarked upon ambitious programs of reforestation, pollution control, the creation of national parks, and education of the populace to environmental responsibility. However, long-term ideals have run into short-term realities, for economic survival continues to depend on the exploitation of natural resources and on agricultural production for export. Further, the contra have ambushed and kidnapped environmental workers, sabotaged reforestation and flood control projects, while the U.S. embargo has halted the flow of badly needed spare parts.[11]

Liberation through education was another Sandinista goal. Plans for the National Literacy Crusade were initiated even during the period of exile in San José. Immediately after the victory, teams of educators began studying the successful literacy programs of other countries, and they invited the reknown Brazilian educator Paulo Freire to visit Nicaragua and offer his advice. As of Somoza's defeat, the overall illiteracy rate was approximately 60 percent, but with widespread variations; for example, for poor, rural women, illiteracy was closer to 100 percent.

The goal of the literacy campaign, planned by Father Fernando Cardenal, later the minister of education, and Carlos Tünnermann, former ambassador to the United States, was to bring functional literacy at about the third grade reading level to 50 percent of the population. The young *"brigadistas,"* as the teachers were called, left their homes and lived in rural areas with the campesinos from March through August 1980. Supplied with mosquito nets, hammocks, chalkboards, and lanterns by which to teach at night after having helped in the fields during the day, the teachers held class for two hours a night with five or six campesinos huddled around the gas lamp.

A second set of volunteers stayed at their regular work in the cities, homemakers, government workers, factory laborers, and taught in the urban barrios during the evening hours. These people were known as popular literacy teachers. In all, the literacy workers reached some 500,000 people, and government figures claim that the Crusade reduced illiteracy to 13 percent. Whatever allowances one may make for exaggeration of the statistics, the achievement is spectacular.

The health campaign followed almost immediately, mobilizing large segments of the general population to serve as volunteer health workers, immunizing against malaria, polio, and other diseases and providing rudimentary instruction in basic hygiene and sanitation. The eradication of polio was a major accomplishment of the campaign. Unfortunately, health workers were special targets of the contra, and health personnel were badly needed at the front. Other health problems, including outbreaks of malaria in centers of refugee concentration, exacerbated the problems faced by the campaign. Still, the successes are significant, and there is an obvious awareness today of the importance of sanitation, hygiene, and of inoculation of children against disease. Effective garbage removal in the city of Managua alone is one of the health victories of the revolution. Today, free medical care is a right of the public, but lines are long and supplies are short.

Another way to recover the national patrimony was to promote the "democratization of culture" as Father Ernesto Cardenal has called it. This was to be achieved through the rediscovery of native arts and crafts, dances, instruments, costumes, the sponsorship of poetry workshops, and a general appreciation of the national culture as against the *imperial* culture of polyester and plastic. Popular book festivals feature affordable editions of classics from Rubén Darío to Karl Marx at what are surely the lowest prices in the world.

The well-known Face the People, or *"De Cara al Pueblo"* sessions, televised nationally, and the Direct Line radio phone-in programs are often exercises in popular democracy. In them, citizens complain loudly and directly to government officials, who must explain themselves and account for their area of responsibility, or somehow get themselves off the hook.

Another accomplishment has been in the area of women's rights.

Women comprised 20 percent of the guerrilla columns in the revolution, and several women led battalions into combat. Women make up 22 percent of the FSLN membership and occupy 37 percent of the party's leadership positions. In both the CDS's and the local militias, 50 percent of the members are women. Women have literally fought their way to a new status, challenging the centuries old preeminence of machismo. The Nicaraguan Women's Association (AMNLAE) claims 85,000 members and is a vigorous proponent of women's equality in the workplace and the home, and a vigilant guardian of the rights already won.[12]

Social services, including social security benefits, childcare centers, orphanages, homes for the elderly, and rehabilitation centers for the war wounded and the handicapped now exist where before there was virtually nothing available. Unfortunately, the war effort now consumes roughly 50 percent of the national budget, and expenditures in the areas of human services, health, education, and culture have been cut back drastically. Such programs today depend heavily on international volunteer efforts.

The Sandinistas like to give the impression that Nicaragua would be a utopia of social equality and harmony if it were not for the contra war; however, such is not the case. There are numerous areas of serious conflict within the country over important issues such as: 1) the government's educational program, regarded as propagandistic and socialistic by its opponents; 2) the proper political role of the church, in a country where church and state have never been separated in practice; 3) the treatment of coastal ethnic and racial minorities who are either indifferent or opposed to the revolution; 4) the abuse of authority by some state security personnel; 5) the incompetence of many government officials at the middle and lower levels, made worse by the flight of educated professionals; 6) the inefficiency of the large, unwieldy state bureaucracy, despite the administrative reorganization of 1988; 7) government censorship and/or monopolistic control of the media, even though the Constitution of 1987 explicitly provides for freedom of expression; 8) the Sandinistas' pursuit of social goals at the expense of individual civil liberties; 9) the government's readiness to identify opposition with treason; and, finally, 10) what constitutes the best economic system for the country. Still, Nicaragua after 1979 did not become a police state. It is rather an impoverished country engaged in a total war at the moment of major social disruption.

Many Nicaraguans have lost family members in the tragic contra war; many feel that in economic terms they fared better under Somoza than under the current government; and all are bone-weary of endless lines and exasperating shortages. Criticism of the Sandinistas is quite open, strong, and widespread. But so is support for the government and, above all, for the revolution.

Notes

1. Storer H. Rowley, "Shootout or Pullout," in *Sunday, The Chicago Tribune Magazine*, August 21, 1988, p. 12.

2. Philippe Bourgois, "Nicaragua's Ethnic Minorities in the Revolution," in Peter Rosset and John Vandermeer, eds., *Nicaragua: Unfinished Revolution*, New York: Grove Press, 1986, pp. 459–72.

3. For more on the history of U.S.-Nicaraguan relations, see Walter LaFeber, *Inevitable Revolutions*, New York: W. W. Norton, 1984.

4. For more on Sandino, the marines, and the creation of the Guard, see *ibid.*

5. *NACLA Report on the Americas*, Vol. 12, (Nov.-Dec. 1978), pp. 6–7.

6. Bourgois, in Rosset and Vandermeer, p. 396.

7. Joshua Karliner, Daniel Faber, and Robert Rice, "An Environmental Perspective," in Rossett and Vandermeer, pp. 393–408.

8. For an excellent account of political developments during the 1970s, see *NACLA Report on the Americas*.

9. Latin American Studies Association, "The Electoral Process in Nicaragua: Domestic and International Influences," in Rosset and Vandermeer, pp. 73–107.

10. David Kaimowitz, "Nicaragua's Agrarian Reform: Six Years Later," in Rosset and Vandermeer, pp. 390–93.

11. Joshua Karliner, et al., in Rosset and Vandermeer, pp. 393–408.

12. Maxime Molyneaux, "Women: Activism without Liberation?", in Rosset and Vandermeer, pp. 478–81.

13. For more general information in English on post-revolutionary programs and problems, see Rosset and Vandermeer, chapters 2 and 3, pp. 389–485. See also Teófilo Cabestrero, *Revolutionaries for the Gospel*, Maryknoll, New York: Orbis, 1986; Peter Davis, *Where is Nicaragua?*, New York: Simon & Schuster, 1987; Mike Edwards, "Nicaragua: Nation in Conflict," *National Geographic* 168, no. 6, pp. 776–811; Sheryl Hirshon and Judy Butler, *And Teach Them to Read*, Westport, Conn: Lawrence Hill & Co., 1983; Thomas Walker, ed., *Reagan versus the Sandinistas: The Undeclared War on Nicaragua*, Boulder & London: Westview Press, 1987; Marc Zimmerman, ed., *Nicaragua in Reconstruction and at War: The People Speak*, Minneapolis: University of Minnesota, 1985.

1   Reinaldo Antonio Téfel (b. 1925)

". . . the people have
learned to speak. *That* is the
most important thing.
It's extraordinary!"

*At first glance, this soft-spoken, bespectacled intellectual seems an
unlikely revolutionary. However, the courtly and refined Reinaldo Téfel's
revolutionary credentials are as impeccable as his manners. It is appropriate to begin the volume with his story because Mr. Téfel's history is,
in fact, also that of the political opposition to the Somoza dynasty beginning in the 1940s. The remarkable events of Mr. Téfel's life not only
provide us with a coherent chronology of the period, but also contribute
a fascinating living history of the time.*

*From his early adolescence, Mr. Téfel, along with friends and cocon-
spirators Pedro Joaquín Chamorro and Ernesto Cardenal, was a leading
and intractable foe of the dictatorship . Though imprisoned, tortured,
and exiled under the Somozas, this gentle man of indomitable spirit has
remained an ardent champion of social justice and has been motivated
and sustained in his lifelong political struggle by his deep commitment to
Christian principles.*

*One of the original "group of twelve," eminent Nicaraguan leaders
who from their exile in San José, Costa Rica sought to gain international
support for the revolution against Somoza, Mr. Téfel is currently a Cabinet
minister in the Sandinista government. As president of the Nicaraguan*

Institute of Social Security and Social Welfare (INSSBI), Mr. Téfel is responsible for all aspects of social security and welfare in a country that until a few years ago had virtually nothing to offer in these areas.

×⊃×⊂⊃×⊂⊃×

I come from a well-to-do family. My father was a businessman and I was educated in Nicaragua by the Christian brothers at the La Salle school, at both the primary and secondary levels. Afterwards came two years at Fordham University in New York, after which I returned to Nicaragua and studied law for three years, but I did not finish because Somoza closed the university and wanted all the students in Managua to go study in León, but, in rebellion, I didn't go. Fortunately, I obtained a scholarship and went to Spain to study political science.

That's pretty much all with regard to studies, but with regard to struggles against Somoza, well, from the time I was *very* young, twelve or thirteen, I participated in all the demonstrations, in everything. This caused some friction within the family, because my grandfather and my grandmother were friends of Somoza and they were pretty upset about me and my activities. Despite their disapproval, I think that my family tradition does have something to do with my precocious political activity. On my mother's side, Vélez, one of the oldest families in Nicaragua, there has been a great deal of participation in politics. For example, a great-grandfather of mine fought in the famous battle of San Jacinto, against the filibusterers of William Walker. He was a lieutenant then, and later was made a general. Such things have had their influence, but it is my education that has been particularly important.

Ever since I can remember, I have felt that my Christian conscience has obliged me to struggle. Even though the Christian brothers offered a traditional Catholic education, still, if one is formed in a Christian manner, one feels the obligation to struggle. That's the way it is, though there were certain contradictions. For example, I remember that when I began to be involved in politics, one of the brothers told me: "Don't get mixed up in politics, you can't win." However, in the classroom, they taught us differently! There was a contradiction between the way they lived and the way they told us to live. I pointed this fact out to the brother and told him that it was the Christian conscience that they had developed in me that motivated me, and that surely he was not opposed to Christian conscience.

I was still in secondary school when I organized a group called Nationalist Action (Acción Nacionalista), which had among its members, Ernesto Cardenal, Pedro Joaquín Chamorro, Rafael Córdova Rivas, and many more youngsters. Arturo Cruz was also a member. All my life I have been a friend of Arturo Cruz. We lived just a block apart; yes, then we were great friends and we would go to school together, everything. I founded Nationalist Action when I was about sixteen or seventeen years old, in about 1941 or '42; I'm not very good with dates.

I graduated from high school when I was seventeen, I was the youngest in the class, and then I came to the United States to study. My father and I made a deal; he wanted me to study in the States, but I wanted to study in Nicaragua. So we agreed that I would study two years in the United States and then I would return to study law in Nicaragua. My father kept his bargain.

For me, studying in the U.S. was a tremendous experience because, first, I had as a private tutor a high school teacher who was at the same time studying for his doctorate, and he became a good friend of mine. He knew a great deal, all the progressive Catholic writers in Europe at that time, like Jacques Maritain, Léon Bloy, Emanuel Mounier, and others. So, he introduced me to their writings.

After those two years, I returned to Nicaragua to study law, but then Somoza closed the university. That's when some of us students and a number of professors founded the Free University, the Universidad Libre. I was the general secretary of the students, but soon Somoza threw out the then president of the Republic, Leonardo Argüello, and with that, the Universidad Libre folded. That's when I received the scholarship to study in Spain.

My Spanish experience was mostly academic because I was already formed in terms of my values, and *franquismo*, the politics of General Francisco Franco, was not going to influence me. Quite the contrary, for I lived in a permanent state of polemics, intellectual and ideological, with *franquismo*. It is interesting to compare Franco's regime with that of Somoza. While *franquismo* was a fascist totalitarianism, Spanish style, Somocismo was a vulgar, rapacious dictatorship. It was a different style but, of course, the same harshness, the same hard hand. It's not so much that Somoza clamped down with regard to intellectual life *per se*. Rather, it was that Somoza did not consider ideas to be important. Strange, isn't it, but none of the Somozas thought that ideas were of any significance; in fact, they were viewed as quite superfluous.

Speaking of ideas, I nearly forgot something important. It was during my time at the university in Managua that I founded a newspaper called *El Universitario,* a weekly, which grew to have the largest circulation of all the newspapers of that time. *La Prensa* existed, but it was very conservative. *La Noticia* existed, which was called liberal, but it too was conservative. There was *Flecha*, which was liberal, but anti-Sandinista, also Somoza's *Novedades* and a few others, but they each had a very small circulation. *El Universitario* had the largest circulation, an extraordinary occurrence. I was the editor, and I can tell you that it was the first Sandinista newspaper in Nicaragua; in fact, we published a lovely article by Ernesto Cardenal and Pedro Joaquín Chamorro on Sandino. That must have been in 1946.

I also founded another organization at the university, the National Popular Action Union (Unión Nacional de Acción Popular, UNAP), in 1948, whose membership was more or less the same as in the other groups I mentioned. The difference was that UNAP was a lot larger, and it also enjoyed some influence in national politics even though it was a relatively small university group.

We were able to organize and meet openly, although this must sound a bit unlikely. You see, sometimes they [the Somozas] would give some freedom which they would let grow until it began to become strong, and then, *pow,* they would crack down again. That's how the two sons operated too, not just the old man; it was the same politics.

Along with other members of UNAP, I participated in the April '54 movement to overthrow Somoza. After it failed, I went underground for more than a year. During that time, Carlos Fonseca, while still a high school student in Matagalpa, wrote me saying that he had organized a UNAP cell there. Later, when I came out of hiding and into the public light, the first two persons to greet me, with no connection between them, were Ernesto Cardenal and Carlos Fonseca. By then, Fonseca, who was now librarian at the Instituto Nacional in Managua, no longer considered himself an *unapista,* or member of UNAP. He told me in all honesty that he no longer read Maritain, but that he now read political scientists and was much more advanced in his thinking. That's when he separated from UNAP and our political paths parted.

It is interesting how I was able to come out of hiding after the failure of the 1954 movement. Remember that a large part of my family on my father's side was Somocista, right? Well, a first cousin of mine, who now is in Miami, used to play poker with the old Somoza, in spite of their great age difference, and one night he said: "General, I would like to ask you please to let my cousin go free. If I win this poker game, will you let him go?" Well, he won and then Somoza took a piece of paper and wrote: "Reinaldo Téfel can go free to dedicate himself exclusively to his work. A. Somoza". So I got out of jail because of a poker bet ! I framed the note and now have it hanging in my house. I will show it to you so that you will have an idea of how the old Somoza was.

His was a carrot and stick policy. He was a complete cynic. He had pictures of Hitler and Mussolini in his office, and when World War II broke out, he took them down and put up portraits of Roosevelt and Churchill and declared war on Germany the day before the United States did. When he found out that the United States was going to declare war, that Congress was going to meet, he hurried, gathered together his Congress and declared war on Germany. A total opportunist, shameless and cynical, but of course, he was intelligent, clever, and he spoke English, which gave him excellent communication with the United States embassy. He had also learned popular English, he knew all the slang, and this made him even more attractive, especially to the ambassadors' wives, with whom he had well-known affairs. At any rate, that's the story of how I was able to come aboveground.

Remember that I was free to come aboveground to dedicate myself to my work. I was working in agriculture with my brother, we grew cotton, and at the same time I had a bookstore with Ernesto Cardenal. We two were partners. The store was called Nuestro Tiempo (Our Time), but of course it did not provide a living, especially as it was a pioneering bookstore in that we stocked all the latest books from all over the world. When Ernesto decided to go study in Kentucky to become a Trappist monk, we closed the bookstore because one person alone couldn't keep it going. As for my farming, I really couldn't dedicate myself to it because I was always either oppressed or in hiding. My younger brother helped me, but we couldn't make a go of it. Then I worked for a brief time with my father.

In 1956, immediately after the poet Rigoberto López Pérez assassinated the old Somoza, I was picked up when they rounded up 3,000 opposition leaders. They took me away in my pajamas, and I stayed in jail just like that for a long time without my family knowing my whereabouts. Pedro Joaquín Chamorro and I shared the same cell, and we were brutally tortured, as described in Pedro Joaquín's book, *Estirpe sangrienta*. (Bloody Heritage).

This was also a time of great polarization between the Conservative and the Liberal parties, and UNAP was losing political ground. We decided, the majority of us, to join the Conservative party, which had a strong popular base then, and to transform it into a modern Christian Democratic party. So, I became the political secretary of the Conservative Party; I was named to this post while I was imprisoned.

The success of the Cuban Revolution had an energizing effect on all of us, and we began to hope that maybe we could create our own guerrilla group. Pedro Joaquín Chamorro and I had the same idea, and we, along with other opposition leaders, went to Cuba to see Castro and to request his support for our plan. He told us that he regretted that he was already committed to a Nicaraguan exile group, and we left empty-handed but not discouraged.

We returned to Costa Rica, where we planned the invasion known as Olama y Mollejones [1959], led by Pedro Joaquín Chamorro, and in which I was leader of a column. This was the first airborne invasion in Nicaragua, and in Latin America for that matter. We landed in Chontales province, and we were to meet up with the internal front, which was supposed to provide us with support and communications, but they failed utterly, and we were soon surrounded by the guardia. Pedro Joaquín and I were imprisoned for more than a year until Somoza declared a general amnesty, the result of considerable national and international pressure.

When I got out, I worked hard in the Conservative party until a *caudillo*, or strongman, Fernando Argüello, began to betray the party. So, I broke with him, left the Conservative party and joined the Nicaraguan Social Christian party (Partido Social Cristiano Nicaragüense, PSC). Soon, I realized that it too was more or less like the others and I left it also.

From about 1965 to 1972, I taught various sociology courses at the Catholic university (UCA). Separate from my academic position but during the same period of disillusionment with the PSC and other existing political parties, I founded the Human Development Institute (Instituto de Promoción Humana, INPRHU), of which I still serve as president. INPRHU satisfied the need I perceived for a structure that was truly revolutionary, one that could bring about deep social change and was not bound by the limitations and traditional weaknesses of the political parties. Through INPRHU we carried out work that was profoundly Christian.

For example, at that time we were dedicated to promoting and supporting trade organizations, cooperatives, community development groups, housewives, youth groups, and the like. It was a grass-roots, popular, organization. We also introduced the method of Pablo Freire in Nicaragua, his consciousness-raising or *concientización*. Of course, this type of work did not provide enough to live on, and the university paid very badly, so I also gave human development workshops to large businesses on the weekends.

I continued with INPRHU working directly with the people, and by about the tenth anniversary my position was completely revolutionary, and I viewed INPRHU as a truly revolutionary coming together of Christianity, socialism, and nationalism. While still deeply involved with INPRHU, I also held meetings at my house every Monday evening of intellectuals, professional people, and workers who all wanted to found a Socialist Democratic party. All those who used to come to these meetings are currently working in the revolution. This was for about a year, and would've been during '77; yes, that's right, because Pedro Joaquín was murdered in January of 1978, and that same month I joined the "group of twelve."

I was also on both of the National Strike Committees, one took place in February and the other in September of 1978. Other members included Sergio Ramírez, Miguel D'Escoto, a Socialist Party leader, a representative of the private business sector, and so on. It soon became clear to me that no labor or business group really had power at that time. Power was to be found in the spontaneous response of the people and in the Frente Sandinista, which was the only political-military organization capable of responding to the circumstances.

Then the Frente sent me in April of '79 to Costa Rica as its representative to a meeting of all the Social Democratic and progressive political parties of Latin America that were in support of the revolution. The Frente decided that I would not return to Nicaragua but would serve instead in foreign affairs. Then they sent me on various missions, as much to spread the word as to raise funds. I went to Mexico, the Dominican Republic, Puerto Rico, Spain, and many other places.

When I was on one of these trips, the junta formed a Cabinet and named me to Social Security; when I returned I was unhappy because Social Security had been very unpopular in Nicaragua, it was a very technical assignment, and besides, I wanted something more political. I remember that Miguel D'Escoto told me this: "All your life you have fought for the poor, with INPRHU, now you are going to have the opportunity to do something at the national level, and that is why you have been chosen." And now, I would be very unhappy if they took the job away from me!

Before the revolution there existed the Nicaraguan Social Security Institute (Instituto Nicaragüense de Seguridad Social), but it only existed in Managua, León, and Chinandega, and there was no social welfare. The Social Welfare Ministry (Ministerio de Bienestar Social) was founded in 1979 upon the triumph of the revolution, but it was closed in '82 and the Instituto absorbed all its functions and became the Instituto Nicaragüense de Seguridad Social y Bienestar, INSSBI, which we are today.

Radical changes in the social welfare system have been a major objective of the Revolution, and I think that fact illustrates well the principal influences and inspirations, Christianity; Sandinismo; that is, the historic legacy of the thought of Sandino who desired an effective democracy with social progress and justice; Marxism, which has influenced some youths; democracy; nationalism, all these factors converge and form what Carlos Fonseca called a national revolutionary ideology. Thus, the synthesis of all those currents, that's what the popular Sandinista Revolution is. It is, to me, a democratic, pluralistic, humanistic, Latin American path to socialism. That is our revolution and I believe that that is what will be reflected in the new Constitution. I am a member of the National Assembly, but I don't have time to attend. I was able to keep up when there were only one or two meetings a week, but now that they are working on the Constitution, it is day and night and even on weekends, and I would have to abandon INSSBI, which I can't do.

But I believe that from the new Constitution there will come a democratic state based on social justice, that is, with a qualitative, profound difference from the other "democracies" that exist in Latin America, which are capitalist, bourgeois democracies where the rich become richer and the poor poorer, just as President Reagan has done in the United States and wants to force us to adopt too. Then, it is for these reasons that I think that ours is a new Latin American way, democratic and pluralistic, toward socialism, and that is what has awakened such hope, such sympathy, not only among the peoples of Latin America, but throughout the world to the extent that we have in Nicaragua volunteers from all over.

Nicaragua is a laboratory of social change, discarding old molds, creating new ones, and awakening great hope, for the new molds depend on the combination of many principles: political pluralism, nonalignment, a mixed economy, anti-imperialism, Latin Americanism, Bolivarism. In all this Marxism plays a role, not of a dogmatic religious nature, but rather a scientific role as an instrument for interpreting social reality. Now, many of us have come to the revolution motivated by our Christian conscience. There are others who have come motivated by their study of Marxism. Still others, simply by their opposition to Somocismo and to Nicaragua's dependence on the United States. This confluence of currents is producing something new and different, and it is a source of inspiration for many peoples.

I am often asked about the Cuban influence in our revolution, and, without doubt, since it was the first socialist revolution in Latin America, the Cuban Revolution has come to enjoy much popularity and since the Cubans have been a help to us, of course they have been an influence as well. But it is not that we are copying the Cuban Revolution, no, ours is different. Fidel Castro himself in two speeches that he gave in Nicaragua spoke about these differences.

For one thing, we have various political parties and in Cuba there is just one. Further, in Cuba clergy cannot enter the party, whereas the Frente Sandinista has welcomed the participation of Christians not only in the revolution, the first revolution in the history of all revolutions in which we Christians have participated significantly as Christians. For example, in the United States, the people were Christian, but there was no clear consciousness that they were participating in the Revolution as Christians, but here there is; it is a Christian militancy. So, that is another important difference, and one that is considered dangerous from the ultra-conservative viewpoint of Reaganism, and that's part of the reason for the effort of the most conservative sectors of the Vatican and the United States to do away with, to crush, the reality signified by the saying, "Between Christianity and revolution, there is no contradiction."

The roots of this Christian activism are to be found in the events of the 1960s and 1970s, the Vatican II Council, and the conferences at Medellín and Puebla, which have given great impetus to liberation theology and have been very influential with a large sector of the Nicaraguan church and the Nicaraguan people. By the time of our revolution, there were many Christians who were not conservative as they were in the time of the Cuban Revolution, and there were many Marxists who were not dogmatic as they were in the time of the Cuban Revolution.

There were specific individuals during the period who had a big influence as well. Beginning with the martyred Colombian priest Camilo Torres; and, of course, "Che" has had an impact, and he is the one who predicted that the day the Christians of Latin America become revolutionaries, no one would be able to stem the tide of revolution. Dom Helder Câmara of Brazil, and Gustavo Gutiérrez of Peru are sources of inspiration, as have been certain Nicaraguan personalities, such as Ernesto Cardenal and Uriel Molina. These factors have made this revolution different from others.

I prefer to say from "others," rather than specify the Cuban Revolution because it sounds as if we were in some sort of conflictive position with Cuba, when in truth, there is a great sense of brotherhood and friendship and, perhaps, there is more Nicaraguan influence in *Cuba* than vice versa.

I think that the Nicaraguan experience has had something to do with the lightening up by the Cuban government in its attitude toward religion. For example, take the remarkable book *Fidel and Religion* by Frei Bento. It would never have been written had it not been for our revolution. So, there is a reciprocal influence, and that is only reasonable, and a great friendship between both countries. Cuba is probably the country that has helped us the most, with primary schoolteachers, doctors and nurses. And those medical teams have gone into dangerous mountainous regions. Of course we also have help from Mexico, Spain, North America, and Europe, from all parts of the world. In INSSBI alone we have fifty-seven foreign volunteers.

These volunteers usually stay for one, two, or three years with us and many work in dangerous regions. Lately, the government has had to require those who are in the most vulnerable areas to pull back a little, because seven helpers have been murdered. The deceitful propaganda of President Reagan and West German Chancellor Kohl is that we send these volunteers to dangerous places so that they will be killed, but that is in no way true.

I have given something of an overall view of the philosophy and context of this revolution. In the first two years it had a great social goal, the results of which were that the number of students doubled, the rate of illiteracy was reduced considerably, and many health centers were created in the countryside where before no services had ever existed.

In 1982 the Social Welfare Ministry (Ministerio de Bienestar Social) and that of Social Security (Seguridad Social) merged into one integral concept, an innovation that currently is being talked about in the majority of world congresses on Social Security. We have done it and we cover not only salaried workers but the entire population. In Somoza's time, about 202,000 people were tended to, but now we are taking care of some 1,600,000 individuals. That's out of a population of a little less than three million, and in spite of the war.

Now, however, the war has obliged us to place our priorities in defense and production, and we have had to freeze social programs to a certain extent, or to depend on funding from abroad. For example, if we are going to build a childcare center, we must be given all the construction materials, equipment, and maintenance for a whole year, because otherwise we just can't do it. So, as you can see, the first thing that we must do is defend ourselves, and the defense budget, which in the first two years was just about 8 percent, now is more than 40 percent, maybe even 45 percent. The budget for Social Security and welfare is 10 percent, for education more or less 10 percent, and for health, about the same or slightly more. All in all, in the social areas we have roughly 30 percent of the budget in spite of the war. Not too bad, considering, but we have huge problems, such as a serious shortage of professionals and technicians, because under Somoza very few such people were produced. Only now are a few new professionals beginning to appear, and this after more than seven years of revolution.

The kind of technicians I am referring to are university-educated individuals who have expertise in medicine, dentistry, agronomy, engineering, rather than in the liberal professions, because now, what we need to emphasize are the areas that are most economically productive for our people. You see, now there are shortages of everything, especially food, because there are zones that are traditionally agricultural and cultivate basic grains, but now they are unable to do so because of the war and the embargo.

People react to these hardships in very interesting ways. There is a very good illustration that a Chilean philosopher and sociologist once gave. He says that there is a psychological and a social or political consciousness. The former manifests itself in the people's expressions of discontent, in criticism, for example, when one is standing in line, finally, it's his turn, and they're out of what he wants. And the social or political consciousness is that which analyzes events and determines their causes, and sees what the fundamental problem is. In Nicaragua it is foreign aggression. My friend used the example of Chile, saying that a similar thing occurred there to what is happening in Nicaragua. There, the polls made it look like the Allende government was going to lose the upcoming congressional elections. There was a demonstration in which a woman carried a placard saying, "This government is shit, but it's ours!" So, there you have both, the psychological consciousness and the other, which was expressed in the elections which saw discontent increase 10 percent, and that was the pretext for the coup.

A similar thing is happening in Nicaragua. Nicaraguans have always been very expressive and very critical. We feel free to say whatever we like. Of course, a foreigner stands in a line, listens to all the people protesting, and perhaps takes it too seriously. Nevertheless, when we had our elections, we still won 68 percent of the vote. Henry Kissinger comes for four hours to make his famous report, and there occurs a spontaneous demonstration in opposition to him. There you see the expression of the political consciousness.

You see it also in the military service and in the reserves, because some do evade the draft and escape it, but most serve. Between eighteen and twenty-four years of age one must serve for two years. For the reserve, the ages are between twenty-five and forty. Reservists have three weeks of training periodically, after which they return to their daily lives.

People criticize the draft, the shortages, and the government; that is because criticism is completely open in Nicaragua. *La Prensa* was not closed for being critical; it was closed for treason to the country, especially because they came to the U.S. to lobby for the 100 million dollars for the contra.

What people complain about most is the scarcity of everything because it makes life so difficult, but they also protest whenever an important official does something wrong. Then the criticism on the radio, in the press and on television is very harsh. For example, *Barricada* and *El Nuevo Diario* are sharply critical of government officials; sometimes they go overboard, and if they are radio journalists, they are even more extreme. You might say they have more psychological than political consciousness. So, yes, criticism is extremely strong in the country. This is very important because it is part of the revolution.

In the "Face the People," or *De cara al pueblo* programs, the public takes the president and the ministers to task, and they express themselves freely. We officials have to answer for ourselves, right then, on the spot. Actually, people hardly ever ask me questions anymore. At first, they used to ask me about health because they thought I was in charge of it. Later, rather than criticize me, what people did was to ask for child development centers, rural day care centers, and I had to explain that because of the economic situation of the country, because of the aggression, that we couldn't provide what they wanted. I had to give accounts, so many millions of *córdobas*, and so forth, and now, hardly anyone asks me questions about my area. But these "Face the People" programs are carried live on national radio and taped for TV. They are quite an experience.

From my vantage point, I see many concrete achievements of the revolution. Certainly, doubling the student population from 500,000 to one million, the literacy campaign, the enormous proliferation of unions and cooperatives and of community organizations, the neighborhood CDS's (Sandinista Defense Committees) throughout the country, the participation of the people, the fact that the people have learned to speak. *That* is the most important thing. It's extraordinary! The humblest people are not frightened in front of the TV; they are put before a camera and they answer. Sometimes the TV abuses that because they repeat and even bore, but the point is that all this is a *huge* success.

In my area, the biggest victory is to have been able to extend Social Security to all the country, an amazing achievement when you think about it. For example, we now cover all the urban areas, and all the agro-industrial area too. Where we are currently extending coverage is in agriculture and cattle-raising. Coverage consists of Social Security like you have in the U.S, but with one advantage. In spite of our poverty, we have revalued pensions already ten times in these seven years!* In no other Latin American country have they been able to do this.

Besides that, before the triumph there were three child care centers in Nicaragua, and now we have 170.**

Of course, if we were at peace, we would have perhaps 1,000! These are day care centers with excellent programs, so that the children are taught a great deal. They learn to eat by themselves, to develop their skills, to nap all at the same time. You know, it's marvelous to enter and see 100 children sleeping, or 150 children eating. I don't know how the staff does it.

These are examples of the integral nature of the Sandinista Revolution, which embraces the social, political, economic, and cultural areas. I have given you some concrete programs and goals in the social area. But, in the cultural sphere, the Ministry of Culture has done a phenomenal job and so has the Sandinista Association of Cultural Workers (Asociación Sandinista de Trabajadores de la Cultura, ASTC), which Rosario Murillo, the poet and wife of Daniel [President Ortega] directs. A fantastic job! So that if you go to a neighborhood, any one, you will see artistic groups there, folkloric groups, singers and composers and poets, in all of Nicaragua. That's why I prefer the word "integral."

With regard to social goals, the objective has been the eradication of poverty rather than the complete reorganization of the social class system. That is what the Constitution [of 1987] in its Preamble is going to say. To eradicate the exploitation of man by man, but in our own unique way,

---

*[Ed. Note: As of June 1988, pensions had been revalued sixteen times.]

**[Ed. Note: As of June 1988, there were 190 child care centers.]

maintaining a mixed economy in which the fundamental objective is not profit but rather service to the people.

Though one may say that it is part of human nature to be selfish, we believe that we can bring about our goals through the law and through education, consciousness-raising. Of course, he who has a million dollars doesn't want anyone to take it away from him. The enemies of the revolution are those who have seen their economic status reduced. They are above all the enemies, and many of them are still in Nicaragua. This is a big problem; it is the biggest obstacle to a mixed economy. The thing is that many big businessmen are hoping that Reagan will crush the revolution and restore Somocismo.

But on the other hand, there are many other big businessmen who work very well, even millionaires. It's not that such people are with the revolution, but rather that they have stayed in Nicaragua; they work in Nicaragua and they have big businesses. Of course, many live part-time in Nicaragua and part-time in Miami, and travel constantly. Generally, their families are in Miami, but they all have their business in Nicaragua and their wives visit too. There are also a large number of medium and small farmers as well. These are with the revolution, and they form the membership of the UNAG, the Nicaraguan National Farmers Union (Unión Nacional de Agricultores de Nicaragua).

Of course, now with the disruption caused by the war, we have campesinos coming into the city, approximately 250,000 displaced by the war who are relocating. We have also received about 20,000 Salvadoran refugees in the past seven years, but they have been absorbed by the Nicaraguan economy and society to such an extent that we are now only attending to about 900 refugees, directly that is. They have for the most part been incorporated into mixed cooperatives in which half are Nicaraguans and half Salvadorans. I really doubt that many of them would return to El Salvador if the political situation allowed, because the economic problems there are tremendous, and the economic differences between the classes in El Salvador are much greater there than in any other Central American country. Of course, in its last years Somocismo was producing a similar gulf in Nicaragua. Ours was a country in which land ownership was, compared to the rest of Central America, of course, fairly well-distributed, but with the heyday of cotton, it became concentrated, especially with the desire of the Somozas to usurp property. Toward the end of Somoza's epoch, the imbalance became very aggravated, very serious.

The greatest limitation we have in carrying out our projects at INSSBI is the lack of dollars, because there is a long list of things that we would like to do, but the only way to do them is with dollars. For example, regarding eye care, we are experiencing serious problems because we simply cannot get the dollars that we must have to be able to import the materials that our opticians need to serve the public. Another example is in the field of information, computers; we are constantly in need of different parts and repairs and materials, and it is virtually impossible because we lack dollars to buy them with.

The funds for developing our social programs come partly from the assessments that workers and employers pay, and, for the social welfare part, the state, and the lotteries that we run. But's that's all in córdobas, our national currency, and there are a lot of things that one can *not* do with córdobas. We receive much assistance from abroad, from nongovernmental bodies, churches, solidarity committes, labor organizations, political parties. I don't know the exact percentages, but it is a limited amount in the face of the great need. However, international aid allows INSSBI to establish child centers, social centers, and without that support we could not initiate any new programs. It is a constant effort to go around trying to raise funds; you see, we receive practically no funds from governments. That type of assistance goes to other areas, not INSSBI, to production, health or education. Besides, governments are more interested in big economic projects, development programs and the like.

Development assistance is badly needed because there is a tremendous need to increase production, which has declined significantly, especially agricultural production. Industrial production is in the cities, where there is no war, but agricultural production has seriously deteriorated. Now there are great efforts being made, including many meetings of the revolutionary leadership with popular organizations, for example like UNAG, and ATC, which is the Association of Rural Workers (Asociación de Trabajadores Campesinos), to try to increase working hours.

As you might imagine, people respond in different ways to the request that they work more, but gradually they are coming to understand the need and are cooperating. Of course, the campesinos who are now in cooperatives and have their own lands that the agrarian reform has given them, work more voluntarily. It is more difficult with the salaried agricultural employees, because you have to convince them that they ought to work, but there is a lot of consciousness-raising going on in the countryside, very efficient and well-organized.

And don't forget that there is still the great need for technical training, which also requires funds. Where do the funds come from if the shortages are so great? There is a 2 percent tax levied on the salaries of the workers, which the employers pay; it is intended for technical training of the workers. We collect that tax together with Social Security, and with that sum, the Ministry of Work has a General Training Office (Dirección General de Capacitación) where they train people for their positions.

Because we have so many serious problems, many people think that the Nicaraguan public must be very demoralized now, what with the low-intensity warfare, the continual shortages, the endless lines. Of course, things are extremely difficult for everyone, and if the Nicaraguan people were introverted, probably they would be depressed. But since they are an extroverted people who complain about everything, even about things that there is no reason to complain about, then really, they are not a depressed people. No, I would definitely say that they are not a depressed people.

I prefer to regard ourselves as determined and positive; for example, we hope and believe that the North American people may learn the truth about what is happening in Central America and Nicaragua, and in all Latin America in general. I deeply hope that the people may become aware of the role that a great power like the U.S. can play in bringing about peace in the world. Once we are left in peace, we will be able to enjoy an integral democratic development toward a humanistic Latin American socialism, which, sadly, is exactly what the U.S. government wishes to crush. An authentic democracy in Latin America brings independence; this is the *threat* to U.S. interests, but it is the promise of hope to others.

2 Violeta Chamorro (b. 1929)

". . . there are thousands of Nicaraguans right here who are opposed to them [the Sandinistas], to their Marxist, Leninist, communist ideology. The government claims that the Revolution has been for the people . . . but it is all brain-washing and lies."

Waving away the crowd of reporters who habitually wait outside, the strikingly attractive silver-haired doña Violeta smilingly ushered me into her comfortable, but simple, office. There, a prominently displayed crucifix and a large national flag immediately caught my eye, powerful symbols of Mrs. Chamorro's arch-conservative political stance. Our lengthy conversation was animated and extremely cordial. When we met again several months later to resume her life story, Mrs. Chamorro reinforced my initial impression of her as a very likeable woman, but one obsessed by a political ideology that divides the world into "them" and "us."

Widow of the martyred journalist, opposition leader and national hero Pedro Joaquín Chamorro, whose assassination in 1978 galvanized support for the revolution against Somoza; former member of the Directorate of the Government of National Reconstruction created after the overthrow of Somoza; mother of a family which has been bitterly divided by the revolution; staunch defender of traditional Catholicism; tenacious owner and president of the Board of Directors of the embattled La Prensa; *the outspoken Violeta Chamorro here narrates her biography and expresses herself unequivocally on a number of issues, including the tense relations between her newspaper and the Sandinista government.*

If we place doña Violeta's reminiscences of her life with her husband Pedro alongside Reinaldo Téfel's biography, we gain a fuller picture of opposition activities during the long Somoza years. We also see first hand the polarization of Nicaraguan politics today, for until the revolution, the Téfels and the Chamorros had a great deal in common, while today they share only respect for the memory of Pedro Joaquín.

I am from Rivas and I am fifty-eight years old; that's a lot of years given in love to my country. When I was young, I did not have the slightest idea of the many responsibilities that would be placed upon me, nor of how my life would become so identified with Pedro's and with *La Prensa*. I was not prepared for any of this, but, when one loves one's country, one does all that is humanly possible.

La Prensa is sixty-one years old and it has come through numerous crises. Somoza closed it many times, once for two years [1944–46], and my father-in-law, the founder and director of *La Prensa* at that time, had to go to the States, where he worked for a long time as translator for the New York Public Library while my mother-in-law worked as a seamstress. Their oldest son, Pedro, my husband who was assassinated nearly ten years ago, with the little that his parents could send him and his grandmother could provide, finished his university education here and went to Mexico to study further, taking with him only his two changes of clothes. It's a lovely story and true. The Somozas closed *La Prensa* many times, but they didn't confiscate it like the Sandinistas.

Ortega says we are financed by the CIA. That's the pretext they [the Sandinistas] used to close the paper from June 16, 1986 to September 19, 1987, when they allowed us to reopen, only after intense pressure by the international community. The government closed the paper right after the U.S. approved the 100 million dollars for the contra. What the Sandinistas don't realize is that there are thousands of Nicaraguans right here who are opposed to them, to their Marxist, Leninist, communist ideology. But what happens is that the North American and the European who come down here are *mareados*, "snowed," overwhelmed by the propaganda machine. Ortega is very good at that; he wins them over and they go back saying that there is freedom in this country, but it is a lie. Like the new Constitution [of 1987], which sounds pretty, but it is just another deception, an *engaño*. And now they're talking about an amnesty, but you can be sure that it won't be for the Nicaraguan who has left the country!

Oh yes, this paper has seen it all. I remember well that my husband was one of the few people who wrote in favor of Sandino, and Somoza called *La Prensa* "*amarillista*", yellow, and "*comunista*", and now we are called imperialist, bourgeois, "*vendepatria*", or sellouts. We have been through a lot. What we were, and are, are the only ones not toeing the government line. Look at the TV now; all you see is government propaganda. For example, remember the trial of the captured CIA pilot, Hasenfus? Daniel Ortega talked and talked, all this baloney about the government having such a big heart and wanting to see Hasenfus reunited with his wife and kids for Christmas, and so on. If the government has such a big heart, why don't they let all the *Nicaraguans* go free too!

Imagine, Ortega saying that we deserved thirty years in jail, the penalty for treason, and that we got off easy with the closure. That we have to pay all employees during the time of the closure, even though most left, some are now working for the government, we have practically no funds, and we are having to sell some of our furniture. He says we're enemies of humanity and deserve thirty years. I can hardly *believe* the lies they tell about us on TV! All these lies, from having been repeated so much, no one believes them. It's like any dictatorship; they lie so much that the day they finally tell the truth no one believes them.

Here, let me read to you from my letter to Ortega in response to his accusations: ". . . if you wish, Comandante, with pleasure I will hand myself over to my captors so they can impose on me the jail sentence you threaten me with. In this way, I would follow with pride the example of my husband, Pedro Joaquín Chamorro, for whom the previous Somoza dictatorship had only one strategy, jail.

"How quickly you have forgotten my firm, nationalist position when, in 1979 in San José, Costa Rica, I was the only one to oppose the suggestion that the Nicaraguan political problem be solved by seeking outside help. What I said then I repeat now: Nicaragua's grave crisis must be resolved among ourselves without the influence of Cubans, Soviets or North Americans. . . .

"You will never convince anyone that I am a traitor to the country or that I received money from the CIA or that I am part of the Reagan administration's terrorist plan."

Ortega never answered me. The "answer" to my letter did not come until March 26, *1987*, from the Ministry of Work; that's the letter saying that we had to pay all the workers, as if we had the money.

This government's so-called rationale for closing *La Prensa* was that we were collaborating with the enemy, which is absurd, merely a pretext to close the paper because we won't follow their Marxist-Leninist line. We have our own line, democratic and pluralistic, open to all the political parties to express themselves. But go ask the parties who aren't with the govenment how they express themselves. They closed us because they don't want us to criticize them, and that's that! And the role of a newspaper is to criticize for the good of the country.

The news is so controlled. What you see on TV today you read in *Barricada* tomorrow, period, that's it. If before, Somoza owned one half of the country, now the Sandinistas own it all! Usurpers! Because if you own a cattle ranch, and you want to sell an animal, it has to be to the state and then they sell it. If you're a coffee grower, the same thing, you turn your crop over to the government. Total control. They say that this is because of the war. Bah! It's because of a betrayal, and the war is the product of a betrayal. Further, they say that the terrible shortage of food and basic goods is because of the war, but we've experienced scarcity since the beginning of this government and the war came later. However, those of us who complain about these things, well we're with the CIA! Many have left, but my place is here at *La Prensa*, doing what I can.

La Prensa is not in favor of the Reagan government's policy toward Nicaragua. No, because I live here in Nicaragua and because I am a Nicaraguan I'm not in favor of any external plan. But we have a strange situation here in my country with regard to the contra because so many families are divided. My son, for example is with the contra and lives in exile. I also have here in Nicaragua a son who is becoming a communist, and a daughter who is too. *Comunistas nuevos*, "new communists," they're called. And my family situation is not unique, but is repeated throughout Nicaragua. My son is the editor of *Barricada*, and my daughter is ambassador to Costa Rica. That makes for tension at times, but we manage well because we are a close-knit family. I do worry about my children here because they are bombarded by government propaganda. That's a concrete and personal example of why *La Prensa* is so important.

It is interesting to see who has supported *La Prensa* during our ordeal. Not one Latin American intellectual or writer has come to our aid. Not one of them has defended us! And in Nicaragua, the writers are all Sandinistas or communists, except for Sergio Ramírez [the Vice-President of Nicaragua], who is a Somocista. *Yes!* I know him and his family too well.

But other international groups have been very supportive, such as the World Interparliamentary Union, which held its international meeting here in April 1987. We put out a sheet welcoming them to Nicaragua. Then the guards came to "close" the paper again, as if we had reopened. Well, it so happened that I already had a meeting planned for that same afternoon, April 30, in my office with a French delegation. They came, saw the guards, the guns, the big outer door closed. Later, they held a press conference to tell people what they had seen. I didn't know about it or I would've supported it.

That "occupation" was a comedy of errors. They didn't close the paper right away because they were taken aback by the sheet we put out on our poor, broken-down rotary press. They had to find a pretext for occupying our building. The whole thing was a foolish mistake by the Voice of America representative in Nicaragua because he should have come here to find out the truth. There I was at home in the solitude of my room, listening to the VOA on the radio, and I hear this late-breaking news from Nicaragua that *La Prensa* has begun publishing clandestinely. Imagine that! I couldn't sleep, there was no one to talk to, and I didn't have a driver until the next day. The following morning I arrived at the office about 9:30 to find it had just been occupied by about thirty armed soldiers. I demanded to know how come they were here. They said they heard on the VOA news that we were publishing again. "Well," I said, "Nicaraguan state security is *so* good that it depends for its information on the VOA." After a three-hour occupation, search, harassment of the few workers who remained, and the confiscation of some pamphlets and printing plates, they left.

The offical report finally came out and said that the 3,000 sheets we put out, many of which had to be thrown away because they were of such poor quality, did not constitute a violation of the Ministry of the Interior order closing *La Prensa*, because a greeting is not a newspaper. So there you have it, the whole ridiculous episode.

I don't think people realize just how much propaganda and pressure there is here. At my friend's school, a special school for retarded children, the government took away the teachers because the school wouldn't become Sandinista. The school is named Manolo Morales, and is right across from the diplomatic store. The school keeps going because it is financed by individual contributions; they now have fifty-seven students. Recently, they used the donated money to hire a cleaning lady, because my friend and her sister are the only teachers and they live on practically nothing. It breaks your heart to see their dedication to the children. They are very well-prepared; its an excellent school. When they [the Sandinistas] told my friend to display the Sandinista flag, she refused. Instead, in the very place where they wanted her to put the flag, she and the children built a shrine to the Virgin. My friend is dedicated like a true nun; I say a *true* nun because many now have another ideology. But one who really has faith, doesn't lose it. I don't believe in those people like Fathers Ernesto and Fernando Cardenal; they have gotten off the right track. The Nicaraguan people love the true Church and their Cardinal Obando y Bravo, and they are not fooled.

I never lost my faith during the time that *La Prensa* was closed. I would like to tell you about when they lifted the punishment, about the nineteenth of September [1987] when Daniel Ortega visited my house along with the vice-chancellor of the Republic, Rodrigo Madrigal Nieto. First, I received a telephone call from Rodrigo, who told me that the president wanted to come and talk to me about the newspaper. At that moment, I didn't know if it was going to be good news or bad news, so I simply had to wait and see. They arrived at 10:15 in the morning and we began to talk, and Daniel said that he wanted to take advantage of the friendship that the chancellor had with me and with my husband, in order to talk about the newspaper, to put his point of view forward, and see what we said to him. I told him that closing the paper was a grave error, a completely totalitarian act that he had committed against the Nicaraguan people, and that I didn't retract a thing.

I think they finally realized that there are just too many people in Nicaragua and in the world who do not want to see this country plunged into the abyss. He came with the intention of lifting the punishment, which he did. I say punishment, becaue that's what it was for the Nicaraguan people, for all the personnel, for the press, because for one and a half years we were closed. We had to sell furniture, everything; now, having just opened again, we are *trabajando con las uñas*, working with our fingernails, as we say. The machinery is aged, broken-down, and we have an ancient rotary press. But even so, the paper is coming out, and without *any* censorship or pressure from the government.

All this is a responsibility that has come to me; I did not seek it, but as I said, one does what one can. And although I am half crippled from osteoporosis, and we are getting along by the skin of our teeth, at least I can say: here I am, doing what I can. Unfortunately, the people here in Managua cannot receive the paper now like they used to, through subscription, because we don't have any transportation since we sold everything earlier. So, paperboys walk around selling now. Before, it was a motorcycle, and people would hear the vroom, vroom of the *moto* and would come out and buy their *Prensa*. It's also coming out late because of the lack of equipment, much ruined from lack of use. It should be coming out about 5:00 p.m., but often we can't get it out until 8:00 or 9:00 p.m. But with the problems of machinery, what can you do? We are trying to get some money so that we can send our equipment out to be repaired, to another country of course, as here in Nicaragua we have no facilities for that type of thing. That is what we are working on right now.

We do not share with or borrow from other papers, such as *Nuevo Diario* or *Barricada*. No, we do nothing with them. If the government closes us, then the government itself has to supply us. That is, the government has to sell us paper, ink, and so forth. They have usurped everything. The day we opened the newspaper, we didn't even have a flash, and we had to call the person that Daniel Ortega indicated to sell us a flash. One can't go on working like that. Mostly what I do is try to get help, donations, to keep us going.

As you can see, *La Prensa* is an all-consuming passion for me. But I have a personal history as well, and I am delighted to tell you about it. It gives me great pleasure to recall my past.

First, I love the countryside. I told you that I was born in Rivas and I grew up out in the country, for my parents on my father's side owned land and cattle, and I always spent school vacations on their estates. All my brothers and sisters did too. There were six of us, four are still living. All are married and live here in Nicaragua. My sister lives part of the time here and part of the time in Miami because she is very sick with arthritis; her four daughters live in Miami and are married to Nicaraguans. Having her family there, she can go back and forth easily. My mother is living in her house too; she has just turned eighty-six, poor thing. She is in poor health, and has just suffered a stroke and can hardly talk. Earlier, she had a thrombosis; she is an invalid, and we have her with a nurse until such time as God wills otherwise. I called her just a little while ago to see how she was doing this morning. We are very close.

My parents had a tremendous influence on my development. My father's parents were landholders, and my mother's father was a businessman who had an establishment in Rivas. One sold cloth, and the other raised cattle, sold wood, and bought things, and that's how they made their livelihood. They never cheated anyone; they are decent people, thank God. That is our heritage. My father died in 1948 at the age of fifty.

When he died, I was eighteen years old and was in the U.S., supposedly studying and learning English at the same time. But I couldn't do either one, and I would've loved to learn English because it is a necessary language, the international language, everywhere in the world they use it, even in Russia I believe. But unfortunately, I couldn't learn it because the school where they sent me, Our Lady of the Lake College in San Antonio, Texas, didn't have special English classes, and it is very difficult to learn just by hearing. We were eighty *latinas*, imagine! I wrote my father, "Here I am, and I'm happy, but there's no English language classes for people like me. What do I do, do I come back to Rivas?" He answered, "No, stay there, it will be better for you in the long run."

He was very influential and well-to-do, and he would come with my mother and spend vacations there with me. Then we would go to New York, because they would visit my grandparents, both my grandfathers, who were living in exile during the time of the Zelaya government. One, my paternal grandfather, went to the north of the U.S.; and my maternal grandfather went to Costa Rica, where my mother was born, in Punta Arenas. Though my father spoke Spanish perfectly, without any accent, my mother would always have to correct his letters, because he had virtually grown up in the U.S., from the age of three until he was twenty he lived there. My grandfather used his money to educate all of his children, my father and my uncles, in good universities, such as MIT and Cornell. He later moved to San José, Costa Rica, and died there. He called my father, who was at MIT at that time, and asked him to move closer to home so that he could administer one of his *fincas*, or farms.

So, we are country people, we love the country. Before, people used to go horseback riding; now they go riding in a car, but I prefer the former. I love horses, and I ride perfectly. I love the music of the countryside and the people. I have such beautiful memories; what a lovely childhood, although I was an internal, or resident, student it didn't matter. I remember first I went to school in the city of Rivas. Later, I would take the steamboat *Victoria*, and cross the great Lake Nicaragua to go to school as an intern in a *colegio*, or secondary school, in Granada, called the Colegio Francés. That crossing was *bellísima*, extremely beautiful. During the time that I was interned there, Anastasio Somoza García bought a boat, a second boat for the crossing, called *El Somoza*. How's this for a funny coincidence: those two boats ran into each other in the Lake, and the *Somoza* sank while the *Victoria* emerged triumphant! I was very young, but I remember the collision well, being an internal student in the Colegio Francés.

From there I transferred to the Colegio La Imaculada, also Catholic, here in Managua, with the Mother Cabrinis. What saints! Now they have beatified Mother Cabrini in New York I believe. I was there two years, and then during the fifth year of secondary they sent me to the U.S. to another Catholic school, the one in San Antonio. I loved the atmosphere in San Antonio, though I was there for only one year.

Then they transferred me to another school, a college in Virginia, where I stayed a year and a half, both auditing and taking classes for credit too, and somehow passing them. I can't remember the name of that small college now, in Blackstone, Virginia but it was very beautiful. I adjust to everything. I think I have always been independent; you have to do your own things in life, and at that time I was studying to be an executive secretary.

Then my father died and I had to return home. He died on January 1, 1948, but I did not return to Nicaragua until February because I caught pneumonia in New York and I had to spend a month there. When I returned to Rivas, I met Pedro, my husband, by coincidence. The world is so small. I remember that occasion as if it were yesterday. My brother Carlos was coming to Managua to make some purchases that he needed for the *finca*. You see, he also had to leave his work and come back to Nicaragua. He had graduated in electrical engineering from the University of Texas at Austin, and had done postgraduate work too and was working for Westinghouse. But he had to come back home to help manage all my father's landholdings and properties. When he was in Managua in March, during Holy Week, he went to a popular restaurant, on what was then called Bolívar Avenue, since destroyed by the earthquake, and there he ran into Pedro. They had been schoolmates earlier, both interns at the Jesuit-run Colegio Centroamérica in Granada, where they became good friends. They affectionately called each other *cuñado*, or brother-in-law.

Pedro's parents were waiting for him in San Juan del Sur, a resort on the Pacific. Our *finca* was off the highway to Costa Rica, on the shore of Lake Nicaragua, with a very beautiful view of the lake and of the mountain too. Pedro greeted my brother and asked what he was going to do that weekend. My brother Carlos José, or "Charlie," invited Pedro to the *finca* to go deer hunting, but said that first he had to stop at the house in Rivas to pick up his little sister. Later Pedro told me that he was expecting some little kid, not a lovely young woman. He said that he fell in love at first sight. But I certainly did not! It was over a year before I accepted him as my *novio*, or sweetheart. Now I'm sorry, because I lost a year of my life with him, but what can you do? We were married December 8, 1950, and lived twenty-seven very happy years together, whether in jail, hiding, in exile or on the run, because when there is love all things are possible.

In 1951 our first son, Pedro Joaquín, was born. We baptized him Quinto Pedro Joaquín de Nuestra Señora de la Merced, because he was the fifth Pedro Joaquín and because Pedro wanted to recognize the saint on whose day his first son had been born. He was very *hermosote*, beautiful, that baby. Now he is in Costa Rica, working against this government and for the resistance, trying to bring about the democratization of Nicaragua. In 1952, the year after our first son was born, Pedro's father died and Pedro became director of *La Prensa* from then on, with others such as his brother Xavier taking over when Pedro was in jail or in exile.

Then Claudia Lucía was born, prematurely. We didn't know whether she would make it or not, but thanks be to God, she lived. When she was born Pedro was not here in Nicaragua but in Costa Rica with two of my brothers, who had taken him to see a football match, so that he would "put his mind on zero" as we say, and relax, forget about everything. Claudia was born in Rivas where I had gone to visit my mother; that was March 7, 1953.

Eleven months later Cristiana was born, *una marimba espantosa*, a three-ring circus, right? During all this time of births, Pedro was in and out of jail. He would be released from one jail and I would get pregnant, and then he would be jailed again. That period was very difficult, for our lives were always in turmoil and Pedro was always in danger from Somoza. We were living here in Managua; for a while we lived in my parents-in-law's house, but then we got our own because I believe that every married couple prefers to have their own place. Then came Carlos Fernando, on March 1, 1956, with a little more "margin," shall we say, than the first three. When Pedro would come out of jail, where he would spend eight or ten months at a time, the Somoza dictatorship, instead of giving him freedom, would keep him under house arrest. So, that's when I got pregnant again and Carlos Fernando was born.

He is now the director of *Barricada*, the Sandinista paper, but we get along fine, beautifully. The problem is that politics tries to divide families, but our bonds are too strong. Anyway, Pedro and I managed as well as we could, Pedro in jail and I, taking care of the children. All the while I tried never to make my children's hearts bitter or sad about life, or about what was happening to their father, never anything like that. When they took Pedro away, they took him to La Aviación prison, and my oldest, Pedro Joaquín, asked where they had taken his papa. "He's working," I told him, "in a place called La Aviación," and that *chavalo*, that boy, loved airplanes. So when I was allowed to visit Pedro, but not conjugal visits like they have now, but every three or six months, he would make airplanes out of those Eskimo ice cream sticks and tell me to tell papa to keep them as a remembrance.

That was my life with my four children. The last one, Carlos Fernando, at birth also had a very grave problem, because none of the doctors who attended me during that pregnancy gave the test, and I didn't know about it either, for the RH factor. It turns out that I am RH negative. So, there was a blood incompatibility, and that had been the problem with Claudia's birth but we didn't know it at the time. She had so many difficulties that by three years of age she still wasn't, well, it's not that she was abnormal, but Cristiana for example, who was born *after* Claudia, walked first. We were doing everything possible to help her develop, but we didn't know about the problem.

Then Carlos Fernando was born in 1956, and of course Pedro was in jail and couldn't be with me; and Carlos was born as black as a Negro from the Atlantic Coast. I told my mother-in-law to tell Pedro that he had a son and that he was black. Pedro answered that black Chamorros are very strong and brave. I went home almost immediately with the baby, hoping for the best, but right away he began to turn yellow. I called the doctor and he said to bring him back so that he could examine him. They did lab tests, but they didn't know what was the matter and the baby was dying, urinating blood, it was horrible. But, God didn't want to take him then, and he was saved. The doctors operated on him and changed his blood. When they gave him the first transfusion a cousin of Pedro's who was a friend of Somoza's told Somoza of the problem and he gave Pedro permission to go to the hospital, without guards, just on Pedro's word as a gentleman. But thankfully, Carlos was saved, and after that, I determined that I would not have any more children.

This is how our lives went on, with Pedro in jail, first from 1954–56 when he was arrested for participating in the failed coup against Somoza García, the first Somoza. Then he was freed for several months in 1956; but when Somoza García was murdered by the poet Rigoberto López Pérez, they arrested Pedro again and tortured him brutally, even though he had nothing to do with the assassination. Imagine what it was like! I was worried sick about Pedro, but having to take care of the kids, to educate them, and to go on with everyday tasks. All the while I tried to maintain a facade of normalcy, but it was a strain. Every day I begged for permission to visit my husband, and whenever it was granted I ran to the jail with my basket, carrying his breakfast, lunch, and dinner too, in the rain, in the sun, in all circumstances whenever they would allow me. So that my oldest, Pedro Joaquín, wouldn't see my daily anguish, I sent him to be an internal student at the Jesuit school in Granada. It was a good school then, but from what they tell me I don't think I would like to have anything to do with it now. He was just eight and a half years old, and every Sunday I came to visit and changed his sheets, made his bed, arranged his closet, and so on. That was my life, running from here to there all the time, constantly, that is how I lived.

One day I went to the jail and the guard told me to wait, because they were going to move Pedro. So I stayed, and at 7:30 the next morning they moved him from La Aviación, which the Sandinistas have now changed the name of, like they change the name of everything. Anyway, I saw Pedro come out and I embraced him. "They're sending me to San Carlos," he said, "I'm to be confined to San Carlos". That's a port on Lake Nicaragua and the San Juan River. I begged the captain to let me talk to my husband for a minute before they took him away. Then Pedro told me to leave immediately for San Carlos on whatever was available, any old piece of junk. At that time, both the boats and the airplanes were very unsafe, but at least the airplane would get there faster, if it got there at all. So I went to San Carlos by plane.

Those were dark, threatening times; that was in 1957, and Luis Somoza, son of the first Somoza, was in power. I left my children, two with my mother and two with my mother in-law, and I went. Pedro did not want me to go there alone, so I went with his brother Xavier who was running things at *La Prensa* then, and who is now at *El Nuevo Diario*. When we got to San Carlos, I had only very few clothes but I had my statue of the Virgin, because I cannot separate myself from her; I have a very strong faith in her. Pedro was there in a *pensión*, a tiny hotel, and after two days Xavier flew back to Managua while I stayed looking for a house. I thought we would be moving there, since we did not know for how long Pedro would be confined to the town, but we thought it would be at least for three years.

But Pedro knew right away that he could not stay there at all; he was constantly harassed, followed, pursued by the guardia, even though he had the town for a jail. He told me, "Violeta, my love, I'm sorry, but I cannot remain here. You return to Managua and take care of the kids; I must flee this country." I told him that the children were fine, that nothing was going to happen to them, but that if I returned to Managua, I might be taken prisoner, and I would have to try to find refuge in an embassy. With four kids that was not going to be easy, so the best thing to do was for us to flee together. After much discussion, he finally agreed, and we set out together in a rowboat for Costa Rica.

A month later my children joined us, brought by plane by two *empleadas*, or maids, and we lived for two years [1957–59] in exile in Costa Rica, where Pedro wrote of his imprisonment in *Estirpe sangrienta: los Somoza* (Bloody Heritage: the Somozas). He also had to get a job in order to support us, so he went to work for a paper called *La Prensa Libre* at that time. It was dying, and he brought it back to life. He was just an employee, but he revived it, and we lived on his salary and the little bit that our families sent us. We rented a small house, then later we were able to buy a car. We lived there happily, all things considered. The kids went to school, some to La Asunción, and others to the Colegio San Francia, but Pedro was always restless, uneasy, eager to return to his country.

During those two years there occurred a very important event, the first airborne invasion of Nicaragua, that of Olama y Mollejones, which Pedro directed in 1959. Along with Reinaldo Antonio Téfel, his close friend with whom Pedro had suffered imprisonment earlier, and Enrique Lacayo Farfán, another faithful ally, Pedro had traveled to Cuba trying to get arms and help from Castro and Che Guevara, whose revolution had just triumphed. But they received no support from Castro, perhaps because their political line was different, I don't know.

Anyway, the expedition failed miserably for many reasons. The idea was to land men and arms in an isolated area where runways had been prepared and where radio contact could be made with the internal front in Managua. But the radio never materialized and they had to depend on sporadic mail service; further, the only airfield that was built was the one at Mollejones. At a given signal the peasants were to join in the revolution, there would be a general strike countrywide, and Somoza would be driven out. Instead, along with everything else that went wrong, two peasants informed on the expedition and told the guardia their exact location. Pedro and thirteen others, including those mentioned above, were captured and jailed. These experiences are described in Pedro's *Diario de un preso* (Diary of a Prisoner). When I heard that Pedro was in jail in Nicaragua again and that the invasion had been a disaster, I packed our things and left Costa Rica for Managua.

I almost forgot, another child was born during that two year period in Costa Rica, a baby girl, *un angelito*, a little angel, because she died only a few hours after birth. During the pregnancy, my doctors had examined me and discovered the RH factor and advised against having the baby. But since Pedro and his family were so Catholic, an abortion was out of the question. We went to talk to representatives of the church, to priests and so forth, but the outcome was that the child would be born come what may. Pedro never even saw her, because at that time he had gone to Cuba looking for arms for the Olama y Mollejones invasion. In San José I buried my *angelito*, whom I named María Milagros. I was not too sad, because of course I had known for a while that she would die, and my mother came to help me out and keep me company. That's life; one has to have faith in God, that's the only way.

Pedro continued his opposition during the reign of the third member of the dynasty, Anastasio Somoza Debayle, who had himself elected president in 1967. Then came the earthquake in December 1972, after which *La Prensa* published a series of articles exposing the corruption, the shameful traffic in relief money and goods that Somoza was openly dealing in. He kept for himself millions of dollars of international aid that was intended for the victims of the disaster. My husband was one of those who exposed Somoza's profiteering.

In December 1974, Pedro, along with Reinaldo Téfel and others, helped found UDEL, (Unión Democrática de Liberación, Democratic Liberation Union), a political party proclaiming ideological pluralism, and composed of all those, except for the "ultras" on either extreme, who opposed the regime. With the combined efforts of *La Prensa* and UDEL, Pedro thought that Somoza could be defeated. But, as luck would have it, later that same month [December 27, 1974] the FSLN commando raid on the hated Somocista Chema Castillo's house took place, and Somoza cracked down on *La Prensa* with a heavy censorship that lasted for three years, until 1977.

That's how it went, publishing on and off, at the whim of the dictator, having to close, receiving death threats, Pedro being carried away to jail while I waited for news. However, in spite of the censorship, Pedro and the UDEL members continued doing whatever they could to publicize Somoza's abject corruption, even resorting to mimeographing and handing out flyers when there was nothing else available to them because of the government censorship. Finally, in 1977 as a result of international pressure, Somoza lifted the censorship he had imposed in 1974, and immediately *La Prensa* resumed its inquiry into the use of earthquake relief funds, such as those from the Agency for International Development.

Also in 1977, *La Prensa* ran a series of articles exposing the unbelievably shocking scandal of the plasmapheresis center in Managua. Poor

Nicaraguans would go there to donate blood in exchange for a few córdobas and a meal. Then the plasma was separated out and sent to the United States. The business was owned by Somoza and a Cuban exile, Dr. Pedro Ramos, who together made millions of dollars as parasites, sucking the life blood of the Nicaraguan people. After the exposé, Ramos sued my husband for libel, lost, and moved to Miami.

On January 10, 1978, Pedro was murdered and all Managua spilled out into the streets. During the wake at *La Prensa*, the guardia and the Somocistas began throwing tear-gas bombs and shooting, trying to disperse the crowds, but it was impossible. The people were shocked and angry. One group of mourners burned the plasmapheresis center. I truly feared a holocaust, because I saw how inflamed the people were. I saw at once that Pedro should be buried as soon as possible to avoid further violence. So, I had his body brought to the church, and during the service in the midst of all the shouts of *viva!* (long live!) and *muera!*, (death!). I stood up on a pew and said, "Please, no more *vivas* or *mueras*. I ask you only to sing the national anthem with me from beginning to end, until we have buried Pedro. Let's not do or say anything more; let's just sing." There was a respectful silence, and then everyone started singing the anthem in the most moving and dignified manner you can imagine. I will never forget it.

Here I am nearly ten years later trying to carry on my husband's struggle. It's the same story. The current government claims that the revolution has been for the people; they claim so much, but it is all brainwashing and lies. I remember right after the triumph they said that no longer would anyone beg. There had been much begging during Somoza, and it was a source of great shame. So the Sandinistas loudly proclaimed that no longer would anyone have to sell gum on the streets. But now it's even worse than before. I remember when they accepted my resignation from the Directorate, they gave me a big *despliegue*, a ceremony honoring me, expressing gratitude for my service, including some women from AMNLAE, the national women's organization, and others from similar organizations. But I knew in my heart that all that falderal was pure hypocrisy. Anyway, one of the topics that was brought up in all that effusion of words was that no longer would anyone sell gum on the street, because that belonged to the imperialist past. "But why should this be an indignity," I said, "if it helps support the child and his parents, and it's the only way?" At any rate, now they sell gum and more.

They [the Sandinistas] have such a closed attitude; that's why I resigned from the government. From the beginning I could see it, but the people had faith in them. We were coming out of a dictatorship, and we were trying to enter into a democracy without worrying about political parties, about this or that affiliation. But I knew what was really coming; I sensed how they felt about me, and I felt a great deal of tension. When I offered my resignation, they accepted it immediately and took over the newspaper. Well, there's more, it's really like a novel or a soap opera. At the beginning, when I was in the junta, they said they were going to find my husband's assassin. The most popular of all the comandantes came to my house, and he said that everything was all set, that he had retained lawyers and it was all arranged. I asked what he meant, and he said "Violeta, why don't you authorize me to have him killed?" Imagine my shock; I was just sitting there drinking a Coca Cola. I said "I'm not a murderer; the person wouldn't even have a chance to defend himself, to speak." And it's not that the comandante felt the death of my husband so much either, the *hypocrite*! But they're all the same. I'm *hastiada*, fed up and disgusted.

If they [the Sandinistas] would only leave people alone and stop propagandizing, then we could have peace and freedom, but they don't. Look at this headline today about a new life for people in the city because the government is giving them housing and taking them out of their miserable shacks. What *really* happened is that the government has realized that these squatter settlements in the center of the city look very bad, so they send in their bulldozers, raze them, and relocate the people to new homes provided by the government. These poor families have nothing to say about it. They *have* to move; they are uprooted and they take their few possessions to their new life. Yet, the headlines dare to proclaim "*De los escombros a una nueva vida,*" "From the rubble to a new life." That's all political propaganda. It's completely *maquinado*, manipulated; none of this is coming from the people themselves.

As for the vaunted educational campaign, the famous literacy crusade. It always had *their* [the Sandinistas] ideological stamp, and if you didn't see eye to eye with them, well then, too bad for you. And now many young people are telling their parents that they just can't go on any more in their school, even though this decision is unpopular and causes them to lose friends, even though it isolates them from their peers. Still, many are saying that they have *had* it with the schools, their teachers and some priests who have changed their ideology, with the *servicio militar patriótico*, and they are leaving the country any way they can.

They are going to the U.S., Mexico, El Salvador, Costa Rica. But often they can't get visas so they have to pay 600 dollars or more to a *coyote* to cross them illegally, and then passage to the U.S. where they have relatives who have gathered clothes, funds, and have things waiting for them. Once there, they manage, they use their skills and their wits and they work hard. Rarely do you see a Nicaraguan immigrant in one of these countries who is on the dole or who is a burden to society, because the *nica* is very adaptable and very hardworking. These people, many of them very simple, even manage to send money back to their families here, and in these hard times too. It's so sad, things just can't keep on like this. In the meantime, one must never give up. My job is to stay here in Nicaragua and to carry on with *La Prensa* at all costs.

3   Doris María Tijerino (b. 1943)

". . . my personal, intimate life, which has been difficult, has always been limited or determined by my political militancy. It couldn't have been otherwise, because we were responding to a cause and an ideal; that was the most important thing, and everything else was subordinated to that goal."

I was not prepared for the contrast between the elaborate and always unsettling security measures that awaited me and the retiring figure who softly bade me enter her office. Other contrasts were to follow as Doris María Tijerino, hands quietly folded in her lap, recounted with self-effacing modesty a singular life of outstanding valor and deep suffering. Her gentle manner and shy smile mask a remarkable resilience and a constitution of steel.

This disarming heroine of the revolution and current chief of the national police force has distinguished herself nationally through her leadership roles within the Frente Sandinista, her acclaimed military prowess as guerrilla leader and as comandante, and her stoicism in the face of sadistic torture by the guardia. Comandante Tijerino's powerful story, told with unusual warmth and candor, provides a vivid portrait of the life of a revolutionary.

Comandante Tijerino's life story broadens our understanding of the Somoza decades and of the work of the opposition during the period. It also illustrates with blinding clarity the total commitment of the small bands of Sandinista revolutionaries who early in the 1960's accepted armed violence as the only way to rid the country of Somoza. Finally,

Doris María Tijerino's narrative sharply focuses the precarious drama of the post-revolutionary period, in which individuals like herself struggle daily to keep from losing a revolution paid for so dearly.

I come from a very wealthy family, whose background and possessions afforded me an extremely comfortable life. My family have been large landowners, proprietors of many businesses, and, a long time ago when I was very young, my father was also owner of various radio stations. I was born in the north, in Matagalpa; my mother was from Matagalpa, and was also born there, but my father is from the west, from León. My mother had strong personal values and principles, and she played the crucial role in the constitution and development of the family. Her centrality in family decision-making is probably what determined that we would leave León for Matagalpa and live there. I have fifteen brothers and sisters. Eleven are from my mother and father's marriage, and the other four are from my father's second marriage, after my mother died he married again.

When I was very young, we lived for a good while in the countryside, because, as I mentioned, we had land, and even when we didn't, we would still visit the holdings of my aunts, uncles, and grandparents. When I was in secondary school we lived in the city and we had a business, a big business, a commercial house that represented other large commercial houses that were located in Managua and ,they sold everything, cloth, refrigerators, cars. Ours was a very large store; in addition, my father was the owner of a radio station called Radio Musón, named for a very high, imposing hill in the Matagalpa region.

All my development took place within the framework of an extremely affluent life-style. I was educated in a very traditional nun's school; nevertheless, perhaps because of the way that family life develops in the countryside, there was evolving in me, spontaneously, as part of my own character, a deep interest in knowing the life of the poor, the marginalized classes. I wanted to become involved and try to solve some of their problems from a Christian perspective. Though I didn't realize it at the time, mine was a very bourgeois, individualistic approach to the problem. I was about nine or ten years old, and I had as my charge a poor family, for whom I obtained food, medicine, clothes, and whom I also visited regularly. All this made me feel good; it soothed my Christian conscience and my political conscience, not that I had developed any ideological position then, but I *was* aware that the phenomena of poverty and marginalization were political realities. Nevertheless, I never focused on the issue from an integrated perspective. I was unable to view the situation as a whole, to see it as a product of the system or of the repression of the dictatorship.

Part of the problem was my education, which tended to develop a kind of Christian awareness that was based only in charity; now I see that it was offensive for those on the receiving end. They were educating us from very young to assume the role of wealthy charity ladies when we grew up, used clothing, a handful of food, that's what Christian helping meant to the sisters of the Order of Josefina at the Colegio San José, and to most others at that time. But, it all seemed wonderful to me then.

That approach tends fundamentally to soothe the guilt of the one who has, but what it reveals is that one *has* precisely because someone else does *not* have, and no one wants to think that about themselves. Nor does he who has wish to scrutinize the system as a whole; so it is easier just to perform individual acts of charity. This, then, was one way in which the system was able to keep on reproducing itself ideologically. However much I may criticize the motivation, I have to say that because of that experience I really got to know what misery is like, and I was shocked at the contradiction of people living in subhuman conditions in such a rich, fertile, coffee-producing zone, and of those who had nothing living along-side the great landholders who had an abundance of everything, and who even had their own banks. My mother's family were coffee planters, while my father's family were more in electronics, commerce, and radio. I have a brother who is still a coffee grower, but, as you might imagine, today I have almost no relationship with him; we do not understand each other. Politically, I developed my awareness in the bosom of my family. In the first place, my mother's family was of English origin, and they suffered serious economic displacement when the *yanquis* took over the coffee market here. You see, the coffee markets and plantations had all been owned by Europeans, Germans, Danish, English. But when the North Americans displaced them, beginning early in World War II, there developed a fierce anti-American sentiment. It was rooted in an economic, not an ideological base. Although my mother herself never felt this way, others in her family just did not accept North Americans. They were considered as inferiors and usurpers. Perhaps they especially felt that way because they were English. Anyway, it was there, in the family circle, that as a young child, I heard stories about General Sandino.

I will talk more about that, but first I want to tell you about my mother. I was fortunate to have an exceptional mother, because even though she was from an extremely conservative milieu, that of the English landowner, she was most progressive. My mother's father was English; he came here when he was in his twenties, and the Haslam family was one of the first English families to settle in Nicaragua. They came in the 1800s, established themselves in Matagalpa, and started a hotel. Later, they acquired land through my grandfather's marriage to the daughter of an Irishman named Macy, who was married to a Nicaraguan woman whose family name was Pérez, of Spanish ancestry. The Macys had extensive holdings in the north, and because of this marriage the Haslam family acquired coffee lands.

By the time my mother was growing up, the Haslam family was established, and she was being prepared to fulfill the role assigned to her as a woman in an upper-class, conservative environment. She went to primary school and learned the basics, addition, subtraction, reading, and so forth. After that she began a course of study in a school run by some French nuns, where girls were instructed in *culturas femininas*, feminine culture, embroidery, knitting, high cuisine, how to set a fine table, how to be ladies within the value system of the wealthy classes.

Fortunately, my mother had very little of this type of education. After she finished primary school, she was sent to the countryside, which was a good thing, because my mother had very different ideas, and a great tendency for self-affirmation. There, she began to develop her character, and because of the relationships that the more open members of her family had with North American intellectuals, she began to read world literature. She was very much interested in progressive readings, which gave her a world view very different from that of other women of her class. She read all the classics of poetry and the novel; I remember she particularly enjoyed Gorki. And a very special thing for me, when she was only sixteen years old herself, my mother dedicated her books to her first daughter, who would receive them on her fifteenth birthday. But she gave them to me when I turned thirteen, because she understood that I would not be content in a traditional role, and since I already had had more schooling than she ever did, I was in secondary school by then, she gave them to me.

Why did she put those books away for her first daughter and not for her first son, or simply her first child? She told me that she had suffered the consequences of being a woman in a wealthy family of English background. Their main concern was what and where their sons should study, since they one day would manage the family fortune and compete in the world of the coffee market and international commerce. The daughters were of little consequence, were relegated to the house, to being a good mother, an obedient wife, and an accomplished hostess. All this seemed terrible to my mother. She decided that since men had more possibilities, her male children did not need her books as much as her daughters did. So she turned this gift over to me and, at the age of thirteen, I began to read world literature. Without doubt, this experience helped me considerably to interpret the political phenomena which I heard talked about within the family, for example about the struggle of Sandino, and which, otherwise, I would not have been able to place in a framework. My mother gave me a framework, that of anti-imperialism, not anti-Americanism, which was more common, but anti-imperialism, because the root problem was the economic struggle.

To be anti-imperialist was to be pro-Sandino, because many Nicaraguans realized that so much of our suffering, the history of our invasions from William Walker on, was the product of the bourgeois and the pettit bourgeois ideology. Sandino represented for a large portion of the Nicaraguan people the national expression of our feelings, certainly for my mother, but not for my father.

I think that being born in 1943 helped my development a lot, although my brother was born in '42 and it didn't help him at all. But it helped me in the formation of my personality and my positions with regard to what war is, the arms race, imperialism, because my first years were spent under the influence of the terrible psychological and ideological war against communism. Here there was a tremendous campaign against communism, which I began to perceive with some awareness as early as four or five years of age. By '46, I was well aware of what a world war signified, of the principal aspects of fascism, and of what the war meant for the German people.

You see, we had many international radios in my house; we lived in the country then and my father was always listening to the radios. That's how I heard the anti-communist campaign against Stalin from such a young age, and I asked my mother who Stalin was. She answered that he was the leader of the Russian people, who had had to face fascism. Then I asked her what fascism was, and so on. And I heard on the radio the stories and reports of what fascism meant for Europe, about concentration camps; all this was coming together to form my ideological consciousness. My mother had a great deal to do with the whole process; because of her, besides hearing the news and feeling a true terror of fascism, I could also receive an *explanation*. She interpreted things for me, told me what a concentration camp was, what racism was, how the Germans did away with the Jewish people and with all those they thought were inferior. My father was interested in all this too; after all, they were his radios and he was always listening. But in the Nicaraguan family, instructing the children is the responsibility of the mother, so my mother was the one from whom I learned about the world.

My parents argued a great deal later, maybe earlier too and I was too little to realize it; but I remember it well when I was older, and they eventually separated because of political differences. They disagreed totally about the positions that we, each one of their children, should take regarding the dictatorship. My mother encouraged our political participation against Somoza , but my father, no. He was not in agreement; he said that we had no reason to get involved in politics, especially as women, and that we should stay at home, that these were men's affairs. But now he is different. He has changed so much, but in those days he was that way, and the point is that we children owe our formation almost exclusively to our mother, not our father, as was surely the case with many other Nicaraguans. That's why the woman, the mother, is so vitally important in the Nicaraguan family.

We can say that my life developed in the city knowing what the system was and what its effects were on the marginal classes, and in the countryside seeing the exploitation of the campesino, which was terrible. I saw it on the haciendas of my own relatives. I saw children die needlessly from their illnesses, the elderly dying of hunger. I saw how they worked, how they made my grandfather rich, while they became poorer and poorer. All these things contributed to the creation of my own political definition in the face of the factors that generated this situation. I was becoming aware, for example, that the guilty party was not really my grandfather, but that he was part of the existing system, and that there were many, many more worse than him in the treatment of their workers.

My mother's books had an impact on my development. The book that most affected me, and there were many including *Los miserables* of Victor Hugo, but the one that most influenced my political and ideological awareness was *La madre* by Maxim Gorki. That book helped me to understand many things. What stood out for me was that it was about the participation of a woman who had a minimal cultural level and really no preparation to understand what was going on politically in her time. She had only a woman's sentiments and a mother's heart to help her understand her son, who participated in the syndical movement, and to support him. I identified with that book, with that mother and that son.

You can see what the formative influences in my adolescence were, and how I came of age in a country in which the dictatorship was so terrible that if one were a decent human being then one had to stand up and be counted. One couldn't remain apathetic, alienated, or isolated from the Somoza horror in this country. This is what gradually dawned on me as I was growing up, while I was still a child really.

I was looking for a way to participate, to do something, and in 1960 I joined up with the Juventud Patriótica Nicaragüense (Patriotic Nicaraguan Youth). It was a huge organization, very broad. It was so broad that the contradictions among the various groups that composed it—students, workers, campesinos, professionals, women, liberals, conservatives, communists, socialists, Christians, atheists, could not be resolved. Afterwards, most groups went on to try to find organizations more compatible with their beliefs. The Juventud lasted just a year, but it was very important for the participation of students and women; it was open to everyone who was against the dictatorship. I joined as an anti-Somoza youth.

It was open, as I said, but not legal, so every meeting was threatened by the guardia, broken up by blows from rifle butts, and there were injuries and people taken prisoner every time. That meant, of course, that we became more and more radicalized. As positions hardened within the group regarding our harassment and persecution, we became more polarized within the Juventud, and the organization collapsed as an entity. But it awoke in many of us the desire to participate and I, for example, afterwards joined the Juventud Socialista Nicaragüense (Socialist Nicaraguan Youth), the sector that represented the party of the proletariat here. In this way, I began to develop an outlook that, while not exactly Marxist, I was still very young and I didn't understand Marxism very well, was at least compatible with Marxism. I was about fifteen or sixteen at that time, and still in secondary school.

After finishing my secondary studies, I decided to go on to university. I applied for a scholarship and studied Agronomy and Agricultural Administration for almost three years in the Soviet Union, from 1963 to the end of 1965. Already in '63 the Frente had had its first armed experience and I had begun to feel sympathy for the guerrilla movement. In the first place, for merely emotional reasons, because I had a first cousin, Charlie Haslam, who had been head of a guerrilla unit in '59. The guardia killed him and did away with Charlie's small group, but I felt a natural identification with the armed struggle ever since that event.

I found out about the scholarship and appplied for it through a friend who was studying in Mexico. He helped me a great deal and at some risk, for of course, all this was clandestine. I chose the Soviet Union because it represented for me, from the time I was a little girl, all that was opposed to North American imperialism. From my earliest radio days, when the family would sit together and listen to the news from all over the world, I felt a great sympathy for Stalin and for the Soviet Union. This sympathy had absolutely no objective basis, because I knew nothing about Russia, but that was not the point. I also admired Russia because Somoza proscribed anything and everything that had to do with communism. So I said to myself, "If Somoza doesn't like it, I have to believe in it. Further, if those who have always invaded us, the North Americans, criticize the Soviet Union, I have to believe in it." I know it's not rational, but it does have its own peculiar logic.

I had just turned eighteen when I left for the Soviet Union, and at first it was terrible, separating myself from my family, especially from my mother because we were so close, but she wanted me to educate myself. It wouldn't have mattered if it had been France, Spain, England, or wherever, she would've encouraged me. But my father, no. He didn't want me to go to university, much less in the Soviet Union. He was ferociously anti-communist. At that time, he was pro-Somoza and was working in the Somoza-owned television station. Later, one of the times when they captured and tortured me, my father broke with them; but at that time, my decision brought a complete break between us. That's why my mother's support was so important to me, and to my development as a woman and as a person.

I went to the Soviet Union, with the idea of armed struggle taking shape in the back of my mind. I began to think that the Juventud Socialista was not going to be able to stand up against the dictatorship; I started to gather information about the Frente Sandinista, and came to see that it was a more viable alternative. I had a friend who was a fellow student there, who later was one of the national leaders of the Frente, and who had also been a militant in the Juventud Socialista, compañero Oscar Turcio. So I put it to him, asked him whether he thought we should become involved in the Frente, and he agreed that we should. He returned to Nicaragua in '64, and he wrote me later saying that he had linked up with the Frente, that he had told them of my interest, and that they wanted me to come back and work for them. In December '65, in spite of the fact that I loved my studies in agronomy, I returned home without finishing the program.

I applied to the Frente and they responded on February 21, 1966, through compañero Oscar Turcio and Comandante Daniel Ortega. There was a ceremony that day in commemoration of Sandino's birthday, and afterwards they called me aside to tell me that I had been accepted. Later, I met with Carlos Fonseca, who had influenced my decision to go to the Soviet Union, because when I was younger I had read the book that he had written after his visit there, *Un nicaragüense en Moscú* (A Nicaraguan in Moscow).

I already knew Carlos Fonseca because he, too, was from Matagalpa, and he had worked in my father's radio station. He was born in '36 and was older, but I knew him from when I was young because his father's family were great friends of my father. He was very much admired in Matagalpa because he was so intelligent. All the wealthy people, the common people, everyone, recognized that he was an unusually capable and intelligent young man. He had been a university leader, he had been to Moscow, he had been taken prisoner, he had been in the battle at Chaparral, he had been wounded by the guardia. I was one of the many townspeople who knew him, cared about him, and respected him greatly. Therefore, the meeting with Carlos on February 21 had special meaning for me.

At that time, he assigned me the job of political organizing within the student movement. So I registered in the national university here in Managua, and began to carry out my task. From then on, I have performed many different jobs within the Frente: as student leader; as grass-roots organizer; as intermediate, or regional, head; as leader of the women; as base community organizer with the Christians; as campesino coordinator; as member of the national directorate in 1966–67; as chief of a group of military cells that carried out various urban military activities.

My personal life from '65 until today has been militancy within the Frente. Though this has been my principal reason for living and working, I, like most people, got married, and I had two children. My son is now twenty-two years old and lives here in Managua. He was born in the Soviet Union where I was married, and I brought him back here when he was just an infant. My mother, again, was fundamental in enabling me to continue my political life, because she took care of my son until he was five years old. I don't know what I would have done without her, because sometimes I was clandestine, and other times, many times during this period, I was prisoner. She was always there to take care of him.

I separated from the father of my child, he is an Ecuadorian poet, because I was coming back to Nicaragua, and he was going back to Ecuador. I had already decided to join the Frente, so we broke the relationship, and I kept the child. Later, I was married, though not formally or legally, to Ricardo Morales, a member of the national directorate of the Frente, and with him I had a daughter. She died in an airplane crash two years ago. Ricardo died when I was two months pregnant with our daughter.

You could say that my personal, intimate life, which has been difficult, has always been limited or determined by my political militancy. It couldn't have been otherwise, because we were responding to a cause and an ideal; that was the most important thing, and everything else was subordinated to that goal. Our own development as women within the Frente was very important because we developed independently of men; that is one of the biggest achievements as regards women. We know that we can be someone on our own, and not have our worth be determined by the husband we have. This is one of the tragedies of many middle-class women and also of many women in the working-class sectors; their intellectual, political, and social lives are still defined by their husbands. We women within the Frente realized that it was up to us, and we threw ourselves into the task of creating our own identity.

My children grew up with me and they shared this same vision. My son, Fyodor Humberto—Fyodor because I am a great admirer of Dostoyevsky's books, and Humberto for his father; but nobody calls him Fyodor and he doesn't like it anyway—shows in his dealings with others that he shares my philosophy about being your own person. When he was growing up he always took into account my criteria, my beliefs, because he respects and admires me very much. Humberto visits his father for brief periods from time to time, but I have always been his reference point in life. However, he does *not* do what I tell him! That really annoys me, because

I want him to be like I think he *ought* to be, right? Nevertheless, he is like *he* wants to be, and that is fine.

He likes military life; he has military training because he went to military schools, and he was a soldier for a while; but he doesn't have enough personal discipline to make a career of the military. He is very independent and very revolutionary. He also likes to drive, to shoot, to fish. Sometimes he wants to be a pilot, but he had an automobile accident and has injuries that make it impossible for him to be a pilot. He says he likes agronomy, but I think he says that because he knows that I like it. I've certainly never seen him plant even one little shoot or sapling!

My daughter died in a Cubana Airlines crash as I mentioned. She was just eleven years old. What a special child she was! She too was very independent, had her own ideas about everything, like her brother. She was born in Cuba, where I had been sent for care during my pregnancy and for protection from the guardia. I made a conscious decision to have this child, because Ricardo had died, and I wanted her to live. I named her Doris María. She loved Cuba so much, Nicaragua too, but she really considered herself Cuban, since she spent her first five years there. Humberto was in Cuba too, until he finished seventh grade. My daughter loved Fidel very much, and she wanted him to come to her birthday parties, but as you might imagine, he never was able to make it.

She was very revolutionary, and, for one so young, she had a remarkable conception of what constitutes revolutionary values. I remember once, during a conversation with some of her friends, she came to me and said that she was upset. One of her friends had called another boy a counterrevolutionary. She said that counterrevolutionaries do bad things, but that that boy had not done anything wrong. It seemed to her that the real counterrevolutionary was the one who had made the accusations. I asked her why she thought that and she told me: "First, because he hurt that boy by calling him names, and that is bad; and second, because he wastes toilet paper, and that is definitely counterrevolutionary!" She was a child who knew very clearly what she thought about things.

Doris María was very bright; she had a great facility for languages. She learned French when she was quite young, and by the time she was in the third grade, she spoke it well. Then she began studying Russian, while continuing French. She wanted to work as a translator for the leaders of the Frente. She did so well in Russian that she participated in a contest in the Soviet Union for children all over the world who were studying Russian, and she won a bronze medal. She had her life planned, that child; she had calculated that by the time she graduated from high school, she would be fluent in French and Russian. Then she would begin English, and after she had that under control, she would take up German, all to prepare herself to be a translator for the Frente leadership.

She made that decision so early because once on TV she saw a program that made a lasting impression on her. It was an interview with a member of the national directorate of the Frente, and the translator had a very shrill, sharp voice, which gave the interview a negative, disagreeable tone. She told me that she could do better than that and that the national directorate had to communicate through a more pleasant voice. That's when she decided what she would be when she grew up. As for me, I understand Russian, I read it, and I speak some, but I'm so timid about speaking anything except Spanish; not true for my daughter, right?

I should return now to the struggle and the times they took me prisoner. The greater my responsibilities within the Frente, the more I was wanted by the guardia, and the more precarious my life became. I was living legally, aboveground, in my house, but carrying out subversive work having to do with the guerrilla movement. I was also in charge of publishing our bulletins, leaflets, and various propaganda materials, of securing funds to support that activity, and of locating safe houses for our militants and for members of the leadership.

After I had carried out these duties for a while, about the end of 1966, I was distinguished by Carlos Fonseca. He and other compañeros in the directorate decided to encourage the leadership of women, and in recognition of what I had done, they invited me to join them as a member of the national directorate, before they went away to the *montaña*, or mountains. They gave me the task of providing logistical support for the urban guerrilla effort, which was a very difficult charge because I had to coordinate and keep in close touch with all the collaborators , with those who lent us houses, vehicles, and money. And I also had to administer *all* the money that we took in our armed raids. I still lived legally, which was a real pressure for me, because while all my activities were conspiratorial and subversive, I had to maintain the appearance of an aboveground life, justifying all my movements; continuing to study economics; keeping my grades up in order to retain my position as a student leader, I was secretary general in '72, for example. I had to do all these things to provide at least a thin cover for my real activities.

After '73, which was when I began to study Marxism-Leninism in an organized fashion, I came to understand that that is my ideological position. I don't mean that I have a sophisticated development, or that I have even understood the theory well; but yes, I identify fully with all that ideology. This development was more decisive for me than Sandinismo, because Sandinismo was broader, and we arrived at it in Nicaragua through many different paths, Christianity; anti-Somocismo, through conservatism for some; for others, through shame, as Carlos Fonseca called it; and through the socialist party, which was in reality the Marxist-Leninist party.

All these groups could feel themselves part of the Frente because of the nationalistic postulates of Sandino, the program of the Frente, and the leadership of Fonseca, all of which provided the only realistic alternative for confronting the dictatorship. This very breadth has characterized both the Frente and the revolution. Nevertheless, the Frente is a single entity, and we don't worry about whether we are Christians, Marxists, and so on, because now what we all are is Sandinistas. Not that Sandinismo is an ideology, but rather a majority expression of our national interests, as first symbolized by Sandino in his epoch.

After '66 and the carrying out of all those functions that I mentioned, I had serious run-ins with the dictatorship. I first fell prisoner in January '67; they captured me at home as part of a general sweep they were making. Then they mistreated me, but they did not torture me much. It was rather abuse by those who consider anyone who opposes them as subhuman and communist. If you were also a woman, that, for them, made everything worse. It was a *vagancia*, something that made you totally useless to society and thoroughly despicable. For them, political participation for women and prostitution were one and the same thing. They regarded women prisoners from their *machista* perspective, and we were treated twice as bad; first because we were anti-Somocista, and second, because we were women. They submitted women to a series of humiliations, sometimes only verbal, at other times, physical. I suffered mostly psychological abuse; for example, they threatened to take my son prisoner, and he wasn't even two years old at that time. They kept telling me that they were going to rape me; it was that kind of mental cruelty.

They never made any accusation against me. I protested, my mother went searching for me in the various jails, and they told her that I was prisoner because I was plotting against the national security, a very broad, catch-all accusation that they used when they did not have enough evidence to make a formal charge. I was detained briefly that first time, about a month.

Later, but still in '67, in November, I was captured again in my home. They conducted a series of raids in the city, and captured various clandestine houses of the Frente. That's when they captured Daniel Ortega and gave him that scar he has on his forehead. A few hours later they captured me too. That's when they used a great deal of violence against me, physical and psychological, as was their custom, but more so with the women.

Besides beatings, at times with the hand, at times with objects, they made me do exhausting physical exercises, such as maintaining impossible postures for a long period. For example, I was made to stand on tiptoes, with knees flexed, and hands outstretched; then they would put a heavy weight in my hands, and tell me that I must not let it fall. Directly underneath my buttocks, they placed a bayonet, so that if I fell, I would be run through. This was physical torture, but the psychological aspect was terrifying and degrading. They made a big show of placing the bayonet, and they would have me touch it to see how sharp it was. Then, when I couldn't see, they would take it away .The mental anguish was terrible, because I thought that when I could maintain the position no longer and fell down, that I would fall on the bayonet. They did this with other prisoners too. Of course, they varied the torture so that one wouldn't become confident or outsmart them.

There was a whole series of atrocities; for example, they threatened to rape me with a grenade that was very large and thick. They said that they were going to violate me with that, and then they hooded me; but they wanted me to raise the hood to see, and then they started beating me, trying to force me to open my legs.They did this to other women too. Another thing that they used a lot is the electric cattle prod, which has three points on the end which open and close. This they would apply to the women's nipples, the clitoris, rectum, the tongue, the most sensitive parts where the electric shock would be strongest.

The third time that they captured me was after a battle. By then, the persecution was ferocious, and I was, of course, clandestine. They had orders to kill me, and had decided to do away with me slowly so that I would suffer more, and they began with brutal beatings. They even sent out an international cable saying that I had been captured in combat, wounded, and taken to the military hospital where I had died in surgery. But they did not realize that a journalist had been there when I was captured, that he had taken some photos and recorded a brief conversation with me, in which I had said that I was not wounded. He asked what the blood was on my clothing, and I told him that it was from a guardia who had fallen on me in combat. After the notice came out about my supposed death, this recording began circulating in all the churches and schools, because, of course, the media were censored. And that's what saved my life. But they had already tortured me horribly, inflicting bruises and wounds in the genital area from forcing me to open my legs, and injuries on my face from the beatings. I had deep cuts on my knees because they made me fall down on finely ground stones that they had put on the floor. They would make me get up, brush my knees off, and fall down again. This they called the Vietnamese torture. I was naked and hooded the whole time, and they manhandled me; it was part of their way of degrading the person.

They kept telling me grotesque things that they were going to do to me, all related to sex, because that was the way to torture me. They threatened to bring in my mother, my son, and my sister. One of them told me that he had just come from the United States and had received training in Vietnamese torture. These were the mechanisms they used to terrorize me. The one thing that I dreaded above all else was that they would put splinters under my fingernails, and hammer them in with little blows. I had read *Boinas verdes*, (Green Berets), where they tell about that torture as a means of interrogation. Of all the things they did to me, that was the one I feared most and felt that I couldn't bear. But it was a defense mechanism, and maybe I was able to make it through everything else because I was concentrating all my fear on the fingernail torture.

One day a doctor or psychologist came; he examined my face and head, ordered them to lift the hood, and told me to keep my eyes closed. He kept his hands over my eyes so that I wouldn't open them, because the guardia gouged out the eyes of those who did. The doctor said that I did not weep or scream because I was in a state of shock. You see, I talked, but nothing else; I would tell them my name, but I never cried out because of any treatment. He said that I had been traumatized from the combat and that I had blocked everything because of seeing how they had killed my compañero. That last part was true, because there was a certain compañero and Frente leader, Julio Buitrago, who had been in the house with me, who heroically and singlehandedly held out against Somoza's tanks, troops and air power for several hours before being killed, and whom I was very close to. Nevertheless, the doctor's statement was not totally true, because I remembered everything, the combat, and later, the hours that I sat waiting, wondering how they were going to kill me.

What had me in shock was when they said that they were going to do the Vietnamese torture on me; I was remembering the torture that I told you about that in that book. So the thing that made me tremble with fear was the thought of the splinters, and the hammer with each question that I would refuse to answer . Dreading this, I was able to stand everything else without going crazy or dying. I spent sixteen days like that, thirteen of which they gave me absolutely nothing to eat, but after a while I felt no hunger. They kept me naked and without bathing for the full time.

One of Somoza's sons would come and watch when they tortured me; I think it was Julio. He also brought guests. When he arrived, the attitude of all those who were torturing me changed, and they would say señor to him. At some angles, even though I was hooded, when the light reflected against them I could see the silhouettes, and I could tell from the shape and type of clothing that they were not guardias. During one of these visits, a torturer violently forced his hand inside my vagina, inflicting deep cuts and causing me to hemorrage. They gave me sanitary towels to staunch the flow, and Somoza's son ordered me to stand there naked while they began to throw me from one to the other, like a ball. One would grab me by the breast, another by the buttocks, and so on, and then pass me on to the next one.

I thought that I was going to die, but first I was going to put up a fight. When Julio Somoza saw me bleeding, he said that I made him sick; and I asked him why, when he was the one who had ordered that all these things be done to me. I also told him that I knew who he was. And I did, although I never saw his face because of the hood, I remember his hands and his ring. To this day, I could identify them anywhere. After that, he left and he stopped coming to the torture sessions. But meanwhile, the guardia was moving in on me; one had already given me the first blow. I jumped on him, grabbing his face and kicking him in the testicles; that particular guardia did not try to hit me again, but there were still the others, and so on. I was saved that time only because of the publicity from that reporter's interview.

Another torture that was typical and was the most terrible, was that they made you witness the crimes they committed against others. They made me watch while they tortured a campesino, Catalino Flores, and others, so that I would become more afraid. When you are the one being tortured, defense mechanisms can help, but when you are watching others, it's much worse.

I had never in my life been beaten by anyone, or even punished; my father had never used a belt on me, or even laid a hand on me, and my brother had never beaten me. No one had. I always thought that if the guardia would ever beat me, that I would simply collapse; I never thought that I would have the capacity to withstand it physically. One thing that they were never able to do was to make me faint. I had a fear of fainting because that's when they would inject a type of drug for interrogation, and I always wanted to be conscious to know what I was saying. I never fainted; I don't know why.

I have many physical problems as a result of the tortures. I suffer from a neurological disorder, a kind of stroke, brought on by the trauma of the beatings, and I am permanently under doctor's care . It seems that one of the blows to the head caused an imbalance in the brain's electrical impulses, which manifests itself in intense headaches, strong electrical currents, and if I am not careful and do not take proper precautions, the whole right side of my body feels as if it were permanently electrified.

Later, in '78, I was taken prisoner again, also after a battle with the guardia; this was in the mountains on the Honduran border. But I was held only a short while because a commando group liberated me; that was the unit in which Dora María Téllez, now the minister of health, participated. They liberated me and sent me to Cuba on a plane with other prisoners. The Mexican government also received me kindly, and I stayed in Mexico until '79 doing publicity and solidarity work, and representing the Frente.

I wanted to go to the U.S., but they wouldn't give me a visa. I also tried earlier, in '78, but they wouldn't let me in even through I had a passport from the United Nations. Later in '79, after the triumph, I did get to go to the States, in November and December. I went to San Francisco, Los Angeles, and another place in California, visiting solidarity committees and places where there were many who wanted to return to Nicaragua. I think that I could go back again; I believe that they would let me in, but I don't know for sure.

Shortly after the triumph, I was put in charge of international relations work for the Frente. I spent a year doing that, in '80. Then I applied to be relocated, because that assignment obliged me always to be on the go, outside the country. I had just spent four years away, and I wanted to be here. I began with the Frente in '66, and worked hard for the day of the triumph, but I could not participate in it because I was not here, having been captured in '78, and then forced to flee the country after my escape. I returned to Nicaragua in '79, and in July at that, but I missed the triumphant entry on the nineteenth, because I arrived the twenty-first or twenty-third. I returned officially with the Mexican government, with their delegation. At any rate, after so much time away, I asked to be reassigned from international relations. In '80 I began working with the minister of the interior himself, Tomás Borge, in political activities, and in the organization of the Frente within the MINT.

In '81 I applied to become part of the struggle against the counterrevolutionary bands, which had begun that same year. The Frente sent me as head of the first group that went with the army to confront the contra. We were called the Omar Torrijos brigade. They didn't let me get involved in the actual combat, because my compañeros in the army were scared that I would be killed, and they wouldn't let me go anywhere alone. Of course, I was a comandante, and the head of the army unit was only a first lieutenant or a captain, but he was a magnificent compañero. Pedro Argucia was his name, and so I went with him supervising the combat units, but not participating. Once I did escape though; I slipped away from him and the four soldiers who were always accompanying me. They found out right away and brought me back. I told them that they were all *machistas*, that they didn't think I could take care of myself, but they said no, no, it was just that felt extremely responsible for my security.

I continued to cooperate with others to try to overcome the counterrevolutionary threat. We did political work among the campesino population, the people who had contact with the contra, and explained the revolution to them. I did this in many places, in El Cuá, in San José de Bocay, in Jalapa, and in a zone on the border with Honduras. I went to some very remote campesino communities, accessible only by helicopter.

One day, near the end of '84, Comandante Borge invited me to come see him, and he asked how would I like to be chief of police. Then, all at once, I was it, without ever having imagined that I would direct such an operation, because I had always been in organizing and political activities. At first, I was very intimidated, because the police is a huge responsibility; besides being the largest group within the MINT, it is very complex because it has a lot of specialties. One has to confront countless social situations which have their roots in cultural, economic, and political problems, like delinquency or robbery, for example. That's where politics come in, because many of these people are deprived; they've been stealing for years, they've never had access to any form of education. Economic and social factors enter too, for people who come from the marginal sectors. The dictatorship always relegated them to the sidelines and they lived by robbing.

It's a complex job because of all this type of thing, but also I was worried because I didn't know anything about police work, and I didn't know how I was going to resolve all these problems. But I learned little by little, and now I would not like to give it up, even though I myself have said that a police chief should not stay many years in that job. The job is very tense and difficult. I feel that in the three years that I've been here that I've aged more than in the forty years that I had already lived. In this position one has to see all the violence that human beings do to each other, the violation of children, murders, wife beatings, beatings of the elderly. It is also distressing at times to find such lack of understanding about the kind of work the police do. There are satisfactions too, but it is mostly draining and tense.

At times, I think, and though I have no right because we revolutionaries have no right to this, I would like to be able to have a little more time for my family, for my personal life. I am forty-three years old, I have a three year old daughter and I have my grandson living with me. I would like to be able to give them a little more time, but police work does not give that time. The only way is to involve your children in your work, and that is what many police have done. They have a baseball game on Sundays with their kids, and now they're trying to organize a championship of the children of the police in different sports, swimming, baseball, basketball. That way the police can link their children to their work, and the children can begin to learn what the job of the police is like, because it is totally absorbing.

A typical workday for me is between twelve and fourteen hours. I get up at 5:30, because of the small children, my grandson and my daughter. I have to get them ready to take them to school. I leave my house at 7:30, and at 8:00 I inspect the police. Then we pledge allegiance to the flag and the national symbols, and we receive the orders of the day. I demand punctuality, so I have to be a little early. Most of the police come in by bus or on foot; they don't have cars, and it is hard for them to get here on time. But they do, and I, who have the use of a car, have to be here earlier. I can never leave before 7:30 or 8:00 at night, because crimes can occur at any hour. Generally, the morning is calm, and I use it to brief myself on what happened the night before, to take a look at the tasks I have before me, review cases that are pending, call an advisor to inform me on due process for the detainees, etc. I have advisors who are lawyers, and often in the mornings they advise me on certain trials and cases, such as child custody for example.

Now that our new Constitution is in place, we are studying and reforming all the laws. This is an interministerial task, and we are participating as police and representing the MINT as its largest member. That's the sort of administrative work I do in the mornings. I also inspect units, such as the traffic police, and visit cells to see how the detainees are doing. I do that regularly because we have to turn in a monthly report to Minister of the Interior Borge. He sends people over periodically to check out our reports on the treatment of prisoners, and they find everything almost always in good order.

Whenever there are accusations of excessive use of force by the police, the people know that we will listen and investigate. We have more than 4,000 requests now to look into police conduct ourselves. What that means is that the population trusts us to investigate and sanction our police. And we do, because if we let a member of the police get away with mistreating a prisoner, that generates an entire chain of mistreatment.

We receive regular visits from the government commission on human rights, under Dr. Vilma Nuñez, who also comes and gives us talks about human rights and the law. The commission on human rights of the National Assembly visits us as well; they interview the chiefs, inspect the jails, and so forth. Similarly, the military auditor evaluates us periodically, inspecting the cells and asking the prisoners if they have any complaints. When a prisoner complains, we are the first to want to investigate, because it is completely against our interests not to do so.

Theft is the most common crime for which one is put in jail. It is not usually a question of the poor robbing the poor, but rather of the thief selecting his victim carefully. In fact, we had a situation recently in which the head of a district had to talk to a group in a residential neighborhood in which there are mostly foreigners. It is the Quinta neighborhood, on the southern highway, where many diplomats, foreigners, and technicians live. There has been a rash of thefts there. In poor neighborhoods, one generally knows who the offender is. It's not a question of a neighbor stealing your chicken or something. The kind of theft we're concerned about is when they break the window and steal your car, and this happens only in the good neighborhoods. Some thieves also steal dollars from foreigners, and then sell them.

There also have been isolated cases of groups of youths beating people up. When you add to that the movies and TV, which make a god of violence and of the gangster, the man who by force solves all his problems, then it gets complicated. That's part of the ideological bombardment of our youth by European and North American films and trends. For example, our young people admire Michael Jackson very much and imitate his style of dancing. The international media have a big influence on our youth.

But sometimes the media make the problems bigger than they are. Also there's the "he said that she said" problem of hearsay. One time on the radio, someone called in complaining that they couldn't leave their house, that people were being assaulted on the street, through car windows, and so on. So I sent out to have that person brought to me in order to follow up the accusations. Turns out that it hadn't happened to her, but that someone at work had told her about it; we found the woman who had told her at work, and she hadn't seen anything either, but a neighbor had told her, etc. We went to the *barrio*, the neighborhood, and interviewed five neighbors, but no one ever saw anything. Sometimes I say to myself that there are people who have bad intentions, to say things that cause our fears to run away with us. This is not to say that the problems of theft and assault don't exist, because they do. There are youths who drink and go around together attacking people, but rumors don't help the situation.

Another problem concerns those who dress in police uniforms. Not long ago, there was a group of four; one of them had a relative who had been in the militia and who gave him a pair of olive green pants and the police shirt he got from a volunteer policeman. Dressed like that, they would stop vehicles on the highway and assault the drivers. This sort of thing happens, criminals wearing police uniforms. We later clarify it in the papers, as in this case, but not everyone reads the papers, so some people probably still think that they were police.

Relations between the people and the police are generally very good. Of course, the traffic police have problems because the drivers always think they're right. And in cases of petty theft, of hitting a wife or a neighbor, or of shooting a gun in the air, many times the people don't understand that the police have to intervene in that type of situation. But for the most part, we have very good relations and we work at it. Right here in my own office, I have a person whose sole job it is to hear complaints from everyone. There's more. When we hear that a policeman vas rude, not that he hit anyone, just that he was rude, we oblige this person to go and apologize, and afterwards we sanction him with what the regulations require.

Part of our problem is that our cultural level is very low, and we have a long way to go, but as I said, we are working on it. For example, let's say that a man passes a woman on the street and makes an insulting comment. She can come here and file a complaint. Then we go and find that person and bring him in, even though it's not a crime to insult someone in public. But we give him a lecture, so that he will know that it is antisocial to behave that way.

But mostly, people are respectful on the street, especially to foreigners because so many of them are here to help us and we are a grateful people. That's why it saddens me when I hear that some people in the States are afraid to come here because they have heard that they would be assaulted. I have two sisters in the United States. One has three children and she has visited here only once since the triumph. She was married to a policeman there, a Nicaraguan who had become a U.S. citizen, but he abandoned her some time ago. I always worry about those three kids living almost completely on their own. Since there are three, they have trouble renting an apartment, and they live in a camper in the country, always moving from place to place. I think they are in Texas. My sister works two jobs, one as cashier in a pizzeria, and I don't know the other job; and the kids have to fix their own meals.

The time they were here, I saw that they were not used to eating food cooked at home, but just instant, frozen things. Two of them already have anemia and they never eat meat, just starches. My sister said she wanted to come to visit and see her kids, but that she was afraid, and also afraid to let them stay here longer. She had heard that they snatch North Americans off the street and beat them. Such ignorance for a person who lived here until she was twenty years old! She has forgotten how we Nicaraguans are, and she believes all this propaganda.

The fifteen-year-old daughter of my other sister is here with me. She likes it here. She speaks good Spanish, but had to study grammar a little more. At fifteen she feels grown up and wants to work, but I want her to study. She helps me a lot, especially in caring for the two little ones. She wants to stay here because she too lived all day closed up in an apartment while her mother worked in a factory, in Miami I think. She would heat a frozen dinner when she got home from school and basically lived alone. So she loves being in a family and she calls me mama. My sister says that she can stay with me or come back, whatever she wants.

I have very good relationships with all my brothers and sisters except for two, the oldest brother, and one of the younger sisters who is now in Miami, not the mother of the fifteen-year-old. We got along well at the beginning of the triumph, and we did not talk about politics. But little by little, they began to distance themselves from me, until one day they vehemently told me that they no longer wanted to have anything to do with me. Yes, it was a blow at first, but since they were not in agreement with the revolution, but rather with the counterrevolution, it was for the best.

My brother is a big landowner and produces much coffee; the government gives him his incentive in dollars, like they do all coffee growers to encourage them to produce. They make large loans available from the bank to help him maintain his machinery, vehicles, and equipment. But he is incapable of investing one single dollar in this country. Instead, he takes his money out of Nicaragua; every three months he goes to the U.S. to deposit it there, in Miami. He also has bought property in Costa Rica. At first, these things hurt me, but later no, because I have emotionally separated myself from him and from my younger sister too. The revolution allowed them to keep their capital; it hasn't done anything to them. Their attitude is unfair and mistaken, but I can't make them understand.

4   Lino Hernández (b. 1953)

". . . we try to teach people their rights and how to stand up for them."

". . . there are violations . . . which they never hear about in the U.S. because . . . there is a whole structure of disinformation that supports the Sandinista party."

It is only 7:30 a.m. and already the poor women have begun to arrive at the shabby, graffiti-covered building. They come seeking the help of don Lino and news of their missing husbands or sons. Don Lino listens with patience and concern, trying to determine whether the men have abandoned their families, simply stopped writing, or whether this may be a human rights violation. Mr. Hernández is president of the Permanent Commission on Human Rights (Comisión Permanente de Derechos Humanos, CPDH), founded in 1977 during the Somoza dictatorship.

But the CPDH is not the only such organization in Nicaragua. Most foreign visitors are surprised to learn that there are two rival human rights commissions, a testimony to the complete political polarization of the country. The other organization, the Nicaraguan Commission on Human Rights (Comisión Nicaragüense de Derechos Humanos, CNDH) established in 1980 and headed by the highly respected North American nun Mary Hartman, is part of the government and concerns itself primarily with documentation and investigation of allegations of human rights abuses by the contra. Lino Hernández's commission, on the other hand, is an antigovernment, or "independent," group committed to publicizing and investigating alleged abuses by the government.

Though once a Sandinista supporter, Mr. Hernández for some years now has been one of the government's most zealous and vocal critics. He and his organization enjoy friendly relations with U.S. representatives with whom they cooperate and share information. While CPDH statistics are not generally accepted by international human rights organizations, such as Amnesty International or Americas Watch, they are the most quoted source in the U.S. press, and the commission's reports and pamphlets are widely disseminated within Nicaragua where the commission's work is highly regarded by many people.

Mr. Hernández's story gives us an insight into what life was like under Somoza for the poor youth determined to receive an education and for the university student involved in the pro-Sandinista movement. It also tells us a great deal about what life is like now for the individual who has become alienated by the Sandinista's goal of a total revolution, and who has incorporated the U.S. position as a natural component of the internal political dialogue.

I am from a poor, working-class family from Managua. My father is a mechanic, my mother is a textile worker. I started work when I was fifteen, also as a worker in a textile factory, where I became a textile mechanic. I repaired the machines that made the cloth, *máquinas circulares,* circular machines, they were called. I studied in the mornings from 6:00 until noon and I worked in the afternoons from 2:00 to 9:00, on a fixed shift for about six years; this was at the Nicaraguan Textile Factory (Fábrica de Textiles Nicaragua). After I entered the university, my schedule there was very full, and I had to quit the factory. After that came the earthquake, and then we had to leave Managua. So I went to work in a cotton hacienda as an *apuntador,* the person who records the number of pounds that the workers harvest. Being a campesino was one of the worst paid and most difficult jobs at that time; it still is.

I have three sisters and one brother; I am the second. The oldest, a sister, is a teacher here; we have all stayed here. I also have a brother who is a military man, a Sandinista, and he spent three years in Russia. He's been back for about a year and a half now, and is an officer in the army, a first lieutenant. He has ascended rapidly because they have promoted him three times since he has been back.

He is well trained in communications techniques; that's his area. I have a sister who is a psychologist, Rosa Argentina, she is the next one after me. She works in the Energy Ministry as director of social work, something like that, I don't know exactly. My third sister, like the oldest, is also a secondary teacher. But one has just finished her course of study and now is *licenciada*, or certified, in education, while the other is still studying. They both have been teaching and studying at the same time. I don't remember where they teach, but it's somewhere here in Managua. We hardly see each other and have become distant. Every one is married except the youngest, thc soldier, who has his common-law wife and child. You know that many men here do not like to get married officially; that way they still feel like they are single and have their freedom!

The psychologist sister married another psychologist. The other sister who is a teacher is married to a public accountant, but he has just gone to the U.S. to live, looking for better conditions. Although he was manager of a bank here, he decided to leave, and now he works in a gas station and in a supermarket in Miami, he has two jobs. Here he had his own nice office with his own auto and his own chauffeur, but he preferred to leave and go there. He keeps in touch by phone, and has been there about four or five months now.

These are the things that happen these days. One relative went to the U.S., while another one went to Russia. When my brother came back, we did talk, but he saw everything there as beautiful, perfect, for him Russia is the best. But he is young and has nothing to compare it with, no parameters. He was also six months in Cuba learning radio communications, and then he went to the Soviet Union after that. But Russia is the perfect society for him. Well, we don't agree at all; it was hard at first, but one becomes accustomed. The truth is that we hardly ever see each other any more, any of us. I have almost no time, and the little free time I have I keep for my own family.

My parents live by themselves, which is a good thing because I don't know how they would manage with all our different ideologies. My papa is a mechanic in communications for the army chief of staff, the *estado mayor*. He's about to retire now; he runs a repair shop, a *taller*, and sort of keeps to himself, not involving himself in our lives very much. My mama is very religious, and is a person of much initiative. She is now looking for a way to start her own little *fábrica*, or industry; she bought a few machines with the money she won in the lottery. She already has a very small *empresa*, or business concern, but she is looking for a way to develop it, hire workers, and so on.

My mama has had a big influence on me because she has taught me initiative, even though her great deals invariably go awry. She always has something cooking, some business scheme; they all fail, but then she just looks for something else. For example, on one occasion she started a little shoe business. She took out nearly all their savings, mortgaged the house, and afterwards, she began to give shoes on credit to all her friends. My papa was left with a bunch of credit notes that nobody paid, and we almost lost the house besides. On another occasion, my mother bought some machines, she invested considerable money in industrial machinery for making cloth, but now this too is at a standstill. She always goes around looking for a business to start. Things are better for her now because she no longer has to maintain us and she can dedicate herself to her failed business pursuits!

I attended a number of different schools, almost all of them public because of my family's economic condition. I was in San Jacinto school for the first three grades. Then, my father got a job as a civilian mechanic in a guardia station, or *dependencia*, and I was able to go to the First of February school. It was supposedly for the children of the military, but I was able to go there because of a recommendation from my father's boss. It was very demanding, and it competed with the best in the country.

The only problem was that it was very strictly disciplined, military style, and the punishments were fierce, such as running around the grounds thirty times when one misbehaved, or doing an unbelievable number of push-ups, things like that. For the girls it wasn't so bad, but for the boys it was extreme. They also pushed for you to go to the military academy after you graduated from there. Also I remember the preparations for the fifteenth of September, the independence day parades. It was terribly rigorous; for two or three months beforehand, we had to march two hours a day.

Discipline helps one, but I had problems in that school. When I graduated from the primary to the secondary section, where the military atmosphere was more pronounced in political terms, I wanted to leave, and I did, but the circumstances were not favorable. A big part of my problem there had to do with the Juventud Liberal Somicista (Liberal Somocista Youth), which, of course, the military sons all joined. I had my own ideas, and they were not in accord with those of many there. On one occasion a young guy arrived to tell me that I should sign up for the Somoza Youth; he started handing me the forms, but I told him that I was not interested. Right there was sufficient motive for them to expel me from the school; they recorded *aplazado*, failed, for the first three subjects, and as a result I lost a year of study there, just for that.

I was about seventeen years old when I began looking for another school. Unfortunately, the military school had given me a five in conduct for my "problem", for the *whole* year, and other schools did not accept students with a five in conduct. Luckily the director of the Francisco Morazán school accepted me saying that it was a political issue, not one of behavior, and I finished the last two years of secondary there. Two completely different schools, like night and day. The director there was a doctor of Marxist philosophy, one of the few in the country, his name was René Lacayo, and he helped me a lot. He too was demanding with regard to classes, but not so much with regard to conduct. I felt the change immediately; this was in 1968, 1969, the school was very pro-Sandinista because they were the ones who were fighting and dying.

The director had to hide the fact that he was a Marxist, but he gave us some Marxist theory. There were other professors who were also involved with the Frente, and nearly everyone there was a sympathizer. They were not simply in opposition to Somoza, in fact most of the faculty were revolutionaries. They hid revolutionaries there; I remember one artist whom they sheltered. When I was at the high school, it was through the teachers that I met members of the Frente, through meetings of the CUN (Centro Universitario), for example. I made contacts there, ironically, through the person who just recently held me prisoner, which I will tell you about later, through Doris Tijerino, because I wanted to join the Frente. Yes, I did, and they asked me to take two other persons to form a nucleus, but we lost contact, and the teacher we were working with left for France, but he is back here again. We participated in strikes, in the taking of schools and churches, in demanding freedom for political prisoners. That's where my inspiration to become a lawyer came from, so I could defend political prisoners. I graduated from Francisco Morazán in 1971; it was private, and I paid for it through my work. That school was full of life!

Then I went to the Catholic university, UCA, which was more expensive than UNAN, the national university, at that time, though now they are the same. With the Jesuits I had another interesting experience. I came into contact with the revolutionary Social Christian Youth, identifying more with them more than with the Marxists. We began a protest movement in the university when they raised the price of milk and we took to the streets. Then came the earthquake and I had to leave.

I had already met my future wife, Patricia. The last year that I worked in the factory she was working there too, *bien chavala,* a young thing, just sixteen, and she also was working and studying. We started going out, and then after the earthquake, I left with my family for Chinandega, that's where I worked as recorder at the cotton plantation, and she and her family went to Granada, but we stayed in contact.

After I returned here and resumed my studies, I went to visit Patricia in Granada. I also continued my political activities at the university. There I met José Esteban who was the founder of this very human rights office. Manolo Morales was a professor of mine, of constitutional law, and leader of the Social Christians. He was very politically committed; we did many *pintas* together; that is, we painted slogans on buildings, fences, many of them very clever. We mounted many campaigns; for example, we went to the *municipios,*the towns of the department of León, between five and fifteen of us, visiting all the houses one by one, just like the Jehovah's

Witnesses! Sometimes the people were about that glad to see us too; but gradually, we gained their trust and people would talk with us openly about their problems. At times the guardia picked us up and took us prisoner for a few days, but we kept on, because what was important was not to be a quiet opposition, but to go out and *do* things. Operación Hogar(Operation Home), was very successful; just delivering the bulletins asking people about community issues got them started in consciousness-raising. There was still time to study because I was no longer working, and my mama was somehow helping me with tuition again, from her collapsed enterprises, or rather, from her loans at 20 percent interest per week!

I remember how in my third year at the university, in '75, I tried to find other contacts with the Frente, although I was still with the Social Christians. But their civil, pacifist position was not enough for me, and I tried to make contact with the Frente through the very same director of my secondary school I mentioned earlier, René Lacayo. He was in charge of workers' organizations because he was in the Marxist rather than the Sandinista line. He asked me to work with him but I said no, for I would have had to abandon everything, studies, family, everything, and commit myself totally.

In the end, I never made the right contact at the university to become a member of the Frente. So we formed a more radical group of young people within the Social Christian party, and called it the Christian Democratic Left (Izquierda Demócrata Cristiana). After that, we entered into contact with a Frente representative, and by 1977 finally, I was collaborating with the Frente. In '78 and '79 as well, though I was never formally a member, we had a group, especially in '78, a political cell of professional people. I had requested that we be involved more directly , but they said no. Our work was to obtain safe houses, information about where there were arms, to work on commissions. I visited Somoza's security headquarters for example, and made a list of all the license plates of his security vehicles.

I graduated from UCA in '78, but before leaving we had formed a *bufete*, a law practice, called Manolo Morales, that was in '77, which was for assistance to the poor. We charged them practically nothing, it was like social work. Also before graduating, I met again with José Esteban, who was with the Permanent Commission on Human Rights, and almost immediately, still in '78, I left the practice and began working here for the Commission. I started as an advisor with a salary of 1,000 córdobas a month, which was totally useless. I worked part-time because they couldn't afford a full-time position, but in reality I worked full time, and at night I would visit the universities and make contact with the people who were in touch with the Frente.

They were going to mobilize in '78 in what they thought would be the final offensive, and I was going to join them except that a very personal circumstance came up. Patricia had some family problems at her home and we decided to get married, so I postponed everything. I went to my friends with whom I had been working, and I asked them for a few days to arrange my personal situation, but they said no, that they had an order to mobilize. So that was that, and who knows, maybe I would not be here now if I had gone.

When the war came, I still had not been contacted by the Frente. I remember that I stayed in my house at first, waiting, but after a while I couldn't stand it any longer, and I went out. I had no weapon, but I went out into the firing lines waiting for someone to fall so that I could take his weapon. Crazy, right? But I had participated in everything else, and I wanted to be part of the culminating event. I had done all that work in the preceding years: organizing in the poorest barrios; getting demonstrations together; doing *quemas*, or burnings of tires, vehicles, houses; we were involved in all the demonstrations, often under a hail of tear gas bombs and bullets, and here the great moment arrives and I had to be involved. Of course it was ridiculous to wait for someone to fall so that I could pick up their weapon, especially as the people had very few bullets, so I went back home.

Soon, however, the guardia began bombarding our barrio and we went to a seminary for safety, my wife and I. But there someone pointed me out, saying that they had seen me in the fray, and the guardia almost killed me on the spot. These were from the School of Basic Infantry Training (Escuela de Entrenamiento Básico Infantería, EEBI), the most brutal, criminal, and repressive of all the guardia. A drunk from the neighborhood turned me in, saying that I participated in the burning of the house of a lieutenant. They took me to an officer who was going to kill me, he already had the orders. After they had put me in the jeep, another officer told me to get out. They made four other youths get into the vehicle, took them away, and killed them all. They were found later with their fingers broken and their throats slit. Who knows why that guardia changed his mind at the last minute and let me go. After that, we ran back home.

After the revolution things began to change, and since then I have stopped working for political parties and have dedicated myself exclusively to the commission. Certain sectors that identify with the government regard us as an opposition organization, but we want to maintain the best relations possible with the government so that we can obtain their cooperation in the cases that we have to investigate.

Of course you know that there are two human rights commissions here in Nicaragua. It is accurate to say that ours investigates Sandinista violations while the government one investigates contra violations. We are the independent commision; that is the basic difference between us. Our commission has been functioning since April 1977 under Somoza, working in two directions: the promotion and the defense of human rights. The promotion work we do through publications and lectures, but a big problem is the low cultural level of our people in general, and more specifically, they have no clear awareness with regard to human rights. But we try to teach people their rights and how to stand up for them.

Right now we are involved in an education campaign on the rights of prisoners. We are giving lectures and we are trying to reach all levels of the population with our publications, leaflets, and booklets. We also have some drafts prepared that may be ready in a few months on broader themes. These materials will be for those who want to learn the basics about the study of human rights, the philosophical and historical foundations, the different currents that there are in the world, when they were formed, the international organizations for the defense of human rights, things along these lines.

We are affiliated with the International League on Human Rights (Liga Internacional de Derechos Humanos), which has its base in New York, but we are independent. And we maintain relations with the principal human rights organizations, although we have little to do with Americas Watch or Amnesty International. With regard to the educational department, we publish international documents, such as the Universal Declaration on Human Rights, (Declaración Universal de Derechos Humanos), the American Convention on Human Rights (La Convención Americana sobre Derechos Humanos), also known as the San José Pact (Pacto de San José). We have translated these into the Miskitu dialect; it is minimal what we have done, but at least it is something.

We give seminars too and inform people about the principal national laws, what they mean and how to interpret them. We still have not published anything on the new Constitution, as we are very behind schedule with our publications. We have had many problems; for example, we have some publications that are waiting to be printed, but the government requires that all materials go through the censor first. They say our materials are disinformation, and they refuse authorization, so then we have to xerox or put them out in miniprint, which is more expensive and slower.

The other aspect of our work, the defense of human rights, consists of presenting requests to the government, letters or oral requests that we have received. This is, of course, where there is the greatest conflict with the government. We have five lawyers who study the cases that are brought to us, and each complaint has to be signed. The majority are from people with little or no resources.

Under Somoza, a torturer in his security police was one with criminal instincts, a mentally ill person, who vented his basest instincts against an inert prisoner until he beat him to death. Now, though there are serious, not just subtle violations, they are more under control than in Somoza's time. It is very rare now that a person dies from blows while being interrogated, but they may have food or water withheld for a time. Sometimes, however, they lend you a hand while you are in jail. More often, there are violations like the ones I mentioned, but which they never hear about in the U.S. because there is much disinformation about what is happening here.

There is a whole structure of disinformation that supports the Sandinista party. For example, you can talk with the government Human Rights Commission; with the Central American Historical Institute (Instituto Histórico Centroamericano); with the Antonio Valdivieso Ecumenical Center (Centro Ecuménico Antonio Valdivieso); you can visit the prisoner rehabilitation model experiment, the Open Farm, (Granja Abierta); you can go to the agricultural cooperatives in the north of the country. These are normally the tours that well-intentioned persons take. They spend their own hard-earned money to come to Nicaragua, but they are invited by people who indirectly are working for the government. I know that the North American religious, and those who wish to be sister cities and all that, are motivated by Christian principles and want to help the poor in Nicaragua. However, those who invite them are working one way or the other, for the government.

Witness for Peace is a good example, but no, it's not just them, rather it is many, many people who bring delegations here, and not just from the U.S. but from Canada, Europe, from all over. Sometimes we are on their tour, but normally we are not. If people do find out about us, it is difficult to get together with them because the organizers pack the tours so full that there is little time. It is either early morning breakfast or after 8:00 p.m. that we can meet them. All this is part of the structure of disinformation. There are people who take others to the open jails, and they think that the prison system here in Nicaragua is the most advanced and humanitarian in all the Americas. They go back to the U.S. and say how impressed they are, and that they know what they are talking about because they have seen it. They don't realize that they have been part of a plot.

On the other hand, while human rights organizations in the U.S., such as Americas Watch, the Washington Office on Latin America, Witness for Peace, may do a passable job in other countries, they have a great limitation with regard to Nicaragua: they are in a constant confrontation with the U.S. administration for its aid to the contra. They have all the right in the world to do this, but they have no right to alter our reality to achieve their ends, and that is what they do. They try to minimize the human rights violations of the government, and to magnify those of the contra. We, returning to your original question, like any human rights organization should be, are basically dedicated to dealing with charges of violations by the government.

If you pick up any book and read about the theory and philosophy of human rights, you will see that it deals with the rights of people before their governments. The contra in this case are at the margin of the law; they are not the government. Therefore, you cannot justify human rights violations by the government by talking about the crimes that a marginal group commits; whether they are contra or gangsters, they are special cases. The responsibility of the government is clear, especially when they have subscribed to and ratified the International Human Rights Convention (Convenio Internacional de los Derechos Humanos). As I say, we are open to receiving complaints about the contra, although we have received very few, but that is not what most interests us.

Since we have to live with this government, we have to ask people to come in person to the office to make a signed declaration, to give us an address and some identification. If we receive a letter from jail, we assume it to be authentic when a relative brings it. In this way, we are receiving one hundred thirty or forty cases a month. As you can imagine, it is extremely difficult to substantiate them all. Last year, we received approximately 1,300 complaints of government violations for the whole year, and only about eighteen or twenty against the contra. At times, we have the impression that there is much publicity in the U.S. about the contra cases, but little about the government's; so we communicate our findings as much as possible in order to have a more balanced picture.

I don't know if you received the paper today, but there was a story about one prisoner who stabbed another. We have reports, letters sent from jail, letters written by lawyers, which tell us that they [the government] are punishing a group of prisoners that are considered dangerous, and among them is the one who was killed in jail. We believe that the government, through the penitentiary system, is using a new tactic against prisoners, introducing prisoners controlled by state security to beat other prisoners. That way it is not the authorities who are doing it, but the prisoners. We don't believe that the government can be so ignorant of what is going on, and we have sent them our publications on this matter. The government does not permit us to visit the jails, just their own human rights commission. There are some excellent people in that group, but they are not independent.

There are international factors, such as the war, such as pressure from the U.S. and from Russia that influence the human rights situation here, but the origin is strictly internal and there are things that this government has been doing on its own, the violent *turbas divinas*, or "divine" mobs in '81 and '82; the restrictive laws on expression, which date from '80;

the desire to have one sole syndicate for the workers, with a Marxist ideological orientation; the controls on our education and on our means of communication. They can't say that these are all because of the contra. It's one thing to be at war and to have limitations on freedom of expression, but it's another thing to have absolutely no independent communications media. On March 15, 1982, they imposed a state of emergency, because of the contra they said. They took twenty-one independent news spaces off the air, and they have not returned since.

With regard to my recent imprisonment and the hunger strike, as I have mentioned, I belong to no political party, I just work for the commission, but for the fifteenth of August [1987] we were invited as special guests of the Coordinadora Democrática, the political opposition to the Sandinistas, who were inaugurating their office. There were also other guests and representatives of international organizations. We were there mostly as observers from the commission; it was expected that there might be some disturbance there against the people. But everything was going along very smoothly, and at the end the directors of the Coordinadora made a call to the people who were there to go out into the streets, and march around the building in support of the Guatemala accords [the Arias Plan].

So, we all went outside where the police were waiting with big dogs, a German Shepherd and some Dobermans which they had chained, and with rubber batons. They gave us two minutes to disperse, and then they began to beat the people, trying to get them to go back inside. A policeman came up and told me to leave the scene right away. I identified myself as a member of the commission and said that I was not committing any crime being there, that I was an observer of what was going on. Then he hit me with an electric instrument, like a cattle prod, and he also hit me in the stomach. A lieutenant came up who knows me and said, "Lino, get out of here, right now!" Some lawyers also told me to leave, and as I started away, five individuals dressed in civilian clothes grabbed me and started beating me. The police came right away and stopped it, but I think the ones in plainclothes were from security.

They put me in the vehicle and they took me to the station; the second chief of state security arrived, Jacinto Suárez, who had been Nicaraguan ambassador to Russia for three years, I think he was doing nothing diplomatic there, just learning repression, right? He asked us who we were and all that, although he already knew. Besides myself, there was my colleague Alberto Saborío and two women. The women were released almost immediately, but Alberto and I were sentenced to thirty days, charged with disturbing the public order. The people who accused us bore false witness, saying that I had attacked a policeman.

The first days we were in a cell for military people; there were hygenic facilities, very dirty, but at least they were there. The bed was the cement floor, but they loaned us a mattress. They permitted visitors, and many delegations arrived. They let us have books; I'm studying English, and they let me have my English books, my dictionary, the Bible. They brought us food from the office, and from a nearby restaurant.

But when our sentence was confirmed, we began a hunger strike in protest. Doris María Tijerino, the chief of the national police, visited us to see if we were okay, other officials of the Frente came to see us, no one wanted us to get sick. Doris is a good person, a person with feelings; she was concerned about us. She even had them lend us a typewriter and paper to write our appeal for the sentence to be overturned. So you have the very chief herself coming to ask us if we are going to appeal, and when we said that we were, because you have to fill out official forms, her help allowed us to do it. An official of the Ministry of the Interior (MINT) told us in the jail that the comandante of the police, Doris, was not in agreement with the sentence, and that she had planned to let us out, but that an order had come, probably from Borge, saying that the sentence should be confirmed. I imagine that Tomás Borge did not like the tough language of our appeal.

That's when we started the hunger strike. Immediately, they took me aside and said that I was influencing Saborío, that I could stand up to a hunger strike because I was younger, but that he couldn't because he was fifty-four years old. So they moved me to a dark cell with a metallic door and a little window. They kept saying that they were going to find a new fuse but they never did, and they took away my books. I had some candy for the hunger strike, because your body needs the sugar, but they took it away. The toilet was a hole in the floor; that was also the bath.

I was fifteen days on strike, and I was a big problem for them. They brought me food every day, trays full. They would say to me: "*Mira, Lino no seas tonto, comés; lo que no queremos es que te enfermes aquí aden- tro*". (Come on, Lino, don't be foolish; eat, what we don't want is for you to get sick inside here.) I told them, "Let me go free and I will eat; you can take me to any restaurant."

They even got my mama to come and beg me to eat. I refused, my mother was confused and didn't know what to do. After she left, they said I was close-minded, and what was the matter with me, and they took me back to the cell.

The next day, my mama comes in with a huge melon. "What do you think you are doing with that melon?" I asked her. "No, son, you must eat," was all she would say. Then one of the *militares,* in exasperation, took the melon and told another just to leave it in my cell. After that, my mama went away less worried, but I was stuck with that melon and what to do with it. In the roof, there were some holes through which I communicated with other prisoners, and I gave them the melon. But first, in order not to show disrespect for my mama, I took a tiny bit, about an inch square, so that I could truthfully tell her that I had tried it. I divided the melon and the other prisoners were delighted.

Finally, they put me with Alberto again; we were now in an office from which they had removed the furniture. It had very clean hygenic facilities, cots with mattresses, pillows, everything. They told us to stay dressed all the time, pants, shirt, shoes, socks, because at any moment someone might come visit us. We had our visiting privileges restored, and three days later they let us out, when U.S. Senator Tom Harkins came. They wanted us to shave, but we refused, we were determined to leave the way we were. We met with Harkins, with the U.S. ambassador, and there were demonstrations of solidarity. I received more than 300 letters from all over the world, which I still haven't answered.

There is much more that I would like to tell you, but I have to meet a reporter now from the *Miami Herald*.

5   Leticia Herrera (b. 1949)

"I guess you could say that the two constants in my childhood were extreme poverty and extreme political activity."

"I had become a prime target for the guardia . . . they were after me specifically. . . . It was my caution that saved me, because, really, I never believed that I would survive the war."

"A result of the embargo," she said wryly, indicating the empty space where the window glass used to be, and sliding behind the wheel of her slightly beat-up Lada. Leticia Herrera had invited me to her modest home for lunch, which she prepared herself, to meet some of her children, and to continue for several hours more a conversation that had absorbed most of the day already. As she spoke, her bright yellow Wrangler T-shirt highlighted her expressive face ringed with dark curls and set off her intelligent black eyes. So warm was her hospitality and so typically loving her interaction with her young daughter, that I had to remind myself that this was a pistol-packing comandante.

The dynamic comandante is currently vice-president of the National Assembly, but at the time of our meeting she was national coordinator of the Sandinista Defense Committees (Comités de Defensa Sandinista, CDS) grass-roots organizations that were closely related to the Christian base communities and were centers of resistance to the Somoza dictatorship during the 1970s. More recently, the CDS have become distribution centers for rationed foods, sponsors of community projects, such as local clean-up campaigns, as well as defenders of the neighborhood and keepers of Sandinista ideology at the barrio level.

Comandante Herrera was a natural choice for CDS coordinator, for she has dedicated herself to political activity as organizer, strategist, commando, military instructor, and coordinator of opposition and revolutionary groups at the local, regional, and national levels since her days as a high school student in Costa Rica. Widow of the martyred revolutionary leader René Tejada, and former wife of Nicaraguan President Daniel Ortega, Leticia Herrera is currently married to Dr. Juan Carlos Castillo, and is the mother of four children.

<hr />

My father was one of the very first labor organizers here in Nicaragua. He was a true mestizo, the son of a Spanish father and an Indian mother from Monimbó, Masaya. When my father was just a teenager, he emigrated, went to work in the banana plantations in Costa Rica, which was a very common thing to do at that time, and the workforce there was largely Nicaraguan. Just as there have always been many *nicas* who have gone to the U.S. looking for more and better jobs; not just now because of ideological and political differences with the government, but historically, the U.S. and Costa Rica have been places where *nicas* have gone to seek their fortune. I myself have an aunt, my father's sister, in the U.S. She's been there about thirty-five years. So, Nicaraguan citizens have traditionally gone elsewhere looking for work and better pay.

My parents met in Costa Rica while my father was working there. My mother was the traditional Latin American woman, busy with the domestic chores, the children. She helped her husband a lot, but she never left the circle of what was accepted for women of her time. My father was deported from Costa Rica after the Civil War of 1948 for his radical role as a labor organizer. He came back to Nicaragua with his new bride, and they lived at my grandmother's house while my father immediately began to work actively in syndical politics here.

From the time I was very young, I avidly absorbed my father's political energy, and I lived all his adventures as if they were my own. Our house in Nicaragua was a center of anti-Somoza conspiracy, a place for secret meetings, for planning logistics, and for smuggling medicines to the poor. All this allowed me to see how oppressed the people were, yet also to observe that there was at least an embryo of a solution to the problem.

I remember that in 1956 immediately after the assassination of Somoza García, the first Somoza, there was tremendous repression here, and since my father had already been arrested once for his political activities, he was in big trouble. You see, he was convinced that the only way to bring down the Somoza dynasty was through armed revolt. He directed all his energies to this end as he organized the workers' movement. After the death of Somoza García, things really got hot for him, and he fled to Costa Rica just a few steps ahead of the guardia.

In Costa Rica he had to begin all over again, in extreme poverty. My father was a shoemaker by trade, and in Nicaragua he had had a position that was at least comfortable, providing a nice life for us six kids. But there we were starting from nothing in Costa Rica, and it was hard. I was just about seven years old in 1956 when all this was happening, but it made an impact on me, not on my brothers and sisters, because they were younger, the second oldest was only five years old. And too, there we were in Costa Rica, so they began to grow up in another atmosphere altogether, another environment, and with other conceptions. So I was really the only one of us who built upon that base determined by my father's activities in Nicaragua, and when I was about thirteen years old I joined the student movement in Costa Rica to help further my political development. What I always wanted was to return to Nicaragua, but this wasn't to happen until I was twenty years old and I joined the guerrilla movement.

I attended primary and secondary school in Costa Rica, and received a good education. I had to get a scholarship for my father to be able to afford even the public schools, and I had to maintain good grades to keep it. On the one hand, my studies were a route to personal realization and to preparation for the future, but they also corresponded to the serious exigencies of my family situation. Although we lived in misery because my father made practically nothing as a shoemaker, and although the life of a student is difficult, I have very fond memories of that time as lovely and tranquil. It was also a childhood environment saturated with political participation, because during this period my father joined the Communist Party of Costa Rica. I guess you could say that the two constants in my childhood were extreme poverty and extreme political activity.

My father was a very contradictory man. He was quite advanced ideologically, but was very conservative in other ways, especially where his daughters were concerned. He was terribly strict in that he jealously guarded me, but he also imparted to me many beautiful values. I say in *me* because, really, my brothers and sisters grew up with another mentality. He gave me the ideology that allowed me to belong to the Frente Sandinista and to participate in the struggle; I owe it to him. But he also instilled in me a series of values which I hold very dear; for example, reverence for the mother, belief in the principle of truthfulness, and the importance of a life of personal honesty and integrity. For many people, such things are indeterminate and without much value, but for me they are basic; I treasure them, although they have cost me much grief.

Another thing my father gave me is the belief that a marriage is based on mutual trust. From my earliest memories until I finally left my parents' home, I never saw an argument, or even a mild altercation between my parents. My father inculcated in us children a veneration of our mother, but he as a husband also revered her. Not that he was a saint, a *santo varón,* or anything. He already had five children by another woman when he met my mother, and he also drank a lot. But once our family became established, he got himself together and became a responsible husband and father, and he always repected my mother and taught us to do the same.

This was a great lesson for me, because you see, the common thing for Nicaraguan men is to establish extramarital affairs once they are married; that is the norm. His faithfulness to my mother was so important to me that one day I dared to tell him that if I ever found out that he had other children after marrying my mother, that from then on I wouldn't recognize him as my papa. There were never any children outside their marriage, thank goodness, or I would have had a tough problem. Of course my parents had their differences, but we never knew about them. So that's one of the important things that he taught me, about marriage, and respect for the wife and mother.

However, when I became an adult and had to fend for myself, it came as a big shock to find out that real life was not that way. I had an idealistic conception of marriage based on what I lived all my childhood. This was a double-edged lesson that my father gave me, in that I never knew the way people ordinarily treat each other in a marital relationship. So when it came to me to live it, I failed miserably, and it hurt me ten times more than it should have. I also felt guilty about what I had done wrong. Though the example he set for me turned out to be a painful one, I mostly remember it as very beautiful.

My father also provided the great model for all my political activities during my school years. For example, at my high school, Liceo Leonido Briceño in Guanacaste, there were four teachers who were with the Peace Corps, and they were extremely conservative. I saw how they tried to undermine the students' political expression, and how they tried to mold us to think like them. I was an honor student, and I was invited to go study English in the States for a year, but I refused because of what the Peace Corps symbolized to me. I was also offered a chance to study in France, but my papa wouldn't allow it because he thought that three years was too long for me to be away. Besides he needed my economic help with the family. I wasn't working while I was in school, but since I was a scholarship student I was not costing him any money either, and this was a great help.

When these Peace Corps teachers began to learn more about me and my political positions, I was also an organizer of the student movement at that time, they began a campaign against me. On two occasions they took me before the Faculty Council in order to try to have me expelled on political grounds. What saved me was that the teachers there, even if they weren't progressive, were very honest. For example, there was a civics teacher, a Chinese, who, although he did not sympathize with my views, he stood up for my right to hold them. Also, the fact that I was an excellent student helped a great deal. In the five years that I was in secondary school, I was one of a handful of students whose grades were consistently between 95 and 100. I don't feel any resentment about those years or what happened, or the Peace Corps teachers either, for that matter. I look at it this way: the experience made me learn better English and French, because these were the two languages that they could converse in.

I also remember that during this period, when I was about sixteen or seventeen, I had a boyfriend. He was an excellent person, and was also in the Socialist Youth (Juventud Socialista), but he had such a crush on me that he tried to see me all the time, between classes, after my volleyball matches, and so forth. And my father was so strict that the only time that I could leave my house, except for school or sports activities, was to go to student cell meetings. So this boy began to frequent the cell meetings as a way for us to be together.

The administration found out about it, and once during class, I looked out the window and saw a group of boys, including this youth, being marched across the yard to the principal's office. There, the principal, vice-principal, and several teachers gave them a brainwashing. They threatened to take away my boyfriend's scholarship unless he quit his political activities. After that, I broke up with him. I knew that my political positions were clearly defined and that his were not. They never called me in like that; all the teachers knew me and knew that they couldn't inspire fear in me. Later I had a close girlfriend, but even we were not on the same wave length with regard to the strength of our political convictions. I came to realize that my beliefs were unusually clear and strong, and I never found anyone there who completely shared them.

It was my father who helped me form my convictions. He never stifled me, but always encouraged me to read and to question. He was self-taught, never had any formal education, and had many problems learning how to read. But he learned, he learned by reading anything that had to do with the workers and with the revolutionary movement. His materials came from the Party, they gave them to him. At that time the Communist party was legal in Costa Rica, and very active. He also read the Bible, and had been an acolyte in the church in Monimbó. Papa would read the Bible, he would give it to me to read, and then we would discuss it together. For example, he would say that the Beatitudes of Christ are revolutionary principles, and that Jesus was the first revolutionary. The problem is that His principles have been instrumentalized, and put to the service of a system of oppression and exploitation. That was papa's way of thinking. At school I also studied the Bible, even though it was a public school, and I had a progressive Spanish priest for a teacher. I was the student who had the most discussions with him about the Bible.

My father admired the Soviet Union, but with a very practical vision. If we analyze the political content of the communist parties of Latin America, we're going to find that one of the problems that has stymied them has been their dogmatism and their extreme theorization of things, because so many of them are blind followers of Russia. I admire the Soviet Union a lot, but when I see something I disagree with, I say *but*, and I'm not afraid to say *but*. My papa was like that too. If he hadn't been, he wouldn't have linked the revolutionary principles with those in the Bible. That's another thing that he taught me, respect, but not slavish obedience to any ideology. When I was clandestine, I worked a lot with the Christian base communities, and I still feel a deep identification with them today; in fact, if I had more time, I would dedicate it to base community work.

Well, returning to my main story, before I finished the *bachillerato*, [secondary school degree], I was in a few more political scrapes. For example, that was about the time that the fascist Costa Rica Libre movement began, and some of those who now are leaders of that movement let themselves be used in a series of maneuvers against me. On one occasion, they sent a package of subversive literature to me at my school address, thinking that the school would expel me. But then I spoke with the principal and said, "Look, I have my own home, and everyone knows my house, why on earth would I have anything like that sent here to the school? Besides, everyone here knows my political position already." My father never knew about this, because I didn't want him to get upset.

Another example was the written *bachillerato* exam in Spanish, for which I was given an open topic. So, I did a exam in which I criticized the U.S., the political and economic system, all the things that I didn't agree with. The Ministry of Education in this type of exam always sends a special delegate to work with the teachers in grading the papers. Well, they gave me a zero on this exam.

My other teachers intervened, including the civics teacher I mentioned earlier, and then they changed my score to two, this on a scale of zero to ten. But since I had tens on all my other exams in Spanish, such as literature, grammar, composition, and so on, my score averaged out to an eight. I had told my father before the exam that if I did not graduate here at the end that it would be because I had put into practice my political beliefs. I said that I hoped that he would not be angry with me if I failed to graduate for that reason, because he already knew the outstanding quality of my work. At any rate, I did graduate despite everything, and with very high marks.

I wanted to keep studying, but it was financially impossible, so I worked as a substitute teacher to help my family out. Would you believe that I taught for the next two years at the very school that I had just graduated from! There was always a teacher who was sick or on maternity leave, or whatever, and I taught history, chemistry, and math. I actually loved teaching, and though I earned very little, it was a help.

The first year I taught, I thought it would be just for one year, so I applied for a university scholarship to study medicine. I took an exam, and I won the scholarship. But my sister was just about to finish high school and she wanted to go right on to the university too. In Costa Rica, scholarships are transferable among brothers and sisters, and my father, in a very egotistical way, said that I should give my scholarship to her, so that she would not have to interrupt her studies like I did. Of course, I acceded to his request and gave the scholarship to Diana, who went on to study nursing while I continued working. It was very difficult for me, but I had such respect for my father, and I had always received the most support from him.

This experience made me even more determined somehow to find a way to keep on studying, so I applied to the Communist party (Vanguardia Popular), for a scholarship to study in the Soviet Union, and I won that scholarship too. I didn't tell my papa. It was the first thing that I had ever done without consulting him, and he made it clear that I would have to get my things together without any help from him. He asked me not to go. He said that he was about to start a new job in which he would earn more money, and that if I stayed things would get better. But that was not the problem, because I too had an offer of a new teaching job in which I would earn more, though it was in the capital, San José, about eight hours away by public transportation. Then, he became even more upset and stopped speaking to me. I told him that I had decided to leave, that I didn't want to be a teacher, that what I really wanted to do was to go to the university, and that if I stayed at home I would never become anything more than a village schoolteacher. This really bothered him because although he didn't want to let me go, he did want me to make something of myself.

So, I packed my one bag and left home, with papa accompanying me to the airport. I told him that if I finished the course of study in the prescribed five years, I would return home afterwards, but that if I did not succeed, I would not return, period. I know that papa's real fear, other than my being so far away from him for so long, was that I would not stay in Russia, or even Costa Rica, but would try to return to Nicaragua as soon as possible. He had always blocked me from going to Nicaragua, and now he would no longer be able to do so. That's why, when I made this decision to study in the Soviet Union, my father resisted it so vigorously. And he was right, for almost as soon as I arrived in the Soviet Union, I began looking for the means to get back to Nicaragua.

I was there a year only, from 1968–69, as a chemistry student, but for most of that year I had to take language courses. I met many interesting people, made friends with students of different nationalities, political positions, backgrounds, including people from Africa and Asia as well as from Latin America. It was a great experience, but, to tell the truth, my energies were focused in one direction. At the earliest opportunity, I joined a cell of the Frente Sandinista and soon after returned to Nicaragua.

But first I married René Tejada, who was also studying in the Soviet Union. René was one of two brothers who have a special history here in Nicaragua. They were from a poor family and they went to the military academy as the only way to acquire needed military knowledge and skills, which they would later transmit to the Frente as part of a conscious plan. David, the older brother, became a lieutenant in the guardia nacional. He played the double role of a guardia and a member of the Frente Sandinista. He was a link between a small sector of the guardia that was a little more aware, a little more nationalistic than most, and the resistance.

Unfortunately, there were elements that were suspicious of him and this small group, and, though the guardia was never able to prove anything against them, they punished them anyway, just on the basis of suspicions. The members of the Tejada brothers' group were taken prisoner and tortured; David died during the torture. The doctor of the guardia seemed to be a decent person, and he helped bring the murder to light. It caused a great scandal, with much publicity and then a trial. It was thanks to this public outcry that they did not kill the second Tejada, René. He managed to get out of jail, and once out, the Communist party of NIcaragua smuggled him out of Nicaragua. That's how he came to arrive in the Soviet Union where we met and were married.

We returned to Nicaragua together. It was a real odyssey because we had to come semi-clandestinely, with the help of various solidarity groups in Europe and Latin America, and picking up other people along the way. When we arrived in Honduras early in 1970, there were ten in our group, five of us returning from the Soviet Union, four men and myself; three who had been studying in Germany, one of whom is Comandante René Vivas, the current vice-minister of the Interior; finally, two more arrived in Honduras from Nicaragua, Juan José Quezada and Pedro Aráuz who was the leader of the group. Of those of us who left the Soviet Union, only two are still alive, Comandante José Valdivia of the army, he's now chief of a military region, and myself. And of the three who were in

Germany, René Vivas is the only one left. The two who joined us from Nicaragua are both dead now too. Of that group of ten, three are still alive.

The journey was very long, and once we arrived in Honduras it still was not over, because we had to split up, and I spent a good deal of time in Mexico. As it turned out, of all of us, I was the only one who could enter Nicaragua legally, because I had a Costa Rican passport and because in Nicaragua no one knew me, since I had lived most of my life outside the country. This was a great advantage, but it also meant, inevitably, that my marriage to René was over, especially as he was much more *quemado*, or wanted by the authorities, than the rest of us. So he joined up with the guerrilla forces in the mountains, while I left for the *guerrilla urbana*, the urban effort. We separated, aware that we would never see each other again, and we set each other free to remake our personal lives as we saw fit.

We parted without my realizing that I was already pregnant with my first child. I entered Nicaragua in June 1970, about a month after René, and soon discovered that I was pregnant. I was so ignorant of everything, my mother was one of those super-conservative women who never told me anything. I didn't even know the *symptoms* of pregnancy, and I went through thousands of problems. I was incorporating myself fully into my revolutionary work, and did not know what I was going to do when the baby was born. Where would I leave him? With whom? At that time, I could count on no one. I was pregnant, alone, clandestine, in a country in which I was considered a stranger, and to make things worse, I spoke like a *tica*, a Costa Rican. It was so easy to detect me that my *responsable*, or superior, Pedro Aráuz, insisted that my first task was to learn to speak like a *nica*, so I began to work on it right away, in the indigenous community of Subtiava in León, where I was sent to live for a while.

That's where I was when I had the child. As luck would have it, I was in the hopital at the moment that the nurses went on strike. It's ironic because this action was the positive result of all the mobilization efforts that the Frente had been carrying out in León. But there I was having just had a Cesarian, unable to move, and with no nurse to help me. To make things worse, about midnight I saw that the baby was terribly congested, coughing hard and breathing with great difficulty; I was afraid that he was going to choke to death because I could not get over to him, nor could I scream for help, nor was there anyone to hear me if I did. By chance, a campesino was walking down the corridor to see his wife who was also in the hospital. When he heard my faint cries, he came over to me and I told him what was wrong, so he picked the baby up, pounded him on the back, helped clear up his congestion, and saved him.

I named the baby Ernesto David, Ernesto because I always admired "el

Che," and David, for his uncle, David Tejada, the one who died at the hands of the guardia. By the time he was three months old, I had resigned myself to sending him to Costa Rica to my parents, with whom I had renewed my relationship by letter during my pregnancy. However, his father thought that it would be better if the child stayed here in Nicaragua with some trusted friend, because then I could see him from time to time and develop a close, maternal relationship with him. He also thought that I should make it clear to those taking care of him that the child should never be taken out of the country without first telling me or his father. Well, the upshot is that I left Ernesto David in Managua as an infant in the care of his grandmother, René's mother, in April 1972. The following December there was the earthquake in Managua, which devastated the part of town they had been living in, and I lost touch with them completely. For almost a year I didn't know if they were dead or alive, even though the Frente did everything possible to help me locate them.

After a year, we found out that they had somehow made their way to Panama, along with a number of others displaced by the earthquake. I don't know how they saved themselves, but they went from Managua to Masaya, to Costa Rica, to Panama, where my son stayed for a while with doña Velia Peralta and two of her children. Even when they returned here I did not go see them. My work area was León-Chinandega, and if I had to go to Managua for any reason, I first had to communicate with my *responsable,* for security reasons. But since I was so strict with myself in discipline, I never saw them in Managua. And although I knew their neighborhood well, I stayed away for fear of putting my son and his grandmother in danger. We communicated by letter. But when doña Velia Peralta returned to Nicaragua the guardia began to harass her; they would surround her house, shout insults and hound her. It was difficult wherever she went, for everyone recognized her because she was the mother of the Tejadas. As a result, she decided to go into exile, to Venezuela, with the boy. I did not see my son again until he was seven years old. But if I had broken with that rigorous discipline, I would've placed many peoples' lives in great danger.

I began my clandestine activities in '70, and worked in the cities for the next seven years, helping organize political resistance in the barrios. I was involved with all kinds of neighborhood groups and committees; I worked very closely with the Christian base communities, and I helped mobilize the student movement. In '74 I formed part of the Juan José Quezada commando unit, under the direction of Eduardo Contreras and Tomás Borge. They chose people for this unit taking into account various criteria, such as our past activities, perspective, extent of participation, and the strength of our political and ideological convictions. Then they gathered us together secretly in a safe house in El Crucero, where we spent about six weeks receiving military training.

On December 27, 1974, we took the house of "Chema" Castillo, one of Somoza's leading henchmen. We achieved the release of many of our compañeros who were political prisoners, the publication of two Frente Sandinista documents, the delivery of five million dollars, and safe passage to Cuba. The operation was a complete success, and it showed that we were now strong enough so that the regime had to meet our demands. I left for Cuba right away, on December 30, and I stayed there until October 1975. In January 1975, while I was still in Cuba, I received word that the guardia had killed my husband, René Tejada, in Waslala. We had lost contact for about two years, but when I was receiving commando training he wrote me. During the four years that he was in the mountains, he established relations with a peasant woman by whom he had another son, whom I now have living with me. I changed his name to René, after his father.

When I returned to Nicaragua in October of '75, I definitely entered a new phase of my life. Up until then I had been semi-clandestine with at least some freedom of movement, but now everything was different. The commando raid had received a great deal of publicity; the persecution was terrible, and I had to go underground completely. The Frente even changed my work. I could no longer take the risk of doing organizing in the barrios or with student groups, and my first job on my return was as an instructor in a political-military school with Carlos Agüero, who was one of the guerrilla leaders in the mountains. Our job was to prepare people politically, militarily and psychologically to go to the montaña. From October of '75 to January 6, 1976 this is what I did, until I had dispatched everyone including Carlos Agüero himself, because I was not only a military instructor but also the administrator of the group.

Then they sent me to work in Masaya because it was a place I knew. There I began to work with Camilo Ortega, Daniel's brother; Daniel was still in Costa Rica at that time. Camilo and I became very close, and we worked extremely well together; the two of us formed a work team in what is now called the fourth region, the departments of Masaya, Granada, Carazo, and Rivas. Camilo and I organized and put together the contingents that would later constitute the northern front, and we secured the *puntos ciegos de salida*, or safe crossing points, for people and materials along the Costa Rican border.

Around April or June of '76, Daniel entered the country. Eduardo Contreras, who was the *responsable* of the command was already here, and by then the divisions in the Frente were growing. We were splitting into those who wanted a more moderate, political approach and those who felt that armed resistance was the only realistic alternative, and among those who wanted to depend on the peasants, those who wanted to concentrate on the urban workers, and those who thought we could get support from all sectors. We were searching desperately for a way to keep these differences from breaking us up. It was a very difficult internal problem, and there were bitter personal differences as well. With many of our compañeros falling prisoner, and others dying at the hands of the guardia as the pace of the repression increased, our divisions became a concrete fact; but we, each one of us, had to keep on working in order not to destroy ourselves.

I was reassigned to Managua, even though it was very dangerous for me there, but I knew the city and all the structures that we had created. Also I was very well acquainted with all the collaborators because of my years of community organizing. This was an important assignment for me, because I worked directly with Comandante Daniel Ortega. I became indispensable to him, for he had to depend on my knowledge of the groups, neighborhoods, support systems, and so forth that we had developed in Managua, because he no longer knew the city. You see, he was taken prisoner in '67, and the earthquake that destroyed Managua was in '72, so all his familiar landmarks and points of reference were now gone. Because of the intense nature of our work, we developed a very close relationship, one of mutual respect, which provided the basis for our later union.

I felt a strong sense of responsibility for Daniel's security; he could leave the safe house for only a few hours at night, so I was the one who always went out. There was one occasion that stands out in my mind; it was an extremely trying time for us all. We were looking for someone who would lend us 150 *pesos*, not a large amount, but we had to send the mail to the interior, to Comandante Tirado and his men and we needed *reales*, cash, for someone to make the journey. Daniel made contact with some Communist party members who had been friends of his papa. They had also been friends of my papa, and they were going to lend us the money we needed. At 1:00 sharp I was to meet someone and pick up the money. I arrived on the dot, because I was very punctual, and five minutes could cost your life. I even waited five minutes, but nothing happened. I left and returned twice more, and then I said to my compañero, a collaborator who had loaned us his car and who served as driver, that this man was not coming. I didn't like the atmosphere; things didn't feel right; and I did not want to be seen on the street. I thought it was better to let him keep his *reales*, and to get out of there right away.

Sometimes you wonder about ESP; I knew something terrible was going on, but I didn't know what or where. It so happens that at the very minute I was saying these things to the driver, a battle was taking place not far from us in which three compañeros fell, Eduardo Contreras, the other *responsable* besides Daniel; Roger Picado, who was the messenger we were going to send to the mountain; and Eduardo Contreras's driver, Silvio Reñazco, who had recently returned from studying in Germany and was from Masaya. The guardia killed the three of them in Satélite Asososca, in Ciudad Sandino.

I returned to the tiny safe house in which we had a minuscule bedroom, about two meters by one and a half meters, which we all occupied as if we were a family so as to appear more natural to the outside. I told Daniel that the man didn't show up, and he was very upset, because we needed those *reales* for the mail and to send communications to Comandante Tirado. I told Daniel that tomorrow I would go look for someone else, but that right then I didn't want to move from that spot, because I felt something, a presentiment.

That same night, it was a Sunday, near the house where Eduardo lived, which was Silvio Reñazco's house, they also killed another compañero, Carlos Roberto Huembes, from another political tendency. What happened was that as soon as the guardia had killed our companions in Satélite Asososca, they traced the car registration and found out their addresses. Then they surrounded the houses in that sector to see who came and went and who looked suspicious. That's how Carlos Roberto fell that night. We weren't aware of this either. The guardia couldn't identify Carlos Roberto right away because he carried no papers. He had worked with me in the student movement.

The next day, about 6:30 or 7:00 a.m., I was supposed to take Daniel to a house where he was going to meet with Eduardo Contreras, who was now dead but we still didn't know, because the guardia, in order to catch the rest of us, did not publish the news right away. This house was very near where Carlos Roberto had just been killed. Daniel wanted to go alone, and wanted me to let him off at a distance from the house, but I told him I didn't think he knew the territory well enough and that I wanted to get him closer so that I could orient him. I also wanted to pass by the house first just to check it out. So I gave instructions to the driver, Alfredo Sánchez, and then we came upon a BECAT, or antiterrorist squad, of the guardia in a place where anyone who passed by would be seen. Well, since I knew this zone very well I told the driver that the guardia was up to no good, because it was not normal for a tank to be in that location. I told Daniel not to get out of the car, and I directed the driver to take him to a safe place, a school that I knew well where some nuns were collaborators.

Then I instructed Alfredo to get as close as he could to the squad and see if he could get any information. So he got out of the car and talked with one of the guardia, who told him that the night before there had been an assault on a jewelry store and that they were waiting in case the thieves returned. "But are you from the Department of Robbery Investigation?", asked Alfredo, and the guardia became angry and asked him who he was to go around asking questions. The driver answered, "I just have friends who live in this neighborhood and I saw all the commotion, and thought I'd ask, that's all," and then he left quickly. But we knew that something terrible had happened at Vladimir's house, Vladimir was the code name for Silvio Reñazco.

That same day, November 8, 1976, when we were involved in this, they killed Comandante Fonseca in the montaña. I felt like I was dying and Daniel was in great anguish. But we all had to keep our emotions bottled up, since we couldn't tell anyone how we felt and we could only wait until things calmed down and the guardia went away. That was a terrible moment, one of the really horrible times that we lived through.

Then Daniel came to be the *responsable* for Managua, because before it had been him and Eduardo. At my suggestion we decided to find safe houses in the countryside and travel back and forth when we needed to. Camilo helped us find a place, and the three of us worked together nearby in Masaya. Soon Daniel left with Tirado for the northern front and I stayed with Camilo training people to go to that same front. When I had pretty much organized things, I too was sent up to the northern front because I was very *quemada*, wanted by the guardia, here, and they were following closely in my tracks. So I told my *responsable* that if he didn't want another murdered worker, he had better get me out of there.

I had several *responsables*. First was Pedro Aráuz, then Eduardo Contreras, then I was a *responsable* along with Carlos Agüero, and then I was under the direction of Comandante Fonseca. Afterwards, I didn't have a direct *responsable* but I shared authority with Camilo. We constituted a work team, but both of us answered to Tirado and Daniel. In '77 Camilo came to assume all the responsibility in our work, and I left for the northern front. I knew and worked with lots of people, but now so many of them are dead, including a number in the Christian base communities. Of those who are still alive, you have Rosa Marina Zelaya, who holds an elected office; Alvaro Baltodano, now a member of the army chief of staff; Joaquín Cuadra, the army chief of staff; there is Alvaro Baltodano's wife, María Eugenia Monroy, who was very active in the base communities; there is Mario Martínez, who works in the ASTC, the Cultural Workers' Association, with Rosario Murillo; and, there is Estela Mayorga, who is in the rearguard of the army. But beyond these, most are dead, especially those I worked with in the base communities.

The local civil defense committees are the result of the community organizing that the Frente Sandinista was involved in over many years. In '71 and '72 we began organizing in earnest; that's when I worked so closely with the Christian base communities at the grass-roots level. These structures kept on growing stronger as alternative organizations for the people, and later, in '77 and '78, they became the Sandinista Defense Committees, the CDS. They were composed fundamentally by people who were in opposition to Somoza; that was the common denominator. Therefore, they incorporated base communities, students, trade union members, individuals struggling for redress of grievances they had suffered, and those merely fighting to stay alive in the face of the apparatuses that were at the service of the dictatorship. Later, the Frente counted on large numbers of such people as collaborators, to deliver medicines, drive cars, take messages. All this was a collective effort. For example, the Rural Workers' Association, (Asociación de Trabajadores del Campo, ATC), is the result of the massive mobilization work of the Frente in the countryside during the entire decade of the 1970s.

I participated in the northern front, which was when I served as Daniel's guide, as his eyes you might say. Because of his poor eyesight, he could not see well when we had to travel at night, and though I was pregnant with our child, I went before him, tripping and falling but making sure that he would not stumble or lose his way. I came down from the mountain when I was six months pregnant, and went to Tegucigalpa, Honduras, which was a lot easier than going to Managua. Daniel came with me, but on February 26, 1978, after we had been in Tegucigalpa for only five days, Daniel had to go to a meeting in San José, Costa Rica, which is where his other brother, Humberto, was. That's the same day that Camilo was killed in Monimbó, Masaya. I stayed in Tegucigalpa, and I sent a note to doña Lidia, their mother, saying that yes, Camilo had fallen, but that she was going to have a grandson, and that I hoped this would be of some comfort to her. You see, anything that had to do with her children was for her an object of veneration, and she has a great deal of affection for me too. Besides, she knew that I had loved Camilo like a brother. I stayed a while longer in Tegucigalpa, dedicating myself to my work, which was to form support groups for sending others back inside Nicaragua.

The child was scheduled to be born in June, but at the beginning of that month I received orders to go to San José. I thought fine, because Daniel was already there, my parents were there, Daniel's mama, doña Lidia, was there, and everything would be easier if I went there to have the baby, especially if I were to have any problems. That rough journey did cause me problems, and I had to have another Cesarian. Doña Lidia was a great help to me throughout; the baby was born in San José, and I named him Camilo. As soon as I had recovered, I had to go back to the struggle, this time to the southern front.

I felt great pain at having to leave the baby, but I had no choice. In the southern front, we made significant incursions into Nicaraguan territory.

Besides myself, there was Daniel, Comandante Tirado, and Edén Pastora. It was difficult, because I had recently given birth; but I was accustomed to long marches, and I had always done rigorous exercises to stay in top physical condition, which I still do, and this discipline helped me a lot. But I could see that a large part of the people comprising the southern front had little physical endurance, and that was a problem. Soon I was transferred to the north, to Honduras again. And of course I left again without Camilo, who stayed behind in Costa Rica with doña Lidia and his godmother, because doña Lidia had already had him baptized.

I returned to Honduras and began to help organize the insurrection of September '78. The first general uprising took place in September, and after that, many of those involved fled for Honduras, crossing the frontier to escape the reprisals, which were brutal and indiscriminate. Then what I and some other compañeros did was to regroup all these people, send them to underground schools for military and political preparation, and return them to the country to work. I was in charge of all this with a few other compañeros, Hugo Torres, Aracely Pérez, and Marta Lucía Cuadra. We did this work in Tegucigalpa, but the first thing I did when I arrived there was to look for a house. I found a tiny but very pretty one, and then I went and brought my baby back with me. There was a peasant woman who had had a child by Comandante Tirado, and she cared for the two kids for us.

This was a very difficult period for me, because when I left for Honduras, Daniel and I separated over a personal matter. My father told me that I was too intransigent, and that I was the one responsible for destroying that marriage. He said that I was insensitive and didn't understand men; but he also had a conception of the woman as submissive, and I was just not that way. After all, I had already held many leadership positions, made difficult decisions affecting a number of people, traveled all over on my own, and I naturally had my own criteria for personal relationships. I also knew myself well, and I was the one who made the decision to dissolve our union. Our son Camilo now lives with Daniel and his family.

By March '79 we had trained, regrouped, and returned to Nicaragua all those for whom we were responsible, and I was ordered to re-enter the country too. This meant that I would again have to separate myself from my son. I felt great sorrow at having to leave Camilo, not knowing how we were going to survive, either of us, and what would happen to him if I died. When I arrived in León for assignment, my anguish deepened, because the situation there was very bad, and I was very concerned about inadequate security arrangements. To my horror, during the days that I was there, the guardia murdered the entire leadership of our León headquarters. It was just luck that they did not kill me too, because I also had been in the house where they were gathered.

On that occasion three of us escaped: Ana Isabel Morales, now in charge of the Office of Migration at the national level, Fanon Urroz who died in '79, and myself. I escaped because I didn't like the location and the lack of security at our safe houses; I asked to be authorized to find my own place, which I did. I urged them all to move, and to let me find them a safe house, but they didn't take the danger seriously enough. One of them knew my house, and the day that we were going to have a meeting, they were supposed to pick me up at 6:00 p.m., but they didn't show up. I did not move. I could've left, but since I had been away from León for years by then, I knew that I was not current on the situation there, so I stayed put.

That night, I was in the back part of the house, asleep on the *tijera,* or cot, and I felt a gust of extremely cold air. It was very strange, but it was so cold that I woke up with chills and began to scream as if I were delirious with a fever. The owner of the house woke up, came to me and asked what was the matter. I told her, "*¡Los muchachos están muertos!*" ("The boys are dead!") This was about 1:00 a.m., and at 5:00 they were announcing the deaths on the radio. There were five who fell: a Mexican woman, Aracely Pérez; Roger Deshon; Carlos Mandar; Daniel Fernández; and Edgard Lang.

After this tragedy, I was asked to stay in León and build a new team, so I then became a chief of the military staff. Other members of the new team were Comandante Polo Rivas, who is now with TELCOR, the telecommunications company; Comandante Dora María Tellez, now Minister of Health; Fanon Urroz, the one I mentioned who died in 1979; and Isabel Morales. Later they added Mauricio Valenzuela, who is in the Ministry of Construction now, and María Lourdes Jirón, who works in the regional headquarters of the Frente in Managua. We were seven, and four of us were women. During the development of the insurrection, I led around 60 troops; by June 19, 1979, when León was secured, it was the *first* city to be liberated, I had about 1,500 under my command.

When the government junta was installed, when Daniel arrived, Sergio Ramírez, Arturo Cruz, and so forth, we moved our staff office to El Chipote, Somoza's old guardia headquarters. In one part of El Chipote, the arsenal, which also housed the office of Somoza's son, "el Chigüin," I was looking through some papers and files, and I found three orders for my arrest, *three* separate orders! I can tell you that I felt very frightened on seeing these because the fact that they were in "el Chigüin's" office meant that I had become a prime target for the guardia, and that they were after me specifically. I remember laughing nervously as I realized how effective and how necessary my security measures had been. I have always had a terror of being captured. I knew of the barbarities the guardia committed, and I didn't think that I could withstand the torture.

I was afraid that I would tell everything I knew and implicate my compañeros. Because of this fear, I was always scrupulous in anything having to do with security and risks, and I still am. It was my caution that saved me, because, really, I never believed that I would survive the war. This was the nineteenth of June, and we were here in Managua until the twenty-sixth.

I had to return to León, because I was the one in charge of organizing the forces there, and a few days later I received a telegram from Ocotal, saying that Camilo was there, that the collaborators had brought him from Honduras. Even though it was already late afternoon, I jumped in a jeep, pausing only long enough to grab his cradle, and I didn't stop until I got to Ocotal. It's funny that that was the item that I thought was indispensable; "I have to take the cradle," I said to myself. I arrived about midnight and began looking for him. Imagine that, and there were still guardias everywhere, but I, the cautious one, went from house to house looking for my *chavalo*, my boy, until I found him in a house with a lot of junk piled up all over the place, and he was covered with mosquito bites, all inflamed. Well I took him home, took care of him, and we lived a sort of normal life, with me working as the army chief of staff there through the rest of '79.

In 1980, I worked to help strengthen various party structures at the regional headquarters of the Frente. In February 1981, I was assigned to be coordinator of the CDS, the Sandinista Defense Committees. That's when I came here to Managua. I had been commuting from León for a good while because I didn't have a house here. Doña Lidia invited me to come and live at her house, but of course I said no, that I couldn't do that. So I looked for a house, and Daniel helped me find one. But the first house was not secure, and on two occasions, they came and tried to kidnap the boy. After that, at doña Lidia's insistence, the comandante got me a house here nearby, one half block away, so that security could keep an eye on my house too.

I married again in 1981, and one year later my daughter was born. Another Cesarian. My husband, Juan Carlos Castillo, joined the Frente in '77. We met when I was in Honduras, pregnant with Camilo, and he smuggled weapons to us; he drove vehicles that had camouflaged bottoms for carrying arms. During the insurrection, he too fought in León where he was the chief of a column. My husband is a medical doctor, and is currently the director of the Manolo Morales hospital.

Family life is difficult for a comandante. For example, my oldest son, David, lives in a different world from me. He has a lot of problems. He is very introverted and highly critical of others. In fact, he has a negative, antisocial character, and I worry about the time when he has to be on his own, because I'm afraid that he will be very lonely. He says that I don't love him, that I love Camilo more, that I love everyone else more. Our relationship is strained. You see, it was interrupted for so many years, and it's not that easy to pick up again as if I had been caring for him since he was a baby. And, naturally, his grandmother instilled in him her own ways of thinking, and some of these are hard for me to deal with now. Actually, I think that David is a bit like me; we have both suffered and we have both become *endurecidos*, hardened, and neither one of us express our feelings freely. But I can tell you that he resents being the child of a *dirigente,* a national leader, because I never have the time to give him the human warmth that he needs.

My daughter is resentful too. Just yesterday I was talking with another mother who told me that her daughter wanted her to be a *jefe,* a chief, like me. The mother asked why when she already had a good job working as a legal consultant at the National Assembly. The child answered that as a comandante, her mother could come and go at any hour of the day or night and not ask permission of anyone. That way, her mother could take her to school and come see her there any time she pleased. Well, my daughter was listening to all this, and she said to the mother, "Marcela wants you to be a comandante, but I don't want my mama to be one. She never has time for me; she is always in meetings, and she can hardly find the time to take me to school." My daughter then told her friend that she really wouldn't like it if her mother were a comandante, and that she wished that I would stop being one, as if it were a job that I could quit, just like that, and not a public trust. She doesn't understand, but these questions hurt. And they hurt doubly because I know that to be the child of a comandante is to live enclosed, prisoner; it is to want, but not be able, to live like other people. These are the costs.

6 Manuel Calderón (b. 1954)

"In Sandinismo, we are pragmatic, but we are also theoretical, because we have an ideal."

"There is plenty of room . . . for political pluralism, for one who is not Marxist, Christian, or Sandinista, for one who is totally uninterested in politics, and even for the pure capitalist."

Why, I wondered, did I agree to come back tonight to the dark fourth floor of the cavernous Ministry of the Interior (MINT) building with its brusque guards and strict security? Why, when I had been sick that day and knew that neither the elevators nor the toilets in the entire building worked? But I had found this slight, good-natured comandante so disarmingly honest and forthright during our previous, lengthy conversation that I determined to accept his polite invitation to return.

Here was a government representative who gave genuine, considered responses to questions about Sandinismo, rather than the canned rhetoric of a party line. Whether by accident or design, the Sandinistas chose well in appointing this sincere, thoughtful revolutionary of humble extraction to the important position of Director of Political Development for the Third Region. As such, he sees to it that the official Sandinista ideology is imparted to the thousands of soldiers in his area of responsibility.

A practical, reflective campesino, Comandante Calderón is a strong believer in both traditional values and the ideals of the Revolution, which he often equates. He is also a realistic man who sees that accommodation is an important part of life, whether it be to the harsh demands of nature that he experienced during his years as guerrilla fighter, or to political

*realities that one simply has to accept as given. Comandante Calderón's
flexibility and openness, as well as his down-to-earth wisdom and humor,
serve him well in his current post, in which he must communicate with
recruits from the montaña as well as with those from more sophisticated
backgrounds.*

My mother's name is María Estela Chévez Vega and my father's is
Licímaco Manuel Calderón Araus; they are both campesinos. My papa is
from Niquinohomo, Sandino's birthplace; he is the son of Manuel Calderón, who was related to Sandino. My mama is from Telica, a small town
in the department of León. My parents lived a short while in Telica before
moving to Pueblo Redondo, where I was born, on the slopes of the hill
named Telica. My mama is both very religious and very revolutionary.
She prays the rosary every day; my grandfather too. We are eight brothers
and sisters, and mama used to make us all say the rosary every day with
her, and I also helped the village priest as acolyte.

My family roots are eminently religious, Catholic. My sister Socorro
is a nun of the Spanish Puerza de María order. They're the ones who gave
her a scholarship so she could study. She has lived in Spain for many
years, but she is is coming home this Saturday to work in Nicaragua.
Mita, that's what we call mama, wanted me to become a priest. I went to
the local elementary school and made very good grades. But when I
finished I couldn't go to the promotion because you had to wear a tie, and
my parents couldn't afford to buy one. It was a state school, but you still
had to buy things like that. I finished sixth grade in '68 and that would
have been the end of my schooling, but my mother asked the priest to
help her get me a scholarship to go to the national seminary in Managua.
I was there three years. The Canadians were in charge of it at that time,
but there were Jesuits, Capuchins, and priests from other orders giving
classes. Really, at that age, I wasn't very clear about whether I wanted to
be a priest, or what I wanted to do.

The only thing I knew clearly was that I had to do something to help
the people, because they lived in misery, and the only way I could think
to help was through religion. Since I was poor, I felt it myself; I was really
hurt by not being able to go up and receive my elementary school diploma,
especially since I was such a good student. And I've had to do everything
since then all on my own as well, to gain recognition for myself. Another
time, during a school ceremony, I had to go up in front of everyone
without the proper clothes to receive an award, an academic recognition
that they gave for good grades. They called my name and I felt ashamed

because of my appearance, but I had to go up. You should realize that my family was by no means the poorest; the poorest couldn't even go to school at all, and here I was graduating from primary school. Perhaps because of things like this, I was interested in becoming a priest; at least those experiences made me think about the world.

I thought that being a priest I could do something to help people. In Telica there was an Italian priest named Ensofencio. He was *very* hard working; he did everything and worked with everyone, bricklayers, carpenters, electricians. He himself was something of an electrician. Once he made an electric clock to put in the church, and then the whole town could hear when it struck the hour; the bells rang and everything. He was very progressive. The people had great affection for him. Also, he was very fond of us kids, in spite of the fact that he used to get angry with us, because sometimes we would refuse to take the host or drink the wine. Then he would get angry and cuff us; but at other times, he played with us, and he taught us soccer. We spent a lot of time with him, and he influenced us a good deal with regard to helping people.

Padre Ensofencio was always furious with the curia of León, because he would send all our money and alms to them, but they never gave him anything for the village in return. I can hear him complaining, "I have to be on my own here and make do, figure out how to get things, how to fix things, and here I send everything we have to *them*!" In fact, he complained so much that they reassigned him to the boys' reformatory. It was probably punishment, because they gave him two weeks vacation time to go visit his family, and when he came back they had already sent another priest here and forwarded his papers to the reformatory. I used to visit him at the reformatory when I was in the seminary. He was a very humane person.

In the seminary, I spent my first year studying and getting along well as a scholarship student. But there was no student organization or club. So, the second year, together with my friend Denny Tenorio who later died in the war, we began looking for a way to organize the students. We wanted two things: to help students improve academically, establish a kind of tutoring program; and to look for ways to make some changes in the school rules. For example, in the seminary, there was a TV, but we could only see the programs that the rector determined. What we wanted to see, we couldn't. Then the newspapers arrived, *Novedades* and *La Prensa;* generally *La Prensa* did not arrive whenever there was any social convulsion because it was the paper of the middle-class democratic opposition, but it was at least something. Another thing that we students didn't like was that we couldn't smoke; so everyone did so secretly, and some even smoked marijuana. We presented these problems to the priests, but they rejected everything. So, when we got to the third year, we at least established a central committee of students, and since the students were all behind us, the priests couldn't do anything about it; and they had to look for a way for us to get along together.

My third year, I had arguments with my parents because the priest got me together with them; we all sat down, he was very astute, asking them how they were, praising me for my discipline and intelligence, and then he tells them that the school has decided to name me as second director of the seminary for discipline. When I hear this, I realize that if I accept, I'm coopted, and they've got me. "No," I said, "I don't want to be that." "What!" says mama, "How can you say that?" We had a big argument, and I walked out of the meeting with my folks and the priest, who was a short, thin Canadian but very sharp! Then they called me back and asked me to think about it. Mama went away mad, and later called me, asking me what I had decided, saying that she didn't understand what was the matter with me, and so on.

The priests were clever to make me a leader in different tasks and activities. For example, on Sunday afternoons when they would take us out to the Piedrecita park, I was always the second in command after the priest. Also in my third year, '71, there was the taking of the cathedral here because of the professors' strike against the dictatorship. I was a leader of the students, and we were able to suspend classes at the seminary. We were about to march from the seminary to the cathedral, but the priests were very shrewd. You see, there was this math teacher named Rogers, a great teacher, and a wonderful father figure. Naturally, the priests got him to talk to us. He told us how he remembered when he was young, and so on, and spent over an hour talking to us. After that, our enthusiasm passed, and no one was in the mood to have a demonstration.

We finally did get the priests to let us smoke, watch the TV programs we wanted, and to see that the papers would always arrive. We achieved those things. Really, it seems to me that the priests let us do all this because, in a way, they trusted us. We had this spiritual director who was also a psychologist and he was capable of guiding us in the way he wanted us to go. I remember many conversations with this man; he would begin by telling me that my student concerns and activities were insignificant, that what really mattered were my studies, my preparation.

One time we had an argument, and he asked me why I was the way I was, so rebellious. I told him about the cigarettes, the TV, etc. "But," he said, "we gave these things to you already, so what's the matter with you?" I said that I was unsettled and upset because I didn't know what to do about the misery of the people. He told me that that was not my problem, but rather a problem of the state. "What are you going to do about it? You're only a student. Besides," he says, "if those are your concerns, then you should be somewhere else; those are not the concerns of a student here." We had such a heated discussion that, at the end, he angrily told me that, with my recalcitrant spirit, I would never be in agreement with anything and that I would never even find a woman who would have me! I think he told me that because he had run out of things to say, because it's absurd to say that sort of thing to another person, especially to a kid.

We did a survey of student complaints in '71 and practically no one returned to the seminary after that. We did another one in '72, and of the 70 students that were there, only two said that they wanted to continue. Then comes the earthquake. That saved them; if it hadn't been for the earthquake, they would've had to close the seminary, because they couldn't keep it open just for the 25 new students. What they did was to divide into the *seminario menor*, which is the seconary school, and the *seminario mayor*, where they do philosophy. For theology, one had to go to Honduras, Guatemala or Colombia. I don't know if they have theology here now.

At that time, all the protests, surveys, and so forth that we did, we carried out on our own initiative. We had no link with anyone else. But I was already wondering how I could join up with the Frente. My friend Denny Tenorio and I said to ourselves that all these strikes and demonstrations against Somoza can't all be spontaneous; they have to be organized and directed by someone. That's how we figured out that we were the only ones who were not linked up with the Frente. We asked ourselves a series of questions about our goals. Then, when we separated, because we were more or less kicked out of school, we exchanged addresses and parted. Our plan seems absolutely crazy now, but it was to create our *own* organization and then to join up with the Frente.

They expelled me when the rector of the seminary called me to come talk to him, and he gave me a sermon. He said the same thing that the psychologist had already told me and that I would never amount to anything; he even repeated that I would never find a wife (which was not true by the way). When he finished, I said nothing. So he continued, saying that they didn't kick me out earlier because I was such a good student and they didn't want to prejudice my future. Then I responded saying, "If you kick me out now, it's the same difference; I will be blackballed everywhere. Please continue being kind and give me a letter so that I can go to another school." He gave me the letter and told me, "It's up to you to do something with your life. We have given you our advice." He was quite cold, but the letter was in very good religious language.

When I was in the seminary I used to read a lot, and I still like to read. I remember reading *War and Peace* by Leo Tolstoy. A great book like that gives you so much to think about. I learned quite a bit of math and physics because we had to study hard. I also read stories, and I enjoyed literature very much, especially Spanish Golden Age literature, Lope de Vega and Calderón. I also loved history, but I didn't get to study it much. What absolutely fascinated me were physics and math; I was good at them and would have liked to go further. I only have a high school degree, although I am trying to improve myself by taking university classes part-time at Ricardo Morales, a school of the Frente. This is my second year of studying social sciences.

After I was expelled from the seminary, I went to the Colegio de Lima in León, where the director registered me as a fourth year student without *mita* having to come, fortunately. The second day, I began a literary discussion with the teacher, something about Cervantes or Quevedo, and, after that, a compañero who has since died, Felix Carrillo, invited me to work with him. He was with the Student Revolutionary Front (Frente Estudiantil Revolucionario, FER). I said that I wasn't interested, that I had to study, but he kept asking me. Although he was not with the Frente at that time, he had relations with people who were, but I didn't know that until later. He invited me to a meeting where I was given the job of working in the poor neighborhoods and with the campesinos in and around the area. Though the student sector was fundamentally a support group, that experience was a valuable initiation.

Later, I participated in the taking of the cathedral in León, in 1973–74, and in the campaign for the ransom of Chico Ramírez, a *guerrillero comandante*, and of a Salvadoran professor who had been part of the teachers' movement in El Salvador, and who had been taken prisoner by Somoza when he left there for Nicaragua. Both men were in jail. We took the cathedral, there were only a few of us, unarmed; we just occupied it. The group included Mónica Baltodano; Omar Cabezas; Ana Isabel Morales; Ivan "Churumbel"; one other person and myself.

We took the cathedral on December 23. It was beautifully decorated for a wedding that afternoon. There was a magnificent red carpet that covered the entire entrance, all those wide stairs, and ran all the way from the street to the altar. There was also a pretty floral arrangement at the altar and the whole church was decorated with white lace curtains, and there were red, white, and yellow flowers in all the pews. I imagine that that was going to be a fine wedding; no poor person could get married in that style. Padre Areas was going to perform the ceremony; he was in the sacristy when Comandantes Cabezas and Morales went up to talk to him. The rest of us were closing the doors; luckily, the people hadn't arrived yet for the wedding. The padre at the begining was upset, but afterwards he said, "If I have to, I have to," and then he left.

We made some decorative banners to hang and stayed a month, until January 23, 1974. We would leave at times to coordinate with other compañeros who were organizing in the barrios and with the students. That was very important because, at that time, the students were on vacation, and we were able to mobilize around 8,000 people, students and residents of the working class neighborhoods. The guardia responded with shots, jail, rifle butts, beatings. For example, I saw a woman, a simple vendor in the cathedral square, who began to argue with a guardia. He threw a smoke bomb which landed in her bag of yucca. So the woman grabs it, and throws it back at him. There were three guardia together, and when the first one caught it, he threw it to second, and the second one to the third, and then it exploded. They beat that woman, dragged her away and took her prisoner. The next day there was a demonstration of all the *mercaderas*, the women vendors of León, and the guardia released her.

The vendors were very supportive of us; they passed us all our food, cold drinks, and cigarettes. In the back part of the cathedral which looks out onto the market, there are some little windows. We tied a rope to a basket, which we would lower and the people would fill for us every day. They took care of us. Those of us who were inside took shifts; at times there were four or five of us, but once there was only *one* of us inside! The thing is, we had to mobilize the barrios too; I did a good deal of that, because the people knew me in Laborío and El Collolar for example, where I had been organizing before. After the siege of the cathedral, they recognized me as a *militante* of the Frente.

After the *toma*, the taking of the cathedral, everyone went home or to the barrio to keep working. I was beginning my fifth year of secondary school then, in '74; and somehow, I finished. Then I worked even more in the neighborhoods, and the guardia had different ways to pressure one. In my case, they never were clear about what I did because there were times, for example, when I would leave school and someone would follow me. Or, I would be walking in the street with a girl, say, and then a car with three or four men would be going along beside me. They knew my route, my schedule and my habits, because I would turn a corner and they would already be waiting for me. I changed routes, of course; they did these things to frighten me.

They arrested me at the end of '74, but they still didn't know what I was doing. It was a Sunday, and I was in the Laborío vicinity, where I had gone with several compañeros to a *finca*, a farm, to practice target shooting with a .22, which we often did. It was about a ten kilometer walk, but it kept us in shape and we enjoyed the company. That day, one of the boys didn't show up. We went on anyway, and on the way back, a jeep full of guardia comes up and they start shouting at us for walking on the road. One strikes me with his rifle butt, calls me a son of a bitch, and jumps on me. Then another comes up and they try to decide what to do with us. Luckily, we were ready; we had already prepared a story about ourselves, how we met, what we were doing, who we were, so that we would all say the same thing. Then I offered one of the guardia cigarettes and a box and a half of .22 shells that we had left. We wanted to get along with them and not get in any trouble. Then one of them told me that our friend had denounced us, the one that didn't show up, and that's why they stopped us. I said, "We haven't done anything wrong; we're just friends, going out to practice target shooting on a Sunday." That was in the morning; they took us to jail and late that night they let us go. The officer who interrogated me didn't have much experience. That was lucky for me because he didn't beat me too much, and because he told me all the information that he had about me. They knew everything about my schedule, but they didn't know about my backpack in which I carried not only my notebooks for school, but also my Frente materials. They let me go and I kept on working.

I didn't go underground until '75, about six months after that brief run-in with the guardia. I went to a secret military school in León for about a week, a house in the San Felipe barrio, then to a training center in Managua for about two more weeks. Comandantes Tomás Borge and Carlos Agüero were in charge of the exercises, while comandante Carlos Fonseca was in charge of the political end. From there, I went directly to the mountains, with about three weeks of training. We were with Comandante Tirado's men for a while, and then with Comandante Ruiz until September 1979.

From then on, life was like an odyssey. From the political point of view, the most important thing about the montaña was to have maintained alive the hope of the FSLN. That, to a certain extent, helped us win people to our cause, because everyone thought that in the montaña there was a big army. But we weren't big at all; we were small, very small. Counting the groups I knew about, there were about 100 to 125 of us, and most of the time we were divided up in groups of 10, 15, or occasionally 30. The headquarters was more remotely located in the interior of Soslaya. Our tasks were political work with the villagers and campesinos, reconnoitering, and just subsisting. We were in practically no military activity for a long time. In fact, we were isolated, cut off from all communication from the Frente from June, '76 until December '77. We had supplies, and there we stayed without having any encounters, shots, or anything.

You know, the history of the Frente has not yet been written; there are books about the Frente's urban work, but practically nothing about the work in the montaña. There's only the book by Comandante Cabezas, *Fire from the Mountain*, in which he tells a story. He narrates his participation, mixing a little literature with his rural experiences. That's just fine, but the people here in Nicaragua with the most authority to speak about the guerrilla and the development of the FSLN in the monte are Comandantes Henry Ruiz and Victor Tirado. They know more than anyone, but they have not written, and we can't pressure them to tell the story. What I am relating is not so much my adventures, like Cabezas did, or an overall history, for which I am not qualified. Rather, what I say about the monte is my perspective on events and activities, how I saw things. I just wanted to clarify that.

We climbed up to a high place in the montaña where we did much physical exercise. We were in excellent condition, but it's not the same, doing hundreds of sit-ups and push-ups, hiking or jogging in a clean space, as it is to be slogging through a thicket, scaling or descending a steep mountain, and carrying heavy packs. We were on mule and cow paths, with many potholes; it was very muddy and slippery, and one fell down a lot especially at night.

Once I counted how many times I fell in one night and it made me ashamed because I fell down more than most. It was 125 times! Of course, you could never use any light because of security; and we also learned to speak down in our throats so our voices wouldn't carry. There was one weak compañero who would cry; he felt abandoned, thought we would never make it, and nature was too much for him. He couldn't deal with its permanence. Nature doesn't understand us or change for us, the mountain is simply there; the hill is there; the rain is there; the animals are there, whether we like it or not and however much we may protest. If you weaken in the face of all that, you are finished; then the morale weakens, and that is perdition because you could die or betray others. One has to become strong in order to survive and to comply with the mission. I am not brave; it's life that teaches one to have courage.

In critical moments, in the beginning, I would smile somewhat ruefully to myself and remember that when I was in my fourth year of high school in León, they offered me a scholarship to study in Mexico, but I was already a *militante*. And Somoza, through the Ministry of Education, offered me a scholarship too, to study in the U.S. and get me out of the country. The church also offered me a scholarship to study for the priesthood. When I put all that to one side, it was a blow for my papa. On that same occasion when we were discussing these offers, and he saw that he couldn't do anything with me, he said, "Well, since you don't want to be what I want you to be, at least be good at whatever you want to be so that you don't bring me shame." Now, since the triumph, he is proud of me.

Anyway, I would think about that in the monte in the beginning, and what it means is that if one gets involved in something very big, a cause, an ideal, then one has to give up other things. And now, for me for example, life outside the Frente has no meaning, none, because that is what I have cultivated. Why? Because there is a commitment that I've made for half of my life now, and that gives one certain values. I know that to people who have never been involved in anything similar, such dedication seems crazy, but that's the strength of the ideal. I don't believe that psychologists, sociologists, anthropologists take this into account when they analyze societies. That's where they are mistaken, because they are not able to understand why a worker, a campesino, would die for his land or his country, to make things better; and sometimes it's just for the hope that things will be better.

Our standard of living here in Nicaragua is very low and it is deteriorating; nevertheless, if the people were not disposed to defend their country, we would have been gobbled up by the gringos by now. The revolution and the example of the sacrifice of all our compañeros who fell is engraved in the memory of the people. It is a kind of well-spring that nourishes the revolution and makes the people feel and understand our current problems. What I mean to say is that the experience of the monte, in and of itself, helps one to understand, just as the experience of being clandestine, or of being in jail, also give one a special understanding of the revolution and one's mission.

After a while, our most acute problems in the monte were supplies, injuries, and illness. I said before that it was an odyssey, and it was; we had to go and try to find help for what we needed, which was everything. With regard to supplies, especially in '76 and '77, I remember that they were at such a low level that we spent about six months eating one or two *guineos* a day if we were lucky, you know, those little bananas. We ate them peel and all so there would be more to eat. I imagine that our stomachs came to be like iron, for we ate anything, *ojoche*, breadfruit, when we could find it; *zapote*, the fruit from the marmalade tree, which we ate green or ripe, any way we could get it; *flor de pacaya*, the bitter flower from the pacaya, a palmlike shrub which we ate in winter. We also ate something similar to an avocado, and a whole series of foods that animals eat, like carob beans, raw corn, and so on. You had to eat these things and your stomach had to adjust or you wouldn't make it. Two of our compañeros died of hunger; they were two older campesinos who had come with us fleeing the guardia.

You remember in 1975 there began a cooperative military maneuver between Somoza and North American troops in the north, along the Atlantic coast, and it lasted for three years, 1975–77. It was called Operation Aguila VI, and it really hurt us badly. That's when there was lots of fighting and we lost many compañeros in combat. Others had to flee to Honduras; some went to Siuna, and toward the end of '77, others died trying to reopen the route for contact with the city. There were just *11* of us left by the end of '77, and remember that counting all of us at the beginning, we were about 100 or 125. We suffered terribly, but then the Frente was able to open the Carlos Fonseca Amador front in the north. That gave us the break we needed to recuperate some, and we left for Las Minas, Rosita, and Siuna, all on the Atlantic side of Nicaragua, in the north.

Comandante Ruiz left to participate in the reorganization of the Frente, because that was the height of the divisions within the Frente, with the three tendencies as they were called. Because we were isolated, the split wasn't very clear to us, and we only learned about it through the news on a small radio someone had. We knew about some correspondence that had arrived in '78, but all we knew for sure was that Comandante Ruiz was the chief of all of us. He did not know how to clarify the problem to us, and it just didn't enter into our ranks as an issue. During all that period there were many, many confrontations with the guardia.

We believed that the most important role that the montaña played were not the big combats, those came more in '78 anyway, and there were not many big battles, except perhaps the taking of Waslala and of Río Blanco, and some ambushes in other places such as El Plátano, San Isidro and El Naranjo. Mostly, however, they weren't big confrontations of 300 men against 300 guardias, but rather of seven compañeros against a large number, *un montón*, of guardias. They were small hit and run operations because, since we had so little ammunition and supplies, we had to calculate everything down to the last item. But our being there was the important task we fulfilled. That is, staying there, being a constant presence permitted the Nicaraguan people to keep alive the hope that the Frente could help them.

The campesinos were on our side and continued supplying us as long as they could, but the reprisals of the guardia were such that by '77 we had to stop asking for food because the guardia would come and murder the poor campesinos for helping us. They even exterminated entire towns, just wiped them out. For example, there were these two villages that we passed by, but we did not make any contact with the people so as not to put them at risk, but the guardia took them off the face of the earth anyway. They were medieval torturers; they skinned people alive, speared infants with their bayonets, a whole series of horrors as a way to inspire fear in the rest of the population. That was a time of enormous panic in the countryside.

The movement was going forward in the city, but we in the montaña bore great hardships during those years, running and fighting, running and fighting. We were barely surviving, because we were without contact with the population for about two years to avoid reprisals for them. We suffered most from malaria and fevers at the beginning, and then from mountain leprosy, which made walking and carrying things very difficult. I got it on my wrist and my hand , but I was lucky. Others had it on their feet and back, and it would become infected. Mountain leprosy is a virus; mine finally went away by itself after about a year and a half, except for these dark splotches that still remain. There was some medicine for it that came in from Costa Rica, but the guardia found out and cut off our supply.

Another serious problem in the montaña was learning humility. The only way we could overcome our situation was through our physical, animal qualities. That's the only way some of us made it, while others didn't. One's survival depended on one's ability to orient himself in the mountains, to withstand long marches, to carry heavy loads. But that common condition helped give humility and human sensitivity. We each understood the other's physical weaknesses, for example one compañero couldn't carry much, so the others helped him out. Food was completely rationed and we all helped each other to have the political and moral maturity so that we didn't fight over rations. To tell the truth, I didn't think about God or pray much in the monte. I don't know, I am not a career Marxist-Leninist, I've not studied it. But on my own, I have read some basic books, and I have my personal criteria, but I didn't think about theory or pray during those hard times.

I was in three especially difficult moments; one was when I got lost while I was reconnoitering with another compañero. When it was time to return to camp, we discovered we were lost and we spent nine days trying to find our way back. On two other occasions I felt that I was going to die. Once, they wounded me and I crawled away by myself, away from my compañeros, to die, but I didn't die, I'm still here! The bullet went through my lung and I bled through my mouth and nose, but the bullet left my body and I was saved. At that time I spent five days trying to find my compañeros again.

Another time, we were in a surprise attack against the guardia, and I was unarmed because that was another problem: many times we had weapons that didn't work, that jammed, or that would fire only one or two shots. The only thing that *worked* was our morale. In 1977, they sent me and two other compañeros, one of whom died in combat later, from Cerro del Toro to another place, and the guardia picked up our tracks and followed us. It was pouring rain and we were looking for dry wood about 4:00 p. m. One compañero carried a carbine which shot badly; another had a Browning with no magazine, and a Browning with no magazine doesn't fire, and I had nothing at all. Suddenly, I saw a dark figure in the dense undergrowth; I thought it was an animal, but then it turned around and I saw a rifle and a face. We were eyeball to eyeball with the guardia, and they started shooting. I jumped over a ledge and landed in the crook of a tree; then I climbed down and fled under a hail of bullets.

That was the second time that my compañeros gave me up for dead, and the second time that they informed my parents that I had died. While they had gone to advise my parents, I was alone for about three months in the monte without contact with anyone at all. I would steal raw corn from a vegetable patch, or perhaps a little yucca, but that was the reality I was living; it was absolute misery.

I thought only of finding my compañeros and that we were going to win. I had no reason to think either of these things; it was just pure faith, confidence, because it's illogical. If I said something comparable now, people would say I was crazy. I had no arms, the area was crawling with guardia, and on three occasions I nearly bumped into them, stumbling by accident onto their encampment. I didn't have a compass, I oriented myself by the sun, and when it was dark, or when it was the rainy season, just by luck. I think that, being from the farm and Cerro Telica, I knew a bit about life in the mountains; it wasn't so foreign to me as to others, and that helped me adapt to that inhospitable and interminable *monte*.

Three months later I joined up with my compañeros again, near El Naranjo and Siuna; there were eleven of us. Nearby, in Las Minas, there was a congregation of Capuchin fathers. They were very good and very poor, and they had an organization of delegates of the word, lay readers who in this instance also alerted villagers to the guardia's activities, better than the information network that the guardia had. In fact, they were the ones who spirited Comandante Ruiz out of Bluefields to Rama, and from Rama to Managua to protect him. He had been hiding out in the seminary in Bluefields, disguised as a seminarian, and he even gave sermons in church and everything. Father Teodoro, who was North American, Father Agustín Sambola, and a nun who later went with us, Dorotea Wilson, smuggled him in and out, and then they worked with us after the triumph.

Also, in La Rosita I spoke with another nun, who would pick me up in her minibus on the highway and take me to town or to Siuna; sometimes I left town and just went to chat with her in the curia. That was in '78. We left for Las Minas, and our plan was to make contact with sympathetic priests and nuns to help us out. I used to have a good friend named Sambola back when I was in seminary. He was from the Atlantic Coast, and like these people, he was more Moravian than Catholic, and he would sing and play pretty religious songs on the guitar. I liked religious songs and country music, so we would sing together while he played the guitar.

When we arrived there in Siuna, I asked for Father Sambola, but it wasn't him but a brother of his. I told his brother that we had studied together in the seminary, and I blew our cover, because we were all supposed to be poor campesinos. "Some campesinos, studying in the national seminary in Managua!" he said. But he helped by changing two bills for me. That was important because campesinos never carried large bills, so it was dangerous for me to have them. The religious community of Siuna was with the Frente, and much of the congregation of La Rosita too. There was just one reactionary priest that we stayed away from; he didn't even agree with the way the priests and nuns were teaching catechism.

We worked with the campesinos there, in and around La Rosita in '78, preparing for the final offensive. But there were really only three of us, since some had left with Comandante Ruiz and some had stayed in El Naranjo. The three of us were René Vivas, now vice minister of the interior, Comandante Muñoz, now in the leadership of the army, and myself. We stayed and gave military training to the campesinos. Comandantes David Blanco, Hugo Torres, and Roberto Calderón had all been with us in the montaña, but they left for other parts. When Comandantes Blanco and Vivas returned, they led us in the definitive taking of Bonanza, after which we left for Puerto Cabezas. There the guardia did not fight but gave up, as in Siuna. We arrived in Puerto Cabezas on July 19, 1979, the day of the triumph, but when Somoza left on the seventeenth, the guardia collapsed. Some Moravian pastors and a few Capuchin priests arranged for the chiefs of the guardia to surrender, and there was no confrontation.

After the triumph, I returned briefly to Las Minas from Puerto Cabezas because my assignment was to do the political and military organization work of the Frente among the populace there. I got that under control quickly, putting different chiefs in each post, and went back to Puerto Cabezas to work with the religious and the padres there, and we got along well. I didn't know English or the Indian languages, but most everyone either spoke or understood Spanish when they wanted to. A few didn't, and that was a limitation in some communities. About July 22, Comandante Ruiz came to Puerto Cabezas, where Blanco, Vivas, and I already were. Blanco was chief of the military base and I was the political and administrative head for all the Atlantic Coast, Bluefields, everything.

Some problems came up; for example, the Simón Bolívar brigade, which entered from Costa Rica and came to Bluefields causing mischief, wrecking everything, threatening all our gains and making the people confused and troubled. So we had to send some compañeros, like Evaristo Vásquez who fell just about a year ago, to help fix things and repair the damage. They took the brigade members prisoner and sent them to Managua, where they expelled from the country those who were foreigners, from Panama, Costa Rica and Colombia. They were Trotskyists, extreme leftists who wanted to impose their will on everything and everyone, without realizing that things have their own rhythm. As for the Nicaraguans who had gone with them, we put them in a school to clarify things for them.

I stayed on in Puerto Cabezas after they had transferred Comandante Blanco to Managua to direct the police force, and I was there alone in charge of everything. Then they sent Comandante Lumberto Campbell, who was a native of Bluefields, to be in charge of his home town; and then they sent Comandante William Ramírez to the Atlantic Coast too, to be political administrator. So he took my place, and I kept only the job of political organization for the Frente. Then they sent Glenda Monterrey to take charge of the party, and I was left only with the army.

By the end of '79, they took me out and sent me to Cuba for a one year course of study for generals, at the Máximo Gómez school. I was there only four months when they returned me to the Atlantic Coast as a delegate of the Ministry of the Interior to set up the Ministry there. I was there until mid '82, when they transfered me to Managua to be second in command of the Institute of State Security (Instituto de la Seguridad del Estado), and there I stayed until the end of '84. In '85 they moved me to political headquarters with Comandante Cabezas. In '86, they transferred him to Region Three, and I stayed in charge of political leadership here.

I confess that if I had my choice, I would like something else better; however, it is not a matter of personal taste, but of responsibility. One has to put other considerations aside in order to carry out one's responsibility, or else things turn out badly. My principal function is to work in the political and ideological development of the thousands of soldiers who make up the fighting force of the Ministry of the Interior. That part of the work I really enjoy, because then I get to be among the people; I go around talking with the compañeros, seeing them, listening to their problems. I try to bring them officially into the organization, but above all, to assure that they comply with the mission of the Ministry, to help the compañeros understand their political mission, to see that they have to comply not because of any personal obligation, but because the revolution depends on them, whether we get out of this war alive or not depends on them. Fundamentally, what we inculcate in everyone is love for the people, respect for the people, loyalty to the revolution and humility of the people and of the Ministry.

Those are the fundamental bases of the political and ideological work that I do. Humility is a very important aspect to me, so that the compañero does not think that just because he has a uniform and a weapon that he is better than a campesino, or a worker, or a woman, or an old person, or a child, or an intellectual, or someone from the private sector. We teach them to respect the population as a whole and to feel brotherhood, love for the revolution, and the sacrifice of those who defend it. Another thing we tell them a lot is that, in the final analysis, who pays the price for everything is the people, because they are the ones who make the sacrifice for the revolution. This is the fundamental ideology; these things are Sandinismo. What I am saying is an official perspective, because that is the objective of my work, which is institutional.

Marxism and Christianity are mixed in too. Someone may call himself a Marxist-Leninist, but he doesn't know, and that person really isn't, in practice. By the same token, some people in the communist or the socialist parties here in Nicaragua say they are Marxist-Leninists, but their attitudes leave much to be desired. Similarly, there are those who say that they are Christians, but whose attitudes leave much to be desired. There are some who spend all their time worrying about whether God or heaven exist or not; but I say why concern ourselves with things that we can do nothing about and can never know for sure. Rather, we should take the Gospel lesson where Jesus says that when you gave drink to the thirsty, food to the hungry, clothes to the naked, that when you visited the prisoner in jail, that when you did all these things, you also did them to me. Officially, we don't give ourselves headaches over the ideology of Sandinismo. We have *militantes* who are Christians, priests and so on; the *militante* is the one who is capable of defending the interests of the people before his own personal interests.

In Sandinismo, we are pragmatic, but we are also theoretical, because we have an ideal. We have to analyze reality from the theoretical point of view; that's where Marxism-Leninism is useful, as a scientific theory for understanding the development of society and its contradictions. But it is just a guide; you know that you can't force a square peg into a round hole, so if our situation doesn't fit, then we have to find another model. What we have is a theory in which to place the real world and try to make something better out of it. Marxism and Sandinismo are complementary you could say, but not the same thing. Sandinismo is the uniting thread, the navel, so to speak, of the Nicaraguan people—Christians, Marxists, atheists, and so on. You will find people who don't believe in anything except their tiny plot of land, but they believe in Sandinismo. You will find people who say the rosary every day, like my mama, but they believe in Sandinismo. In real life, it is the concrete, personal example that motivates people, the example of those who have given their lives, the example of the mother, who though in great sorrow, sends her son off to fight.

There is plenty of room within this ideology for political pluralism, for one who is not Marxist, Christian, or Sandinista, for one who is totally uninterested in politics, and even for the pure capitalist. There are people from the Superior Council of Private Enterprise, COSEP, for example, who openly go to the United States embassy, and officials of the CIA who openly go to those people's houses. Some of the COSEP people are spokesmen for the White House, but it's not correct to say that and leave it at that, because many COSEP people are a legitimate opposition, with different ideas from us about how to run the country. The important thing in this country is that one *produce*. Production has priority over ideology.

Sometimes I think part of the problem is our own mistakes, maybe not mistakes strictly speaking, but our lack of clear explanation and reasons to support certain of our policies. When you don't give reasons or handle things well, people feel cornered, caged. But, little by little, we're improving our relations with the opposition. Our dealings with COSEP, though, become tense when our relations with the U.S. become tense.

We have other things to learn too. For example, we can learn some things to admire and some things perhaps to do differently from the Cuban Revolution. I was really impressed with the comparatively high standard of living that they have achieved there for the population generally; I was touched by the wonderful warmth of the Cuban people toward us Nicaraguans, and I was amazed at the unity of the Cuban people. One of the things that we have to learn from the Cubans, the Vietnamese, the Soviets is discipline. They, in times of economic crisis more serious than ours—because however terrible ours is, it isn't as bad as it was for Cuba during the blockade, or the crisis of the Soviet Union during World War II, or the crisis which the Vietnamese still suffer from the war—have shown exemplary discipline. It's hard to learn from the Vietnamese because their culture is so different and they're so disciplined already, while we are more soft, more like the Cubans culturally, but the Cubans have learned it.

This is just a personal impression, but it seems to me that we Nicaraguans are more open politically, more daring and bold too. Perhaps it's only out of necessity that we are that way, just as it may be from necessity that the Cubans are the way they are. In the beginning, when I didn't have the analytical skills that I have now, I felt almost a mystical admiration for the Cuban Revolution, but as one develops, one can see certain things. And, personally, I would not like for us to become closed like they did in Cuba, because I know that if we become closed, we will die.

7   Gilberto Cuadra (b. 1934)

"To be frank, working for the [Somoza] government had its advantages. That [1960s] was the time that Nicaragua really began to develop. Almost everything that we have that is new or modern is a product of that epoch."

"For an engineer, modernization on that scale was an exciting adventure."

The out-of-date Time *magazines, sent over by the U. S. embassy and neatly stacked on the coffee table, suggest accurately Gilberto Cuadra's admiration for the U.S. and his support for its policy in Nicaragua. As president of the Nicaraguan Development Institute (INDE), vice-president of the Superior Council of Private Enterprise (COSEP), and civil engineer in the private sector, Mr. Cuadra is a leading critic of the Sandinista government.*

Soon after the revolution, Mr. Cuadra became disaffected with the full-scale reforms that were envisioned and with the restrictions on private enterprise. He has for some years now dedicated himself full-time to political advocacy, sacrificing his once lucrative engineering firm in the private sector in order to lobby against the Sandinista government. He is aided in his efforts by his organizations' close ties with the U.S. government and with conservative U.S. groups, such as as the Heritage Foundation, as well as by the increasingly desperate economic situation within Nicaragua today.

In his autobiography, Mr. Cuadra discusses openly and amiably his politically divided family; his education in Nicaragua and in the U.S.; his work in construction during the Somoza years; his increasing political involvement and his imprisonment by the Sandinistas in 1981 for "public agitation." Throughout, the good-humored Mr. Cuadra expresses his overall economic and social philosophy, in which capitalism and individual liberties are inextricably linked.

I am an authentic Managuan, something you don't see very often. For five generations at least, my roots have been here. My father was originally a farmer, and for a while he worked as an administrator of a coffee hacienda at the same time that he had a small finca of his own. He was unsuccessful as a farmer. I was born about 12 kilometers outside Managua, on that coffee plantation. In the past, my brother and sisters had always gone to school in Managua and stayed in my maternal grandmother's house. But, my grandmother had just died when it was time for me to go to school, I was the youngest, and so my father felt himself obliged to move to the city proper for my education and that of my brother. We are six; I am the only one who has been able to have both a secondary and university education. My parents had only a primary school education, while my brothers and sisters made it through a few years of secondary school, but they did not graduate.

One of my brothers is a technician in highway construction; he is better known than I am, and many people know me because of my brother. Many of my best friendships and connections have come through him. Though he is not a university professional, he is of such quality and ability that he is well-recognized and accepted in both government and private business circles. Another brother is chief lathe operator in the largest lathe establishment in Nicaragua, in the Ministry of Construction. One sister is married to a businessman and she is a homemaker; they live in Honduras. Another sister went to the U.S. and returned with a young daughter, to whom she has dedicated herself; now she is a grandmother and takes care of her grandchildren. Another brother is the most unsettled of all of us, with regard to ideas, abilities, interests. He is an artist; he sketches, paints, does engravings and etchings. Unfortunately, I have to tell you that he has turned out to be a Sandinista; he's the only one in the whole family.

I studied in public schools, graduating from the Instituto Nacional Ramírez Goyena in 1953. At that time, it was the most rebellious and irreverent secondary school in the country. Perhaps that helped me, because it made me become a little eclectic. The year after I graduated that institution was completely transformed, and it became the number one institute in Nicaragua. This was made possible by a massive infusion of money, talent, and material. It was like Cinderella turning into a princess.

The school got its own buildings, a swimming pool, everything. The new director was Guillermo Rothchuh, of socialist leanings. He was the one who you could say provided the ideological incubation period for a great number, 20 to 30, of the political leaders who are running the government today, including comandantes like Bayardo Arce. Carlos Fonseca was there too, though I didn't meet him, because he arrived as I left. He came not as a student, but as a librarian; Rothchuh gave him help and guidance, while Carlos read and absorbed everything in that library, all of which influenced what he later became.

Then I went to UNAN, the national university, for civil engineering. While studying there, I also began giving classes, not at the university level, but tutoring young elementary and secondary students who were having problems with their studies. Their parents would contract me to help them. I still get together with some of these people, and they are very proud that I was their tutor. During the first year, I had some difficulties with my studies, especially the first six months. In secondary school you see, I was the star student, tops, and I was very confident of myself. But the first months of my first year at the university, that confidence tripped me up, because I thought that I could do everything without studying much. But, whenever I took an exam, I found that I could only come up with answers, and grades, that were not satisfying to me. The fact is that it was a big shock for me, and for the other students as well. The drop-out rate in engineering was phenomenal, from 220 first-year students (all in the same classroom if you can imagine) at the beginning, to 12 at the end of the year! It was very demanding.

The class I liked most and was best at was descriptive geometry; I liked it because it required a good bit of imagination. I did very well in that course, but the other classes were a struggle for me. So, I made a deal with my fellow students, that I would explain the geometry to them and they would explain the other classes to me. We would get together for three to four hours every evening, including Saturday and Sunday evenings. At the end, we were part of the twelve who passed to the second year.

That first year, in addition to my tutoring, I worked as a draftsman's apprentice in a construction company. During the vacations between the first and second year, thanks to my brother who had very good connections and friendships in the Ministry of Construction, I obtained a position as draftsman. I continued working there as a draftsman, and also as chief of a section, because thanks to my father, I had learned some English. My father, in one of his crazy raptures, enrolled me in English classes from the end of my primary school years through the third year of secondary school. The program was sponsored by the American embassy and there was a small library attached, which made checking out books easy and convenient. So I learned English, which served me well in that job. I was made editor of the monthly reports that were sent to the Inter-American Bank on the progress of various highway construction projects for which Nicaragua had contracted loans. All that was in English, and the fact that I could do it gave me more status.

Thus passed my years of education. My brothers grew up in a slightly different time than I did, although the years between us are short, I'm fifty-three and my oldest brother is sixty-four. But my papa, when he came to Managua after having been a farmer, had to learn to become an office worker. It was not easy, and he had never had much business sense anyway, or a head for figures even when he had his own finca; he just was not very good at it. This meant that there were serious financial limitations in my house, and my brothers, perhaps, decided early that instead of trying to struggle through school, they would go to work. So when I came along, we were a little better off financially, and my parents could, with difficulty, keep me in secondary school. Though my secondary school was public, there were still meals, clothes, books, and so forth to take care of. Later, I paid all my expenses at the university myself through my job.

In '58 I finished my studies at the university here, and there appeared an announcement in the newspaper that the American embassy was going to make available some scholarships to study in the U.S.; they were sponsored by the International Institute of Education. I applied, presented myself, and since I had more knowledge of English than most others my age I did well, and they gave me a scholarship to do graduate work in Lexington, Kentucky. I went immediately and did my master's there.

I experienced no culture shock at all living in the U.S. because in my free time then (and still now), I was a great moviegoer. The movies taught me American life without living it. Many of the things that are common there but that we don't have here, I knew about from the movies, and I didn't have an adjustment problem. Almost all our movies were American.

The problem was that my English was not of a university level, and I had to spend entire nights without sleeping, writing reports, trying to adapt myself to courses of study that weren't in my language. But, I really didn't have any insurmountable problems. I managed to work a little, legally and illegally, because the professors let me help them in their work, although I was not listed on any payroll. This helped considerably, because the scholarship was for one year only, while the program at the university was for students to study six months, work six months, and so on. That made the program longer. I found myself without any more scholarship, but the professors helped me get a university scholarship. With that, and with what I earned, I could get by. Meanwhile, the government here maintained my salary of $115 a month, which I turned over to my parents.

I'll tell you something about the random events that determine our lives.

I returned to Nicaragua in 1960, around the fifteenth of October, during a week of prodigious, copious rains. There were great floods in the west, which downed all lines of communication, washed out bridges, and damaged highways. Immediately on arriving, I went to the office, very early in the morning, to present myself to my boss. He explained to me that since the government was spending money fighting the guerrillas, funds that had been earmarked for construction projects had been diverted and were no longer available. He released me from my commitment, which was to work for two years for him (he worked for the government) after returning from the States, since it was the government who paid my salary those two years I was away. He told me that I was free to do as I wanted.

I began making plans to return immediately to the United States, but before I could make the arrangements, the U.S. government gave aid to the government of Nicaragua to repair all those damaged highways and bridges. They put me on the project right away and, since it was an emergency, I worked like a crazy man day and night for two years. I learned in that period so much as an engineer, because I was practically alone. I had to make decisions on the spot without advice or consultation, and some I made very badly. At night, I would read my textbooks to see what I should do next, and I learned that way in a concentrated form, a mountain of facts and information.

That experience put me in a very good position technically, and I came to feel that there was a roof over my head that wouldn't let me grow. My boss was very competent, but after that experience I wanted to be my own boss. As a result, I formed my own business in 1964 and made myself independent, though I also continued working on outside contracts because my business was very small, with just four partners.

I had my first job with the government in 1954; it was a small assignment, with no connection to politics. I continued doing work for the government until 1967, when I left to become director of a construction company and an employee of another company, from which I received a percentage of the profits. I knew Somoza slightly, just a little. To be frank, working for the government had its advantages. That was the time that Nicaragua really began to develop. Almost everything that we have that is new or modern is a product of that epoch. We progressed because of the labor of many people, but especially through the mechanization of agriculture, which allowed cotton production to increase; the technical improvements in coffee-growing; and a more scientific approach to cattle-raising. Production in these areas meant that the country needed to provide more electricity and better means of communication and transportation. All this was a sudden, swift development for an extremely underdeveloped country.

For me, and for many others, those sweeping changes permitted us to develop ourselves much more than we would have been able to do in other countries. For an engineer, modernization on that scale was an exciting adventure. The good and the bad of it is that I still feel that way about myself and about that epoch. It was a privilege to live at a time when I felt like I could be a pathfinder; and I honestly feel that I can perform that same function today.

I married when I was thirty-three, but my wife never had children from our marriage. She was a widow and had a daughter, who I also consider my daughter because I have brought her up. She married, and her two children are now my children as well. Unfortunately, this daughter, who is now in her late twenties, has become a Sandinista, and this has been a thorn in our side, but that's part of life. She is a professional psychologist, and I don't know exactly how it came about, but I attribute a lot of it to her marriage to a young man in whom she put all her trust. He was a very different sort of person, and that difference finally took the shape of Sandinismo. He became involved in all that, then the marriage failed (he was always a little unstable), and now my daughter lives in her own house. Her daughter lives with us, and her son practically lives with us, he spends so much time at our house, but he lives with his mother.

I have feelings for her, and there are no major resentments, but we can't keep up our affection, because I do not feel comfortable with her. It's not so much because of her as it is her uniform; she wears a uniform. I have never dared to ask her why or if she has to; she works in the Ministry of the Interior, and I don't know what type of work she does. She travels often, going to other countries, so I suspect that she has an important post, but I don't ask her so that she will not feel pressured. I don't ask, first, because she never asks me why I am what I am; and second, though I have much affection for her, she is not my own daughter and there are limits to what one feels one can do and say. I know she regards me as her father, and her children do as well, but there are some barriers one cannot pass.

Perhaps it has to do with her husband, and his early influence; I don't know. I think that her husband participated in the revolution, because during the difficult moments she practically lived in my house, but she herself did not participate. Her little girl is the same age as the revolution. No, this Sandinismo is a recent development. The two were students when they met. She studied psychology at UCA, the national Catholic university. I don't know all the causes really; perhaps, well, I remember that she used to speak ill of the nuns where she had studied before. Maybe her rejection of their authority was the beginning and has something to do with her later attraction to Sandinismo, but who knows? It troubles me, but what can one do? It hurts me, and it hurts my wife terribly, but she is a free person and must be allowed to practice that freedom.

My granddaughter is in the second grade at the American School, and is already speaking a little English. She is a good student, considering all the difficult moments she has gone through. Last year she was on the honor roll, but this year she probably will not make it because of the emotional problems that have come her way; but that's okay, her grades are better than average.

As you can see, we admire the United States, and we look to them for information. For example, the professional organizations I represent are given out-of-date books and magazines by the American embassy, and we use them. I'm not ashamed, because we still benefit from the information from a two-week old *Time* magazine; their economic sections and world news are still of help to us in our work and in the seminars that we sponsor. It keeps us in contact with the outside world. We also have good relations with other embassies and try to keep up through them too.

The thing is that we are cut off from other currents because there is so little information or freedom in this country. Lately, I have been trying to get the message out about the kind of life that we would like to be living here in Nicaragua. I no longer dedicate much time at all to my business. Rather, I spend about twelve hours a day on this kind of work. I still have my firm and a partner, but I hardly have anything to do with it now. It's no longer my first interest, having been replaced by work on behalf of my country. I was blind for so long, really from about 1960 to 1978, dedicated only to my profession. But, maybe my business skills and my experience in decision-making (I'm very decisive) have been a help to me as president of INDE, the Nicaraguan Development Institute, and as vice-president of COSEP, the Superior Council of Private Enterprise.

Let me explain a little about COSEP. There are six branches, five of which are professional associations. For example, there's the: 1) confederation of chambers of commerce; 2) industrial component; 3) construction component; 4) farmers' group ; 5) then there's the professional persons' association, CONAPRO; all these five are professional organizations under the COSEP umbrella; and 6) INDE of which I am president.

COSEP was formed in 1974, and until about a year and a half ago the president of INDE was also the president of COSEP, but we decided to pass the honor around. Now the delegates from the six chambers elect the president of COSEP, the current one being don Enrique Bolaños, and I am the first vice-president of COSEP.

COSEP's funding comes from a variety of sources. Four of our six branches receive no outside funds. Two, INDE and CONAPRO, receive outside help for their programs; INDE needs funds to help maintain the

75 cooperatives which operate in 14 of the 16 states, and to support the technical personnel who advise and direct these programs, and who have to travel to visit and supervise all of these areas. Since Nicaraguan capital is so weak, we have to seek outside assistance to keep these projects going.

The source of the funds is no secret; they come from the Conrad Adenauer Foundation, which provides German marks that facilitate travel and transportation within Nicaragua. Additional help comes from the Inter-American Foundation, which gets funds from the Inter-American Development Bank, a U.S. nonprofit organization, but not part of the government. The remainder of the financing is from Nicaraguan companies. We also receive a little bit of assistance from Latin American foundations, mostly for seminars for business people. We send managers and trainees to Argentina, Colombia, Costa Rica, and Guatemala for leadership workshops. They are very important because so many of our educated people have left the country that trained personnel here have practically disappeared. That's why CONAPRO, the organization of professional people, holds so many seminars.

COSEP has tried to cooperate with the revolution. In 1979, we felt that the revolution would benefit everyone, but it has not turned out that way. In the beginning we thought, well, these are young, inexperienced muchachos, "boys" as they were popularly called, straight from the mountains; the only experience they have is as *guerrilleros*, rebel fighters, but soon they will learn that you don't govern with arms. We waited a while. Our relations, while not friendly, were not tense either. So for about a year and a half, we tried to work together. But they began to regard us as a class that should disappear, as one that had exploited workers, and, of course, this was true of some individuals, although it was not the common denominator. So our relations became cooler and cooler, until finally they became cold. For example, we would send correspondence which they never answered. Then they would attack us in the papers, accusing us of causing all the evils that plague the country, and this alienated us even more, but we still kept hoping that things would improve. By 1981 relations were very bad.

Then we wrote them a letter, I was vice-president of COSEP at the time, saying that the economy was in terrible shape and that we saw their clear alignment with Russia, that there was no pluralism, that there was too much emphasis on the army. Then Humberto Ortega said things like they were going to hang from the trees all those who made public declarations against the government, awful threats like that. We wrote Daniel Ortega a letter October 20, 1981, he was coordinator of the junta at that time, and immediately, that same night, we were taken prisoner and we were each kept in separate, solitary cells for twelve days, all of us who signed the letter, the six presidents of COSEP. Then we were condemned by the tribunals to seven months in jail for public agitation and provoking chaos in the society. What we said at that time has sadly come to pass, and the economy is on the floor.

It so happens that at that time the government also had troubles with the Communist party which was calling for strikes and protests, and they rounded up the commmunists and put us all in the same cell, thirty-one of us in all. When there are so many people in one small room, you can't avoid them, and there is plenty of time to talk and get to know one another. Since the communists had a few privileges, they could get books, and then we would borrow them and pass the time reading and discussing with our ideological enemies. I read a lot of their books and became very good friends with the communists, outside of politics.

The prison held all kinds, everything from hardened criminals and drug addicts to petty thieves. But I got along with all of them, and it was very educational. I was treated just like any other common prisoner; in fact, we were *all* treated the same. At 4:30 a.m. it was my group's turn to go the bathroom *al aire libre,* that was the worst part, the open air collective baths, in full view of all the others, including the women prisoners. Every now and then they took us all out for "fresh air," as they said, but really it was to search the cells for metal objects, salt, tobacco, etc. During those occasions everyone mixed, chatted casually, and even became friends. After all, rich and poor, capitalist and communist, we were all dispossessed of liberty, so we had a great deal in common. This was all in the seven months following my imprisonment on October 20, 1981. I stayed on as president of CONAPRO, the Association of Professionals of Nicaragua, for about a year after that. Then I withdrew and reflected for a year or so about whether to continue my political activities.

But returning to the history of relations between COSEP and the government, the imprisonment was the definitive rupture. Earlier, in 1980, we had suffered a serious blow when the president of COSEP at that time, Jorge Salazar, was murdered by the security police. He was implicated in a possible military revolt, which was totally contrived by the army with the purpose of involving Jorge. The real reason that they killed him is that he was a very charismatic leader, and much beloved by the campesino, and they didn't want such a leader in Nicaragua. Since then we and the government have been criticizing each other mutually. We have been trying to argue in favor of the capitalistic system as the only way for us to get along in the world. We can't ignore that we are a poor country and we need the help of others. This activity has polarized things even more, so that when any difficult thing happens in the market or in production, they say we are responsible. There was a speech that Daniel Ortega made recently in which twelve times he said that the yanquis and COSEP are guilty of all our ills.

We hoped briefly that things would improve when elections were announced for 1984. But in the end, we boycotted the elections because we believed them to be invalid. There was no public information, education, or opportunity to have all sides presented through radio, television, press, or live coverage. And to us, an election is more than just depositing a ballot or pulling a lever. Since then there has been no dialogue at all between us and the government. We've tried above all to keep alive the principle that it is possible in Nicaragua to live in peace.

The government has recently invited us to participate in a few very large public meetings similar to the *De Cara al Pueblo*, or Face the People, question and answer sessions that the government sponsors. The current president of COSEP, Enrique Bolaños, appeared once and I also appeared once, and what we both said is that there can be no economic solution without a political solution, that is, that things can not improve until there is more freedom.

Many people think that COSEP and CEPAD, the Protestant Development Commission, should have better relations, but the problem is that CEPAD is part of the government. I'm not saying that the *evangélicos*, or Protestants, in Nicaragua are part of the government. But the leadership of CEPAD is, to such an extent that some of them are members of the Sandinista Assembly. The only relation we have with CEPAD is that about every week we see one or two groups of American religious people, and either Enrique or I receive them. They come polarized, convinced that what the government says is true and what we say is false, and of course, they come to us after going to CEPAD. I can't convince them of anything, but I tell them what I think anyway, and that I have a right to my views.

Look here at my calendar, the upcoming delegations, the pro-government religious groups from the U.S.; it's amazing how the government manipulates them. Some are violent and won't listen to me but start shouting and accusing. They return to the U. S. as convinced as when they came, because they see and hear only what they want. See, I have three U. S. delegations coming up in two days. They all come and ask me about our relations with CEPAD, and when I say "terrible," they're shocked and say, "Why, since CEPAD is helping the country?" But if I try to argue with them, I become involved in a religious dispute.

But it's much more than that. You see, what's happening is that CEPAD is undermining the Catholic church. Whatever the Catholic church says, CEPAD says the opposite. We're not in the Middle Ages; we should not be having these struggles. We should worship Jesus Christ as we wish, because one Christ is not better than the other, but the same. However, the CEPAD leaders who are members of the Sandinista Assembly breathe first the air of Sandinismo, and only second that of Cristianismo. All of CEPAD's funds and projects go to help Protestants and pro-government groups. In all fairness, I have to say that CEPAD has good relations with the Atlantic Coast bishops, and that they have done good there, and also in the interior of the country. In these areas they get on well with the Catholics, but here on the Pacific Coast it's a confrontation like in the time of the schisms.

Some people say that both groups have been inflexible and dogmatic, but since I believe in one side, I say no. I find that to the degree that I've grown politically, I see that those who are on the side of the government no matter what, do not act wisely, because no government should depend on sectarian groups, whether they're religious, trade unions or what. They should count on the sympathy, or *buen criterio*, of all. But this type of sectarianism in a government is no good, and that goes for Catholic sectarianism as well as Protestant.

Let me say two things about the religious aspect : 1) the Protestants, except for the few CEPAD leaders in the Assembly, here in Nicaragua are sincere people who show their love in Christ in a special way, whereas, 2) the Catholics who are pro-government, I don't respect them because they're acting for state, political reasons, not Christian ones. Many of them say they're Catholics, but at heart they're not. Maybe they are Christian, but if you're in a religious denomination, you have to follow its rules, and if not, join something else. That's what's happened with the two Cardenal ministers, Ernesto and Fernando, in culture and education respectively, and with Miguel D'Escoto, the foreign minister. They say they're Catholics, but they're in complete disobedience with their religious authorities. They're Christians, okay, but not Catholics.

If you were to go to Cardinal Obando y Bravo's traditional mass in the morning and to Reverend Uriel Molina's campesino mass in the evening you would observe many differences. You will observe many foreigners and many Nicaraguans at both services, but there are far more foreigners at Uriel's. You might say it's a mass for foreigners, especially North Americans. That's why we say that this "popular" church is not popular at all because it doesn't reach our people, just foreigners. But most Nicaraguans attend neither service, preferring to continue going to their local, neighborhood church where they worship pretty much in the traditional way, and they love the Cardinal.

It's strange, but many of us who are on opposite sides of the fence used to go to the same churches, schools, and our families knew each other. I guess to some extent there are ties still. You greet each other, and you don't avoid each other, but you really can't recapture the warmth you had when you were friends. For example, you try to have such and such person over to your house, then another guest or you yourself, says something imprudent, and the other answers and suddenly it's no longer a party but a polemic. So we don't invite each other; where we see each other socially is at embassy receptions, such as at the Spanish embassy. Then we chat agreeably enough, but soon each drifts to his respective group. Another example is when someone dies, we go to the funeral, but that's about it.

The biggest problem with the revolution is that they talk pluralism, but it does not exist, it is just a *ventana de exhibición*, window dressing. But people are taken in by it. For example, I was talking to a Dutch woman who was asking about the mixed economy, and she said rather defiantly, "Give me an example to show there is not a mixed economy but a state-run one." So, I mentioned the instant-coffee plant. Its ownership is private. But this plant receives its coffee from the government at the price the government decides; the government provides the raw material which is then made into instant coffee and turned over to the government for export. So, you have a private enterprise, all right, but completely in the hands of the state, because the government supplies the materials, helps with repairs, maintenance, etc., and then buys all the product.

There's no free enterprise here, but theoretically it is privately-owned, so you can say that you have a mixed economy. Another example is the rice growers who are predominantly private. They had formed a private organization for distributing their rice. The government comes in and and tells them that they must sell all their product to the state, just like with the coffee, and that the government will sell them everything they need, fertilizer, seed, insecticides. Recently, since the rice distribution cooperative was working so well, Jaime Wheelock, the minister of agriculture, said that the state was now going to be part of it and that he was going to be its president. Just like that! So, is this a mixed economy? It's complete totalitarianism!

And the poor campesino; the government says they're redistributing land because the peasant has none. Well, then the people from the city ought to be moving out to the country where they could have land. But the reverse is happening, they're all coming to Managua. We've gone from a population of 600,000 in 1980 to 1,000,000 now. Also, if the peasants had been given land, there would be greater production. But now there is much less, we are exporting less than before, and it's not that we're eating it!

The thing is that they manipulate statistics, blame everything on the war, and deceive people that way. The fact is that the agrarian reform is a failure and production is decreasing. What's increasing are cardboard shacks and problems in supplying water, electricity, transportation, and health services in the city. All this is more difficult now, and all this shows that the cooperative business is a failure, a pure Sandinista invention.

The Sandinistas hide in these cooperatives, especially those in dangerous areas. We say that they hide *entre las faldas de su madre ocultos*, behind their mothers' skirts, so that when there is a battle and campesinos are killed, they claim that the contra kill civilians, when in truth, there are Sandinista armies in the cooperatives themselves. Another problem with the so-called cooperatives is that many peasants received land that was efficient and productive *before*, maybe it had forests and water on it. But instead of working it, the peasants cut down the trees to make their simple homes, which leads to erosion and aridity, both now serious ecological problems. These, then, are the "improvements" of the revolution.

8   Verónica Cáceres (b. 1954)

"I think that Frente members ought to attend to their families. Some members dedicate themselves exclusively to political life and I think that is a mistake. If we don't take care of our children, who will? "

"I am concerned about how difficult life is here in Managua. . . . Life is more peaceful in the country. Other people may be coming to the city, but I am looking forward to going back to the country."

The pale blue cotton dress with the ruffled collar made the slight psychology professor seem even more like a young girl, as did the barely audible whisper in which she spoke. Appearances are deceiving however, for the shy, retiring Verónica Cáceres has already experienced enough action, danger, and difficult choices to last a lifetime. Involved in clandestine activity for the Frente in the mid 1970's, she suffered capture and torture by the guardia, and was a blacklisted teacher under Somoza. Professor Cáceres is quietly proud of her university education, the culmination of a lifelong dream, and something previously unheard of for a girl from the remote village of Somoto on the Honduran border.

In her spartan office at UNAN, the national university, Verónica Cáceres describes softly her cloistered upbringing, the once-hostile incomprehension of her domineering Somocista father, her dedication to the Frente and to her young daughter, the increasing difficulty of life in the city, and her strong desire to return to the countryside.

Professor Cáceres' s story highlights not only the deteriorating quality of life in the capital city, but also what she terms the "dialectical relationship" between life as a committed Frente member and life as a devoted mother.

The first thing to say about my life is that if I had to, I would do everything all over again; I have no regrets. I was born and raised in Somoto, a tiny town about 20 kilometers from the Honduran border, a town that has suffered many attacks in recent years.

My father was a campesino, and my mother was a rural schoolteacher. My father was a very drastic person, strict, and extremely concerned about our upbringing. Mama had fourteen children, eight of whom lived. Since it was a rural area, there was almost no medical attention and my brothers and sisters would die shortly after birth; I remember the deaths of the last two. My youngest brother was born when my mother was forty-three, and she had to stay in bed for the whole pregnancy. He's very important to us; we were overjoyed when he was born, and we treat him specially. I am eleven years older than he is; I am the fourth daughter of those who are still living. We children were, and are, very close.

My parents were married for forty years; they were brought up with the idea that marriage was forever, and they were married both in civil and church ceremonies. We were never hungry because papa was a hard worker. We always got a toy for Christmas, and a special meal for our birthday, usually chicken and a *gaseosa*, a carbonated drink, that always meant a party, and some article of clothing, a blouse for example. The same was true for Holy Week; in all, there were three times a year that we each got a present.

Our family was well-known in the community for my father's ability and hard work. He had his own small farm; they gave him credit and loans at the banks so that he was able to prosper enough until he had a little coffee farm and some cattle. He never went to school because they lived in the mountains, but my grandfather brought someone to their house to teach my father to read and do sums. So he had that advantage, and he read all the time, about World War II, Napoleon, Hitler, the Kaiser. He liked history the best, but he also read everything from the Spanish language *Reader's Digest*. We would always talk about national and international issues; after the revolution we would give him biographies of some of the comandantes and he enjoyed them too. He always told us that his legacy to us was the desire to study and learn.

My father is a very interesting example of someone who was forced to change because of events; it was nearly impossible for him because he was so rigid, but he did it. He was of the opinion that women shouldn't have a university education, and his greatest hope was for his sons to become engineers or doctors, so he put all the emphasis on their preparation and interned us daughters in a normal school so that we would beome teachers. All my sisters are certified elementary teachers, but we all came to Managua to go to university after completing normal school. We worked in the mornings and went to school in the evenings, all of us. It was a constant struggle because of the concept my papa had of what constituted a proper education for women. It turns out that his *sons* did not achieve what he had hoped for them, they did not follow a university career, but we *daughters* all did. Both things were big disappointments to him. One sister is a market technician; another is a teacher, and another is a nurse psychologist.

My father's death in 1982 was a big blow to my brothers. Shortly afterwards, one began preparing himself by studying engineering; another is about to receive his title as a veterinary doctor; and another is in the fourth year of law study, having gone back to school after dropping out earlier. My youngest brother has been in Russia for four years, studying civil engineering. That would've been my father's great happiness, seeing his sons all with university careers.

Before he died he had changed much with regard to his views about women. He suffered many blows that made him change. Another problem in our relationship with him was that he was a Somocista, whereas all of his children were involved in the liberation struggle. My youngest brother, the one who is in Russia, was taken prisoner by the guardia at age twelve as a *tirabombas*, a Molotov cocktail thrower, which he was. They came and dragged him out of the movie theater. My father was able to have him taken out of jail after about fifteen days, and he sent my brother to Honduras, which was safe and nearby. However, by the time of the war of liberation, he had been in a guerrilla column for several months. This was very hard for my father as it was to know that we were *all* against the system. He knew that we were against the regime, but he did not know that we were active collaborators with the Frente when we were all living in the same house in Somoto.

The thing that made him change most was when I fell prisoner. I came to Managua and I joined the Frente when I was eighteen without telling my father. I will tell you more about that but first let me tell you about my mother. My mother was very wonderful to us through all this, where my papa was so drastic, she was beautiful. She had to adapt herself to his character, but at bottom, she was very different from him in that she had a greater capacity for change. She was in the middle in our problems. She always read a lot too, and wanted to improve herself, but papa never let her. She was a rural schoolteacher, as I mentioned, but all that meant is that she had finished the sixth grade herself. In those days, that was the major career a woman could aspire to in the rural zones, and besides, her family was very poor. Further, at that time the first woman still had not graduated from a normal school; it wasn't until the 1950s that the first such teacher graduated.

My mother's temperament is totally different from my father's. She loves to chat, tell stories and jokes. She is an artist at conversation. Papa was the opposite, very taciturn. Mama is more religious now, but not fanatic; she reads the Bible every morning and has the tradition of her saints. Papa was very religious, but in a strict and fanatic way. Mama is very happy; she's about sixty-five years old now, but it is as if she became young, or maybe it's that she became herself again, when papa died. Now, when we invite her to go to the movies, the circus or the seaside, she says, "Okay, let's go!" My father never liked for her to go anywhere. As for us girls, hardly any boys ever dared to come over to the house because he was so strict.

My father definitely had the greatest influence on me, for better and worse. He had his negative aspects and all of us children were socially very backward, repressed, timid compared to other children. My career in psychology has helped me enormously to come out, overcome thousands of things, including the feeling of disloyalty and guilt regarding my feelings toward my father.

For example, I remember when I went to play basketball, which I loved. Papa had enrolled me in a typing class; I went to secondary school in the morning, and in the afternoon I studied typing. He had registered me at that hour just so that I could no longer play basketball. I would tell him that I was going to typing classes, but I would go instead to practice with the team. When he found out, he beat me with a belt; I was fourteen and that was the last time he hit me. We were eating dinner and he said to me, "Some day, I'm going to beat you good!" I was *malcriada*, very bad-mannered that day and answered, "Why don't you just do it then!" He did, and I still remember how angry we both were.

Mama supported me about basketball. The coach we had there was very well respected; further, a girlfriend of mine, whose father was a doctor was also on the team, so he relented. After that my friend would come by for me to go play basketball. I also learned to type, because they changed the hour of the practice.

When papa learned that he couldn't control me totally, he sent me as an internal student to the Instituto Normal de San Marcos, a girl's school known for its strictness. A big blow for me, because I had gained a measure of freedom at the public high school, the Instituto Nacional de Somoto, where I had been for two years. It was coed, I participated in poetry workshops, chorus, and basketball, and I loved it.

My father sent me to San Marcos in Carazo, which was a long way from home for a fourteen year old. But it was precisely because I was fourteen, a delicate age, that he sent me, thinking that there would be less danger there than in a coeducational school. The same thing had happened to my older sisters; they had gone there too and hated it. But it was an especially big step backwards for me, and I regressed, crying all the time. I despised the rigid discipline that was the school's hallmark. It was a state school but with all the characteristics of a religious school in that we went to mass on Sundays, prayed in the mornings, and in the afternoons too, daily, and we also had religious readings in the mornings, *lecturas matutinas*. I was there for four years, and then I graduated as a teacher.

If the atmosphere was unbearable, the education was excellent. Like my parents, I love to read, and I devoured the materials in the library. I read Asturias's *El señor presidente* (Mr. President) for example, *La iliada* (The Iliad), *La odisea* (The Odyssey), all on my own. I read *El corazón de Alicia*, (Alicia's Heart) a lovely book about a native Guatemalan woman who married a North American anthropologist, and about how they both grow and change in their relationship. I remember being especially impressed at how she had to struggle to gain her identity. I also read *El pequeño príncipe* (The Little Prince). I read widely there, and, as an intern, there was not much else to do anyway, but in my case, I loved it.

In the classroom we read some, but mostly the teachers oriented us to use the library. Of course, we read Rubén Darío's poetry in class, also the classic *María*, by Jorge Isaac. We also had what they called vocational orientation. I remember in my last, or sixth, year, a nun came from Jinotepe to teach that class. She was special, a nun with very advanced ideas. She talked to us about sex, the situation of the woman in Nicaragua, the national political reality. This was in '73, and they got rid of her right away as subversive, but I remember her for her progressive thinking.

I had already formed some revolutionary ideas of my own by the time I had her as a teacher, because I remember back in Somoto there was a special person who influenced me, Augusto Salinas Pinell. He was a rural teacher and, we later found out, a Frente member. We were all friends with him. He was a guerrilla chieftain and died in 1976. After I went away to San Marcos, I would see him when I came home for vacations. We would meet and he would lend me books. He loaned me *Pedagogía del oprimido*, (Pedagogy of the Oppressed) by Paulo Freire, and *Educación y liberación*, (Education and Freedom), also by Freire. So, I was already becoming acquainted with the ideas that the progressive nun espoused.

Augusto would also give me flyers and bulletins about the Frente; I remember bringing them back to the colegio, which was very bold because the school was arch-conservative. When Carlos Morales fell in Nandaime in 1973, I had some Frente publications that he himself had loaned me. I became very nervous in case they came to search my room because others knew that I had subversive literature. I remember hiding the papers under the mattress. I still had basically a fuzzy outline of my political beliefs, but my girlfriends all said I had crazy ideas.

I had one outstanding teacher, not of literature, which was my favorite subject and my brother and I both used to write poetry, but of mathematics. Her name was Lidia, and she created an orderly atmosphere in which you could learn. As a result, in the fourth, fifth, and sixth years I did very well in math. I also learned more than just math from Lidia. I remember having an exam with her, and she left us alone, telling us not to copy. Well, there were only about four of us who did not copy, and of course, we got the lowest grades on the exam. But Lidia told us that it was better to receive a bad grade on your own than a high grade and cheat. That was a good moral lesson. I graduated in 1973, the same year they got rid of the radical nun, but I still just had sympathetic ideas about the Frente, no clear judgment.

I went back to Somoto after I graduated to try to get a job, but that was very difficult because my sister and I were already considered subversives. My oldest sister had already been sanctioned, and could not get a job; another sister who also had graduated as a teacher had no job either, she had been four years without working. When I arrived in Somoto, they first placed me in a rural school near the highway, but when they found out more about me, they sent me to a school that was 35 kilometers from town. I had to walk 8 kilometers on foot because no vehicle could reach the school, as there was no road.

There I worked my first year. It was a one-room school with a dirt floor attended by four grades. As a teacher, I was a figure of great respect to the villagers in this remote area. My papa put some doors up, and constructed hygienic services for the children. The school had been falling down, and we did what we could to restore it. My oldest sister was in Managua, without work, and she began to try to persuade me to come join her. That possibility was very attractive to me as I sat there in that isolated rural schoolroom, dreading at age nineteen the possibility of being stuck there forever. In the back of my mind, I had always wanted to go to the university, and that thought was like a magnet to me.

A good friend of my sister's had a teaching position that he was about to give up, but before he did, I put in my application. He practically bequeathed the job to me and I came to Managua to teach primary school in a very poor barrio called Monseñor Lezcano. There I worked a year, but I was unable to begin the university that first year; I missed the registration period and I didn't have the money for the tuition anyway.

In '75, my second year, I was transferred to another school, El Instituto Loyola, run by priests but subsidized by the state. Loyola was both primary and secondary, and is the place where the sanctioned teachers were sent. Really, the treatment thay gave teachers there was tough, almost belligerent, and we were under constant surveillance. It was a very strict school, and I taught there for six years, from 1975 to 1981, because, politically speaking, it was practically impossible to change schools.

In '75 I entered the university and also the student movement. I didn't just join, I actively sought the Frente out so I could be a part of what they were doing. By then my disquiet and nonconformity with the system were significant and undeniable to me. This was at the same time that I was working: I worked from 7:00 a.m. until noon giving classes; and then from 1:00 p.m. I was here at the university. When I began specializing in psychology, I came at night because that program was only offered at night. I began to work more and more with the student movement.

By '77, that's a very important year for me, I fell prisoner in a neighborhood in Managua, then known as La Fuente, now known as Ariel Darce. In that year, comandante Borge was prisoner and was being cruelly tortured. The day I was captured was the day that we in the student movement were going to do *pintas*, wall paintings, in the neighborhoods in solidarity with Borge's decision to suspend his hunger strike, which had been going on for fifty-six days. Our action was to be a big show of support for him. All the Sandinista prisoners had been on hunger strike on behalf of Borge, as had many mothers and other groups. There were many strikes during this period and into 1978. The purpose of this particular strike, which ended January 29, 1977, was to get the guardia to suspend the isolation and torture of Tomás Borge and Marcio Jaen.

My job was to cover the barrios Primero de Mayo, Catorce de Septiembre, and La Fuente. The operation consisted of putting Sandinista flags up, asking for the cessation of the isolation of the two compañeros, and for their freedom. I had been working around the clock trying to get things ready, organizing people and material; I ate very poorly, and I was exhausted by the time of the operation. We were still on vacation from teaching, and so I dedicated myself full time to this task. I was with two other compañeros; we were experienced and that was why they gave us the three most difficult barrios. The two companions I was with fell in the insurrection in '78.

When our operation was over, one compañero and I were hungry, and we went to get a glass of milk. I remember there was a fat lady about two blocks away talking to members of BECAT, an antiterrorist squad of the guardia, and then she pointed to us. *Run,* I shouted to my compañero, "they're after us!" That compañero was my novio, my sweetheart, and he had already been prisoner twice. A third time would be horrible, unbearable, so I told him to run while I distracted the guardia, which I did and they began firing at me. I ran away, and then I circled back hoping that the BECAT would pass by and I could duck into a house. But when I was circling back, a red Volkswagen pulled up beside me; a man opened the door and shouted at me to get in. I was confused, is this security or what? I decided that I would rather be captured by BECAT than by these people in an unmarked car. I tried to hide in a nearby house but the guardia was waiting for me at the door, and they took me away to Tipitapa prison.

There, they interrogated me for twenty-three hours straight. I fainted many times during questioning, because I was already on the point of exhaustion even before the operation and I had had nothing to eat for a long time. But I tried to think up an alibi and to maintain my concentration so that I would not get mixed up and would not give up. I was there for two weeks, during which time they tortured me repeatedly. They beat me, they pretended to execute me, every time they would do this, I didn't know if this time it was real, but they thought it was amusing; they burned me with cigarettes; they applied electric shocks. They wanted to know all about my friend Augusto who had fallen. Remember, he was the rural schoolteacher back home in Somoto who used to lend me progressive books.

They had a complete file on me, all my background, acquaintances, everything. Since my boyfriend had been a prisoner previously, they had already investigated everyone who had any connection with him, including me. They had also investigated Augusto and his friends, so security had a complete record on me. What they most insisted on knowing about was who was in the red Volkswagen; it turns out that they were compañeros from the Frente. I didn't know that at the time, nor had I ever seen them before, I guess they had been totally clandestine, anyway, I had no idea who they were. My other partner had been captured too, but my boyfriend had not; he had, however, seen them take me away. What saved me was that my father had some connections in Somoto, and the priest there helped a great deal to get me out.

After that, I continued working with the Frente, with even more dedication than before, and I married my boyfriend, Aníbal. We were married April 3, 1977, and he left May 13 for clandestine work. I didn't see him again until he fell prisoner in the mountains. The guardia captured him, and he was prisoner all the rest of '77 until June '78. I had a very agitated, tense life during that period; I was still working, and I was also doing everything possible to get him out of jail.

When I had been taken prisoner, my father behaved very well. It was a tremendous blow to him, because he never dreamed that I could be so involved in the Frente. But when he found out that I was prisoner, he immediately set about getting me free. He went to the officials pleading with them, begging them to let me out, the local security chief in Somoto, the priest, everyone. Then he came to the prison with the order for my release, and when he saw me he burst into tears.

He took me home to recover, and both he and my mother cried during those days. They wanted to send me to Mexico where I would be safe and where I could continue studying at the university there. But I told them that I had a commitment to the Frente. After this episode, my father changed dramatically. He stopped participating in the program of terrorism of Somoza; he rejected all of it, completely, right then. He wanted nothing more to do with those who would torture, especially when he had been unconditionally supportive of them, whenever the regime needed something from him, he would give it. When I refused to go to Mexico, he told me that he didn't know whether I was right or wrong in what I was doing, but that he would always be with me.

I returned to Managua and my coworkers at the Instituto Loyola knew what had happened; classes had already resumed when I was in jail. They had written a letter saying that I had malaria, so that they would not take my job away, and they didn't. I continued working there, but security followed all my steps. By June, '78 my husband was set free, but he went immediately into hiding again, so we hardly lived together at all, and in September of '78, he died in combat. After that, my situation was even more tenuous, and I had to leave the country with the help of the Frente.

They sent me to Honduras, where I was near Nicaragua and my family, and there I continued working for the Frente. I entered the university there also, but the Frente could not support me, so I maintained myself giving private classes. A Nicaraguan woman living there got me the tutoring jobs. And since I had already completed two years of psychology, they allowed me to enter the third year in Honduras, in the Escuela Superior del Profesorado, in Tegucigalpa. I crossed back to Nicaragua several times, secretly, but on July 20, 1979, the day after the liberation, I entered the country and immediately became part of the revolutionary process. In Tegucigalpa on July 19 there was a tremendous celebration of the victory; there were many Nicaraguans there, students, exiles, people working with the Frente, and there was a great feeling of euphoria.

The first year of the revolution, I did not resume studying because I participated full time in the crusade, the literacy campaign, working with the teacher's organization, and we directed the entire crusade. After the crusade ended in 1981, I continued my career, working in the normal school giving psychology classes. I also participated in political work, and I studied at night. I made a great effort to finish my degree because it was very important for me.

During the literacy campaign, I was in a very difficult zone, called Río Blanco, in Zelaya. Then we could move about freely, but if the crusade had been a year later, it would've been impossible because of the contra. The crusade was something marvelous, when I hear the anthem and when I think of it, I can still feel the same emotion I felt at the time. We reached so many people, and the dedication, motivation, enthusiasm of the young people was phenomenal.

Something very lovely happened to me during the crusade. I was a technical advisor, and I had a student teacher who was very young, about thirteen. Our mission was to educate adults, but this youngster was so inexperienced that all of his students left his class; they just walked away.

In his desperation, the youth gathered a group of seven and eight-year-old children and taught *them* to read, but he didn't tell me. When I went to supervise, almost at the end because there were so many to oversee, I asked him where the adults were. He said that adults didn't like his teaching but that the children did, and he proudly demonstrated that they indeed had learned to read and write. I was impressed that he had not given up and had shown such initiative.

I returned to Managua to continue studying after that and to continue working, teaching classes in general, educational, and social psychology. I graduated as an integral psychologist, which means that I could've gone on to work in clinical, labor or social psychology as well as in education. But since I was a teacher, I already had much experience in the classroom, and they asked me to teach classes here at the university. I have been teaching here at UNAN for four years now.

I would like to stay here because I love education, but I have family problems now. Life in Managua is very difficult for me in my situation, because I have a two and a half year old daughter; I have her here in the CDI, the childcare center, at UNAN. She spends all day here because I have to. I drop her in the morning, and pick her up at the end of the workday.

Next year she goes to preschool, and then life will get more complicated for me because, currently, I live with my sisters. I am married, but there is a serious housing shortage, so my husband and I each live with our respective families, whose houses are tiny; we have not been able to get a place for ourselves yet. I live with my two sisters and my daughter. My husband lives with his mother. My husband's name is José Arana; I met him in the Frente at the end of '78, and we were married in '79.

I spent many years without having children because when my first husband went into hiding, I was pregnant, but as a result of the torture, I aborted. I was three months pregnant at the time. I think the torture and the miscarriage caused physical harm so that for eight years I was unable to become pregnant. Finally, I went to the doctor and had a series of tests; my husband went too and cooperated in the tests and everything, because they had to rule him out as the reason I couldn't conceive. By then, I wanted to adopt a child, but my husband said, no, not to give up yet, but to wait and keep trying these tests. Whenever people would ask him why we didn't have any children, he would always said that it was because he had a medical problem. He gave me great moral support. Anyway, after all that time, our daughter was born, Claudia Verónica; Claudia because I admire Claudia Chamorro a lot—a *guerrillera*, a woman from a rich, respected family, who gave it all up and risked her life—and Verónica, because having wanted a child for so long, I thought that I deserved having my name present too.

The problem with the preschool is that it does not last all day and the nearest one is very far away. I would have to take my daughter by bus and pick her up at noon. But I have no one to take care of her in the afternoon, and it is very difficult to find babysitters. For me, child care and work arrangements will soon become nearly impossible if I stay here. Actually, I am planning to return to Somoto; my mother is there to help me, and it is easier to find a babysitter there as well. My daughter could go to the preschool in the mornings and could stay with my mama in the afternoons. When she finishes preschool and enters elementary school, then I could return here if need be, because arrangements would be much easier by then. I will work as a clinical psychologist in Somoto, but I will also continue working for the Frente. In Somoto, I will have more help, I will be able to do my professional and my political work, and still have more time to be with Claudia Verónica.

I think that Frente members ought to attend to their families. Some members dedicate themselves exclusively to political life and I think that is a mistake. If we don't take care of our children, who will? What will they be like when they grow up? I disagree deeply with those members who are careless about their families, men and women both. When the Frente needs me, here I am. When my daughter needs me, then the Frente waits while I attend to her. If both need me at the same time, then I make a judgment. If my daughter is sick, she comes first, that's all there is to it. But if she is all right, and I have someone to look after her, then I would choose to do the Frente task. It is a dialectical relationship.

I wanted to tell you a little more about my youngest brother, Orlando José, who is studying civil engineering in Russia on a scholarship. He grew up in an adult atmosphere; we talked about literature, politics, everything, and he began participating in the student movement when he was eleven years old, organizing cells. After the triumph, when the contra war began, he was always placed at the head of combat columns. When papa died, he was already mobilized, in a battalion, and he came home for the funeral. After that, he began studying civil engineering here, later opting for the scholarship. At first, he didn't want to apply for it, because he didn't want to go away, but we insisted. The very day that we put him on the plane for the Soviet Union, the cousin who always went everywhere with him, they were in the same column, battalion everything, fell in combat. A mine killed him, this was in 1984 and he was only seventeen years old.

Recently, we all pooled our resources, everyone in the family, so that Orlando José could buy a ticket to come here for the vacations, and in January he will be able to visit. He writes there in the university newspapers and when he writes us, he always says "I know that I am preparing myself, but I will have missed six years of my country's history." We do everything possible in our letters to keep his morale up because that is a long time. He gets very depressed, six years is a long time, but we keep encouraging him to complete the program. It will be four years when he returns for vacation, and we are going to impress on him how important it is for him to finish. That's why we all pooled our funds, so that he could come home for a visit, to help him over his depression and to encourage him to go back. He likes it there but he is very homesick because it is so different. During the vacations he goes to work, he has worked in Siberia, and what he earns he sends back home to help out. He works with the Juventud Sandinista over there too, and he also is a *militante*, like I am.

Meanwhile, for myself, I am concerned about how difficult life is here in Managua. The population has increased to one million two hundred thousand people, and the government policy now is to encourage people to leave for the outlying regions. I want to work at home for a while as a psychologist, and then get a Master's. Currently, there is no Master's program in the country, and I would have to study outside Nicaragua for that, but it is something that I want very much to do in the future. Then I could be more of a help to my own country, teaching others, and so on. There are many scholarships; for example, the programs in Germany and the Soviet Union are excellent, but the scholarships to socialist countries are not family scholarships, and I don't want to leave my daughter for four years. I couldn't do that. So, I will wait, teach in Somoto for a while, and see what develops after that.

My husband too is going to Somoto to try and find work there. We both prefer village life. You have more time to be with your family and to read, and if I do go to graduate school, I have to get back to reading. Here, I stand in line for hours waiting for the bus, but at home I could be reading instead, or playing with my daughter. Life is more peaceful in the country. Other people may be coming to the city, but I am looking forward to going back to the country.

9 Maribel Duriez (b. 1964)

". . . I felt that with the victory, freedom and equality had automatically been secured, just like you win a battle. . . . And, thinking that way, I had some problems, problems in the army, because the majority of the compañeros still had a machista attitude."

". . . these kids come here [UNAN, the national university] without knowing anything about the student movement, its history, or the sacrifices others have made for them."

A revolutionary from the age of fourteen, Maribel Duriez has grown up within the Frente, a fact which gives a unique perspective to the life story of this young physics teaching assistant at UNAN, the national university. Dressed casually in blue jeans and white shirt, Maribel Duriez spoke with confidence and candor about the extraordinary events of her life, including her capture and torture by the guardia; her asylum in Mexico where she went to recover from the emotional trauma of her ordeal; and her return to Nicaragua in a combat role. Since the revolution, this remarkable militante *has worked for the army and the Frente, and she has both taught and studied at the national university. Here she describes her pre- and post-revolutionary activities, her growing feminism, and her concern that for many university students, the revolution is largely a vague childhood memory.*

I am of working-class extraction; my father is a mechanic and my mother is a nurse's aide. They are now living in the fourth region because there is no housing here in Managua. My childhood was normal, common, which is to say that my family was poor and everything, food, money, education, was a struggle. We were three children of my mother, but there also lived with us three other children of my father's; we were eight people in all.

I think that my childhood was very ordinary for a Nicaraguan at that time, and one event that has stayed with me is also the sort of thing that other children witnessed during the period. I was about seven years old when the guardia surrounded the neighborhood where I was living, and they murdered three young compañeros, one of whom was the revolutionary martyr and poet, Leonel Rugama. They were about two blocks away, fighting the guardia, who had conducted a house by house search, terrorizing everyone. That memory is still very vivid. An even earlier memory I have, I guess I was barely three or four at the time, is of my papa listening to Radio Havana. He was anti-Somoza and a sympathizer of the Frente. He refused to listen to any of the national stations because they were all controlled by Somoza. That was an influence on me because I was the oldest.

I was a very precocious child: I entered second grade at six years of age, and I finished elementary school when I was ten. I began attending school with my older sisters when I was about four years old. I would cry and throw a tantrum unless they took me with them. To humor me, they let me come along, and I learned to read. By the time I was officially in first grade, at age six, I already had been reading for a while. They gave me an exam and skipped me to the second grade because I could already read and write. I was always the best student, in both elementary and secondary school. My parents' fondest dream was for us to become professionals, something that was impossible for them. My papa's mother, for example, sold tortillas, and he is a *mecánico empírico*, an empirical mechanic; that is, he taught himself everything through trial and error. My mama, the same thing, her parents could not send her to school, and she struggled to become a nurse's aide.

A crucial event in my development was when Arlen Siu came to my house, this was between '73 and '74. Have you ever heard of her? I can't say that we had a close relationship because I was a child of nine, and she was a young adult, but she was my first direct contact with the Frente Sandinista. She was part of the Christian movement, and she would come to the house and do political work with us, education, discussions, consciousness-raising. She also played the guitar, and we would sing. I loved her, she was wonderful, and she won me over completely. She spent four or five months working in our zone. My memories are that she would visit our home, play with me, give me special attention, and maybe even spoil me a little. I only remember fragments, not a full story of the time she spent with us. When she fell, her death hit me hard. My papa told me that we have to follow Arlen's example, and that was the beginning of my integration into the revolutionary movement.

I had just completed elementary school when she was killed, and it was time for me to begin the secondary level. My papa wanted to put me into the horrible, infamous girls' normal school in San Marcos run by nuns. I put up a fuss, cried, begged, did everything not to go to study with the nuns. I wanted to go to the Instituto Juan José Rodríguez in Jinotepe. Historically, it has been revolutionary. I did not want to go to a nun's school because I remembered when I was in elementary school how, for punishment, they would make us kneel for an hour in the hot sun, or they would slap me on the hands with the ruler, and that just made me more rebellious. That was at the Holy Family (Sagrada Familia) school in Managua, where I spent the first half of my elementary schooling. We moved to Jinotepe after the earthquake, where I finished. I won the battle, and at age eleven I began the program at the Instituto; this was in '75.

As I said, the Instituto was very rebellious and political like myself, and I became involved. Obviously, at age eleven I still did not understand fully the political situation, but I had a revolutionary mentality, and I knew that I wanted to play an active part in the political transformation of the country. I was the youngest first-year student there; the average age was fourteen, and secondary is a five-year program.

In my second year I joined the student movement, and I became more mature than other girls my age. Almost immediately I began meeting with compañeros who are now leaders in the army and in the party, such as Comandante Salvatierra, Raul Arévalo, and many others. Even so, the first three years of secondary went along normally, normal in the sense that I dedicated myself to my studies and to the student movement, for it was a period when the revolutionary forces were gathering strength and numbers, and many students became active sympathizers. We put up propaganda, participated in strikes, and so forth, but that was really all we could do as secondary students.

Then, in '78, my fourth year, they were planning the insurrection for September, and they needed people to go for training in a military school, that is, an underground training center, and we students were needed. The idea of the military school caused a big problem in my family, because my papa had other plans for his intelligent daughter. I really wanted to do it, however, because I knew what was necessary, and I had had more experiences by that time.

For example, in the student strike in April '78, I had seen the guardia kill four of my compañeros in the market in Jinotepe. We were demonstrating on behalf of freedom for Tomás Borge and Marcio Jaen. They chased us, beat us, killed some of my friends, and put the rest of us in jail. You see, after the insurrection of Monimbó we had begun taking to the streets to demonstrate. At first they just laughed at us, but soon the guardia began to repress us brutally, with BECATS, the special antiriot squads, tear gas bombs, truncheons. It was during that demonstration that I had seen my friends murdered by the guardia.

The next day, our friends at school mounted another demonstration to have us released from jail. All the townspeople participated too, and we were released. That was when I decided to go to the military school, that is, to work clandestinely for the Frente. But my papa was furious; he didn't want anything to happen to me. Well, I went to the military school, but it was at a price, because my parents were shocked and angry. I was only fourteen and I didn't even have a boyfriend, and here I was leaving my parents' house for two weeks. In my country, moral and ideological values are very backwards, and what I was doing was looked upon as terribly immoral. I had problems with my parents who were raised according to the old norms, and my mother especially was scandalized. My father beat me, he was beside himself, it was a terrible conflict. But I told them that I was going to participate in the insurrection whether they liked it or not.

Each day my commitment grew. For example, another thing that happened about that time was at a meeting of the university student cell, with which I was associated. I had left the room briefly with a few friends. Whe. we came back, we discovered that the guardia had taken prisoner fifteen of the other members. They also killed the boy who was the leader of the Student Revolutionary Front, FER, which is the intermediary organization of university students between the Frente and the high school students.

The whole town showed up for his funeral; Jinotepe is very small and everyone knows everyone else. For this procession, for Alvaro Sánchez's funeral, I carried in one hand a banner that read, "Cease Repression, Cease the Murder of Students"; and, in the other, the banner of the Frente Sandinista. To do that was an *incredible* crime! The guardia escorted us to the cemetery, and later my photograph came out in a North American newspaper; I saw it myself. Naturally, my defiant act was enough for the guardia to consider me a subversive leader. No one believed that I was just fourteen years old; I have always looked much older than I am anyway. After the funeral, I had to leave town, because they came to the house to find me, and just by luck, I was not there. My father told me that I could not go back to school there, that they would kill me. He sent me to Tipitapa to stay with an uncle, but I didn't spend much time there, because I felt the need to be at my own house, and to continue at the Instituto.

So I returned home, and my father told me flatly that I could not continue studying or that would be the end of me. Because, you see, in the last taking of the high school, the guardia had chased me for four blocks; I was riding my bicycle on the way to the Instituto which had been taken over by the students, and I got caught on the fence when I tried to climb over. Some friends helped me over just ahead of the guardia, but then they arrived, beat us, and took us to jail. Our parents got us out, but remembering that incident, my father later said no to my request to go back to school.

We made a deal. At that time my mama was working in Catarina, in Masaya. She didn't want me to lose the school year, so she asked me to go there and study medical technology. They had a three-month course to be a laboratory aide, and my mama wanted me to take advantage of the time that I was not in class at the Instituto. My papa resisted at first, but then he relented. Turns out that my mama had me stay at the house of some friends who were involved in the Frente there in Catarina. I knew that the insurrection was coming, this was in August now, and there was just about a month to go. So I went there and I distributed materials in Catarina. I worked with the neighborhoods, and basically continued my involvement. My papa took me out of the Instituto so I wouldn't be in danger, and here I was doing this work for the Frente!

I even managed to get useful information from the headquarters of the guardia there in Catarina. My mama worked at the health center, which was next door to the headquarters, and I went around asking them how many men they had, how many guns, how many were on guard duty. I was careful and never asked direct questions, but since I was just the daughter of the nurse's aide there in the health center, they never suspected that I passed that information along. The attack on the headquarters at Catarina was organized, the insurrection broke out, and I left for the insurrection; this was September 1978. I was not involved directly in Catarina, for security reasons, because everyone knew that I was the nurse's daughter. Three of my companions fell in that attack on the headquarters of Catarina.

At the funeral of these companions we had the audacity to go armed. The guardia surrounded us, they knew that there, inside the funeral service which itself was a popular repudiation of the dictatorship, were the elements who had participated in the attack. Plus, the guardia always had their *orejas*, their ears, or spies. They surrounded the procession with tanks, airplanes, yes, airplanes. This was characteristic of the guardia. For example, when Comandante Julio Buitrago fell, they surrounded the house he was in with tanks, and he was just one person, alone in the house. Three hundred tanks and planes for only one person who fought them until his last breath. This was one of the feared guardia's hallmarks.

As I was saying, they surrounded us, and while many managed to escape, they captured me in the cemetery. I did not participate in the attack and the burning of the headquarters, or the killing of guardias, but I had passed information. It turns out that my instructor in the laboratory where my mother worked was a spy, an *oreja* of the guardia. His brother was a lieutenant in the guardia, and he was the one who captured me. He is still here in Nicaragua, he was recently pardoned.

Thus began the most severe trauma of my life. They took me to jail and a group of them brutally raped me. You have to understand that I had never even had a boyfriend or anything, and I was fourteen years old. I knew they were going to kill me and they had already killed my other companions. In my desperation, I told the guardia that I knew the *oreja*, and that he could tell them that I had nothing to do with the attack on the headquarters. I was, naturally, doing whatever I could to save my life. The spy himself saved my life and they let me go, but by then I had been in jail a month and ten days.

In jail, I tried different tactics to defend myself. I would faint, I would pretend that I couldn't withstand what they were doing to me; these were things that I did to survive. I never said anything either, because if they had suspected, for example, that Arlen Siu had been at my house, they would've killed me on the spot. I am telling you about this because I feel such empathy with those who have sacrificed their lives for the revolution, Arlen Siu, Julio Buitrago, Leonel Rugama. In my own way, I hope to contribute my grain of sand together with those of others who have made great sacrifices, such as Comandantes Tijerino and Herrera.

When I got out, I was incommunicado for awhile, as I was severely traumatized. Then I left for the Mexican embassy. I hoped that I would be granted amnesty since no crime could be proved against me, they didn't even know where the pistol came from that I had had, and I hoped that the fact of my age would help. By the time I arrived at the Mexican embassy, my parents too were in Managua, because the guardia was after them also and had destroyed their house in Jinotepe.

I arrived at the embassy on October 31, 1978 , and there were about 500 others seeking asylum, mostly entire families. The person I waited next to for a while was a man who had been burned with acid; the guardia had violated his wife who had just given birth. Most of us there were collaborators of the Frente, not official members, except for Ana Isabel Morales, who today is a subcomandante. She had been a prisoner and she arrived at the embassy via the Frente. But real members were very few; we were mostly sympathizers of the Frente who had participated in demonstrations against the dictatorship and who could not continue living in Nicaragua because of the repression.

I stayed there for two months, leaving December 21, 1978, for Mexico. When they learned at the embassy what had happened to me, they immediately approved my request for political asylum. But there was another case, that of Lidia Astorga, the sister of Nora Astorga, who was with us, I think that now she is a pilot, but to whom they never gave safe conduct. She sought asylum because her sister had helped murder a general of the guardia. The embassy did not give her a visa because of trouble with Somoza, but neither could she leave the grounds because she feared for her life. She stayed there for about a year; I believe that it was not until Mexico broke relations with Somoza that she was able to leave with the embassy staff.

My parents came to visit me in the embassy, and my mother cried and prayed the whole time. She couldn't stop crying when she learned what had happened to me, and she had such dreams for me. I was supposed to graduate at age fifteen, enter the university at sixteen, graduate at twenty, and marry a fine young man. And I didn't even receive my secondary degree, leaving in the fourth year, I was just one year short. My papa was a little stronger, and said to go to Mexico, finish school there, study for a career, and then return home. My younger brother and sister also came to see me during those two months.

There is a person I remember well and with whom I shared a lot at the embassy. The day that I sought asylum, there also arrived compañera Nubia Salvador Aguilar, who was captured along with compañero Pedro Aráuz of the national leadership of the Frente. Nubia and I had nervous crises; we would suddenly become hysterical, we would wake up screaming, and such things as that. She had been held prisoner for a year and was totally worn out emotionally. We were together although she was much older than I was, about twenty-five, because we were the only two women who were alone. Everyone else was with their families; I was like the mascot of the group because I was so young.

Once in Mexico, the Mexican government helped us a great deal, providing us with money, food, and clothing. Some people became comfortable and stayed; they quit working for the Frente and decided to live a more tranquil life. But they were a minority, most were committed to returning to Nicaragua. As for me, I was in such a terrible emotional state that soon after arriving in Mexico I suffered a crisis, a breakdown really. You see, there is a point that I haven't wanted to bring up, but I think that it will help you understand my life better: I was pregnant when I got out of jail.

In Mexico, they assigned a woman psychologist to me, because I would cry hysterically nearly all the time. What was I going to do, I was so young, I didn't know who the father was, I was desperately in need of help. I didn't want to have the baby, but the doctor, Mimi from Argentina, helped me immensely. I would love to see her again. She told me, "When the revolution triumphs, which it will, you will have much to say, and you will have moral authority with your generation. There are very few of your age so profoundly involved in the struggle."

I had my fifteenth birthday there, the *quinceañera*, you know that is the most special birthday for a girl in our culture. That's when the daughter goes to the church with her papa, and you wear a beautiful white dress, and there is a big party. It's such an important event, almost like a wedding, and I felt terrible because I was the farthest thing from what is celebrated in a *quinceañera*. My friends had a party to cheer me up; they bought a cake and even a bottle of wine, and the doctor helped me get through my emotional breakdown.

But my general health and my nervous state were still precarious, and I miscarried. After that, I felt even worse because the doctor had told me that when I went back to Nicaragua I would have much to say to others, but now I felt that I would have nothing to say when I went back. I was very young to think like that, but you can see how emotionally wrung out I was. So, Mimi began counseling me again, encouraging and supporting me, and pulling me through my prolonged crisis.

Then I almost went to Cuba for training, but I was unable to go because I had serious medical complications from the miscarriage and I was very sick. The friends I had come from Nicaragua with left for Cuba, while I stayed in Mexico. But it wasn't a total loss. In December 1978, I attended a fabulous concert that took place in the National Auditorium in Mexico. Carlos Mejía made the debut of his song to Carlos Fonseca. There was also the Daniel Viglieti group; Violeta, Isabel, and Angel Parra; and Chico Buarque. They sang the Frente's anthem, everything was decorated in red and black, and the auditorium was overflowing with people. It was fantastic! I also went to the national university to talk, and I felt very big and important. With some other compañeros, I visited groups of workers and told them about the struggle of our people. We saw the other side of the coin while we were there. For example, we saw how comfortably the Mexican government people lived, and we saw the poor suburbs of the common people.

Soon it became clear that my superiors were going to make me go back to school, but I wanted to fight because I was brave. So in May 1979, I ran away, making my way to Honduras hidden in a tour bus. That's right. I arrived in Honduras and spent a day and a night trying to cross the border between Guatemala, El Salvador, and Honduras. I was completely alone and empty-handed except for a small suitcase. I slept in the bus, and the other passengers gave me some of their food. After I crossed, I stayed in Choluteca, Honduras. The tour bus driver knew some Nicaraguan refugees there and they took me to Campo Luna, as it was called, an encampment of the Frente. I spent a month of preparation there, which was a month lost because I couldn't be in the fighting; in all, I was out for about a year. Perhaps my compañero would have much to tell you, because he was in the guerrilla at the northern front. His name is Omar Obregón; he's a first lieutenant in the army now and he is my husband, but I will tell you about him shortly.

I finally entered the western front in a combat squadron, that was my first time as a combatant. Theoretically, I knew how to do everything because of my training; in the schools I had attended in '78 and '79 I had learned to fire, but as for facing an enemy, no. We were two compañeras there and the others were men. But they respected us completely. The other woman was a little older, she had already spent some time fighting, and she had lost her shyness about certain things. For example, she would bathe in the rivers along with the men and no one paid any attention, she would take care of her necessities along with them, and she was just like them. But I couldn't do any of those things; for me, that was an impossible break with the normal custom that I had grown up with. I was still not over my emotional trauma; I feared that every soldier who came near was going to rape me. The pain from that other experience was still too great for me to deal with.

We were the Francisco Castillo squadron, and we foraged for food for the month that I was in the mountains with them. Sometimes we would find watermelon, other times we would have to go down to the villages and the people would give us something to eat. That, however, was very dangerous for them and for us. We were right along the border where there was a lot of fighting, in the San Pedro sector, in that of San Francisco, also in Cinco Pinos, Somotillo, Santo Tomás. We went advancing like that, from the frontier, liberating these towns, and the columns came after.

We faced the guardia at times, but mostly by then they had practically disbanded and were on the run. They would leave the towns as we would enter. Of course, there were some heavy battles, but they were nothing like what the people in Managua went through. After we liberated Somotillo, then came the triumph, July 19, 1979. Then everyone went to Managua, but my group and my column were assigned to guard the frontier, so I was unable to go.

Meanwhile, my family had arrived at the enormous gathering at the Palacio de la Revolución in Managua looking for me, hoping to find me alive. Someone had told them that I had been killed by Honduran security forces, another that I had died in El Salvador, and still another that I had been sent to the southern front, the majority of people who had been in the embassy and in Mexico with me had gone to the southern front where 80 percent of them fell in combat. My family then circulated a large photograph of me, hoping to find news of my whereabouts. Unfortunately, I was unable to return to my house until September 1979, because we had to secure the return of exiled Nicaraguans along the border. I helped organize the customs procedures, formed part of a border patrol command, and also served as health worker there in Somotillo.

After the triumph, I stayed in the army for a while; they promoted me twice, until I was a first lieutenant. There I met the father of my daughter. I also found myself facing an infinite number of contradictions because of the revolution. First, I felt that with the victory, freedom and equality had automatically been secured, just like when you win a battle. But there are things, for example, with regard to women's rights, that we still have to fight for. And, thinking that way, I had some problems, problems in the army, because the majority of the compañeros still had a machista attitude. They did not want to give women responsibility. They felt that they were more capable than us, things like that.

In the context of these contradictions within the revolutionary process and of my high expectations, I met the father of my daughter, who was also in the army. I married him in 1980, when I was sixteen, which is how old I was when my daughter was born too. It was like jumping from the role of a girl to that of a mother, without going through adolescence, and I had to mature rapidly. I made many mistakes, the most serious one was having married without knowing the compañero well. He was twenty-eight and he seemed to know everything, but we had almost nothing in common and after two years our marriage was over. I stayed in the army; later, I worked with the Frente. Meanwhile, my mama began taking care of the baby, since I was the oldest daughter. Nadiezhda is her name. When I was pregnant, I saw a documentary about Lenin, and I learned that his compañera's name was Nadiezhda. I decided to name my baby Nadiezdha if it was a girl, and Lenin if it was a boy. I am an admirer of Lenin; I read about him when I was in Mexico. Anyway, mama took care of the baby while I was in the army, but she insisted that I go back to school and prepare myself for a career. She said that I could be a revolutionary and have a career too.

First the Frente sent me to study at the Facultad Preparatoria, which is a sort of accelerated high school program begun in 1981 where children of workers and campesinos attend, and where war veterans from the whole country can come study. The school is for those who have already passed the sixth grade; it is a secondary school divided into three levels instead of the usual five. I entered at the second level because I had finished the third year of high school already. I began studying in 1981, but in 1982 they called me up in the army again, that was when Reagan began sending his mercenary bands. I had a specialty in communications and administration within the army, and that's why they mobilized me, so I had to quit the Preparatoria.

I was in Region I, in Quilalí; in the Fifth Region; in the special zones, everywhere. I learned the whole country, and one thing that I learned is that women in the army have to be treated better, because they still do not feel that they are on the same level as the men. But my own experiences were wonderful, above all in the combat zones. I returned home in 1985; well, actually I returned in 1983 because a bus had run over my daughter, and she was in a coma, and for six months she could not walk or speak. It was a terrible shock, and I didn't want to go back to the army, but my mother had been raising her and there was no alternative for me anyway. In 1985, I came back home again, because I had decided I didn't want to stay in the army, I had some personal problems, and besides, I wanted to study. So the Frente sent me back to the Preparatoria.

I began the third year there, which is the equivalent of the fifth or last year of secondary, and in 1986, I finally started here at the university, UNAN. When I came here I assumed some responsibilities with the student movement, I am president of the student group of the faculty of education. It is one of four faculties: medicine, education, *preparatoria* (the accelerated secondary I had just completed), and natural sciences. The education students are the largest group, in the night shift of course. I study at night. In 1985 I assumed the leadership of the student movement, while I was still a student at the *preparatoria*, and I put into practice many of the group techniques I had learned doing political work for the Frente.

In '86, I began to study physics in the faculty of education. My average was 95; there are some compañeros in the army or police and who study at night but who work harder than I do and who had a score of 100. In '87, I started my second year, and since I am one of the best students in the faculty of education, I was asked to be an *alumna ayudante*, or teaching assistant. The idea is to encourage some students to go on preparing themselves to become university professors. They give you education, political, and scientific courses. By now, I already teach the laboratory to introductory physics, during the day. I can't do more than that because I am only in the second year myself.

Remember that I'm studying physics in the faculty of education; physics in the faculty of natural sciences is different. They work more on experiments, in using physics, for example, in geothermal projects. But we study more basic physics. The laboratory was donated and it is minimal, barely enough to help you learn the basics about, say, oscillatory movement, mechanical movement, and magnetism. In truth, there are very few resources, and we need everything. There are some experiments that we cannot perform because the donated materials have been ruined. For example, if you have an electric wave tray, and the power goes out, which it often does, and it is still connected, it is lost. I am also head of all the teaching assistants in the faculty of education; I represent them in the student movement. Three years ago I was named militant of the Frente. Militancy is a big responsibility, and I feel that I have to live up to it.

I met my husband in the army too, but we were just friends. When he came back wounded, I went to visit him, and after that our relationship became deeper. He had a compañera also, and children, and problems, but for almost three years now our relationship has been beautiful. He is one of the few men who has put machismo aside a little. We live in a house; minimal, just a bed, table, chairs, but we are happy. He is an excellent man. He is understanding. He doesn't complain because I am studying, like so many men do. That is a big problem here at the university, men do not want their compañeras to go to school. We both clean, cook, and share the responsibilities at home.

Nadiezhda used to be with me, but it would be impossible now. I agreed to let my mother keep her, because I am here from 9:00 a.m. to 5:00 p.m.; I begin class at 6:00 p.m. and leave at 10:00 p.m. So I couldn't keep studying if the child were here with me. My compañero brings me to school in the morning when he is in town. He doesn't have his own car, but an official one. However, he is often mobilized and is away, so usually I take the bus. The line is very long, and then I have about a twelve-block walk to the house. Transportation is a terrible problem, there are very few comforts.

Another big problem is that many students now do not share my political commitment. I am unusual, not the average, I realize. They support the revolution, but not to the extent that I do. For example, the students who are entering as first-year students now were about ten years old when the revolution occurred, and they have not had much opportunity to integrate themselves into revolutionary activities. The compañeros of the generation that participated actively are now occupying intermediate level responsibilities. But these kids come here without knowing anything about the student movement, its history, or the sacrifices others have made for them. I think that Mimi was right, I do have many things to tell them, I do have a special responsibility.

10   Luz Beatriz Arellano (b. 1939)

"... the Gospel is subversive, if one takes it seriously and identifies Jesus with the most humble. This happened in Nicaragua; we took it seriously and it changed our lives."

"He [Tachito Somoza] announced angrily, 'this nun is a communist!' "

The mural of Christ offered a message of peace and a bright splash of color to the inner patio where the hammock hung and where the deep green of the potted plants contrasted with the drabness of the surroundings. The minuscule courtyard of her very simple home is an oasis of calm and order in the hectic world of this extraordinary Franciscan nun and leading exponent of liberation theology in Nicaragua.

It is appropriate that Sr. Luz Beatriz Arellano should live in modest surroundings in a poor barrio, for she was reared in a humble family and has always identified Christ with "the people." Whether as a student at the Sorbonne, base community organizer, intractable foe of the Somoza dictatorship, or activist theologian, Luz Beatriz Arellano has dedicated herself to narrowing the gap between theory and practice within the church. Ths most striking example of this goal is the historic national encounter of 1972, which Sr. Luz Beatriz was a major force in organizing, and during which teams of religious crisscrossed the country listening to the experiences of the people and creating a ministry based on the popular sense of the national social reality.

Until the administrative reorganization in 1988, this soft-spoken yet formidable sister occupied the dual post of Director of Solidarity Programs and Director of Theological Research at the internationally known Antonio Valdivieso Ecumenical Center, the hub of activity in the new *church in Nicaragua.*

I come from a poor, but not destitute, family. My mother would always tell us that however bad things were for us, they were worse for others. The earliest image I have of my mother is seing her with the littlest baby in her arms, and all the rest of us around her praying, early in the morning about 5:00 a.m., before an image of Christ. My father on his father's side was linked to the upper class. But he didn't study because there was only one boys' school in Granada, and since he had run away from it three times, they wouldn't let him return. So my father basically lived with campesinos, tilling the one *manzana* that my grandfather let him use. When he married my mama, she didn't know they were going to move to the country and it was a very hard thing for her to do because she was from the city and unaccustomed to rural life.

We lived in the country until we were of school age. We were seven children, I am the second oldest. Then mama got a little house in the city, so we could study there; she put us as interns in a religious school at great sacrifice. We would go back to the country with papa during vacations. She sewed constantly because the colegio was so expensive. My father, meantime, rented four to five *manzanas* to plant, to keep us in food. Then the farm grew to twenty-five *manzanas*. But the bank took it all away, because papa couldn't pay the loan. There were bad winters and poor harvests, and the bank took away *everything*. My papa died having a profound love of the land, but without having ever owned any, and we were very sad. The loans always went to big landholders. We were left only with that tiny house in the city of Granada.

What all this means is that I saw and I lived what life was like for the campesino , though we ourselves were not dirt poor. The experience that most marked me was that of giving. When mama cooked something special, she would make us give it to the very poor. When there was a newborn baby, she would make clothes for it. I believe that the poor have a great capacity for sharing. Mama taught us to give away not what was left over, but what we had. When we were about seven or eight years old, we too began making baby clothes for those who were poorer. For me, that was the experience of God. Mama would tell us that God is love, and that was the way she lived her life; it was natural for her, and I grew up believing strongly that love is made manifest in life.

We lived in the city during the school year and with my papa in the country during vacations. I also helped with the planting and with taking care of the cattle on the farm. I loved it and have fond memories. My papa was a happy person; he loved parties, played the guitar, but he didn't drink, which was unusual. He would sing to us from the time we got up in the morning and would joke with everyone. People with problems would come over to our house and he would cheer them up, while mama would give them a little salt or thread, because, as I have said, there were others poorer. Then I began to see how other people lived, for example, my father's family. We saw each other only ocasionally because we were the poor relatives. I don't want to talk about his family so as not to say bad things. But my father, though he had practically nothing, always made them little gifts.

At that time the campesinos, you couldn't tell what color their pants were; they had so many patches that they were dressed in all colors. It cost ten centavos for an arm's length of thread, which they would buy to cover the holes in their clothes, because they had their pride and did not like to go around with torn pants. As for the women, they would dye their one dress different colors. They would buy the dye also for ten centavos. I remember the neighbor woman at the farm stopped me to chat, and I saw she was soaking her dress in a tub. Then I knew why I would see her one day with a red dress and another with a green one, but the patches were always in the same place.

The secondary school I went to was a nuns' school in Granada, run by the sisters of María Auxiliadora. I was an internal student, and it was a strong shock, the strict discipline, the strange clothes, the rigid schedule, getting up, going to bed all at set times. I cried all year, but mama when she would visit us, would encourage us to go on, to be strong. I tried to get good grades because of her sacrifice, and I was always one of the best students. I remember that she and my sister would argue because my sister spent much more money than I did. I had a facility for learning, but the discipline of the school was hard for me to get used to. I compensated with sports, baseball, and basketball. I was at the colegio for seven years. They made us go to mass every day at 5:00 a.m. We had not eaten at that hour, and the mass was long; so sometimes the Virgin would start to sway before my eyes. When vacation time came, I didn't go to mass. I went to the movies every possible chance. Another thing I liked was to dress nicely, and I was especially fond of pretty shoes.

When I was sixteen, something happened that transformed my religious life. A very wealthy lady invited us to spend a vacation with her at her finca, one of the largest in all Nicaragua, where she would always invite poor kids and her friends' kids for holy week vacations. It was wonderful, horseback riding, racing along the shore of the lake, singing, playing guitars in the evening. The second trip out there for vacation, I remember something that impressed me deeply. Our hostess came to the dining room bringing us breakfast from the kitchen, and in agitation saying, "Those campesinos are getting so bold; now they want to eat like we do. The cook has just asked me to sell shoulder roast to her, the best cut! What are they going to pay with? She ought to be happy that we sell the bones!" That sounded vile, repulsive to me. It was horrible because in my house I had never heard words like that, and because traditionally we gave bones to the dogs. I felt physically sick. I left the table and went for a walk. As soon as I was alone, the tears streamed down my cheeks.

Then I went over to the area where the campesinos lived. They had always been there, but I never paid attention to how they lived. There was the whole family in their mended rags, with their animals, all in one wooden room. I began to ask them, "Do you know that God is love?" They looked at me like I was crazy. "Do you know that we all have the right to eat meat?" They started laughing and said, "Yes." Then I asked, "Do you want me to give you catechism?" I thought I would teach God is love and that all things are possible. They answered, "Yes." So, for the rest of the vacation I would ride with my friends in the morning, and in the afternoons I would teach the workers on that hacienda. I tried to apply what little I had learned to their lives. And at the age of sixteen, I began to think that I should put my life at the service of the poor. My friends thought that I was foolish, but I thought that *they* were. "How can we see these things and do nothing?" I asked.

When I went back to the city, I took up my usual ways again, wanting pretty clothes, going to the movies, but always in the back of my mind was the idea of the campesino. I had an internal conflict. I thought that maybe I could give a few years of my life to help the campesino; I didn't know if I wanted to give *too* much! I remember once I went to all the masses I could go to in one day, about four, to hear how the priests interpreted what Jesus said about the poor. But the bishop of Granada, a cousin of Somoza, was preaching: "If you want to give money to finish your cathedral, fine, but I have twenty million in the bank and I do not need your alms." I could hardly believe what I heard. Then I went to another mass, and another, and didn't hear anything as bad, but I did not hear any priest interpret the word of Christ either. I decided that I was going to have to read the Bible myself. I asked grandma if she had a Bible; she told me that we shouldn't read the Bible because the priest had to interpret for us.

The next vacation something good happened. A Nicaraguan priest who had been studying in England returned; he had very progressive ideas for his times and was organizing missions to the countryside; this was in 1956. He came to our house and asked my older sister to accompany him to help catechize the workers on the fincas of the wealthy. That weekend I was supposed to go the seaside, for which occasion I had bought a pretty new bathing suit. My sister said she couldn't go with the priest because she couldn't give up her Sunday, but that *I* could go. I was furious with her! But I went, saying resentfully, "I won't talk to anyone on the way; then they will see that I am angry and they won't invite me again."

But on the trip, I gradually forgot my resolve. The father kept looking back at me through the rearview mirror of the small van, and asking me if I was all right. We got to the finca and began organizing the mass and the catechism, at which point the father would ask me to help with something, and I would say no. He would suggest something else, and I would say no to that too. Finally, the last task was reading the Gospel to the campesinos, and I said yes, on one condition, that he not stand behind me, but leave and trust me to do it. He agreed. What happened was that I began to read the Gospel; then I began to *explain* it. It was completely natural for me because I had seen mama talking to God in our house as an everyday occurrence. Then I felt the priest standing behind me; I told him he had broken his promise, and he left.

After that, he kept coming to our house and and one day he asked me what I liked to read. "Novels, and all things prohibited," I said still trying to reject him. "I don't want anything that you can bring me," I told him. But I read poetry and novels all the time. I wanted to study literature, and I loved the poetry of Rubén Darío. One day the priest brought me a pile of books in case I ever ran out of reading materials. The idea of the religious life kept coming to me and I kept pushing it away. I was horrified at the thought of all that rigid discipline. One day I picked up one of the books at random, almost against my will, fearing that I was going to be interested. It was called *Rabonni*, and was a biography of a young person who was wondering how to become a follower of Jesus. When I finished I was crying; I realized that I wanted to do what he did, but that it was too hard for me. I took a religious card with the image of Jesus on it, and on the back I wrote "Lord, I want to, but it is difficult; I am unable. How long before I will be able?" I was afraid to change my whole life.

Finally, I talked to the priest, saying that I wanted a religious life that was unlike the ones I had seen that were all repression. I had two requirements: one, that the order be modern; and two, that they work for the poor. My father's family offered to help. They felt that the Salesians and the Sacred Heart in Granada were the "family's" communities, because my grandfather's sister was the one who had made it possible for these orders to return to Nicaragua after they had been expelled during a liberal period, along with the Jesuits and the Mother Cabrinis. I began my religious life in the Sacred Heart community, but I don't want to say any negative things about them. It was like a contradiction between what the written rules of the order were, and what it was in practice, between the good intentions and the real acts.

They wanted me, as a novitiate, to continue my studies, and to do so outside Central America. Theirs was a French school and a French order, and I was awarded a scholarship by the French government to study in France. I did not want the scholarship, nor did I want to go. But I went in order to prepare myself for better service to the pueblo. I had to fight within the community to get permission to study what I wanted. They wanted me to study something and come back and teach it in the colegio. But I knew that secondary Catholic instruction in Nicaragua was at the service of the privileged classes. Mine was also an internal struggle because I loved literature, and I wanted to teach it. But I decided to study sociology to understand better what was happening within the church and how to put the church more at the service of the poor.

I was in Lyons at first, then the Sorbonne, in Paris, for more serious studies. But wherever I was, I read everything I could get my hands on to help me understand what was happening in Latin America. There was nothing on Nicaragua, but I found much on Latin America. I read, for example, analyses of the Alliance for Progress, what it meant for Latin America, how it was exploitative and based in an erroneous concept of development. Another was a book on the church in Latin America called *Mi iglesia duerme*, (My Church Sleeps).

Somewhere around 1961 or 1962 I became quite ill and the doctor suggested a change of climate; that's when I went to Paris to continue my studies. I took advantage of everything the city had to offer. I participated in reflection meetings of the Latin American religious, and we founded the Colegio Latinoamericano for students from Latin America, for consciousness-raising. I read voraciously, especially the Brazilian authors, who influenced me greatly. Celso Furtado's economics made an impact with his systematization and rationalization of what had been for me vague notions and undefined feelings of disquiet. If I had been in Nicaragua, I wouldn't have read any of these because of the censorship. We didn't even have the facts about Nicaragua, much less the rest of Latin America. I also read dom Helder Câmara on institutionalized violence; we later read his works in Nicaragua, amazingly enough.

Several of my professors were interested in Central America, such as my economics teacher in Lyons, who was also a Christian, and who treated problems of development and underdevelopment in his courses. Gilbert Blardonne was his name; he was very machista, because he was expecting a male student, not a woman, and certainly not a religious. He asked me why I wanted to study, what possible use it would be to me, and so on. He told me that he was going to be extra demanding of me because Latin America had to solve its own problems. He gave me his books to use, and he required that I take complementary studies at the Institute of Political Sciences so that I could combine theology and politics. He invited me to his house and I met his family. Later, at his invitation,

I participated in a journal that still exists called *Crecimiento de las jóvenes naciones* (Growth of the Young Nations).

My reading and participation were vital to my development during those years, from 1962–69. I read anything and everything that came into my hands, from classical works of French literature, to Che Guevara and Régis Debray, who were much discussed among the students. I participated in everything, including Jacques Brel testimonial concerts and the student protests in 1968, in which the sociology faculty of the Sorbonne was very involved.

But my main interest was always Latin America. I researched the Somoza dictatorship, searching out every last shred of information, friends would even send me clippings they had found, and that was the subject of my final paper in sociology. I participated in all discussions, round tables, and lectures on religion; I began to work in earnest with Christian youth groups, and I had an impact on those French young people. As I became more interested in the sociology of religion, it became clearer and clearer to me that we say one thing and do another in the church. That's why this time of intellectual ferment and questioning opened up by Vatican II was so vital, especially as much of the impetus for change was coming from Latin America. But the South American students there looked upon us Central Americans as, well, very young. Chile, Argentina, Brazil, Uruguay, that's where the real changes would take place! And my professors too would tell me I was dreaming when I expressed hope for Central America; maybe in a hundred years, they said.

In the meantime, I was having problems within the religious life. Many of the members of the order lived in another century and made you feel guilt and shame if you didn't share their views. The discipline was very oppressive, and I was troubled, especially by those who said "So what?" when I expressed my concern about the gulf between theory and practice in the Church. But I also had many friends within the community who talked with me and helped me.

I prepared my final paper in theology on the structure of religious life. I entitled it "Institution and Institutionalization." In it, I presented a "new" perspective on religious life based on the Gospel. I had researched eighteenth and nineteenth century European religious communities and discovered that they began as servants of the poor, only to become gradually absorbed by the Vatican and to lose sight of their original purpose. I used a theological and a sociological approach; of course, all the while I was drawing parallels with the situation in Nicaragua. I was eager to return and to plunge into the life of the people.

The first thing I remember on coming home in '69 is passing by the Catholic university, UCA, and seeing the visible signs of protest, strife and repression on campus. Nothing had changed; if anything, it was worse. Students were held prisoner for no reason at all, sometimes their parents too. Those in jail had no rights, no access to a lawyer; they were beaten, tortured, killed or disappeared. That was the first shocking image on my return, fresh from Paris, with my M.A. in Sociology from the University of Paris and my diploma in Theology and Religious Sciences from the Catholic Institute. I couldn't help comparing that sight with an indelible memory I had: I was fourteen and leaving my house in Granada when I saw a crowd of people; I went over to where they were, and I saw a group of guardias shooting down young boys in the street. That memory came back to me, mixed with phrases from the thesis I had written on the dictatorship, and I rededicated myself to fight so that life here would have meaning.

How difficult then that my first assignment back here was to teach in a colegio for the upper class. Another thing that struck me on returning was that the kids who came to study in our Catholic secondary schools had absolutely no interest in their religious formation. We were knocking ourselves out trying to teach these kids who couldn't care less, while the mass of the population became poorer, more miserable, and more humiliated. I tried, within that limited context, and with a few other religious, to evangelize among the young people, to help them develop in a Christian way. I began, for example, biblical circles for youth. It was very difficult because at first, there was no interest at all, but I kept on anyway. A few other religious who were doing youth work in other colegios and I began to get together to relate experiences, and to discuss how to present an analysis of the social reality about which those young people knew absolutely nothing, and to do so in such a way as to reach them.

We formed a team to share what we were doing with other religious in other places, like León, where they also had *inquietudes*, misgivings, which is to say that they were not in conformity with the status quo. There followed retreats, visits to the seaside with the youth and, ultimately, a national retreat. We felt that if one is sincere about the Gospel, that one has to act. The youth were finally responding, and it was marvelous. Many were from the wealthy and middle groups. For example, Luís Carrión, currently a high-ranking comandante, grew up with this Christian movement. Among the Christian youth, he learned that Christ's purpose, his kingdom we would say, his project, others would say, is justice. To be Christian is to struggle for one's brother; to love is to work for justice. We read the Bible with that meaning in mind. This is the peculiarity of the revolution, that young people learned these things and carried them forward, lived them.

The authorities did not like us. What we did was always with open doors so that anyone could come and see how we were teaching the Bible.

We were without fear because we knew we had the truth. Many, many Christian group members died during the struggle, and many others are in the government now, Carlos Carrión, the brother of Luis, is in a leadership position now; there are also leaders of AMLAE, the Nicaraguan Women's Association, such as Nubia Aguirre; and there is Flor de María Monterrey, director of the Casa de Estudios del Sandinismo, (House for the Study of Sandinismo). The Christian youth movement began very small, but it grew like wildfire. I remember once I participated in a meeting in Guatemala of leaders and advisors of Christian youth, and to my surprise, because we had an inferiority complex in Nicaragua, we were the most advanced and numerous of the countries represented. That was curious, because we were one of the smallest and poorest countries of Latin America, among the three always considered the "tail" of Latin America.

Then we were invited to go to Honduras to share what we had learned. Looking back on this, I see it all as the experience of God. I think that what we have had is an encounter with Christ in history. I think, in fact, that we find Christ as long as we do not deny history, because he speaks to us from history, from the poor, from our forebearers. These youth groups felt this too and were crucial to the change. Somoza did not intrude because he did not believe that Christians were capable, or that they had the strength to fight him from all the angles that were necessary. For example, one of our groups was called Metanoia, and the daughter of a military man belonged to it. One day she said that her father had told her to be careful, that Somoza was asking questions about what these groups were doing. "What is Metanoia; is it communist?" Somoza asked. The father told him that it was a Christian group. "Well," said Somoza, "that's not important then." He didn't realize the strength of what we were doing, or that the Christian youth movement that began in '69 would continue throughout the decade of the '70s.

I was the first religious to take part in, and to help direct, the taking of the cathedral. It was simply not the custom that religious would take to the streets or demonstrate. I hadn't been back three months when I became part of the team that organized the first strike of the Catholic schools to ask for justice for those held prisoner, many of whom were young people. I couldn't remain calmly on the sidelines. I remember two things which stood out: first, how difficult it was to say the Our Father when we weren't doing enough to create a society of brothers; and second, that it was impossible to celebrate Holy Week passively, without doing anything for our people, because that was the passage from slavery to freedom. In that sense, the Gospel is subversive, if one takes it seriously and identifies Jesus with the most humble. This happened in Nicaragua; we took it seriously, and it changed our lives.

We participated in the strikes, the taking of churches, student protests, demonstrations. This was for me a time of consciousness-raising and organization, of work with communities, with youth groups. I was an advisor and a coordinator of other advisors from various Catholic high schools. We worked with the groups we had organized in the schools, and we worked in base communities that were organized in parishes.

We did not have access to the Church directorate, but Fernando Cardenal and I were the first Nicaraguans to attend a meeting of the religious leadership of the church. There, three fundamental questions were asked: What is the mission of the church now in Nicaragua? How can we make the Gospel incarnate in this reality? How can we educate the people in a Christian manner? With regard to the last question, it was clear that in our colegios, we did everything *but* educate students in the faith. One thing we began doing was to go to all the barrios, all of them, from the center to the periphery, and to make it obligatory for students to have "field" experience in the barrios before graduating. Their experience was in helping with literacy. We had inter-school groups and mixed boy-girl teams; many of these kids had gone on retreats together too. Those of us doing the organizing were the same ones supporting the base communities in the barrios.

The bishop of León, after Vatican II, had to invite some of us religious to reflect with him about various questions he had to answer for the Vatican regarding catechism as a part of evangelization. We said you can't have evangelization without a profound study of the reality in which we live. Without that, how are we going to make the Gospel incarnate? The winds that were blowing at that time, 1972, permitted that statement of the question, while politically, it was a very tense period. We talked and prayed, and eventually that bishop invited other bishops to come and participate, and soon pastoral groups were formed in all the different dioceses. It was a major breakthrough.

We divided up into several teams, such as one on the analysis of the social reality, and one on reflection on the church. We went to all the dioceses, to all the parishes throughout the country, with a methodology of popular education that we invented as we went, because Paulo Freire's books could not enter here; they were prohibited by the dictatorship. As I mentioned earlier, we did have some of dom Helder Câmara's works on institutionalized violence. As we went from parish to parish, we were able to go about collecting information on what the people really thought about their situation, their lives, and we presented some questions and a schematic structure for our sessions. First, an introduction; then, the people would reflect in groups; afterwards, we would collect their thoughts for the plenary sessions, which we complemented with what we had. On the basis of the reality that they had articulated, we began a theological reflection, taking up the question of what our role was as Christians. We did this everywhere, in the cities and in isolated rural areas, including the Atlantic Coast. It was the first time that I had been there.

I remember the difficulties that we went through; for example, in the Atlantic Coast, the bishop there called the guardia to "participate" in these meetings. I was on the reality analysis team, and I had to present the ideas we had collected. I was afraid because the guardia was there, and because I also had to communicate all the reproaches we collected in our group about the bishop who had called them. One North American on our team said to me in all innocence, "Well, we have nothing to hide." As if you had to have anything to hide for the guardia to take you away, and besides, he wasn't the one who had to get up and talk! I was the one who was in charge of the entire meeting. Finally, Fernando Cardenal gave me the courage to go ahead. You know, we were disconnected, isolated from all the social and religious currents that were influencing the rest of Latin America; we were just feeling our way along, carried only by our faith that it was right. My knees were trembling, but I had to do it. Not to speak would leave the people exposed and abandoned.

I began to present my analysis of the social reality, but as I was talking I was also trying to think of how to neutralize that guardia. I remember saying that we were all there together as Christians and that we had come to reflect on our lives and our country. Then I added, "If there is anyone here who does not feel that he is a Christian, or who does not want to do this, then he can leave now." I thought that the guardia was going to get up and go, but he stayed, and the local dignitary stayed there too, without budging. So I went on, presenting myself as a religious, standing there in my long white dress, and explaining our procedure, after which I added that at the end, each person could ask one question, hoping thereby to keep the guardia from taking over. I was able to say those things because Jesus and the suffering of the people gave me strength. There were so many things I learned in France that I simply couldn't apply because our reality was so different; the misery here was of a different order of magnitude. I knew that if I backed down then, I would never have the courage to keep going. I thought, "If they kill me, it doesn't matter, because I have delivered my life to Christ."

Well, all the people raised their hands to speak, saying how they hated the guardia, how the guardia treated them, and so on. Then the guardia started shouting, saying that I was lying, that I was getting into politics, and that I was subversive. I tried to make my voice as soft and calm as possible and told him that as I said in the beginning, we had come here to reflect as Christians, and I told him, "You have come as a guardia and not as a Christian, so you may leave. If you have come as a Christian, sit down and be quiet and listen to what others have to say. Afterwards you, like everyone else, have the right to ask one question." He became silent and sat down. After that, at the end, the people didn't ask many questions and I understood. Later, we broke into small groups, and then the guardia left.

The next place we went on the Atlantic Coast, the guardia followed us, took our pictures, and the local official was present at the meeting. From then on, we knew that wherever we were talking or meeting, that they would be listening. Soon they began to threaten us as well, but we kept on, gathering the sufferings and the hopes of the pueblo. The people began to say that the church is changing, that it is doing what Jesus wanted, and that is what filled me with encouragement. That whole pilgrimage is known as the national encounter.

We concluded it with a national pastoral encounter. So many interesting things happened there. We did a number of teaching games, activities that simulate what goes on in society, in this case, to help us see the injustice in our system. For example, we devised a game of exchange of little cardboard coins of different colors but of no designated value, which we put in small purses, different quantities in each one, and which we passed out to everyone. Then, without explaining why, we asked them to trade freely with each other. Some people gave away what they had and ended up with nothing. Others would give a token that presumably had little value, and would try to get in return one of greater value. Some would try to steal from others, or to take their coins by force; soon fights broke out in the different groups. There were many bishops participating in this game, and several of them were among the winners, that is, among those who had managed to take the coins away from everyone else. When it came time for reflection, they figured out that they had put themselves on the side of the exploiters, and in fact, one of them walked out of the meeting. He was angry because everyone was laughing at him. But this is an illustration of our popular methodology that we invented on the spot, because nothing like this existed in Nicaragua.

Then came the actual meeting itself, attended by all the bishops and held at the national seminary. This is still in 1972. This was the first nationwide meeting of clergy during the time of Somoza. It was a very big moment in the life of the church. The bishops began to ask us if the social analyses that we had collected were credible, if the sources were reliable, and if they were exaggerated. Their questions meant that our bishops had not felt, understood, or internalized the meaning of what we had presented. They saw the consequences, but they didn't see the roots. The discussion went on until 10:00 p.m. about whether this was or was not an analysis of reality. The majority said no, and then each one gave his reasons for opposing our findings, some saying that it would only cause more repression from Somoza, and that it was better to remain quiet and do nothing, while others said we had no theological focus.

Our team of twenty maintained, however, that an analysis of reality can not have a theological focus; nor can it arrive at its own conclusions, because everything is articulated, connected, and that now was the time to decide if we really were going to have a ministry based on this national reality. It looked as if we were going to lose everything. Finally, the team convinced me that I should be the one to make the oral presentation of our written report. I knew it would cause me problems with the guardia, but I said yes. The bishops had not yet given their official opinion on the results, though the majority were against it, and even though I was very timid, I spoke before all the bishops of Nicaragua. We had everything all written for them, but I didn't have to read my copy because I had *lived* it.

I told of the hunger and of the lack of houses, of Somoza as dictator, but also as the man who owned monopolies which had a stranglehold on the people, and as an example I told them about the cement monopoly. I said everything with great simplicity, clarity, tranquility, and force. When I returned to our group, they were practically cheering. We had invited to this assembly some people from CELAM, the Latin American Ecumenical Committee, which was then still respectable, later it was in the hands of the right. We had invited Edgar Beltrán, who was surprised at our dynamism and fascinated at how this event would impact in Latin America. We went away very happy, with the impression that the poor would be free to express themselves.

I had begun to sleep at the school where I taught because of problems with my community, and a priest friend of mine called me there saying that he wanted to see me to borrow a catechism book. I finally figured out that he wanted to tell me something, but was afraid to talk on the phone. When he arrived at the reception room, he told me that a friend of his, the director of the cement factory, had just visited him and informed him that while Somoza was at the factory he had received word of my speech. Then he told me that Somoza had ordered that a denunciation be made of what I had said as subversive lies, and that it be published. He left telling me, "Don't worry, if anything happens, we will find a way to help you." But that night I did not sleep.

The next day, I went back to the *encuentro nacional*, the national encounter, and became so caught up in it that I forgot my fear. It was wonderful the way the lay people were involving themselves actively in the meeting. I had to go to Rama a few days later for a meeting, but before I left the full assembly ratified us as a pastoral team. However, some difficulties did arise because certain bishops began to argue among themselves over who was in charge of the national pastoral encounter, who was in charge of the teams, what had really taken place here, and so on. I remember also that Monseñor Obando said, "This analysis of reality, isn't that Marxism?" "No" I answered, "this is what we live; you have heard what the people have said, and we have to account for these things." Bishop Vega too was upset and confused, sometimes acting as a sociologist and at other times contradicting himself.

When I returned home from Rama, the superior of the community called me into her office. I knew that every time she asked me to her office it was to scold me. So I always carried the Bible in one hand, and the documents of the community in the other to defend myself. With a smile she told me, "Now neither the Bible nor the papers can help you." Triumphantly, she produced a letter from Somoza, accusing me of participating in subversive work over a long period of time. The possibilities were three: either I was manipulated by those with exotic ideologies, and we have to find out who they are; or I was ingenuous and didn't know what I was doing; or I did know what I was doing and was dangerous, in which case it was the community's responsibility to send me out of the country or else have the school confiscated, and have me come in for questioning first. At that time, that was very strong, because it was not the custom to question any religious. I knew that this was an unusual situation and that I was left stranded by the community. I went to a group of priest friends whom I had worked with on the team to ask their advice. They had already heard what had happened and had written a letter to Somoza telling him that I spoke in the name of the church, and that since the church was one, the responsible party was the entire Catholic church of Nicaragua.

But the guardia began following my every step, and in 1975 my order sent me to Honduras and told me to keep my mouth shut, to keep total silence. I don't want to talk about Honduras, because the situation there is extremely tense now. But I came to know the religious community there and I was elected their representative, which meant that I could enter into contact again with CLAR, the Confederation of Latin American Religious. They realized the anguish that I was in, and they helped me see that one can change one's community if one is not happy. I began to think that maybe it was possible to find what I was looking for in another order. If I said more about that period in Honduras, there would be repression for the people I worked with; it is already difficult for them. But I worked in the countryside for four years, from 1975–79, doing similar work to what I had done here, except that there I worked more with the women, coming and going to Nicaragua with permission for brief visits. I was exiled, but the government never said so publicly.

You know, they only gave me twenty-four hours to leave the country. I grabbed a few things and that was that. The letter from Somoza came first; then followed a series of repressions by the military; and finally, the choice of either leaving the country or having the colegio confiscated. They gave me fourteen *lempiras* for Honduras, which would buy practically nothing, the hour I had to catch the bus, and some directions about where I was to change buses.

I was so depressed I thought I would die, but I had to appear happy so that my family would not know what was happening to me. But papa was very intuitive, "Why a change in the middle of the year? That doesn't seem very normal." He got together some money as quickly as he could and gave it to me. It was about 400 U.S. dollars, which was an extremely large sum for us and for that time. I don't know where he got it, but he told me to keep it until I needed it. I arrived at the border in a serious state of depression; but I realized that if I crossed the frontier with that attitude, that I would not be able to work there, and that it was useless to cry over the past. But how to cheer myself up? I decided to use some of that money to buy myself a personal gift. I went to the store on the border and I bought a radio to listen to news from Nicaragua and some cologne. And it worked; I felt better.

Besides the pastoral work in the base communities, in Honduras I worked with Indian women and young women generally; I also worked closely with delegates of the word, and I was much more in contact with CLAR. It was during this period that I transferred to the Franciscan community. I also began to think not only of Nicaragua, but of Latin America.

There's something I want to tell you about that happened in '72; then I will pick up my story in '79 with the triumph of the revolution. But I want to relate the following because it will help you understand how thoroughly corrupt Somoza was. It concerns a confrontation I had with Somoza himself. Remember that the earthquake was in '72. I was in the cathedral with a group of twenty or so youths who had occupied it and were fasting to protest the large number of young people who were being imprisoned, murdered, and disappeared. That was a very important event itself, but the earthquake came the day after we had begun our fast.

After the earthquake, there were many thousands of victims in Nicaragua; some of these went to Granada, where we created the only relief committeee that was independent of what Somoza had set up in Managua. This was very important, because the corruption of the government was unbelievable; they stole the aid, the supplies, medicines, blankets, tents, the very *food* from the people. It was shocking! I arrived at the bishopric in Granada about two or three days after the earthquake, and they had already begun organizing the committee there. Volunteers were washing bottles, making things, carrying food to the people, and I began to wash bottles too. Then a padre I knew came up and asked me what I was doing there washing bottles, when everything was so confused and I could be put to better use organizing. So I joined the planning committee and said that I wanted my assignment to be in the food supply center, where they store the basic grains and all the foodstuffs. I knew that if I wanted to be assured of doing something effective, that I had to place myself in that central spot.

The first thing I learned in that position was that I had idealized the people, the poor; I began to see how they were selfish and grasping and desperate like others. I think the long dictatorship had its effect on their behavior too. They fought among themselves, cheated and stole from one other; all those things were very disillusioning for me. In spite of all that, we managed to organize the committee. I had heard in Europe the experience of the two world wars, how they had made ration cards and created a system of distribution of goods. I was wracking my brain trying to remember what they had told me, trying to figure out how to get out of the chaotic mess we were in and give food to 40,000 people.

Then I came up with the idea of printing ration cards by family, which we did. We passed them out, and began to deliver food to the families in the barrios. We divided Granada into sixteen zones, and created a very efficient, organized system, thanks to what the Europeans had told me of their experience. As we shared food, we also did consciousness-raising among the people, reflecting with them on their lives and current situation. Many students were involved in the relief efforts with us.

One day the bishop sent me a note saying that Somoza was coming and that he wanted to see me. For those of us who knew how Somoza was stealing the food and supplies from the people, this news had a big impact. This was both a threat and an opportunity. I thought, how are we going to demonstrate to the people who are coming with Somoza, the international mission, that he is stealing, that the food, clothing, none of the help is getting to the people? We determined to have a strike of silence, that is, that we would maintain silence when Somoza and the committee arrived. We would let him rant and rave like a crazy man, but we wouldn't say anything.

There we all were in committee, the padres with their collars and me with my white dress, and suddenly Somoza arrived, surrounded by guardias in military uniforms and carrying machine guns which they aimed at us. We were completely taken aback; we hadn't expected anything like that, and our plans for the strike of silence fell to pieces. Our fear was so great that we couldn't carry it off; we just collapsed. Some members of the committee belonged to the Conservative party, that is the opposition party, and they began to try to talk to Somoza. I began to feel a great frustration and a rising anger. Remember that a commission was visiting too, and Somoza took them over to our pathetic store of supplies and shamelessly began telling them that we were organized just like the committee in Managua, and that we were part of his operation.

I was so distraught that when Somoza came over to me and asked me to show the commission the record book, saying he was sure that everything was in good order, I didn't know what to do. Should I keep silence? Should I turn over the records? Suddenly, I blurted out, "You are lying!" I said this to his face and in front of the whole gathering. "You know that this committee does not work with you, and that's the reason we have so little to work with." Then he made signs for me to be quiet. I continued, "No, I cannot, because you are robbing the people and this committee is a committee of the church." We were right there in the bishop's palace. He answered, "Yes, I want to thank you for the job you are doing." I responded, "This is the work of the church; you do not have to thank us for anything. Nor do we have to answer to you, because we are working for the people and not for you."

Then the confrontation became really serious. He announced angrily, "This nun is a communist! She has Granada divided into zones!" I was stunned and furious, so I told him before everyone, "I knew that we were a backward country, and I knew that there was corruption and ignorance in the government, but I didn't know that things had reached such a low level. All we did was make a mathematical division for distributing food, not an ideological statement." "Shut up!" he shouted, and stalked out.

Later, he came back with another delegation, a United Nations mission for earthquake relief. The interesting thing is that a member of that delegation was from Switzerland and no one could communicate with him. I asked his language, and it was French, and that was my salvation. I said, "I can explain to you what is happening, but first I would like us to sit and chat a while." So, I told him that I had learned French while I was studying at the Sorbonne. "The Sorbonne?" he says, "I studied there too; we're colleagues." Then I explained everything to him, and in full view of everyone, he gave Somoza a card on which he had written, "This sister is my colleague. If her committee is not given provisions before I leave Nicaragua, then Nicaragua will receive no loans." Then he stated that he was staying at the president's house, and that he had his own direct line. I was to call him immediately to let him know what happened, and he repeated, "No supplies, no loans."

I was terrified because I knew that this meant great repression. Right after they left, Somoza's son, el Chigüin, arrived, surrounded by his guardia, and broke down the doors of the bishopric. He threatened to kill us if we did not keep our mouths shut and stop delivering food to the people. I remember there was a relief mission from Venezuela close by. We ran looking for them to tell them what happened and to turn the people we were serving over to them, so they would be cared for. But they said,

"No, let's combine our forces, and we will participate with you in your meetings so that you will be stronger." That is what we did, and it saved us. The point of all this is to show you what Somoza was like up close. Afterwards, I could not go out alone; I was constantly followed and harassed. Finally, as you already know, I was sent out of the country.

I was the first nun exiled under Somoza. My time in Honduras was very important because I learned much from the women I worked with and it has helped me in my work back here. I think the spirituality of the Latin American woman has been misunderstood. It is based in strength and faith in God gained through great suffering. In Honduras I worked with husbands and wives, sometimes separately, sometimes in groups. The men are oppressed and they often have no verbal outlet; they have to learn how to talk, express themselves to reduce the violence. The Honduran government did not like the pastoral work that many teams were carrying out; in the zone of Olancho, for example, peasants began claiming their land, which led to repression against all pastoral groups. Fourteen people were massacred in Olancho by the army, including one North American priest. I was working in another zone, but the Honduran government cracked down on all of us.

I returned home immediately after the victory in '79 and began helping to prepare materials and cooperate with the Literacy Crusade. To me, that effort and the health campaigns were wonderful volunteer endeavors, common experiences, the construction of our own identity. I see all of this as an ecclesial experience, that is an experience of the church among the people. We are reconstructing our values, but at the same time we are a new people open to the rest of the world, especially to Europe and North America with whom we share cultural roots, particularly North America where people went fleeing oppression to find a new world.

We gave workshops at the Centro Valdivieso about how Christ can help us construct a new life, how socialism can help, how the legacy of Sandino can help, we had many group reflections. I also worked with the base communities when I came back, but many of the members died in the struggle, in my neighborhood alone, Riguero, more than 200 died, and I helped organize a national meeting of base communities to discuss how we fit into the new picture. Many members were working in health, literacy, neighborhood defense committees, and in the harvests of coffee and cotton for example. So we had serious questions of identity to ask ourselves and to determine what was the best way that we as Christians could contribute. The base communities began to renew their mission. The interest among the people was growing, and another task that I undertook, for example, was to go on the weekends to help form new base communities. I would take the bus to Estelí where I would meet with the men, women, and children, there were hundreds, who came from the countryside for catechism on weekends.

Around that time, that would be about '80 or '81, I began to explain to other priests and nuns, from Sweden, Holland, the United States, many places, who came to the center what was going on in this new country. I began to write about our experience because I realized that we weren't doing this alone but with the help of people throughout the world who were and are accompanying us. It is essential always to remember to be open to others; I realized very early the international dimension to our work, and our special relationship with other Christians. That is why I began, it was a very natural outgrowth of my beliefs, to give talks and arrange visits for people who come to the center.

This interaction with foreign visitors has been very instructive to me and I have learned one big lesson from it, that we have to have new eyes for new experiences. For example, sometimes people visit us expecting a perfect new society, a utopia, and they go away bitterly disappointed. Others come looking for errors, very grave ones; of course, they find them and they say that is the whole revolution, just as they had suspected. It is difficult to come and judge objectively, that is what I mean about new eyes for new experiences. But we work in hope and trust that Christ lives in history, and so we do the best that we can with our flawed reality.

My work has many aspects; another thing that I have done, like thousands of others, is participate in the cotton harvests. Let me tell you that is backbreaking work! The cotton plants when they are ready to harvest have very scratchy stems, plus the cotton sticks to the plant, you stoop over all day in the hot sun because the plants grow in the open fields not the shade, and at the end of the day, because the cotton is so light, you find you have only harvested a few pounds and not all of that is good enough to use.

I felt enormous solidarity with the campesinos who work in the cotton fields, because I have walked in their shoes. I also feel great sympathy with their bitter questions about why their work is exported for such a tiny amount of money. They know that the trade relationship is unjust, anyone can see that we sell cheap and buy dear because the labor of the Third World *no vale*, is not worth anything. It's our sweat, but your cotton shirt. Even so, it was a special experience of sharing; we felt mutual admiration and support for each other. On Sundays we would celebrate a very simple mass with tortillas for bread, so that we would all remember that Christ is there where we work. It is the Christ of the *rostro curtido*, sun-bronzed face; that is not a pretty poem of the *misa campesina*, the country people's mass, but our reality, a real experience for us.

Perhaps the most difficult part of my particular ministry is to accompany the women who have lost their sons in the contra war. When you know that these youths have died in an absurd war because of egoism and lack of love, it's impossible to think of what to say. Low intensity warfare they call it, but it is high intensity anguish in human terms. The mothers ask questions that I simply can not answer. So I just sit there with them, embrace them, listen to them. Who are they in the U.S. government to say that these people must die? The image of Cain springs to my mind, after Cain had killed Abel and the Lord said to him, "What have you done with your brother? His blood cries out to me from the ground."

In all my work, particularly in the Theological Research Program that I now head, the Bible and the life of Christ are our constant points of reference. We look to the Acts of the Apostles to see how the first Christians lived, how they shared everything according to their needs, and how important it is to create a society based on sharing and cooperation. When egoism and injustice seem too much, I reflect on the Psalms, the eighth one for example, which says that only God is our sovereign, that only His reign is righteous, and that He rebukes the mighty "silencing enmity and vengeance." It is a lesson of peace and equality under God.

11   César Isaac Gómez (b. 1923)

". . . Sandinismo and Christianity are very basic because in my life they have come to mean dignity for oneself and love for our brothers and sisters."

This diminutive campesino with the large, weathered hands is an avid reader and a reflective, articulate commentator on any number of subjects, life under the Somozas, the historic influence of U.S. policy in Nicaragua, the legacy of Sandino, and the relationship between Christianity and Sandinismo.

Don César has been a hardware store employee for many years now, though he still misses the countryside and would like to return, except for the ill effects he and his family suffered from the indiscrminate use of pesticides during the Somoza era. Don César is a long-standing member of FUNDECI (Nicaraguan Foundation for Integral Community Development) a Christian base community in León, which he regards as a central influence in his life, and he is greatly inspired by the example of the modern "prophet" and founder of FUNDECI, Nicaraguan Foreign Minister Father Miguel D'Escoto.

I have seen a lot and I have many memories. Most of them are of a suffering people. My country, ever since it was conquered by the Spaniards, has had a bitter, martyred life, because the richness of the earth, gold and minerals, has carried with it disaster, illiteracy, misery.

One of my first memories is when I was about ten, and I was on my way to school one morning, I attended the Christian brothers school in León, run by French and Spanish priests, when suddenly I heard machine gun fire and saw the bullets hit about four meters in front of me. I ran back home terrified. What had happened was that a man who said he was coming to bring peace and democracy, to fight for the Nicaraguan people, had fomented the overthrow of the legitimate President Juan Bautista Sacasa, and that man was Anastasio Somoza García.

As chief of the national guard, Somoza had carried out a *golpe de estado,* a coup. He was Sacasa's subaltern, and they were relatives besides, in that Somoza's wife was related to Sacasa. But to Somoza, the Constitution was not important; family, law, the fact that Sacasa was his superior chief, that Sacasa was the legitimate president, none of these things mattered to him.

My papa was a bricklayer, which in those days meant something, because then they made houses of earth and adobe, not out of concrete blocks. He was very religious, so was my mother; we were eleven children and they taught us all our catechism. We are just four left now, all here in León except for one who is in Bluefields and who, when he was young, joined the guardia nacional. As time went on, and Somoza made other coups against other presidents, especially the one against Leonardo Argüello, my brother renounced his position saying that the true, legitimate government was that of Argüello. But Somoza García, brute that he was, sent word that my brother was a member of the army and that was that, anything else beyond that simple fact was *his* problem. So, he stayed in the guardia, and retired after twenty years. He has spent many years there in Bluefields, but with the bad luck that during the revolution, just for the fact of having been in Somoza's guard, the Sandinistas keep close tabs on him. He receives no pension at all.

Everybody has it tough now though, because we lack everything, even the most fundamental foodstuffs. No, it was not that way when I was young because there were more things to buy and fewer people. I remember in 1936 there were just about one million people, instead of the three million we have now, in spite of the great loss of people during the war. You know that to date 40,000 people have been murdered by the contra, who owe their existence to Mr. Reagan. They estimate also that 50,000 were killed in the revolution, plus another 50,000 that Somoza killed or had killed during his bloody dictatorship. It's terrible.

My mother was a very humble woman from Masaya, and she dedicated herself to the home. There were no centers at that time where one could learn sewing or a trade, and there were eleven children to care for. When she was young she learned how to make cigars, working with her parents and brothers and sisters in that trade. My mama instilled in us a great respect for other people, especially for our elders and for our neighbors. She sent all eleven of us to school; we didn't pay a fee, and the teachers were all foreigners, so I guess their orders maintained them. But it was expensive in that when we were in school we could not help at home. All of us graduated from the sixth grade, that is, we all finished elementary school.

There were some parents who could pay and some who could not, both at my school and at my sisters' school, and you could tell from the way the children dressed who was who. I noticed it at the time, because those who paid had prettier school bags, better supplies, and so on. The Christian brothers had two buildings, the one called San Juan de Dios, and two or three blocks away was another building, where the students had nice uniforms and shoes. It was very clean and they had good food, whereas most of us went to school barefoot and with little to eat. So, yes, we noticed the differences at the time; it is not just something that you think of later. I left those boys alone, but I remember that I had a friend, Ulises, who had a good left hook and he would fight with them. He would take on two or three of them at a time if they made fun of him, and he would make them cry. He was named Ulises like the president of the U.S., Ulysses Grant, no? Now, you don't see things like that much anymore, such a large social division among the students.

I was about thirteen or fourteen when I graduated from the sixth grade. My papa wanted me to be a priest, but I said no, that I wanted to be a carpenter. Then he asked me to be a mason when I said I didn't want to be a priest, but I said no, that I was better at carpentry. So I apprenticed at a big shop near my house. There were two branches of carpentry training: one, where you learn to make furniture and so on, and the other, where they teach you to work wood, and to refine and polish what has already been made. That's what I liked, to finish things, to see furniture with its natural wood grain, not painted, but smooth so you can see the beauty of the grain. I have a big dining room table that I made recently and it is so smooth and shiny that you can see your face in it. Anyway, I learned my trade by the time I was a young teenager, but the problem was that there was no money in it.

I had to look for some other way to make a living. Someone came to me and said that they had a chalk factory, and would I like to learn how to make chalk. Sure, I said. So we went, and I spent a short time there, six months or so. Then, another said to me that there was work on the fincas, and I liked that work very much because it was so beautiful. I regret ever having left now. While I was working on the finca, I went *montaña adentro*, way into the interior.

They were virgin lands then, not like now all spoiled and deforested because of the gringos who have exploited the land. They used many poisons which cause serious sicknesses among the workers. The atmosphere was loaded with chemical substances, and my daughter, for example, has suffered from the aftermath. Lately, I have been reading about how we are destroying the ozone from the atmosphere. There seems to be nowhere to run to escape the utraviolet rays of the sun which come through the holes in the ozone layer and burn us and produce cancer. This is a big issue with me, because I have lived with all those chemicals and my daughter has suffered.

After the finca, I worked for several years out in the country with some relatives, but I knew nothing about farming, and they had to teach me. After a while, I became nostalgic for the city, although as I say, now I am sorry because the countryside is so beautiful, although we have very serious ecological destruction. I returned to León and began working in the shop of a master carpenter.

Then a good man who had a hardware store here asked me to work for him, even though I knew nothing about hardware. He said, "Little by little, you will learn." After I had been there about six months, he said, "Now, what were you talking about, not knowing anything about hardware?" You see, he had workers who had been there three or four years and I already passed them up in how much I knew. Maybe it's because in carpentry there are many tools, and that helped me catch on to the hardware busines. The truth is that I loved it in the hardware store and I stayed there; it's been thirty-three years now, and I'm still there.

I have always loved to read, but undoubtedly the constant dealing with the public has been something that I have learned a great deal from. Because you meet all types in a hardware store, everybody comes there, workers, campesinos, businessmen, students, professional people. That way you learn more about the importance of education and culture, you form relationships with people and talk about things; people come to ask you advice as if you were a technician or a philosopher. And when North Americans come, we always talk about the government, because I want them to think about what their government is doing. We talk and joke also because North Americans are very friendly.

I've been married for thirty years now. I have two grandchildren living at home, and a daughter who is a pharmacist, but with the misfortune that about a month ago they operated on her for a tumor, and now she will be unable to have children. It's been a big blow to all of us. My son Francisco is studying; he is married and has a daughter. All my children are professionals. One of them studied to be a dentist; he graduated six years ago and now is in Moscow on a scholarship doing postgraduate work. First he studied here at the University of León for five years and graduated, and he is still on their faculty. Then he got that graduate scholarship. I have another son who studied electronics and who works in Managua, for himself, on his own. First, he studied a branch of metallurgy; then he took three courses in electricity, and now he can do both. That was very smart because there is a big demand for people with technical skills.

The children who are still at home complain about the problems that we are all going through, the discomfort of not having things we need to eat and to wear, but they are aware of the reason for the Revolution. They are aware that there had to be a change in this country. And we see it concretely, the change that is. For me, the best way is to compare it to when Christ came into the world. The first thing that Christ did when it was time to begin his ministry was to to choose the twelve disciples; he educated them, prepared them, and he told them to go out and teach everyone. Well, the revolution came, the new government, and the first thing they did was to prepare the youth, in the sense of giving them the necessary training in order to teach others, the campesinos, through a massive campaign throughout Nicaragua.

I participated in the crusade here in my house, where they held classes. I even got a certificate of recognition for my participation. I have a library in my house, I have so many books, you can't imagine. Anyway, here is where you note the change, this government is interested in its people having a better culture, in their learning and understanding that we are human beings and not just animals that exist for the benefit of others.

Another change is that for the first time the campesinos are receiving medical attention. Before, there was nothing, and you died. Some people had insurance which the workers, employers, and the state were supposed to pay, but if you went to the clinic they would treat you only up to the amount that had been paid into your insurance. However, the vast majority of people had absolutely no health insurance at all, and doctors' offices were not that crowded. Today, that's not the case. Since there is such a great demand and so few doctors, you spend hours waiting and people get very frustrated. They say things like, "I am not being tended to like I was before," meaning under Somoza. And, sadly, there is practically no medicine to treat people with, so some say that things are worse now. But they forget that now *everyone* is served, at least to the extent of what is available. And we do receive donated medicines from other countries, including the United States.

Many people my age do not agree with me, because they have had more comfortable and easy times than we are experiencing now. For example, I have an older sister who disagrees totally, and I cannot blame her because she had a very nice life before. Her husband had a good economic position because he worked with Somoza, and they did very well. They bought a house, moved downtown, across from the Colegio La Salle; they bought a little vacation house; they had a little farm.They now have very little and are bitter; I don't blame them. I see her almost every day; she helps me buy wheat, eggs, bread, meat, the basic supplies.

I haven't seen my brother on the Atlantic Coast since the revolution, but I don't think that he is in agreement with the Revolution because the military pressures him since he lives so near their quarters. Whenever something happens, they spy on him and put him under suspicion, although I don't know what they think an old man of seventy-five is going to do, especially one who was against Somoza!

Because I am in favor of the revolution, I guess you could say that I am a Sandinista. However, to say you are a Sandinista means also to be aware of the government's social programs. Of course, you've got to realize that they have made their share of mistakes. There are many errors, for example, not punishing those who embezzle public funds. There is entirely too much theft. If they catch someone red-handed the police arrest them, the judge sends them to jail, and in a year or two they are back out on the streets doing the same thing again.

Another error is to temporize too much with regard to our international diplomacy. I prefer that our government either say "yes" or "no," and to remember the 40,000 who have died, not to be so afraid of international governments, especially Mr. Reagan's. We say, "We want to talk with you" over and over again to Mr. Reagan, but he doesn't want to talk with us, and we should stop demeaning ourselves by continually asking. It looks to me that Hitler's spirit has become incarnate in him. When Hitler died in his bunker, his spirit ended up in Hollywood!

I am for the revolution because of a whole series of little awarenesses that I have put together over the years. When they killed Sandino, I was about ten years old. I heard that they killed him *por bandolero,* because he was a bandit who had been attacking the Segovias area. I knew nothing one way or the other about that. But when Somoza García overthrew President Juan Bautista Sacasa, I knew that that was a bad thing. One day I was on my way to school, and in the mud I saw a newspaper, which I picked up and I read. There it said that there had been a coup against Sacasa, actually an uprising of many regiments here and in Managua. Then I thought to myself, here I am in León, and I haven't seen or heard anything. What uprising? The town is peaceful. He came with his troops to attack the barracks, Somoza García did. As head of the guardia nacional, he attacked and that was how it happened. There was no uprising.

I began to analyze the attitude of that man who had killed Sandino. Four, five, six years later there appeared a book put out by Somoza García called *El verdadero Sandino, o el calvario de las Segovias* (The True

Sandino, or the Calvary of the Segovias). I read it, and I thought it was the correct version. Then I read a poem of a poet from León who praised Sandino, calling him the paladin of the Americas, the paladin who was searching for freedom, who set his sword against the invading eagle. I was confused, and the strange thing is that this poet was working for the Somozas. But he was a poet and a lawyer, two very respected professions, and if he writes thus, I thought hmm. . . . Another day, I was passing by the university , which was an old building, not the new ones they have now, and I saw that the students were waving a poster of Sandino and shouting pro-Sandino slogans.

I began to read and try to learn more. I read a book by someone named Ramón Romero, I can't remember the title, but he was a Nicaraguan exiled in Mexico, I was about twenty or so by this time. In that book, he spoke about all of Sandino's actions, but, yes, he spoke well of him. Then I read a book by another Nicaraguan exile in Mexico, whose last name is Torres, there were many exiles in Mexico at that time. Of course, these books did not circulate, and that also caught my attention, because Somoza always claimed to be democratic. So, why can't these books come here, I wondered. Why, when people wrote certain favorable things about Sandino in the newspapers were they then taken prisoner? With my readings and reflections, gradually I came to understand Sandino's revolutionary conscience.

There is something else that I remember very well. There was a lieutenant in the guardia, one Abelardo Cuadra, was in the Campo del Mártir garrison. He was young, this was in about '33 or '34, and he rose up against another national guard chief, Anastasio Somoza García himself. This is how it went. Sacasa's government was in a very bad economic situation, and they were trying to figure a way out of their fiscal problems. But Sacasa told Somoza to pay the army, that they had to have a salary, even if it was reduced. At that time soldiers got about twelve córdobas per month, and Sacasa suggested that they be given at least eight, so that they could have something. What happened was that the enlisted men, all those without rank, suffered a greater reduction than the others, and they became rebellious.

At that point, their leader and representative, Lt. Abelardo Cuadra, went to talk to Somoza to ask that the soldiers' salaries not be reduced so drastically. Somoza asked him what he suggested, and Cuadra said to reduce the salaries of high-ranking officers, giving the money instead to the enlisted men. "We'll see," said Somoza, "You go figure it all out and put it in writing for me."

So Abelardo comes back with the figures, saying, "The first one whose salary should be cut is yourself", he says this to Somoza, "because you have the largest salary." What a brave man Abelardo was! Somoza didn't like it one bit. Then Cuadra became involved in the barracks conspiracy against Somoza, but someone denounced him, there's always someone who will do that, and all those who were involved were caught, and many, including Cuadra, were killed. He was the only one that I knew, but there were about sixty in all who died. This was the beginning of Somoza García's dictatorship, in '34. Our current government, I have sympathy with them, because I remember what Sandino wanted, how he was calumnied, and how terrible the dictatorship was.

I see Sandino as an idol, and there are many who think as I do, of course. You realize that by '79 nearly everyone wanted to do away with the dictatorship, but many people did not really desire a revolution; they just wanted to get rid of Somoza. Instead, what we got is a radical change, complete, in spite of so many disasters. It's true that I read a lot, and that I always have, but I am not atypical except for that. I wish my kids read, but they don't; and I don't have much time to read now because I have my little grandchild who takes much attention.

That's another thing I was going to mention when we were talking about changes, that the primary educational program is totally different now. Our little second-grader is learning more than we learned in the old system. It seems that they have invested much in improving primary education, because they learn things in reading and math for example, that used to be taught in secondary school. The readings in the second grade text are short, but they are very challenging for the children. In fact, they are difficult, and I have to pressure my grandson to do his homework; he doesn't really like school very much. But I can see that the education is much better than before, and I believe too that his future will be much brighter because he will be better educated. If you are educated, you can stand up better for yourself in the world. What I think is that we Nicaraguans will never have much money; I don't see that we will have more than just the minimum to get along, in a material sense. We will continue to be poor, but we will have our happiness and peace of mind, and that is the main thing.

The new texts have a Sandinista content, for example, readings describing who Sandino or Carlos Fonseca were, but that is a good thing. I have been told that there is a communist content, but I don't know. I believe that there is a similarity between Sandinismo and what Christ said, that we must always try to love each other and to help our neighbors in their difficulties. Sandinismo speaks of this a great deal. I don't know much about communism, isn't there love in it? I thought that Gorbachev preaches brotherhood, peace, and peaceful coexistence. If he means what he says on TV, then he is in line with what we believe.

Sandinismo and Christianity come together for me, but as I mentioned earlier, everything has come through gradual realizations, including the Christian aspect, which took longer because of the way wc were brought up in the church in my days. At the Christian brothers school, in addition to the usual academic subjects, we also received religious instruction. I think that it harmed me, not with regard to my faith in Christ, but in that it made me see things through the eyes of fear, purgatory, hell, fire, and punishment. We had to be on our knees at mass practically all the time. They had a whole catalog of terrors that they inspired in us. They emphasized hell and not heaven, and it made me very timid. I went to mass every Sunday, scared to death, but I went because the padre told me to and that was enough for me; I was very obedient.

Now, it's all different. But in the morning there was the *misa solemne*, high mass. In the afternoon, another religious ceremony, I can't remember how it was called now. But it was all sin and punishment, and for many years, it struck fear in my heart. When I was a boy, they sent me to catechism classes at the parish church. In the sacristy there was a huge book that attracted my attention, and I started reading it. The priest entered and shouted at me, "Child, what are you doing with that book! That is forbidden for you!" He grabbed it away from me, it was the Bible. "You are incapable of interpreting this", he told me, and I was shocked by that. Then he made me go in the church and pray for forgiveness for that sin. But I also noticed that in another type of Christianity people were going around with their Bible and preaching in the street. I wondered at the contradiction and why it was all right for some to read the Bible, but not others.

When I got married, I started to go to church less and less; I always kept my faith in Christ, but I didn't go to church. Then someone came into my life at an opportune moment, and I consider him a prophet, Father Miguel D'Escoto. He came to León to create FUNDECI as a manifestation of his Christian faith. It was founded in 1973, after the earthquake, as a non-profit organization supported by wealthy and respected Nicaraguans, including Father D'Escoto and his family, to provide low-income housingfor the poor. But, equally important, Father D'Escoto envisioned FUNDECI as a model community whose members would be committed to the common good and would live simply but with dignity. In fact, we are committed to developing ourselves in our Christian faith through worship and Bible study sessions, and to practicing our faith by the way we live with others.

For me, considering my previous negative experiences, Father D'Escoto came as a prophet of a different kind of religion. This was more than twelve years ago, and since that time my life has been very different. It is more integrated than before because my religious beliefs have been strengthened in a positive way. To me then, Sandinismo and Christianity are very basic because in my life they have come to mean dignity for oneself and love for our brothers and sisters.

12 Juvencio Salgado Rocha (b. 1963)

"I saw how necessary it was to educate the campesino. . . . Helping them has been my goal ever since I was in elementary school. . . ."

"I am educated but I am still a campesino."

The care with which he treats his sharpened pencil and his neatly organized folder suggests immediately the seriousness with which this slender young campesino regards both his studies and his educational mission. Juvencio Salgado began his vocation as a volunteer teacher in the famous literacy crusade of 1980, after which he taught in the follow-up program over the succeeding four years. In the process, he postponed his own secondary education, while at the same time strengthening his commitment to education for himself as the way to help other campesinos. For Juvencio, "education and religion have worked together," in teaching rural adults, in serving as a delegate of the word in his Christian base community, and in choosing his course of study at the prepa, *the secondary preparatory school in León, where he is now a scholarship student.*

I live in the second region, in the town of Achoapa. I was given a scholarship to come here to León. I come from a campesino family; my father works the land. When I was about eleven I began working with him, planting corn, wheat, beans. I started elementary school at the age of twelve because my parents could not send me earlier. I went to the Colegio San Nicolás, and I graduated from the sixth grade.

Afterwards, I saw that in the countryside there was no chance to go to secondary school. In the country we had no means to develop ourselves, to prepare ourselves to help others, no center to meet and study, nothing. But I loved school and felt that I had to continue studying, that somehow, someday I must continue. That thought was my guiding star, because I was determined to develop myself. As you can see, here I am finally at the *prepa*, the preparatory school, having received a scholarship from my local district. But before getting this scholarship I spent a long lapse of time unable to go on from primary school. At twenty-four, I am older than the average high school student. Then the war came, and I was stuck, because all plans came to a halt. Then came the liberation and the literacy crusade in '80.

After my work in the crusade, I applied for and received the scholarship to come here and study for the *bachillerato*, the high school degree. I am a third and fourth year student, and I need the fifth and sixth years in order to graduate. The reason I say that I am a third and fourth year student is that I am in the accelerated degree program and I do two years' work in one. It is extremely difficult, but I am a serious student. If you're not very dedicated, you do not pass your exams, and then someone else gets your scholarship. There are so many people who want to study and funds are so limited that we have to do accelerated studies and maintain very high marks in order to retain our scholarships.

I'm studying math; chemistry; national geography, (I already took world geography); Spanish, psychology; and physical education. I like math the best. I wanted to specialize in it but I see a bigger need for Spanish, and I'm right now trying to decide between the two. I believe that I should choose to study a subject in which there is great need, in which I can be of service to the people. I know there is a need for math too, and I enjoy it the most of all my subjects. I can specialize in both math and Spanish; it would be very demanding, but it's possible. In the countryside we need spelling, writing, reading, help in forming letters, help in everything regarding language skills.

After the prepa, from which I hope to receive the bachillerato in three years since that is the time period of my scholarship, those of us in this program will go to the university. That is still like a dream to me. We can study medicine, odontology, Spanish, math, whatever. I'm still trying to decide between the first two; it is on my mind these days. I would like to stay here and go to the university in León so I wouldn't have to be any further away from my family than I am already.

My family has little education, being campesinos. They all have about five or six years of schooling; none have been to secondary school. What was my inspiration to continue? I saw how necessary it was to educate the campesino. You simply can't imagine how forgotten they have been for so long, left in complete ignorance. Helping them has been my goal ever since I was in elementary school, even though for years I couldn't do anything about it. But I kept the spark alive; that was the important thing, to keep that hope going, or else I would never have come this far.

My brothers and sisters, as I said, have little education. There are ten of us, six girls and four boys. They're scattered all over the country now because my sisters married people from other regions and went to live near their husbands' families. Only one still lives at home, my youngest sister, who is seventeen years old. I am the youngest son. My brothers work in different things, but mostly they work the land in other districts. One brother works in a match box factory, where he also loads trucks; then he makes deliveries to general stores in different regions all over the country. He belongs to a union, which is a good benefit for him, but I don't know how it works. That brother is the only laborer, and I am the only student.

All the others work the land, because my sisters all married campesinos too. All my family loves the land, and I do too; I spend all my vacations with my family on their little farm. I always wait until the day before classes start to come back here. My family is very proud of me, and my parents have put their hope in me. It's a big responsibility, but I have never had any fear or doubt about whether I can do it, or about whether to continue studying because classes are difficult, or anything like that. I just know that I must develop myself and that I have to succeed, come what may. One must always have a strong resolution to get anywhere in life.

There are both external and internal students at the prepa, which is also coed. I am an internal student, because I live too far away to commute. I eat and sleep at the school, and the scholarship covers everything for three years. That's why I'm in the accelerated program; it's double the work, but it's the only way. I have to keep my grades up and not get behind because of other activities, such as working in the fields planting corn, and so on. I should say that in spite of the fact that we are students, we also have to plant and to harvest to help out our families. Sometimes we get behind because of these responsibilities, and we are evaluated. For example, if a student works too hard in the planting, he or she will be given a make-up exam after having a chance to study more. Obviously, the need to produce food is great so that the people can eat, especially now when everything is so scarce. But if a student does poorly just because he or she went to the movies, then no, they take the scholarship away. There are many scholarship students at the prepa. Let's see, there are 300 scholarship students, and a total enrollment of about 800 in the school, so that is a considerable number of scholarship students like myself.

I have worked out a very disciplined study program for myself. My usual day is like this: from 1:00 to 6:00 p.m. I have class; then I eat dinner; and then from 7:00 to 11:30 p.m. I study on my own, dividing my study time very systematically in order to get everything done. There are forty of us in each room, so it is often difficult to study there. I have to get away from the conversation and the music, so I go off on my own. My teachers are all excellent; they care so much about the students, and they are all there to help us pass the courses. They really don't want us to go wandering around the street or fooling around doing nothing, but to work so that we will all pass. For example, right now we are in the exam period, and the teachers are working especially hard, in and outside of class trying to give us extra help. They are all lay Christians, very dedicated to their teaching and their students. Everyone works so hard here and the teachers are so supportive that about 95 percent pass their exams, sooner or later and often with lots of outside help and special schedules to take into account planting time, but they pass.

The material resources for the students, well, they are very limited and we lack many things, even basic things. Our economic situation in this country is terrible, desperate really, owing to very concrete circumstances, the contra war in particular, and we understand that. We have very little in the way of books, especially chemistry books. We are fortunate to have a chemistry lab, but we have no books. And in math, at least we have a small library we can use, because we don't have enough books for each student to have one. So we have to do research and go to the library, taking turns using the copies there, which takes up a lot of time. The lack of basic materials is a serious disadvantage for the students and the teachers.

Another problem that interferes with our studies is the planting that we have to do. We have about two hours almost daily for "family duties" as we call them. We know that we must do these duties, but the student feels pulled in two directions. The need to help out in the fields is great and the need to study is great too, so it is a dilemma that we face all the time, and we have to do the best we can in both things.

I want to tell you a little about my work in the literacy campaign, which was a very moving and inspiring experience for me. I began helping when I was about seventeen, during those four or five months in '80 when the campaign was all over the country. Of course, that period of classes was very intense and concentrated, and it was not sufficient for adults. Still, it was thrilling to be able to teach campesinos their ABC's and how to make their first letters. After the compañeros *alfabetizadores*, the teachers with some training, went back to their homes, usually in the city, we assumed their roles in a way. We formed *brigadas de seguimiento,* follow-up brigades, and we kept on functioning just like they had done, only we stayed in our own local areas. There were workshops given for us periodically as well, so that we might receive instruction in how to teach others. All through 1980 we did this, and we used materials provided by the campaign itself.

In the beginning I felt very uneasy, being younger and giving classes to older people. But after two or three times, I became adapted to adults, and they to me. I worked better and more comfortably when I saw the confidence and trust that they put in me. It moved me deeply. I met every single day with these *compañeros,* who would all come to their neighbors' houses for class no matter how tired they were, and that gave me strength. The schedule was from 4:00 to 6:00 p.m., because that way the campesinos could work the land during the day, rest a little and then go to classes. So that's the way I worked until '84, for four years. The follow-up program still continues, but I can no longer participate in it because of my studies.

In my case, what I tried to do was to prepare the best students to take my place if I couldn't continue classes for some reason. I trained a series of campesinos that way, and in fact, my former students came to staff the programs in many different districts, where they in turn would teach others, who would go out and prepare more and more people, and so on. No longer did we sit and wait for people from the urban zones to come and teach us, but rather now we were teaching *ourselves,* providing our own impetus and continuation.

A very important change had taken place in me by '83, by then I had gradually developed a firm Christian conviction about myself and my role in our society. I continued giving my classes, of course, and then afterwards I would visit the churches. Little by little, I found a group of Christian brothers and sisters with whom I felt very comfortable and had much in common. I would tend to my work in the various sectors, for I had to go from village to village in my general area, and then I would go to Bible study in the evenings. As I continued teaching and reflecting on the Word, it became clear to me that the duty of the Christian is to take God's message to all our people. At the beginning, as a campesino teacher, I just taught my classes, and I did not think of religion as being a part of a whole series of things. But after I saw how important religion was in the daily lives of the people I taught, and after I started visiting churches and church group meetings, I saw how important religion was to me too.

I also learned how much happiness faith can bring, being with people who believe in what you are doing and who see Christianity as a joyful way to live. For example, they loaned me a guitar and taught me how to play. Now, I have my own guitar and I sing and play during our worship services here at FUNDECI, the base community here where the Maryknoll sisters work. In fact, my role is very important, and they have come to depend on my singing and my playing. All this is a very emotional and beautiful experience for me. I get together with the sisters every Friday for our base community meetings. On Sundays a priest comes from the parish of León, and maybe 60 percent of the community shows up. For our Friday services fewer attend, but those who come are very faithful and active. This is a community for the very poorest families, and their housing is provided by MINVAH, the Housing Ministry.

Soon after I became involved in the activities here at FUNDECI, I began preparing myself further through training workshops with the village priest. Then I became a *delegado de la palabra,* a delegate of the word, with specific religious responsibilities in the community. Delegates of the word do different things, some help give catechism, others help instruct couples before marriage or before baptism, and still others celebrate the word of God as lay readers, which is what I do. Where did the inspiration come from to be a delegate of the word? I started going to the services just to go, to see what it was like, something to do. But a Christian conscience began forming within me. I was seeing; I was liking; I was being inspired by others; and I was touched by the happy fellowship. All these things nourished my religious vision, which started out as mere curiousity. After I became a delegate, I had two functions: one religious and one educational. By 1983–84, they were coming into conflict, plus I still had to help tend to the planting. I had too much to do, and I knew that something would have to go, but I did not want to make any choices.

Finally, by '84 I had rethought my priorities to some extent, and I made my decision to quit teaching. I had already formed new teaching brigades, as I mentioned earlier, to help replace me in the various villages where I had been working. I myself trained the compañeros who took over after I left. Between '84 and '85, I worked as a delegate and did agricultural work for my family. I worked that whole year tending to the twenty-five communities nearest to where I live. I would visit in the evenings; we would do celebrations of the word; we would reflect on the meaning to us of what we had read; we would sing; and we would enjoy being together for that while. The next day, everyone would go back to their normal activities.

I spent a year completely devoted to this; and in '85 I continued working in the same way, but not with as many communities. I used here the same methods that I had used in teaching, some of which I learned in workshops and some of which I figured out for myself. That's one of the many ways that education and religion have worked together for me. I think perhaps for others too, since delegates of the word and teachers of campesinos are sometimes the same people, because they can read. Even though I did these things throughout '85, I still held to my vision of continuing my own education someday.

In '86, after a long lapse in my formal education, my dream finally came true. I found out about the scholarship from my district and I applied. But just because I can now study does not mean that I have abandoned my commitments in my zone, no; I feel very proud that I have left a whole series of good teachers who I prepared over a period of years. I am educated, but I am still a campesino. The rural areas are of great importance to me, and I would never abandon them. That's why I say I support the revolutionary government, because it has concerned itself very greatly with the zones which in our country historically have been completely abandoned and ignored.

My family and I are from these forgotten places. We and others in the countryside see for ourselves the improvement projects that have been implemented; we know that the government is responsible and that these are positive things. What we are seeing is not just talk or promises, but theory put into practice. I see that the government is trying in a true way to share what there is with the campesino zones. Sandinismo is part of this. To me, it means following the ideas of Sandino, who fought for the freedom of our pueblo, including those who have always been the most left out. My family all feels the same way, but many of my friends' families are of a different opinion. We are positive because we see a development in comparison with the past, and we see a future for people who had nothing before.

My educational goals predate the revolution, but they are now furthered by it, and they are in harmony with national goals too. I have not done military service yet, and I am still in the seventeen to twenty-five age group; my case is now pending. You see, I received an extension because of my teaching work, and later, because of my studies. But I have to comply when the government calls. I do not see it as a heavy obligation, but as a just law for the defense of our country. If we don't defend our own pueblo, who will?

My friends who have done their service tell me of many experiences. Those that go to the city say that life there is hard to get used to because it is so different from life in the country. Others have had to go to the montaña, by which we mean very remote, rainy, swampy places with many mosquitos, illnesses, and hardships. These friends experienced a total change, but they have told me that they don't feel completely bad as long as they look at it as another experience in life. None of my friends feel bitter or angry about it; they simply see it as something they had to do and they did. Some even feel proud, and say that they would do it again, but I don't know how serious they are.

They all said that the most positive aspect was meeting people from other zones. Otherwise, they could go all their lives just living in our district and never knowing what people from other regions were like or how they lived, such as the people on the East Coast for example, who are so different from us. But they also got very homesick for their families and their villages. Most got permission to visit their families after six months, but that is a long time to wait. With regard to visits by mothers, however, there is no restriction at all. Mothers can come and visit any time. Because it is difficult to travel to the remote areas, there are mothers' committees that have formed in the different towns to transport mothers and help them make travel arrangements. These mothers then bring mail and messages for whole groups of people. They help others keep in touch with their families at the same time that they are visiting their own sons. These visits and mail deliveries help to keep up morale.

There are also a lot of deserters. Many don't like the zone that they have been sent to. Either it is too different from what they are familiar with, too hard to find food or to keep from getting sick, or it is too dangerous. I don't think most people desert for any political reasons or convictions, but rather because they are too far from home and maybe food supplies and conditions are bad. They remember how comfortable and happy they were at home, and they say, *"Bueno, me voy,"* ("Well, I'm leaving.") They are easy to find because usually they return to their homes. Some are sanctioned by an existing law, for between two and six months. Others are sent back right away to do their service. Sanctions usually involve not being able to go out for diversions, being assigned to do social work for very long hours, and then being sent back to do service. The months of sanction, however, do not count toward the two years; they are extra.

In my school, I belong to the Juventud Sandinista, (Sandinista Youth), a national student group that primarily sponsors political and community activities. It's completely voluntary; some people have no interest at all or no time, and that's fine. They don't have to pressure anyone to join, because usually people see how much others get out of the organization and they want to join too. That's the way it was with me. I saw what a good time my friends had at the meetings, how they talked about worthwhile topics, how they helped out in social and community projects, and so I wanted to become a part of such a group. There are three levels of membership: aspirant, member, and militant. In the first, you think that you may want to become more involved but you are not sure. You go to the general meetings, the *asambleas de base*; you help out with tasks such as school clean-up programs; and you wait for a period of time before applying to become a member. I am a member; that's my level of participation. The third step of militant is for those who are very active, and it is quite an accomplishment to reach that level.

I didn't join the revolution or participate directly in it. I wish I had, but I was very young, only sixteen. Still, I wish that I had. Another thing that I wish I had done is participate in the various mobilizations, like for the coffee, sugar cane, or cotton harvests. But, I was usually in classes, and they were a big commitment for me. But I feel like I should have participated in the mobilizations. I do volunteer now with student battalions, usually in December for the coffee harvest, and for some of the sugar cane harvest, but that goes on much longer.

Everyone has to work very hard because the country is so poor. For example, it bothers me that in some areas the rural health centers have not been built, and that in others they have not been maintained. I also feel sad when I see the lack of training of some of our health workers, or when I see that the campesino has to walk to a town 10 to 20 kilometers away just to get basic medical help. But I see that these flaws have a cause besides our poverty, and that is the scarcity, for which the contra war is responsible. I see the lack, but I also see the problem that causes it.

I also know how bad things used to be. I am not too young to remember the great fear that everyone had of Somoza's guardia. For example, they would pick up a drunk, beat him, keep him prisoner many months when he couldn't pay lots of money to get out, and they would not allow him to have a lawyer. I remember these things personally because I saw them, and you don't forget things like that. So, although times are very hard now, especially because many people are hungry, they used to be worse.

Everyone works two or three jobs. I principally study, but I also work in the planting, in the Juventud, and in the base community. Yesterday I took my last exam, so I don't have to go and study right now. But classes go on; we have no break at this time. The school year is divided into two semesters, April through July, and August through November. That leaves December through March as vacation months. I love the *prepa*, my studies, and my religious responsibilities. I look forward to receiving my high school degree, after these years of effort and waiting. My teachers are all about twenty-eight or thirty years old, and we get along very well together. I am very fortunate.

13 Oswaldo Mondragón (b. 1936)

". . . they [the Sandinistas] really are out to get me . . . there have even been attempts to poison the communion wine!"

". . . if it weren't for the contra, . . . we two would not be talking. Perhaps we would not even be alive."

His hands shook uncontrollably as with great difficulty he lighted the first of countless cigarettes and in a hoarse whisper asked me to record our conversation by battery power, to avoid the risk of electrocution by Sandinista spies! Rector of the Seminario Menor on the outskirts of Managua, confidant of Cardinal Miguel Obando y Bravo, bitter enemy of the government, and acrimonious foe of the popular church, Monsignor Mondragón has placed himself at the center of religious and political controversy.

This ardent anti-Sandinista and zealous defender of ultraconservative Catholicism was once an active opponent of Somoza and a socially progressive priest. What had happened to bring about such a reversal? The answer emerged as a strange combination of Father Mondragón's own personal development and various external circumstances, especially the the growing "threats" of Marxism and of liberation theology.

Monsignor Mondragón relates here the story of his childhood in Granada; his studies at the national seminary and in Mexico and Chile; his work as a priest; his wholehearted embrace of United States policy in Nicaragua; and, with unrestrained emotion, his peculiar perspective on his encounters with government security.

I am from the city of Granada. My father was Francisco Mondragón and my mother Mercedes Mondragón; they were relatives, second cousins, and had to get a dispensation from the bishop to get married. My family is from a long Conservative tradition. My grandparents were *ganaderos*, ranchers, and my paternal grandfather was an important figure in Conservative politics in the times of don Diego Manuel Chamorro. He was a national deputy, a senator of the republic, and he had a newspaper that was of local importance in Granada, called *El Censor*. The Universidad Católica has it on microfilm; there was a time when it was easy to do that sort of thing. Our family was anti-Liberal, Somoza was a Liberal, so we were anti-Somoza.

By the time I was born, my parents were no longer in the cattle business. They had fallen on hard times and my father went to find work at the San Antonio sugar plantation which was owned by a family from Granada and was the largest in Central America at that time. He got a good job there because my father was very competent, cultured, had many friends, and was an avid reader. He later became a military man, working in the military school, where he was trained by North Americans and Germans. I always wanted to be like him, but I never achieved that goal.

We were four children, two boys and two girls. One sister, Melba, was married but her husband, a pilot, died seven months ago because of this Sandinista war, leaving her with three children. Here is a picture of my niece. And my brother has the most perfect marriage in the world. They have a young son, just one. I don't have a picture of him, but I think I have a picture of my other nephews, somewhere. Here is my mother when she was young, she was beautiful; she looks like a Hollywood star, no? My mother sang very beautifully; she sang in church, and she worked a lot in the church. She also was an elementary school teacher in a Catholic school. Her belief was that you never beat or shouted at a child, but that you had to treat them with much love. I remember that she always danced with the children. Later, she was a trainer of teachers. Yes, she sounds like Gabriela Mistral, whose works she read.

My education was Catholic. I was educated in primary school by the Salesian brothers, where I had a teacher who was still only a priest but who everyone loved dearly, none other than Miguel Obando y Bravo! He was an excellent teacher; he knew all the Greek classics by memory, and he told them to us in story form. Everyone always wanted to have class with him, and we would shout out to him "Tell us the story of Ulysses!" For us, it was the best movie in the world to listen to Obando. He was very *nítido*, crisp in every detail, his speech, his person, the way he dressed, everything.

When I finished primary school in Granada, I entered the seminary here in Managua. I think that the city of Granada thought that we could afford the tuition. But four friends of my mother decided to pay for my way. They also helped me with my expenses, but all so quietly, absolutely in secret, so that when my mother would come to visit me with presents, I thought that they were from her. Financially, my parents were strapped by then; that's when my mother had to work as a teacher.

The seminary was very strict. It was run by Spanish priests from Avila, but I remember them and, above all, the course of study with great affection. It was an excellent program, far superior to other secondary curricula, which was of very high quality generally in those days. I remember after I had graduated my friends were open-mouthed in awe at what I had studied, Latin, Greek, world literature, Latin American literature, Nicaraguan literature, art history; I loved studying art. We read the Spanish and English classics, Cervantes and Shakespeare, everything; I read about four different translations of *Hamlet*. We studied theater as well; that was my best subject along with soccer. In sum, it was a classical humanistic seminary. I entered when I was about sixteen, and stayed until I was about twenty-two, six years.

Then I went on to study philosophy, also at the seminary. The texts were all in Latin, the classes in Latin, and we did all our work in Latin. I used to speak Latin fluently. We were all very familiar with Virgil, Cicero, Horace, in the original language. Today I can't do that. It was wonderful how in classical times they believed in leisure, which they dedicated to the arts and things of the spirit. We also studied Spanish in depth, subjects such as *elocuencia*, or eloquence, and also music; I used to play Schubert's serenade by heart, but now I have forgotten it all. In philosophy, I didn't like logic, but I was fascinated by metaphysics, morals and ethics.

We also had chemistry and physics; we took twice the number of classes in the sciences that they had on the outside, that is, in the secular secondary schools. We even had a laboratory, which was unbelievably advanced in those days. Everything was very theoretical then in all the other schools, but we had a laboratory because we had a priest who was a chemist whose passion was chemistry. These priests were *full-time* teachers, just for the seminary; that too was practically unheard of.

Afterwards, in 1958, I finished that course of study, and I left; I was very unsettled because of the student movement in León. That's where there was an infamous student massacre, and I got involved in some of those riots. Then I went back to my city, and felt that as a Christian I had to be for justice, right? So I, along with a group of other young people, confronted Somoza's guardia. We threw stones and bottles, and in that demonstration they beat me badly and split my head open; I have a scar that covers my head that the guardia gave me with their rifle blows. After I got out of the hospital, my friends gave me a party, and I felt very proud.

"Well," the bishop said, "you certainly have your ups and downs, but I think you have a vocation for the priesthood. Let's wait and see." One day we sat down to talk and he asked me, "Have you forgotten your vocation?" "No, I have always remembered it and I want to be a priest; I just took advantange of the time that I was out to study typing, some practical things." I had been out for about a year during the time of the massacre. Then he said to me: "I don't see any problem." This was Monsignor García Suárez, bishop of Granada. I don't think that people understood him. He was thought to be very hard, rigid, and conservative, but he understood me well and he liked me. You can't categorize a person in two words, can you? The person is something more than the word. "All the crazy things that you have done as a youth, I understand them," he said. I was very surprised. He had founded a prestigious colegio, or secondary school, in Managua, the Rubén Darío, and he taught literature classes up until the last day of his life. He was very given to writing. He told me "When you are older, you will be much more balanced. If you want to become a priest, you have my support."

Then he sent me to Mexico to study theology, but in Mexico they made me take another year of philosophy, for review. So I reviewed philosophy for a year, and then I began my studies in theology. There I stayed from the end of 1959 until 1963 or '64, in Mexico City, in the famous Seminario Conciliar of the diocese. That was a time of equilibrium for me; I loved the Mexicans and they were crazy about me. I loved the celebrations of Christmas, the Virgin of Guadalupe, and Mexican food. At that time, my studies were going well and I was making good grades; I think I was the best student there with the best grades. But I still was not sure of my vocation.

I am going to take you into my very personal confidence: I went to pray to the Virgin of Guadalupe and ask her please to beg God that I not lose the vocation, because right then I did not feel like I had it; I had the desire to quit. I had doubts about whether I could be a good priest. But it seems that the Virgin of Guadalupe did not beg to God, or else she made a pact with Him, and I left the seminary. I remember that I cried and I said to the Virgin, "Why am I leaving?" At the moment that I was leaving the seminary, my friends sang to me in Latin, and I was carried away with emotion.

Now I understand why I left in 1964. It was because 1965 is considered the year of the beginning of the crisis of the priesthood in Latin America. You know, it was between '65 and '75 that we had all the trouble with the communist priests, seminaries in confusion, all that error, a complete identity crisis. Now I understand it all and give thanks to God that I left when I did. I returned to Nicaragua and joined the Christian Democratic Youth at the national university, UNAN, where I was a militant, or extremely active, member. The party was new and small, but I liked it because it had very honest founders and very honest school companions too.

During the administration of Eduardo Frei in Chile, I received a scholarship to go to Chile, where I studied during 1966. There I saw the beginning of the *iglesia popular*, or popular church, that during all this decade we have been plagued with here. Christians for socialism it was called then. Also in Chile I enlarged my Christian social conscience with a political commitment. But my philosophical and theological background helped me not to fall into extremes, although I was tempted to at times. The temptation of Marxism came to all of us youth in those days.

Our course of study was excellent. We were twenty-five Latin Americans, of whom *ten* later became guerrilla fighters, and one of whom was my companion Rubén Zamora. He now is the public relations person for the FMLN in Salvador. He is a very famous man; he is also an ex-seminiarian, and ex-student of this Chilean religious institute, in Santiago, called ORMEU, Coordinating Office for University Student Movements (Oficina Relacionadora de Movimientos Estudiantiles Universitarios) for Latin America. Our professors were from other Chilean institutions, such as the Instituto Pedagógico and the Universidad Católica. There I had the opportunity to be the student of Paulo Freire for one year; he was in exile from Brazil. I adored him. There were two other exiles, Pablo de Tarso, and I can't remember the other one's name. But this exposure gave me a new sensibility, a new horizon and a new enthusiasm for the poor. I think that Paulo Freire taught me more than I learned that whole year in Chile. His seemed to me to be a valid liberation theology, one that I could be dedicated to. If that's leftist, I said to myself, then I'm a leftist, because it is beautiful, to the point of giving one's life for one's brother, like Jesus said. It seemed to me an authentic actualization of God's message.

On my return to Nicaragua, I participated very actively until 1970 in the Social Christian party in Managua, including working in the party's central executive office in '67. In '70 I entered the Central American University, or UCA, in philosophy, and finished my degree in Arts and Letters there. Meanwhile, I also gave classes at the secondary level in Spanish, literature and philosophy, at that time they taught philosophy at that level. Beginning in 1970 when I entered UCA, I came under the influence of a very powerful figure, a Jesuit and a Basque named Santiago de Anítua. He had degrees in theology and philosophy, and was a superb writer. I remember, in the beginning of '74, he made fun of the charismatics, saying "We've got some crazies speaking in tongues; let's study this new witchcraft, what do you say?" Well', we did, and do you know what happened? We became charismatics!

Under the spell of that new fervor, I went to see Msgr. Obando and

Msgr. Bosco Vivas and told them that I would like to be ordained a priest. It was a difficult decision for me to make; this is a long involved story, but basically I told Obando that I did not think that I was looking for a lost paradise, and he helped me as always. He advised, "Lets let things ride for a while. Why don't you take a doctorate in philosophy in Germany? Why don't you go and register for that program?" I registered, but then I spoke again with Obando and Bosco, and decided not to go to the classes in Germany. I went instead to the seminary to live and to give classes. I was ordained August 15, 1975. Msgr. Obando ordained me in the chapel of the seminary. From then until the end of '78 I gave philosophy classes at the seminary, but then Msgr. Obando founded this minor seminary and we came here, where now I am rector. Before, I was vice-rector, because Bishop Bosco was rector.

During the war I had high hopes for the Frente Sandinista because I thought that things would be better for the poor. I did not join the revolution, but I helped them, including hiding muchachos here. When we, that is priests like myself, were in the Cruzada de Alfabetización, the Literacy Crusade, that was crucial for us. I remember that Paulo Freire came to visit Nicaragua, and he left saying this: *"Voy con esperanza,"* ("I'm going with hope.") But I said to myself, Paulo Freire is not convinced, because to say I am going with hope, well a Christian never loses hope, so that is not saying much. That was a blow for me. I saw him, I greeted him. I found him much older, pale, and he became very emotional when he saw me. Then Obando said, "Literacy, yes, we will support it, but ideologization, no, nor massification."

When Comandante Bayardo Arce spoke, it was to call the campaign "the biggest political seminar that has ever been held in Nicaragua." So there you see there were two intentions, or perhaps just one intention, to educate as a pretext for politicizing in just one way. That worried us. Nevertheless, we had a mass for the Catholic literacy teachers when they returned, and Tomás Borge attended. Then there was a minor disturbance by the popular church, and they were not respectul of the then Archbishop Obando. I personally stayed right beside him as bodyguard in case anything happened. It was very tense and a few people were hassled. It was the first brush with danger. We do not have Obando y Bravo for such things as this! We also thought it was no way to treat a man who had been so distinguished in the struggle against Somoza; he saved many people's lives, you know.

They even said in the newspaper that they found photos of us with Somoza. They found a picture of me with Somoza. One had no way of defending oneself. I sent a letter but they didn't publish it. I tried to explain that that picture had been taken the year before when I had gone as an envoy of Obando, with a private letter, to try to intercede on behalf of

Tomás Borge who was being held prisoner by Somoza. I saw the Minister of Government (Ministro de la Gobernación) as it was called at that time, Antonio Mora, and then the chief of the staff of the national guard, José Somoza, the brother of Tacho, asking them to safeguard the integrity of Tomás Borge, which they granted. But anyway, that's how things started, my first brushes with the Sandinista government.

In the beginning I went to many Sandinista meetings in my neighborhood, and I spoke well of the revolution. But I think that in a revolution all is possible if it is guided by love and if one does not lose one's critical capacity. I told this to the people, and to the popular church that was forming at that time, between '79 and '80. Father Uriel Molina, the leader of the popular church, at the end of '79 said, "Obando has ceased being one of us. He is no longer to be trusted, but he can still be rescued." You can see that their plan was different from the beginning.

At the end of the first year of the revolution, July 19, 1980, Fidel Castro came here for the anniversary celebration. They invited me to come and hear Fidel, and to enter into dialogue with him. So I went, and I greeted Fidel, and I thought that he was one of the most intelligent men that I had ever met in my life. What's more, he was a very charismatic leader, very *simpático*. That does not mean that I am in agreement with him, on the contrary. In fact, I don't know what came over me there. I said to myself, "This man is very *vivo*, dynamic, but he is talking communism and totalitarianism. Those people present, nuns and Protestant pastors among others, are delivered over to communism; this is not dialogue, this is not to trying to find common goals." There's a phrase, I don't know if I invented it or the community or what, "The only dialogue with the Marxists is total surrender." And that's what the group was engaging in, total surrender, just saying yes to everything without any critical capacity. I couldn't do that, so I denounced the meeting, I couldn't help it.

Then there came a time when they had more security agents on my case to record me. In a show of support, Obando suggested that I be given the title of Canon of the Cathedral (Canónigo de la Catedral). The Cathedral was destroyed in the earthquake of course, and the title was honorary, but the ceremony was very beautiful. There was a large crowd, the people became very emotional, and they had decorated the church so that there were flowers everywhere. During the ceremony, when it was my turn to speak, I spoke of fidelity to the church. I said, "Let it be clear that I am a priest, faithful to the church and to the Pope, and for nothing in this world do I want to see the church divided. And let another thing be clear as well, that the priests who deliver themselves to Marxism are like a devalued bill. They have lost their worth." The people applauded enthusiastically because they were incensed at the popular church and have hated it since its birth.

After that, I was the target of a series of attacks in the newspapers saying that I was a rightist, ultra-rightist, and so on. Then *La Prensa* published a beautiful article, countering their accusations, and the battle continued. This type of thing went on through 1980 and intensified in '81. I became very involved in the Permanent Commission on Human Rights, the anti-government group, for we have two here in Nicaragua. I was shocked when I began to read of all the disappearances and assassinations that the government has not investigated.

You know that before the rupture, I was invited by Uriel Molina to help found the Centro Antonio Valdivieso, the ecumenical center, and so was Alán Delgado, a father who was here at the seminary with me. The three of us were to be founders with Obando. But we disappeared from the picture because that's the way the Sandinistas write history. It was to be a center of reflection and pastoral work toward a new future. I was delighted. But the *sine qua non* for reflection is freedom. Without it, reflection is a slavish repetition of government slogans. So I asked if we were going to have here seated at the same table Karl Marx, Thomas Merton, contemplative monks, nuns, existentialists, San Juan de la Cruz; and Uriel told me yes, yes. But it has not happened.

Meanwhile, look at the list of those who have disappeared or been assassinated by the Sandinistas. These things must be investigated. It's horrible. The people whose names are on the list were Somocistas. Here's the name of a young pediatrician whom I knew; he was merely related to the Somozas, that's all, and we need trained doctors so badly in this country. I went to the Centro and talked to a Jesuit priest and showed him these things and he responded that these were just little pecadillos, mistakes of the revolution. Fine, I said, and left and then they erased our names from the list of founders. In '81 there began this type of thing.

Also early in 1981 the bishops denounced something terrible that was taking place, the extermination of the Miskitu Indians. Times only got worse in '82 and 1983 with the *turbas divinas*, or divine mobs, Sandinista mobs in the churches, blood was flowing in the churches. I never believed that I could be anything but terrified by such things, but I was very brave. I believe that I was in a state of grace, because I felt no fear. What the government wanted was for us to turn tail and run or hide, but Obando and I were supported by the people. They would come and warn us when they saw security, or when they heard that the turbas were coming. I believe that if the U.S had not started funding the contra, that I wouldn't be here talking to you now. That's my opinion.

In 1979 they entered singing "We will fight against the Yankee enemy of humanity." The communists always have to fabricate a Yankee, an enemy, right? They have to fight against God because they are atheists. They have to fight against capitalism because they are communists. They have to fight against the U.S. because they are pro-Russia, simply. Reagan is not the problem. Reagan is the only leader on the continent who speaks clearly; he calls bread bread and wine wine, and the Nicaraguans know that what he says is true.

In '82 and '83, I dared to go to Europe with a group from the Permanent Commission on Human Rights, and we went all over Western Europe denouncing the errors of the Sandinistas. We experienced everything. Amnesty International gave us a cold reception, although they were printing an article in which they were using some of our data, and they asked us to proofread it, but in a very perfunctory fashion. We began in Spain and went to Holland and Belgium, Austria, and we stopped briefly in Rome. We did not go to England, Sweden, or Norway. In Austria it went fairly well except for one woman who was shouting at us like *una comandante vulgar*, a common female comandante. I told her that she sounded like a Nicaraguan. Then she started insulting me, and I said, "Look, how would you like to change passports? Here is mine, take it and go ruin your life if you like communism so much." She was a fanatic!

On the way back we had to request the aid of the governments of France, Spain, and Italy to reenter Nicaragua. From that day on, there have been many attempts against me, attempts to poison me, attempts to make it seem that I had women and that I liked young boys. According to what I have heard, they have a film of some young prisoner, in the nude, and another figure appears in the film, not clearly distinguished and they say "Mondragón, homosexual." How horrible!

Also, state security has called me in twice. One afternoon, they had fourteen priests brought in, bam, just like that. It took us all by surprise. They took us before journalists, foreigners, and they took our depositions, but I remained silent. It was humiliating waiting in an anteroom where there were common criminals, prostitutes. Then they took us down innumerable corridors so that we would lose our sense of space, they gave us 10,000 turns. Twenty-five minutes passed, and they took us out the same door that we had come in! They also had a flashlight that they would shine on your forehead while one person would take photographs and another would be filming. The seats were very hard, and I was sitting in one that was also unstable, and I kept thinking that I was going to fall. They read an accusation, and then I was released. I went to Obando and he asked me how I felt. I told him that I felt physically exhausted. "I want a drink, a whiskey" I said, and he gave me one. Then he told me, "Be a tiger." I responded that tomorrow he was going to see what a tiger really is.

Right after that, Obando asked me to take a letter to the Pope from him, which I did. The *Santo Padre*, the Holy Father, read the letter, and answered with a personal blessing, and that was very moving. I want this to be recorded because if I die or they kill me, I want it to be known about the immense love I have for the Pope, and about my deep wish that he understand us. I don't know about the Vatican, but the Pope, sí, he is *bien cerca de nosotros*, very close to us, and he knows what we are suffering. And one time I told a monsignor who came here to see us in the Pope's name, without propaganda, to tell him that we love and respect him but that love for the Pope here in Nicaragua has a high price.

Afterwards, they invented other things about me. One night, I was going about my own business, coming here tranquilly to have a retreat with a group of young people who were coming from several parishes. And while I was en route here, there was a big scandal taking place in Managua. I was coming in a bus, calmly, I hadn't heard anything about the Sandinistas' scandalous Operation Alacrán (Operation Spider), which was to clean up the internal front of which I was supposedly the chief! It seems that I had plans to burn the refinery, burn all Managua, kill children, and that I was an enemy of humanity, the very monster Dracula! I even said to myself when I heard the accusations against me on television, "Who is that Dracula monster?" And I am totally antiviolence. I prayed, "Lord, I swear to you that I hate violence; what is all this that is happening to me?" They were saying on TV things like "This assassin," "This priest," "And still he is not detained," "And so many people have fallen."

The next day I was summoned to present myself to state security. I went with a lawyer from the human rights comission, another lawyer from the Social Christian party, and another priest. But security didn't let them come in. They interviewed me all day long, in the same site where Somoza had done the worst things. It was as before, going around in circles, becoming disoriented, walking down long hallways, the guy with the flashlight again, the filming, two photographers, two huge security men. But God helped me. I invoked God's name, asking for strength for myself and pardon for them. God knew that I was innocent, and I felt that Christ was very close to me at that moment, and a calm came over me. One young boy, a security person who had more hate in him than anyone I had ever seen, called me a *hijo de puta*, son of a whore, for wanting to destroy Managua, and shouted that I had a black heart! Then I said to him, "Are you aware that you are repeating lies? I know that Nicaraguan security is efficient, that it is the most efficient part of the whole government, and because of that I know that you know that you are lying." The boy remained silent after that.

Then the comandante came in laughing and wished me a good morning. I responded that it didn't seem very good to me, and that I wished I could see him under different circumstances. I told him that if he had talked to their *pájaro*, or bird, that he would know that they had interrogated me not once but four times, and that I was tired. I also let him know that I realized right away who the security agent was that they had sent to the seminary to spy on me. I reminded him that he knows all about me, and since that is the case, he also knows that I fight the Frente Sandinista in Nicaragua and abroad, but that my only arms are words and books, and they will continue to be. "Even so," I continued, "I say here before God that I would give my life before having you get so much as a needle prick." He stopped laughing and looked at me, surprised.

He asked me if I was nervous. I answered yes because my hands were shaking, I have a problem with trembling hands, but they were shaking even more than usual. I said to him, "I am glad that my hands are shaking, because all Nicaragua is shaking before you. But I am not afraid of you; I am ill." At that moment, I had a religious experience that I will never have again in my life. I felt that, excuse me for the tears but this is a very emotional memory for me, God was there with me at my side and the Virgin was at my other side, and that they were supporting me. This is very emotional to tell this. Incredible!

"I'm going to take you away now," said the comandante. Again, we were right there at the very door, but I was disoriented after everything, and I exited into the bright sunlight saying, "What's this, where am I?" He laughed again and got into his pretty new Lada, with a driver. The comandante then opened the door for me and said, "Come in, Monsignor." He called me by the formal "usted", and my title, "Monsignor." He asked me if I would like a cigarette, and I said no although I smoke heavily, blaming it on my ulcer. Then he talked about how difficult everything was now what with the food situation for people with ulcers. Now everything was more cordial. As he dropped me at the bishops' meeting, I gave him my hand and expressed the hope that the next time would be under more human circumstances. Then he left.

All I remember after that is that I entered the chapel and greeted the bishops, but I don't remember the meeting at all. The fathers told me that I said that I wanted to talk to God first, and that I went up to the sanctuary and cried. Then I went to eat. I have no memory of what I ate, but they say that I ate an entire chicken. Then I came to my office here and went to sleep on this cot, left the door open, and I didn't wake up until the next day. They made such a campaign against me on the radio and TV with photos, newspapers articles, and so forth, that I felt like a prisoner on the stand whose judge was all Nicaragua.

But I have only immense love and gratitude for the Nicaraguan people. They cured me in one day, because the bishops told me to take a walk outside, which I did. I was amazed that the people greeted me with great affection. First, however, a truck full of workers came by, saw me and shouted "Assassin!" I felt like Cain. But as I walked around the neighborhood of the *Conferencia Episcopal* (Episcopal Conference), the people, when they recognized me, would shout from their cars, "Monsignor, we are with you!" Above all, in my own parish I felt that everyone believed in me without even having to hear my story. It was beautiful. No one really believed that I was involved in all that.

Well, they haven't called me back since that time. But they have me pretty well controlled with their people. Some agents are here to spy on me. Are they working on a plan to get me? Let's just say that they are watching me closely and they record everything I say. They know everything about me, if I like the seaside, what brand of cigarettes I smoke, what brand of alcohol I like, if I have North American diplomatic friends. The pressure is just as intense now as it was earlier, and I have to be very careful, because they really *are* out to get me, there have even been attempts to poison the communion wine!

The continuing dialogue between the church and the government has been for me a series of dilatory, long *charlas*, talks, with a Marxist methodology, in order to convince people abroad that there is communication going on. But in reality, there is none. I don't attend these meetings because they are for the bishops. The fundamental problem of the abyss that exists between the church and the state is human rights. That is the basis, the right to life, to information, to expression, to free associaton.

I think there is one other thing too: they can mount all the propaganda thay want saying that the youngsters should do their military service, but it is sending them to their death. And *everyone* knows it. But they oblige all the boys to go. This is the principal problem in Nicaragua and what distances the Sandinistas from the people. In each home someone has died. We all have to have a military card, and the youths who have not done their military service and seek asylum in foreign embassies are not considered political refugees but deserters! And now it's not only the young seventeen-year-olds but up to age forty. We are all military! When you tie up the youth of a country that way, you kill the church, religion, politics, unions. But if one says these things, the accusation is always that you are with the contra. The children, they are organizing them now from kindergarten, as candidates for the Sandinista Youth. This is totalitarianism! The people have no self-determination.

All the excuses about restrictions because of the war are lies. Look, if it weren't for the contra not even the *New York Times* would enter here, and we two would not be talking. Perhaps we would not even be *alive*! The war situation has turned the eyes of the world to Nicaragua. But what happens is that everyone comes here to prove the cruelty of the guerrillas. However, I tell you that the majority of the people here in Nicaragua *adore* Reagan because he is strong. And they adore Cardinal Obando, not just the *burguesía*, or bourgeoisie, as they claim, but everyone.

There has not been one single advance because of the revolution. Nothing! Look, I can't replace the glass in these pictures of my family, because there is no glass in Nicaragua. Health care is absolutely on the floor. Go to a hospital and you will see that it is a *porquería*, a shocking pigsty, and there is simply *no* medicine for anything. I went to the doctor the other day and he gave me a prescription; I inquired at three or four places trying to find it, but there is nothing. In education, there are no teachers. The *bachilleres*, secondary school graduates, are more foolish by the day. The level of professional competence is terrible, and the Sandinistas say that it's because they went to help with the coffee or cotton harvest. How ridiculous! As for mixed business, legally it's possible, but in practice it's impossible. And the campesino is poorer now than before, *including* in the cooperatives. They kill themselves working and the government buys the crop and sets the price. Does that sound like progress to you?

14 Miriam Lazo (b. 1946)

"I believe in this
profoundly human aspect
of the revolution, that it is
capable of changing our
individualistic sentiment,
and I have *seen* it
happen. . . ."

Ms. Lazo seems too good to be true. In fact, she is as close to a modern-day saint as most of us are ever likely to meet. Whether she is working with her colleagues at INSSBI, the Nicaraguan Institute of Social Security and Welfare; with representatives from international relief organizations; with the campesino children in the rural day care centers that she has established; with the destitute Miskitu Indians whose repatriation she is assisting under U.N. auspices; or with the victims of the October 1988 Hurricane Joan which leveled the Atlantic coastal town of Bluefields; Ms. Lazo stands out as an authentic, strong, practical Christian idealist.

Ms. Lazo lives in a tiny, simple, crowded home with her husband and three daughters, two of whom she adopted after they had been abandoned by their natural parents. She works relentlessly and compassionately on behalf of the poor, undaunted by the near-total lack of resources she faces, bureaucratic red tape, and general institutional temporizing.

Eschewing the language of ideology for that of the parables, which is immediately accessible to the campesino experience, Ms. Lazo clearly identifies the kingdom of God with the social justice promised by the revolution, and she works tirelessly to realize that promise. She may be a saint, but she is no mystic.

━━━━━━━━━━━━━━

I was born in Juigalpa in the state of Chontales in north-central Nicaragua, a rich agricultural and cattle-producing region, and life for me was very comfortable there. My mother died when I was born, and I was brought up mostly by my father. All my family are devout Catholics, and my father sent me to a Catholic boarding school when I was very young, so that I would be brought up in a proper religious environment. We were very close and he came to see me every week without fail. The convent school, the Colegio María Auxiliadora in Granada, was run by the Salesian sisters, most of whom were Italian, very cultured and also very conservative.

There, in the school, I came early on to see how one's economic position is related to the way one is treated. For example, I remember well one occasion in which we internal students were helping to clean the sacristy. Some of the other girls were helping the sisters do the chores around the school. Well, one of these girls dropped a flower pot and broke it, and then the mother came and scolded her angrily. Now, when I was helping clean the sacristy, I dropped one of the light fixtures, which broke into many pieces, but the mother did not say anything to me; she did not get angry at all. I wondered what the difference was between what I had done and what the other girl had done. Then it suddenly dawned on me that she belonged to the group whose parents did not pay, and I belonged to the group whose parents did.

When my father came that next Sunday, I told him all about the incident and that I hoped that he would pay for the flower pot because the girl's family could not. I think he realized that this event had a big impact on me, for he said: "*Hijita mía* (My little daughter), you did very well in helping out your friend; I'm going to tell the Mother that you are the child's friend now and to let you share whatever you have with her." That was the most valuable example that my papa set for me when I was a young child, that we ourselves have to act though our caring about others to help lessen social differences.

After the convent school, I continued developing along similar lines. First I wanted to become a nun, then I wanted to become a doctor. But my father wanted me to become a teacher. He said that teaching too is a calling. So, I went away to a normal school, the Escuela Normal de Señoritas in San Marcos, and when I returned, he told me: "I would like for you to help me a bit. I want you to establish a school on the finca and provide the workers' children with an opportunity to educate themselves.

When they are educated, then you can go and study medicine if you still wish." But, as time went on, he said to me: "Why don't you give classes to the adults, the parents and grandparents, as well as the children?" So, as you can see, my father practically pushed me into teaching and, indirectly, into studying the sociology of my country.

Well, after I finally finished with the educational mission on my father's estate, I made my way to the university, but not to study medicine. I would have had to go all the way to León for that, and I wanted to be in Managua. So, I studied Philosophy and Letters there. When I finished my course of study, I taught in the primary and secondary schools, the normal schools too and also at the university, everywhere and at all levels. It was very instructive from a sociological perspective. I saw in each of those different grades the poverty of Nicaragua. Not only the poverty but also the discrimination.

For example, when I was teaching at the university, it was quite obvious that the wealthy students were the ones who went to the Catholic university, and that those who had fewer resources went to the national university. It was a great sacrifice for the Indians from Bluefields to leave everything behind and travel the long distance, both in cultural and geographical terms, to Managua. Observing such contrasts made me keenly aware of how little the government did to promote education for our people, and this while I and everyone else knew that well over 60 percent of the population was illiterate. One didn't have to have any connections with the Sandinista movement to want to change that situation entirely.

Perhaps I would not have been so sensitive to the extreme inequities had my father not taught me so much. He was unusually compassionate, my model and my inspiration. He was always using nature to make wise comparisons with human beings. I remember when I was very young he would say things such as this: "Human beings are like plants. Some plants grow very tall, are strong, and give good fruits. Others are sickly; they do not produce fruit because many times the bigggest plants take all their nourishment and do not give them a chance to develop. That's also the way it is with human beings, and that's why we must share what we have with others."

What I saw in Managua further awakened my social conscience. There I had ample opportunity to become familiar with the vast differences that economic power and the lack of it make in one's life. I saw it in the schoolchildren I taught and in their mothers, who would come up to me and say: "I have no money to buy the uniform or the shoes. What am I to do?" This made quite an impact on me, and so I often provided the students' shoes and uniforms.

I saw children who arrived with empty stomachs and who would faint in class. Then I would go to the family and ask if the child was sick. The mother would tell me: "My husband is an alcoholic, and I have no work, so we have nothing for our children to eat." It is the child who suffers the consequences of this type of situation, which was very common. My sense of social awareness was heightened by such valuable experiences and insights gained from my teaching.

I started to work [against the Somoza regime] little by little, because at that time in Nicaragua it was very dangerous to work openly. After I finished all my studies, I began giving classes in Spanish and Latin American literature at the Universidad Centroamericana, that is the Catholic university, where I consciously strove to teach, say, the poem of the Argentine *gaucho* outlaw *Martín Fierro*, from an openly political perspective. It seemed the only responsible approach to me, as there I was teaching the wealthiest students in the country. There you have my teaching career from about '72 to '78 and a little of '79, when the revolution was born.

I did not participate in the revolution as a Sandinista, because I have no political affiliation, only a religious one you might say. But, yes, I participated as a "friend" of the Sandinistas. I worked with the university youth in a consciousness-raising project. It consisted of a series of classes informing them of the terrible abuses of power during the Somoza dynasty, the corruption, and the persecution of students.

With the revolutionary victory came great expectations, great hope, and great faith that the change would be so radical, so dramatic, that we would be able to feel it from the very beginning, and that was *in fact* the way it happened! I, for example, was no longer the professor in the classroom, although I felt that I continued being a teacher in some ways because I began a social welfare project in which my teaching background helped me greatly.

The specific program I'm referring to was the establishment of childcare centers for the campesinos. I remembered my childhood experiences, my father's properties, the workers, the families and the little school, and I also remembered my father's words about the campesino as "the one who harvests, who makes the land bear fruit." So, in order to help the campesino harvest more easily, I worked to create rural day care centers throughout the country. I was, and still am, the individual responsible for the operation of these centers. Though some still provide meals only, there are others that provide full-fledged child care. Nationwide, we now have about 100 centers, each with around 100 children and 10 teachers. When you think that a few years ago there was absolutely nothing, you can see that the change I refer to has been total.

That's how I began to be involved in national welfare projects, through the rural child centers. The post I currently occupy with the government involves developing further all the social projects for which I am responsible, which are many. In addition to the childcare centers, I also oversee those for the elderly, and the rehabilitation centers for prostitutes, alcoholics, and those disabled through war. It makes no difference what side they were on; if they are in need, our job is to help them, and my task is to see that it is done.

Before the revolution, there were a few very rudimentary centers, but they had a totally different philosophy. People were just dumped in the centers for the elderly, for example, without the hope of anyone ever engaging them, taking an interest, or treating them with the kind of family warmth that we endeavor to give. And of course, these places were all private and expensive. With regard to the treatment of orphans, the orphanage that existed was called a "temporary home," and to my knowledge, the children had no stimulation, toys, attention or education, affective or otherwise, because the personnel were just maids, orderlies, no one with any training. As for the disabled, there were simply *no* services at all. The old concept was that the disabled person was just a parasite to be scorned. Now, we think of him as one who has the potential to be self-sufficient, to be of use in his community, and even to hold a job commensurate with his physical capacity. Nor were there any social agencies for the rehabilitation of alcoholics or prostitutes, nothing. All of this is a result of the revolution.

Not only have we created social services that were nonexistent before, but we have also changed the philosophical orientation of each center and of each service, and, therefore, its effects on the people it serves. The way we helped bring about this change was that there was a team of us, and little by little, we worked with the staff and technicians in our centers, old and new, instilling in them an awareness of the worth of those who were in their care and of the importance of their job. This was between 1979 and '81 and it was very successful. To cite an example, many of the former prostitutes have now formed sewing cooperatives and are reintegrating themselves into society with dignity and an awareness of their value as human beings. You can see that the difference really has been total, and it has affected me deeply. It has caused me to undertake the task of seeking funds to support all our centers. So now, in addition to my other duties, I also search for resources, support. But it is very difficult because Nicaragua is faced with a war situation in which each day the needs worsen, in which there are more orphans, more disabled, more displaced persons, widows, more refugees from El Salvador and Guatemala, a whole gamut of needs which when compared with our resources are very great.

I seek assistance from international humanitarian agencies, from ecumenical groups, such as the Ecumenical Refugee Council in Milwaukee, from international bodies of the United Nations, such as UNICEF and the

FAO. There are many solidarity groups; for example, the European, Canadian, and North American solidarity committees have helped greatly. The Latin American committees have been for us the essence of brotherhood, because they feel and experience the same privations that we do, but still they share with us what they have. Because of that, I think that the work we do in Nicaragua with the refugees from other Central American countries is especially significant. You see, in spite of our serious shortages, we feel a deep sense of pleasure in sharing with the refugees the little or the much that comes to us.

You might expect that there would be resentment toward the refugees, especially in light of the serious, even desperate, scarcity of basic foodstuffs that we are experiencing, but the fact is that the refugees are completely enmeshed in our national productive life. It is a unique but a very human experience. That's why I say that if there is anything that I believe, it is that revolutions are capable of transforming the individualistic sentiment of humankind, and it is for this that I respect them. The refugee feels at home here because we make him feel that this land, Nicaragua, is also theirs, and they should benefit from it just as any Nicaraguan. I believe in this profoundly human aspect of the revolution, that it is capable of changing our individualistic sentiment, and I have *seen* it happen in my work with the refugees.

The challenge is, of course, how to maintain that cooperative, expansive spirit. I think that previous revolutions that have not been able to sustain that corporate spirit were not authentic revolutions, for I do not believe that revolutions can be understood solely in material and social terms. They should be regarded in more holistic and integral terms, and in terms of the development of the human spirit. For example, in Nicaragua what we see now is people learning to live communally, together; this fact perpetuates the spirit of solidarity and mutual cooperation that we wish to strengthen. As we continue to learn to live in this type of system, mutual assistance comes to be seen as intrinsic, or at least as the normal mode of human interaction.

Another area in which I have seen a dramatic change brought about by the revolution, and which, like the others I have mentioned, has directly affected my own life, is in the opening up of new opportunities for women, and I mean meaningful positions in the government, for example. That change is one reason that I am occupying the position that I hold. I am a personal example. The post I hold now is a leadership position within the Ministry; my immediate superior, Lic. Reinaldo Antonio Téfel, confers regularly with Comandante Ortega. Before the revolution, as a woman, I would never have been named to such a responsible post. This then is a concrete, visible result of the revolution.

Of course, the reason that women have been gaining ground is simply that they have been conquering it because of their participation in the struggle, in the literacy campaigns, in the defense of the revolution itself, in the health campaigns, in the National Emergency committee (a voluntary organization of which I am the executive secretary that mobilizes help in the event of natural disasters or war). So each woman gains according to how much she gives. It's not the kind of situation in which you get something simply because you are a woman; no, you have to earn what you have, and you do so through participation. The old battle in which a woman was not allowed to hold a post just because she was a woman, that struggle is over, because women themselves have been actively creating their own opportunities.

There are in Nicaragua, for example, women ministers of state; this is new for us, and exemplary. There are women who are rewriting the laws to reflect precisely this equilibrium between men and women. Laws regarding family welfare are suggested by women, and there we are, present in the assemblies of the government. Women do not just have honorific positions; rather, they have leadership posts. For example, in the ministries that span social concerns, in education, in health, in housing, in social welfare, especially in social welfare, the majority of the leadership positions are held by women. It is very encouraging to see. Yes, I can tell you that the revolutionary process has been of great benefit to the Nicaraguan woman.

The process has also done a great deal in helping to reduce the gross social inequities that have historically existed in Nicaragua, especially with regard to the campesino. You see, the Nicaraguan campesino was always the most marginalized of all groups. Therefore, it is just, and it is recognized to be just, that he be given what he has for so long been denied. You know, the person who has the greatest social conscience of all is the campesino. He who has no social conscience is the one who always has taken everything.

Let me show you what I mean about the campesino. What happens to the Salvadoran, Guatemalan, or any other refugee when they are incorporated into our national productive life? I'll tell you. The campesino accepts them as if they were just other Nicaraguans. That is because the campesino feels a spirit of great brotherhood; he is not egotistical. The campesino, to me, is the purest of all in spirit; he is capable of giving you everything that he has. I see this generosity every time I visit the campesino communities. Though these visits are part of my professional responsibilities, I visit four or five centers a week traveling by jeep, boat, or small plane, I also often go with my family on Sundays, and we treat the visits as a family outing. When we visit a rural center and they see us coming, they bring their chickens, eggs, whatever they have, and offer them to us. And it is not only to us, but to anyone who comes, such is the generous spirit of the campesino. To me, this is a symbol of the richness of the human heart. As you know, Nicaragua is a country of campesinos, not only in terms of social class, but also in terms of largesse of spirit. You can see that I have great faith even though times are so difficult, because I believe in the goodness of our country people.

One of the truly original aspects of our revolution and the one with which I identify most closely is the role popular religion has played. The operative word here is *popular,* yes, that is the word to use. Popular religion, to me, is the basis of a genuine Christianity because it is so much a part of our people and the life they live daily in their communities. Our people are deeply religious, but their religious development depends in large measure on the ability of the pastor to tend to his flock, to be close to them. If abandoned, the sheep will be lost from the fold; but if the shepherd is always there, then the religious spirit of the flock will be strengthened. But, what happens? Many members of the Catholic hierarchy, I think, have forgotten how to become close to their sheep. And the others, those who have opted for the popular church, well, they are often severely chastised by their superiors. And why? Because, of course, the hierarchy think that *they* are the church, that *they* are the kingdom of God. I think that they have forgotten that the true kingdom is in each and every one of their sheep, that is what *I* say!

There are pastors and even bishops who have remained close to the people, and who have helped with regard to issues of social welfare. There are some, I cannot give you names, but if we approach them, they will help us. If we say: "There is great need in this community and if you help us we can obtain food, clothing, and medicine. If only you will sign this voucher, we can seek help from abroad." And they do it. The only thing that such bishops lack is the courage to speak out publicly, but, that time too will come. In the meantime, their signature, their endorsement of our requests, is an act of solidarity and of Christian conscience.

There have been some areas of social policy in which the revolution has made serious errors, for example with regard to the discrimination that the indigenous Miskitu population has traditionally suffered. The revolution mistakenly tried to move the Indians of the Atlantic Coast from their own communities to new ones in which the government had prepared the economic infrastructure, and, well, they were *very* unhappy. The change was difficult and it was precipitous. It was a mistake of the revolution to uproot the Indians, one of many errors. The revolution is made by people, not by angels. But now that this fault has been recognized, the Indians are being given the opportunity to return to their traditional way of life. They can choose either to remain in the new community or go back to their own villages.

Many, those who are very close to their traditions, are returning, and the government is helping them do so. This project is called the Project for the Autonomy of the Atlantic Coast. It is extremely important, so much so that the Minister of the Interior himself, Comandante Tomás Borge, is the one who is directing it. Another thing about the project is that it is very representative; it is the Indians themselves who are making the decisions, and it is the Indian women in particular who are representing the government of the Atlantic Coast. In my view, it is this sort of thing that, in the long run, strengthens the revolution.

There is a delicate balance to be achieved between supporting autonomy for the Indians and, at the same time, incorporating them into the national picture. When the Indians were brought from their home communities to the government creation, TASBA PRI, there was created for them a minimal, incipient infrastructure, health centers, schools, small industries, just something to provide work, a start. But the fact is that the Atlantic Coast Indian lives from the river; separating him from it is like tearing his heart out. We learned that infrastructure is one thing, but that it is totally meaningless if the Indian is taken from that which nourishes his spirit. So, now the government is trying to develop projects that are in harmony with the traditional way of life of the Indian, for example, fishing and farming cooperatives in the villages along the Río Coco. That is the sort of thing that is now being done, for the first time in our history, to bring the Indians into the process of national development, while also respecting their culture and way of life.

There is so much to learn and to do, and we have only just begun. There are also tremendous obstacles to face and to overcome. I think we must always keep in mind the legacy of other, earlier revolutions, the spirit of freedom. It is this spirit that is taking hold and growing among the people of Latin America as a whole, not just Nicaragua. Our country has so many serious limitations, first, the contra war, but we have also suffered earthquakes, floods, droughts, and most recently, hurricanes. In sum, devastating natural phenomena have also rained down upon us.

Considering all of these disasters, you may ask why does Nicaragua continue to resist, especially in the face of powerful external forces that try to destroy the revolution? Because our history is one of suffering and hardship, we know how to resist, that is what we do know. And now that our people have begun to experience freedom, even under these extremely difficult circumstances, their resolve is strengthened.

Some people accuse Nicaragua of representing a danger to other countries and say that the revolution must be destroyed. But that is not the true reason, because Nicaragua is no threat to anyone. Rather, the "threat" is simply in the *example* that is being communicated to the other Latin American countries, this thirst for freedom, for self-determination, that we feel. The message that is being communicated to other Latin American countries is this, we are still struggling, still resisting, still keeping the spirit alive. We all need freedom. If the birds of the air can enjoy freedom, then why not human beings also? We are all brothers and sisters who have been placed here in the same world, not on different planets. We share a common humanity, and we need to learn to recognize that fact.

15 Vidaluz Meneses (b. 1944)

". . . we should not regard culture as something superior to, or subordinate to, the revolution, but rather as an integral component of it."

". . . the revolution is fundamentally a moral option. . . ."

What I appreciated most about this attractive woman with the fine features, fair complexion and ready smile, was that she did not give a "booster club" talk about revolutionary culture, but rather an honest appraisal of current efforts, which must have been difficult to do considering Vidaluz's almost religious identification with the objectives of the revolution.

Raised in comfort as the daughter of an officer in Somoza's guardia, Vidaluz now has a commitment to an egalitarian program that fosters the development of a popular culture. And as the former wife of a leading member of the contra, Vidaluz seems to work doubly hard to realize the "solidarity, love, sharing, and hope" that the revolution symbolizes to her.

Poet, former director of Libraries and Archives , founding member and associate director of the Ministry of Culture until 1988, and current director of the Antonio Valdivieso Ecumenical Center, Vidaluz Meneses has dedicated herself totally to furthering the cultural goals of the revolution, the point of convergence of her acclaimed poetic sensibility and her strong Christian conscience. Here Vidaluz describes her work at the Ministry, in all its frustrating limitations and exciting possibilities, dis-

cusses the role she sees for her own writing, and relates openly the heavy personal toll that her revolutionary commitment has exacted.

The triumph of the revolution created the Ministry of Culture, which is a singular institution in the history of our country, without precedent. Like most of Latin America, we had only a cultural extension department of the Ministry of Education; but since the Revolution there has been a tremendous movement toward promoting culture and shaping true cultural institutions, broadly considered.

Let me give you some very different examples. The minister of culture himself, Ernesto Cardenal, has sponsored one of our best sculptors, Fernando Saravia, enabling him to develop his talent. He has created some beautiful stylized pieces as a result. And that is culture. We also published here in the Departmento de Publicaciones, a book by the poet Fernando Silva, who besides being a poet and storyteller is a pediatrician and director of the children's hospital, La Mascota. His book is called *La Salud del Niño*, (The Health of the Child). It consists of suggestions, based on our own cultural reality and values, on how to care for our children. And that too is culture. Further, we have published a book called *Cocina nica*, ("Nica" Cooking), which contains the Nicaraguan selections from a wonderful cookbook published many years ago by a high society woman who was a fantastic cook, and who wrote on international and national cuisine. In our cooking we see expressed our *mestizaje*, our Hispanic and indigenous influences. In publishing this book we are helping to unearth our roots. And that too is culture.

In addition to all the areas traditionally described as cultural, we felt the need after the triumph to figure out, take stock of, what we had inherited from the past. We went to see the condition of the national library, and of public libraries, for example. Then we took all the books, art objects, archaeological treasures, paintings, and similar items from the homes of Somocistas and declared them part of the national patrimony. We went through the books and distributed them among the public libraries. The houses that the Somocistas left have been converted into cultural houses.

Then we took a kind of census of artists in the country because we wanted to know who and how many were interested in the cultural task in all branches of art. At the same time we also realized that we had the enormous responsibility to promote at the national level a great cultural movement of artists and *aficionados* of culture.

Of course, the Ministry was born with a deficit in educated human resources that we have not been able to overcome, keeping in mind the low level of literacy in our country. With regard to finances, another deficit, beause in the year of the triumph, the U.S. government began supporting those who left and had lost power. So we haven't had the oxygen we need, and we have struggled against the current. For example, wc here at the Ministry have complained because we have not spent much time in theoretical reflection on the cultural project, which is something that we would like to do, but we have been unable because the situation of aggression obliges us to make ad hoc responses. That seems to be a permanent contradiction: we have the political will, the backing, of the revolutionary government, but we do not have the material conditions necessary to concretize that political will, to respond to the infinite demands of the people. Thus, from the beginning, we have had objectives that we have not been able to fulfill.

At the same time, we have helped artists and writers to organize themselves. This step was very important because on the one hand, we writers recognize ourselves as just additional workers, not as an elite; but on the other hand, we achieve recognition of our work as a contribution, as a social product. That's how the Sandinista Cultural Workers Association (Asociación Sandinista de Trabajadores de la Cultura, ASTC), was formed. It is separate from the Ministry of Culture, and is an organized guild, a state institution. It is voluntary, and has many members, but the greatest poet, the one who stands out over all the others, and the only dissident, Pablo Antonio Cuadra, is of course not a member. There are Nicaraguan artists living abroad who also keep in touch with their roots through this organization.

In the past, the Somoza government did not promote artists; on the contrary, they repressed us because we had a different attitude from the official one. When the *Ventana*, or Window, group was formed by Fernando Gordillo and Sergio Ramírez, that was the first time that writers linked their literary labors directly to a political and social commitment. Then we had the Praxis group of painters who, in their turn, rejected the kind of painting that the bourgeoisie had wanted. They just stopped producing superficial, decorative adornments with colors chosen to match the drapes. They began to make of art an arm of struggle and denunciation. With regard to music, it is very obvious, because we all know the rich production of the Mejía Godoy brothers, the Pancasán group, of all the groups who made of the song an example of protest and struggle for all Latin America. Naturally, at the triumph of the Revolution, all these groups and tendencies came to associate ourselves in a common interest group, which is the ASTC.

Now, what do the ASTC and the Ministry have as their fundamental objectives? Just one—excellence in artistic and cultural products. That is really the only condition. Comandante Tomás Borge said in one of his public addresses, "A bad poem is counterrevolutionary." The people are free to choose their themes. And if many literary and artistic works of today reflect scenes of war or specific experiences of revolutionary transformation, it is because the greatest impact on our people in these times is that caused, for example, by the loss in combat of one's son, or best friend, or sweetheart, or husband. I believe that the natural tendency of the human being is to express what he or she lives. Nevertheless, even in these times we may discover primitive paintings like these in my office which represent landscapes, the campesino's daily life, domestic tools, etc. When we have peace, I'm certain that we'll see an explosion of imagination with flowers, butterflies, and the sun brightening all the artistic production now overshadowed by the war.

This is not to say that they are not doing others types of art too. We have art schools, absolutely tuition-free, la Escuela Nacional de Danza, la Escuela Nacional de Música, de Artes Plásticas, which includes the school of mural painting and which we are able to support thanks to the help of the Italians. We used to have a program where we brought students here from all regions of the country as internal students, but it was impossible for us to cover their expenses. So we have cut projects like that. Our aspirations have been reduced because of financial limitations. On the other hand, we have created other areas without precedent, such as the Nicaraguan Film Institute (Instituto Nicaragüense de Cine). We produce documentaries, but we depend heavily on international cooperation. Cuba's help has been invaluable, because they are close, speak the same language, and have a very sophisticated film industry. We also have done a number of co-productions with France and Mexico, but Cuba has helped us the most.

We also sponsor another area which has to do with the preservation of our national heritage (Dirección General de Patrimonio Histórico); it too is a costly service because it involves conservation of historical sites, such as León, the first city the Spaniards founded, and Granada, as well as various archaeological areas. Since the triumph, we have had to learn by the seat of our pants. Someone who knew a little about archaeology would see the historical significance in a building for example, and would teach those who knew nothing at least how to identify a particular style of a certain period.

That's how we've been doing things, working and studying at the same time. Thus, development of programs is limited not only by finances, but also by the low level of preparation and training of our people. Further, many technical and professional people have left the country , and others are working in defense. This situation has left many women and many people with minimal education at the head of production in the cities, yet another difficult aspect of the reality of the state of war that we are living.

Recently, the director of the National Library, Professor Iliana Rodríguez, a very good writer who formerly taught at University of Minnesota, and who is very analytical and profound, wrote about the "state-school" phenomenon. It is a serious problem in that the state forms the people, gives them training, even sends them away to study, and then, shortly after they return they enter the private sector to earn more money. This is an ethical choice that one has to respect, but it is also an economic question, at bottom, because anywhere in the world one pays in order to learn. At the minimum, what these people should do on returning home is to pay back what the state invested in them. We do have a flight of technicians and professionals because we have chosen to live with a mixed economy and pluralism. This is a serious economic problem, and it shows that we have internal as well as external contradictions.

We also have the problem of people, the public, coming to offices not knowing what they want or how to ask for it. This situation is compounded by the bureaucrats who are supposed to be serving the public, but who really don't know any more than the people do. Rather than appear not to know what they are doing, some office workers simply give out misinformation, or perhaps they deny a perfectly reasonable request. We face that problem at the national library too, with regard to public services. We have tried to set up a system of information and orientation for the community, trying thereby to help resolve problems related to light, water, telephone, and similar services. But we see that a great many people are functionally illiterate. They not only need help in reading and writing, but also in formulating questions and in interpreting what they are reading and writing. This is a stark fact of our state of underdevelopment which we confront every day.

The reference librarians at times find it very difficult to figure out what it is that some people want to look up, because they can not even formulate their own topics or questions. Just everyday fluency, ability in using the language is also a problem. Those of us from the middle classes had a similar background and education, we had traveled to other countries; in short, we had the same kind of development that allowed for quick, easy communication among ourselves.

Now, however, we must communicate with a much wider group that does not share any of those experiences, and that comes from a very different background. So we have had to adapt the rhythm, the speed of everyday communication with office workers, for example. Since it is very difficult even for us Nicaraguans, we feel deeply for the North American and European volunteers, who have more development, and who try to work here. We are in a long process of adaptation that begins with establishing communication at the same level as the people you are working with. This is the sad legacy of underdevelopment.

Considered against this background, I believe that there have been remarkable advances. I don't know if you are familiar with the practice of this program *De Cara al Pueblo*, where the people speak their mind in regular, public sessions with the president and high government officials, each time in a different town. I consider it an eminently democratic exercise. It is worthwhile to look at some of these programs on film in the archives of the Ministerio de Información y Prensa. That way, you can compare the first *De Cara al Pueblo* with those that are taking place now, and you will see clearly how the people are making enormous gains in their capacity for self-expression. At the beginning, you will see how timid and fearful they were, after fifty years of dictatorship. Since the triumph, however, many people have learned to read and write; they have gained confidence in themselves, and it is logical that they would have a new attitude and a new-found voice.

You have seen how articulate the people are when they are talking about their lives; they don't get mixed up and they express themselves clearly. I think that the distance between their fluency in this area and their inability to function effectively in, say, an office setting, is perhaps a question of stages and of life-style. First, we can't expect everything to happen at once or even in a smooth, flowing development. Second, many of these people are from the country, and rural and urban ways of conducting oneself are different.

Sometimes I am surprised though; for example, I will see them interview on TV residents of one of the barrios, and those people will know why there was a bomb in Lebanon, or they will talk in an informed manner about the conflict in the Middle East. In other words, the people have grown; they know how to express themselves better, and their areas of interest now go beyond their own country. This is not to say that such a level of awareness is uniform, but you can see it here and there in different sectors.

I believe that the time I am living in is unique and that, since I am one of the privileged ones in my country, I have a responsibility to do what I can to analyze, interpret, and record our moment for our children, the future. Though I am a poet, I am trying now to write a little prose. Perhaps I will be able to write a novel that recreates an epoch. I have copious notes that I have scribbled down about my generation, the '60s, whenever I have a moment.

But think for a minute about the generation of the '60s here in Nicaragua, in which we spoke of the existentialists, who were for many, images of men and women bathing naked in a pool, or of people thinking possibly, let's live it up now because tomorrow we die. But these were postwar European preoccupations, not ours. What we got was not the philosophy, but the external manifestations, the trappings, of a phenomenon deeply lived by other people and appropriate to another culture.

The hippies, for example, belonged to the developed world because they possessed an "anti" position vis-à-vis the economic and material development of their countries, and an enormous spiritual disaffection. For us, however, the hippies were dirty, long-haired young people who experimented with drugs, wore lots of bracelets, and did nothing with their lives. Moreover, they were shocking, and they were a source of inspiration for our writing at that time. One of our poets was moved to write "We are tired of asphalt and whiskey." Really, I'm not kidding! It's ridiculous isn't it, to write of such things and live in such a poor country as ours. That gives you an idea of the degree of alienation and cultural penetration that permeated our atmosphere during those years. I remember it all.

During that period, there was an intellectual named Ricardo Morales Avilés, of the FSLN, who used to be a psychology professor at the university but he became fed up with teaching things that had absolutely nothing to do with our life or with transforming it and resigned. Similarly, Danilo Rosales, a young, idealistic doctor, saw as indefensible what was going on in his university classes because it was contributing nothing to society. They both left, joined the armed struggle, and died for their beliefs. Morales Avilés wrote for the intellectuals of the time, and one of his principles has been very important to us here at the Ministry: that we should not regard culture as something superior to, or subordinate to, the revolution, but rather as an integral component of it.

From this perspective, not only is culture viewed in ideological terms, but it is also conceived of as fundamental, basic. Thus, the series of productions and artistic expressions that we promote are not superfluous or frivolous, but essential. I know that this seems an incredible contradiction in our country where everything is lacking, where there are not enough hospitals or schools, and where people have to volunteer just for there to be a teacher at all in certain towns. It seems a luxury that we would sponsor a chamber music concert, but we do. Moreover, we feel that we must do these things because we are committed to raising the cultural level of the people, to contributing to the transformation of values, to an awareness of national identity and to a sense of nationhood. We must open ourselves up to international influences as well, for we learn from the whole world. For this reason, we promote exchange as much as possible, both at the governmental level and at the level of solidarity groups, so that we have the opportunity to learn about the cultural manifestations of other peoples.

With regard to things like the latest trends in literary criticism, structuralism or deconstructionism, of course we are interested in what North American, French and other literary intellectuals are doing, especially in specialized literature courses. But the problem is in being able to know, to read, the works and the authors themselves. We lack dollars, and such books are very expensive; further, many times we are not able to get them in Spanish translation. Many of the university people read English, but perhaps just as many can only read in Spanish. Thus, there are limitations of language and limitations of dollars. Nevertheless, we promote things, such as the International Book Festival (Festival International del Libro), that we are trying to put together to include the latest examples in world literature.

Personally, and this is just my own opinion, from what little I have read about the new currents in literary criticism, it seems that it is an arid university phenomenon of dissection that runs the risk of losing sight of the human factor or of what the book is trying to do. Excessive analysis can lose sight of the forest. Sometimes I feel like the great poet José Coronel Urtecho, teacher of Ernesto Cardenal, Martínez Rivas, and Mejía Sánchez, who has a horror of the university as this unfeeling monster that kills the creativity of individuals. I think that if we are not careful, we do lose the essence in going after the form. These things can discourage people from reading, because often you can't understand the commentary on a work, and you think, why should I read the work if I can't even get through the criticism.

My generation has often been referred to as the generation of women poets, because there were six or seven of us writing at that period. But I will tell you frankly that the importance of our group was not the quality, but rather the novelty. In a country where more than half of the people were illiterate, it is reasonable to expect that more than half of these illiterates were women, that they were restricted to the home, and that they were subjected to the will of the man with whom they were living. This picture typically included women with money, who may have gone a few years to primary school, but whose most important education was in a decorative art, perhaps embroidery, and in how to give orders to the maids. For these reasons, it has come to be so significant that there are seven of us women poets. That's all there is to it, I think.

We gained prominence individually, not as a group, although we are friends. Last year we gave a public recitation and it was lovely; afterwards we had a warm chat together and it was very moving for me. We are all from the middle class; that's why we had access to the privilege that it was to study at the university. We identify ourselves as women in transition, for we are no longer the women of before.

I am trying desperately to put the benefits of my background and education to the service of the people. Even though I am experiencing severe financial difficulties now because of my salary, I am still in a privileged position. I am also fortunate in that I have had the additional stimulus of representing my own country abroad. I have visited places that I never dreamed I would ever see. Knowing that I have all these advantages makes me want to work all the harder to share them with others, and that is why my frustration is so great when we must work against such overwhelming odds. The war is never out of my mind. While we are here in Managua, calmly talking in this air-conditioned office, the best of our country, our youth, are at the border. When I open the newspaper, or turn on the TV, I hear about a destroyed cooperative or a burned school. All these setbacks, all these uphill battles. That is the most difficult, like swimming against the current. But, I keep on going.

I feel that I can speak very honestly with you, and so I will tell you exactly what I think about the degree of disaffection in the country. I know that some people say that things were better before, and that they mean by "before," under Somoza. It was better in that what they earned covered two pair of shoes for their children, whereas now a pair of shoes is a luxury item out of reach for the average person. I think that there is a strong certainty that we would win in an armed invasion. I believe that in the diplomatic and military arenas it is correct to give that analysis, that we are winning and that we will win.

However, our fundamental problem is economic; this economic wearing down is part of the war strategy of the U. S. government, and has been written about. Because of our sovereign self-determination, the U.S. government would like to crush us like a cockroach, but our international campaign and world opinion will not permit it. So it is in the economic aspect that they attack, and the results are obvious. However, I also think that, considering the severity of the economic problems that we are suffering, the people would have risen up against this government by now if they thought that it was the government's fault. The fact that they have not done so shows a considerable degree of awareness of the causes of their misery.

But it is true that there is also a considerable percentage of responsibility that we self-critically have to accept, and it has two aspects. I recommend to you an article by Gioconda Belli in yesterday's *Barricada* in which she speaks first of *el aprendizaje*, the level of "learning" or skills, a problem that we talked about earlier, the fact that there is hardly any middle class, but rather a huge preponderance of the *clase popular*, or the poor.

In the past, those who did study had a very weak education on the whole. These things are not rectified overnight, especially with the flight of the middle class, and there are grave deficiencies at all levels of education. This means that there are many objectives that we cannot carry forward and many problems that we cannot solve for lack of preparation, awareness, *mística*, or commitment, on the part of the people. So, there is a percentage of fault to bear in which the people simply are not capable.

The other dimension to all this involves the concept and quality of service, and Gioconda writes about that as well. Service includes a respect for the dignity of the person, and things have to be done with delicacy and caring. But cashiers in the supermarkets are not taught this, for example. Neither are some bureaucrats.

There was a flagrant example recently, I talked about it with a good friend of mine in another ministry, and we protested it vigorously, and that was in the distribution of toys, so that all Nicaraguans could buy two toys. Well, they made the people stand in extremely long lines for hours on end, the lines were so long because parents will put up with a lot to be able to give toys to their children. When the people were worn out from standing there in the hot sun all day, the delivery person, when she finally arrived, just started very rudely handing the toys out, without asking the people if it was for a boy or a girl, or what ages, or what the children's interests were. This particular case was also criticized in the paper. It is bad enough that we have almost nothing, but we aggravate our problems through incompetence and inconsiderate attitudes.

Another thing that I wanted to tell you was that in economic matters, possibly since you are a Latin American specialist you have come across it too, and you have perhaps had access to more and better information on this than I, but recently I was reading Isabel Allende's novel, *La casa de los espíritus* (The House of the Spirits). Of course, I identified profoundly with the character of the Latin American woman. But with regard to economics, the author speaks of the terrible moment when they kill Allende, and then, immediately afterwards, the stores and supermarkets are suddenly filled to overflowing with all kinds of goods. That is the imperialistic aspect of things.

We are experiencing a similar reality here in which daily limitations are aggravated to the level of impossibility. Of course, this is the plan. The work of imperialism is as clear as water. Some people even make jokes about it. "Well," they say, "Arturo Cruz is with the contra and Robelo says he wants to come back. Their campaign slogans will be toilet paper and toothpaste for all!"

You know that I have a position of responsibility and that this guarantees me use of an automobile. What you may not know is that this is a very practical measure because in between meetings, phone calls, and appointments today I have to run quickly to the supermarket, because I do not have any food at home, even for lunch today. I take turns with my compañera here at work standing in line for groceries.

Similarly, there are three women here at the Ministry with small children, and they have organized themselves too. Since lines at the health clinics are long, and these people do not have private doctors, and since after seeing the doctor they have to go find the medicine and then stand in another long line to buy it, we have worked out a human, realistic agreement. These three are very responsible compañeras, so what they do is share family and job responsibilities. For example, two cover at work for the friend who is taking all their children to the clinic that day. Otherwise, you could spend all day in line, and many people do.

However difficult, these limitations can also stimulate solidarity. You simply have to cooperate and help each other out in order to get by. I don't want to romanticize, because it is not romantic, but I do believe that the revolution has helped us believe in love and our hardships have helped us to appreciate the most simple things. I realize now what a beautiful thing scented soap is! When I visit relatives in the U.S., I go to a supermarket and I get dizzy from all the array. Maybe one-fourth of what they sell in a grocery store is necessary for living, while the other three-fourths are luxury items.

The revolution has also been hard on marriages, and not just for those who are working in positions of some importance. Since this happened in the Cuban revolution as well, one might be tempted to say that revolution destroys the family, certainly that is the imperialistic propaganda. It is partly a question of work, pressure, and of changing women's roles. But it is more than that too.

First, the revolution is authenticity; it is the quest to rescue and foster that which is true, that which makes our existence worth the effort. And I think that we inherited a very mediocre world, which included many mediocre marriages. A couple that has a solid base finds ways to withstand hard times, extra work, and separations.

Often though, there is a distance between the development of the man and the woman, and the prevalence of machismo still makes it impossible for some men to stand for the woman to improve herself, and those marriages do not last. But if there is a shared base of ideology, values, and ideals and a true relationship of love, the couple will make it through crises. And there are some couples who split up during a crisis but who later manage to find each other again. For example, I had a compañero who married the same woman twice.

The second reason for so many marriages breaking up, and here I will give you the evangelical note of the person of a Christian formation, is that the revolution is a moral commitment, and not everyone is disposed to take on this commitment. So often a marriage will fail because, at bottom, the partners have different values, conceptions of the world and of life. For some, the most important thing is to have your house, your dog, your car, your material comforts, and status. Then the revolution comes along and demands more of you. If you are of the professional middle class, you have two responsibilities: to work and to teach others, because you were privileged. This means working in the neighborhood, helping to develop community, volunteering, giving to others in any number of ways. Everything becomes a collective problem in the revolution, the pain and the triumph. When someone becomes embittered, it hurts us all; likewise, when someone makes a breakthrough, it is a victory for us all.

For these reasons, when you and your spouse don't both feel the same way, then it is unbearable to go on living together. There are some people who stay, and who are in a hermetic position, closed to all the changes. Many of them finally leave. This also happened in Cuba. But here what we also have, unlike in Cuba, are people who claimed certain revolutionary militance, but who weren't able to stand it in practice, because it demands so much of one.

So, the revolution is a challenge and a deep, personal commitment. My own conclusion is that it could cost me my life, but it is worth it. I believe that I was put here on this earth at this time and in this place for a reason, and I can't get that out of my head. Yes, I could go to the U.S. to live with my relatives, eat well, and enjoy many things, but I am not interested in collaborating with a system that has dominated my country. I know that in my country I am going to endure serious difficulties, but it is a moral choice which I have made according to my own Christian conscience.

You are talking with a very religious person; it is through my Christian background and beliefs that I came to the revolution. That's why I said earlier that the revolution is fundamentally a moral option. In the face of all our problems, my religious faith never fails me. I also have faith in the people. I am confident that the people themselves are teaching us every day.

What frustrates me as far as my work is concerned is the war of aggression. Owing to the position of responsibility that I have, I know very well all that needs to be done. I have already listened to the people; I know the cultural programs that each community is trying to put together, and I have heard the expectations the people have. I know what it is that they would like to do, whether it is sponsoring a modern dance group or what; and I know the problems that they have, such as obtaining adequate costumes for the production. I know that part of the problem is that we do not have a network of rural libraries, and our resources are so limited especially now because of the contra war. But the worst frustration is to see the will, the desire, the plans, and even the demands of the people, and not to be able to respond to them. We have promoted a cultural awakening in the people and now we cannot handle it. That is terribly depressing. But I do not lose faith, and I keep on going.

When the U.S. invaded Grenada, it made a great impact on all decent, honest people in the world. It was terrible for Grenada, a tiny island smaller than Nicaragua, and the victim of such brutal arrogance. When that happened, it was like a warning for Nicaragua that we would be next. We want to keep hope, so first we have to think that they are not going to destroy us, that we are going to resist successfully. But, just suppose that all the vast panoply of might is too much for us, and they destroy us. What then? If the world stays silent and does not protest, which I desperately hope would not happen, then it will not have been worth living on this earth in the first place. But if there is a challenge to the human conscience, then it would be worth dying for, and our time here would not have been in vain.

I do not have any trouble traveling to the U.S. The first two years they gave me multiple visas for a year. This last time when I went, my first grandchild was about to be born; my son is married and living in New Orleans. In fact, I just wrote him and sent him a cassette; here is his picture. I have four children. The daughter in this photo is the only one who shares the revolution with me; she is a militant in the Sandinista Youth organization. The daughter in the other snapshot, the one who looks like me, is in Miami working in a bank and studying finance. When their father and I divorced, two of the children stayed here with me, and the two who were already teenagers went with him. They no longer live with him, but are on their own now, living in the U.S.

These two, the ones who stayed with me, I have given them permission to go take vacations in the U.S. and to visit their father, even though he is in the counterrevolution in Honduras; yes, he is working as a lawyer for the contra. I don't know exactly what he is doing, but that's just as well. Anyway, I gave the two children permission to go visit in the U.S.; then, two years ago they went to Honduras to see their father for two weeks, which turned into a month. This year, I told them that they could not go because of the war and the whole dangerous situation. But I gave them permission to go to Panama, where their grandmother, their father's mother, lives, as well as an aunt who also left Nicaragua to work for a multinational company where her husband works too. They are people who live tranquilly and comfortably. The kids visited there and of course they ate well and had plenty of everything.

My daughter visited and returned after two weeks. I told her that she should not have left her younger brother there, but since she had been with him the whole time she felt that there was nothing to worry about. There had never been a problem with their father before; they would always go and visit and return home afterwards.

Then what I had been afraid of happened: they told me that the boy didn't want to return home. I said, "No, send him home!" Instead, they sent me a tape in which he said that he wanted to stay there, would I please give him permission to stay with his grandma, his aunt and uncle, that he was just fine, very happy there, that he was not going to Honduras with his father, but wanted to stay in Panama with his relatives. I hurried down there to bring him back, this was just three months ago, but the day that I arrived, at noon, his father arrived earlier and took the boy away. Yes! And he is still there. I can only trust that his father will change and leave the contra and go to some other place, or at least realize that he is putting his son's life in jeopardy, or give the boy the space to decide for himself whether to return home.*

Do you know what the big problem is? I have always discussed our everyday realities with these two children. No one has written the last word on child-rearing; perhaps I should have told them what to do and what not to do, rather than talking things out together. Perhaps I should never have permitted them to visit their father and his family at all.

On the other hand, I wonder if my sense of respect and confidence in them and in my revolutionary role is not excessive. I know that I can not compete for their allegiance with objects, toys or material things, and perhaps I have gone too far in the other direction. Who knows? I do feel that I must do everything I can to transmit to them the values, solidarity, love, sharing and hope, that one sees here in Nicaragua. They are intangible not only for foreign visitors, but often for the Nicaraguan people themselves; however, we know that the revolution is these values. My son does not share them, but my daughter does.

This youngster of mine suffers, she is committed, she feels the responsibility. She is now at the head of seventy young literacy volunteers who are going to work in the barrios. She has already had enormous responsibilities for one so young. When she was twelve, she went to help with the coffee harvests. Her younger brother also went, but he did not like it at all and was distressed by the whole experience. There are different values expressed here. I have tried to teach what I feel is just and human, but different family members give different responses to the same reality.

I'm telling you all this simply because my case illustrates the dilemma of each Nicaraguan family. My situation reaches back a generation as well, because, as you may know, my father was a general in Somoza's guardia nacional. Our relationship had some very tense moments, since we disagreed totally about politics, our world views were opposed, and I envisioned a completely different type of society from the one that he knew. My religious group helped me a great deal in coming to terms with our fundamental differences. My father and I had a deep respect and love for each other, in spite of everything. On his retirement, Somoza named him ambassador to Guatemala, where he was fatally shot by a Guatemalan

*Ed. Note: As of June, 1989, Vidaluz's son was living with his father in the United States.

guerrilla group in 1978. It was a terrible shock, but my faith has supported me.

Returning to the discussion about my work for a moment, if it weren't for international solidarity groups, things would certainly become even more problematic for the Ministry of Culture. We have learned from experience something that people like myself, who were not very politically savvy, did not know before, and that is the following: we suffer the ups and downs of international politics with the countries with which we have cultural agreements, because governments are very sensitive and vulnerable to economic and diplomatic pressure from the United States.

That's why I tell my compañeros that we have to be alert to international news, in order to know when we are making a good or a bad impression on a government. Solidarity movements, on the other hand, are more firm, for two reasons: first, they are direct; they do not have all that protocol and formalism of government bureaucracies; and second, because the work is carried out by people of good will, who are doing it not for political gain, but because they think that it is the right thing to do.

With regard to my own work, I can't even find the drawer that I have all those notes in. I guess that indicates the priority that my own writing holds for me. It is a personal, individual choice; I really respect my compañeros who value their work as writers. Do you know what the problem is that I have? Honestly, I am going to tell you without false modesty, I have recognized that poetry is a subjective necessity of mine for self-expression. I consider myself an amateur poet, *una poeta aficionada* in that I create, I pause, I reflect, and I hit upon an appropriate theme or inspiration. But I do not have a representative body of work, and I have not given enough time to literature.

What's even more to the point, I feel this moral imperative to use my position to devote myself to reducing the distance between the levels of education of the people, the very problem that we have been discussing today, and that is what I feel drawn to work toward. This is my own problem; no one has given it to me, not the revolution, not the leaders, not the people, no one but myself. Here we get back to what we said earlier, about each person responding to certain internal demands.

I do think that I am accumulating a series of experiences that will be very important to put to paper and pass on, and I have kept an agenda of everything here since the founding of the Ministry. Unfortunately, writing, like everything else, needs its own time and space, and whether I can find that now or not remains to be seen. But we'll see, we'll see.

16 Lidia Saavedra de Ortega (b. 1920?)

"My sons have always been somewhere else, either fighting, in hiding or in jail. For more than eighteen years I had sons in jail, and that's not counting the times that they were picked up when they were still in high school."

"God and the Virgin helped me through those difficult times."

Plastic-covered saints and photos of her sons occupy every wall, shelf, and crevice in the house, symbols of the two points of reference in doña Lidia's life, her religious faith and her "boys." An attractive, silver-haired woman perhaps in her late sixties, doña Lidia is beloved by Nicaraguans for her warmth, kindness, and gentle good humor.

As the mother of President Daniel Ortega, Minister of Defense Humberto Ortega, revolutionary martyr Camilo and daughter Germania, doña Lidia has a wealth of memories and experiences to recount, from her early years in the gold-mining town of La Libertad to her later struggles to improve conditions for Somoza's prisoners, including her own son. Throughout her story, one sees that doña Lidia's deep religious faith and tenacious perserverance have sustained her when times were anxious and the outlook bleak.

I come from a part of Nicaragua that has suffered greatly because of this contra war, the province of Chontales, which was an important cattle-raising area, but which lately has been the site of fighting and of much dislocation. Currently, a number of Swedes have come to help us work to increase production, which is desperately needed. The small town where I was born, raised, and married is a gold-mining area called La Libertad. Fortunes were made and lost overnight in La Libertad. It was a boom town in the 1930s, but during the 1940s the gold gave out, and the foreign companies left. They had built lovely houses, fences, streets, churches; it was a bustling center when I was growing up. But when the companies departed, they left lock, stock, and barrel, leaving behind a desolate town, with more poor people than before. These companies, North American, English, German, just took and took without giving anything back, and when the gold ran out, they pulled up stakes.

Danielito, I call him Danielito to disinguish him from his father whose name is Daniel, was born there too, but we left by mule when he was only two months old. Danielito was my third, not my first-born. The first two children died there in La Libertad of the fever. There was so much malaria there at that time, and huge mosquitos were everywhere. That's how I lost Germania, just before her third birthday, and then Sigfrido after her. I suffered terribly from those tragedies; it was a severe shock to my nerves. My husband gave the children German names because he was very fond of German culture, and also many of the engineers excavating the mines were German and my husband admired their ability.

I was the natural child of don Benjamín Saavedra Montiel, a successful businessman, who decided to recognize me as his own, so he asked my mother, doña Mercedes Rivas, if I could come live with his other five daughters and wife in order to receive a good education. My father was in the dry goods business, but he also helped obtain credit for individuals and businesses. Unfortunately, his North American associate swindled him, and he was broke for a while. This sort of thing happened all the time in La Libertad because of the gold mines, the speculating, and all the foreigners who had come to seek their fortune.

I went to Managua to receive secretarial training and returned home to work for my father. I managed a store and sold supplies to the miners, who would come in to buy their provisions every week after receiving their paycheck. I sold everything from fine cloth to cigars. I also taught elementary school for a few years in La Libertad, but I was too intense. I would become so concerned when the students had trouble with the lessons that I would stay awake nights worrying about how I could make them understand better. I was not suited to teaching, but I loved business. I found it very challenging to keep accounts, order stock, and sell, all of which I had been very well prepared to do at the Colegio de Señoritas in Managua.

My father was quite well-respected in the town; he was the mayor, and he was a supporter of Sandino. I remember once the guardia came and occupied the town trying to get my father to pledge his support to Lt. Solórzano, chief of the guardia unit. But my father resigned his office instead. People knew of my father's resistance to Somoza, and those who followed Sandino would come to town and feel welcome. I remember one occasion when a famous anti-Somocista General named Pedro Altamirano came to father's store in nearby Santo Domingo, I was managing it at the time, and he asked for nearly all our supplies. He came with approximately 300 troops, but we provided what we had because we admired him.

I met my husband Daniel in La Libertad where he had come to work as a cashier and accountant for La Esmeralda mining company. He was born in Los Rincones of Masatepe. He was a natural child but was raised by his father in Granada and educated along with his other children. He was a Sandinista; he was very intelligent; he read a lot, and he was bold, even fearless you might say.

For example, he was working in Matagalpa managing the accounts of a wealthy commercial family when Sandino was assassinated in 1934. He was one of the few who dared protest publicly. He sent Somoza a telegram accusing him of responsibility for Sandino's death, signed the message and included a photograph so that Somoza would know who sent the telegram and would not harass innocent people. Daniel was imprisoned as a result, and the guardia took him from the jail, barefoot and half-dressed, out to the monte, or countryside, where they were going to kill him. But he was clever and a great storyteller. He asked his jailers to sit down and let him tell them a story. "Well, okay, just one," they said, but before long he had won them over with his entertaining tales, and instead of killing him, they took Daniel back to the jail.

Meanwhile, his aunts moved heaven and earth to have him transferred to Managua, and out of isolation. It also helped that don Marco Antonio Ortega, my husband's father, was director of the Instituto de Granada, where many sons of Somoza's cronies were educated. He too asked them to send his son to Managua. That influence had its effect and Daniel was transferred. His aunts visited him daily for the two years that he was in jail. During that time he, like all other prisoners, was required to read that infamous biography of Sandino that Somoza had had written [*Sandino, o el Calvario de las Segovias*], in which Sandino was accused of being a communist, a murderer, all kinds of lies. When Daniel was released, Somoza offered him money, which he rejected indignantly. Soon afterwards, Somoza sent him an insulting telegram. [It read: "Eat shit!"] I still had not met my husband at that time, but I know that it's true, because later he would proudly show the telegram to our children.

Once out of jail, Daniel had to look for a job. Many people from Granada were going to La Libertad to seek their fortune, and he did too, finding work as a cashier for the Hurtado family, owners of La Esmeralda mine. Around that time the Hourvilleur, the Cuadra, the Ulvert and the Paso families, all prominent names, also arrived in big launches that transported passengers and goods from Granada to Chontales.

This would be 1936, when I was managing the store of Adán Guerra, again selling a variety of items from thread to felt hats. The new rich and the dirt poor filled the streets at that time, for the mines seemed to have limitless gold. One day, Daniel Ortega, my future husband, not Danielito my son, you see why I call them by different names, came into the store with a group of young miners and employees of La Esmeralda to buy their weekly provisions. That's how we met, and two years later, in 1938, we were married in the church in La Libertad. My father had died earlier, but my stepmother was still living; she died much later, in Managua during the earthquake when the walls fell in on her.

I told you earlier about my first two children who died of the fever. Then Danielito was born in 1946. By that time, the gold was giving out in La Libertad. On muleback we left for Juigalpa, I had a sister there, and that's where Humberto and Germania were born. There was not much business opportunity there for Daniel and soon he left for Managua, where he found work as a cashier for the Delgado family's stores. But he also kept looking for something better and, before long, he obtained the right to represent the business interests of several foreign commercial houses that wanted to import their products into Nicaragua. After that, he was able to quit the Delgado family job and do quite well, or so we thought. I already mentioned that my husband admired German products. He was working with the Pataky house, a Hungarian concern that produced cloth and wire fencing. My husband was the principal agent promoting that new product, wire fencing. Soon he was gaining clients right and left, but when the business was at its peak, the company decided to turn over its representation to a group of German nationals living here in Nicaragua.

We were all living in Managua by then, and my husband was without work. When we could no longer pay the rent, we were thrown out of the place where we had been staying. Someone offered our family a room in another neighborhood, called Colonia Somoza ironically enough, although everything was named after Somoza in those days, and that's where Camilo, the baby, was born. Despite that big financial blow, my husband didn't give up; he stayed in the import business as an agent and imported a kind of gold to be used in dental fillings. You should have seen the dentists all come running for this new product; they thought it was a marvelous invention, gold for your teeth. Daniel always placed his orders with Germany, because their quality was the best. He recovered his losses to some extent and we got along fairly well, but certainly not comfortably, up until the earthquake, for until then my husband still had enough business for us to get by on.

The important thing is that we were able to send Danielito and Humberto to the Colegio Pedagógico, which was private and run by the Christian brothers. Danielito loved to read. Did you know that he was such a diligent, serious student that the brothers invited him to join their order? I kept their letter of invitation but it was destroyed in the earthquake. After a while, however, my sons' political activities were too much for the school to deal with, too many marches and demonstrations, and the Pedagógico refused to accept Danielito and Humberto any longer. At that point, they went to Masaya to study in the Salesian school. Not long afterwards, Danielito came back to Managua, accompanied by a priest, to participate in a national oratory contest, which he won. Some years later, when Danielito was in jail, he heard about an essay contest in Costa Rica, in honor of the 150th anniversary of the independence of Central America. From jail he wrote his essay and entered it in the contest. Someone sent it to Costa Rica for him and he won that contest too!

Danielito and Humberto were always involved in the political struggle. So was their father. About the time of the Cuban revolution, my husband would defy the guardia every afternoon by sitting in his rocking chair on the sidewalk in front of the house with the radio at full blast listening to Radio Havana. The two oldest dedicated themselves completely to the revolutionary struggle. They were both jailed while they were still in secondary school for participating in student protests against the dictatorship. Danielito was only about fourteen or fifteen when they first put him in jail, for a few days only. That was before he got his high school diploma. After he graduated from high school, Danielito was able to attend university for only a year, at the Universidad Católica before he went into clandestine work, followed by Humberto just a few days later.

Danielito loved oratory and at UCA he made very good grades in it as in everything else. All three sons made good grades in their schools, the Pedagógico, the Salesiano in Masaya, the Maestro Valdivieso, and UCA. Camilo graduated from the Salesiano because he was so involved in student politics that they wouldn't let him in the Pedagógico; Tacho's [Anastasio Somoza's] kids were studying there too you see. So Camilo went first to study in El Salvador with the Salesian fathers at Santa Cecilia in San Salvador, where he stayed for one year. Then he returned to Managua, where Humberto and Danielito graduated from the Maestro Valdivieso, and where Humberto was awarded a prize by the ambassador of Spain. Later Camilo received his degree from the Salesiano in Masaya, as I mentioned. The same year he graduated, he died in combat, in the famous insurrection of the indigenous community of Monimbó, Masaya, one of the first to revolt, in February 1978.

I was in Costa Rica when Camilo died; I had gone there when the revolution broke out. When I got the phone call, I was thankful that at least Camilo had died where he wanted to live and work and where he had gone to school. Masaya is a very picturesque place with charming customs and beautiful crafts. Danielito was working with the Frente on a mission in Honduras when Camilo was killed, and Humberto was fighting somewhere else.

My sons have always been somewhere else, either fighting, in hiding, or in jail. For more than eighteen years I had sons in jail, and that's not counting the times that they were picked up when they were still in high school. Those were very difficult times and I try not to think about the terrible torture that they endured; it makes me shudder it was so inhuman.

Danielito was arrested first for participating in a street demonstration [1960]; the second time was for setting fire to some vehicles belonging to the U.S. embassy [1961]. After he joined the Frente [1963], he must have been about seventeen or eighteen years old, he went to Guatemala where he was arrested and returned to Nicaragua [1964]. Each time he was beaten, kicked, tied up, and subjected to degrading abuse.

The longest imprisonment was when Danielito was held for seven years [1967–74] in La Modelo prison in Managua. That's when he got the scar on the right side of his forehead and nearly lost his eye from the torture. He had worn contact lenses as part of his disguise and didn't have time to take them out before the beatings started. The conditions in the prison were horrible, the boys were isolated; they were not allowed to speak to anyone; they had no exercise; they were kept in the dark and were subjected to brutal, sadistic punishment. We mothers had to fight a long time to have them taken out for sun and exercise and to be able to bring them food each week. Every privilege that was granted was the result of struggle, protest, and constant pressure. There was even a time when the mothers were not allowed to visit at all, but then the Red Cross intervened.

There were many strikes during this period, the biggest and the last one was at Santa Faz church. At that time the prisoners were on a hunger strike in the jail; it had gone on for more than thirty days, and we mothers were going crazy with worry. The students supported us, of course, as did the general population. This was the biggest of all the strikes, as I said before, it was huge. After all, the boys were dying of hunger, and I was on a hunger strike too!

We mothers all went to the church at Santa Faz where we spent the night, although the priest there, Father Peña, was violently opposed to us. He was completely antirevolutionary, I mean with arms and everything.

He has been expelled since the revolution, but at that time he was the padre of this church, and he was a pure Somocista. But still we begged him to take our letters, and to intercede on our behalf. He refused to let us in the church and threatened us with the guardia. We cried and screamed, but we did not move; we stayed there without budging. The guardia came at night, but they were unable to dislodge us either.

All the people from the neighboring communities rallied to our support. They burned tires, made bonfires, threw stones, lighted fireworks, all in defense of our cause and against the dictatorship. There was one special case of a young compañero who had completed his sentence, which was for giving a rifle to the muchachos, or boys as the Sandinistas were called, but they wouldn't let him out. Finally, because of all the uproar they released him. The struggle was for better living conditions, letting the boys go outside in the sun, giving them exercise, allowing them to have visitors, to speak to each other and not be isolated. It took *twelve* strikes in order to obtain these minimal privileges for Danielito and the others who were imprisoned with him.

It was a long struggle, and nothing was gained except by repeated protests. But finally the boys were allowed to be taken out to the patio to do exercises, and finally we got to visit on Sundays. We would come early in the morning, and often we had to wait all day, until about six to get to see them. When the Sandinista prisoners were finally allowed to read, study, and talk, each one dedicated himself to learning something different and then sharing it with the others. All those boys were *bachilleres*, secondary school graduates, and they devoured the reading materials that we brought them. I don't remember them all, but they were stories, history books, and the *Bible*. You remember how Danielito had always loved to read and how serious he was about his studies. Often in prison he would refuse a game of chess in order to study; he has an iron discipline. At any rate, Danielito and the boys would give themselves specific assignments in their books, just like a class, and then they would discuss them. That's how Danielito came to enter the history essay contest in Costa Rica that I mentioned earlier.

I don't know when Danielito would have been freed if it had not been for the Sandinista raid on "Chema" Castillo's house. He was one of Somoza's men [the minister of agriculture] and he was having a Christmas party at which many important Somocistas were present. The commandos broke in, held the guests hostage, and didn't release them until they agreed to put Danielito and the others on a plane to Cuba. Then Danielito stayed in Cuba for two years [1974-76] doing political work for the Frente, writing pamphlets, and studying; he returned secretly to Nicaragua in 1976 to continue working underground for the revolution.

Perhaps the worst time for me was earlier, when Humberto also fell prisoner, in Costa Rica. I went to San Jose, but I also kept visiting Danielito in Managua at La Modelo. When I had returned back here to Nicaragua, I received word that they were denying treatment to Humberto, he had been wounded in the arm when he was taken prisoner, and I knew that he was in excruciating pain. So I returned to San Jose and demanded an accounting from the warden of the prison. He blamed it on the hospital, saying that they were the ones who had refused to admit Humberto. Then I went to speak to the director of the hospital, who told me that the warden had lied. After eleven days of struggle, in which the international Red Cross intervened along with many *ticos,* or Costa Ricans, and *nicas,* the authorities were forced to treat Humberto, who barely avoided the loss of his arm. A few days later Humberto obtained his freedom.

Then came the earthquake in 1972; by then my husband was ill with diabetes and we were having serious financial problems as well. So with our daughter Germania we moved to the farm of a friend in Juigalpa. It was from there that every Sunday at 4:00 a.m. Germania and I would set out for La Modelo to visit Danielito until he was liberated in December 1974. The following year my husband died of diabetes. In 1977 I moved to San José, Costa Rica; remember that's where I was living when I was told that Camilo had died. He was in charge of the work for the Sandinistas in Masaya and all the surrounding area. He was always so happy and generous, and completely dedicated to the cause.

Meanwhile, Germania, who was married and living in Costa Rica, decided to return to Nicaragua. A few days after her return, a Sandinista commando unit assaulted the National Palace [August 22, 1978] and, immediately the guardia captured Germania. They tried to get her to reveal Humberto's and Danielito's whereabouts, but she would not tell them anything. Thanks to international pressure she was freed, but she had to seek asylum in the Mexican embassy. Months later she was reunited with me in San José, shortly before the triumph. God and the Virgin helped me through those difficult times.

The thing that kept me going is that I always knew that what my boys were doing and what they believed in was right; what they were fighting for was human and Christian. I also knew that in life, one must give without expecting recompense. The Virgin lost her son, and compared to that my situation wasn't so bad. I'm very religious; everywhere around the house I have my saints as you can see. I especially love the Virgin of Carmen. I gave Danielito a scapular of her when he was young because it has so much power. My children were all baptized and confirmed and made their first communion. I used to have pictures of these events, but they were destroyed in the earthquake, along with the diplomas and other memorabilia.

Do Danielito and his family go to mass? I think the best answer is that they have their faith. They baptized all their children. Father D'Escoto, the foreign minister, baptized them. The important thing is to practice one's faith, not necessarily to go to mass, but to be a good brother, a good compañero. And as long as one is not offending religion or offending God, they're good Catholics. And my children are good Catholics.

I am thankful that my family is not ambitious or covetous. Many people think they are getting rich, Danielito and his family, with lots of money and property in Costa Rica. But Danielito's only ambition is to govern the country in order to help the people. He is concerned about the poor, about providing them with farming cooperatives, health care, and education. These are the things that are important to him. Those other stories are terrible lies. Why don't they mention some of the well-known reform efforts, like the agrarian reform, in *La Prensa?* Do they think back in the U.S. that all those lies that paper prints are true? Why does *La Prensa* print gossip and scandalous stories when there are so many people who are working selflessly for the revolution? And what about people like Arturo Cruz, Alfonso Robelo, and Violeta Chamorro? When they were in the junta, why didn't they keep on helping the country? Why didn't they criticize constructively and try to help instead of going over to the contra? But I know that the eye of God sees all, justice and injustice, and we can take comfort in that knowledge. I have great faith in God. And I know that people can change, because I have seen members of the wealthiest, most reactionary land-holding families turn out to be generous supporters of our farming cooperatives.

I also have faith that things will improve over time. When Obando became Cardinal, Danielito went to congratulate him and there we were chatting with him. And as we were leaving I said to him, "Monsignor, don't you believe that it is the work of God that this boy is where he is after all that he has been through and suffered? With all the physical and psychological torture that he has sustained for so many years, and to keep going on like this, don't you think that it is God's work? It is God who gives Danielito the courage to go on." "Yes, yes," he answered. "Please Monsignor, ask Mr. Reagan to stop this aggression," I continued. *"Vamos a hablar,"* he said, "We'll speak." That's all he responded, but that's something.

I think that things will improve in the future. I have great hopes for my grandchildren, that they will grow up practicing the principles of the revolution and doing everything they can for their country. As I have great faith in the Virgin, so I also have faith that this country one day will overcome and prosper.

17   Ernesto Flores (b. 1930s?)

"It's not the same, life here and life in the country. I don't like it here. The difference is that in the country, everything is more favorable, easier, and if a person wants to plant, well, he just plants, and that's that. It's up to him."

"My kids can all read and write some. . . . As for me, I'm the last illiterate left in Nicaragua!"

His dirty undershirt, stubble beard, and gold tooth retreated and advanced as the hammock swayed back and forth, and don Ernesto's words kept steady pace with the accustomed rhythm. His wife had prepared a tortilla and a small portion of rice pudding for me, the family's meal for the day, and as guest I was obliged to eat it all. Miriam Lazo was right, the campesino's generosity is overwhelming. I hoped that someone in the barrio would soon bring a hog for don Ernesto to butcher, his only work now that he has moved back to the city.

A woodcutter by trade, don Ernesto Flores has moved often in his life, cutting, hauling, and selling wood to the highest bidder in times of plenty, and enjoying the sense of independence that work provided him. Now, times are thin; soil erosion is a serious problem and scarce natural resources are tightly controlled by the government. Moreover, the contra war has frustrated don Ernesto's efforts at subsistence farming and forced him, grudgingly, to flee to the crowded capital.

Now, with nothing to do, don Ernesto sits in his hammock outside his humble ranchito for hours on end. He does not possess the skills or the desire to hold a regular job; he is unable to adjust to working for someone else; and he is unhappy about being separated from the land.

However, don Ernesto is naturally good-humored and greatly enjoys telling jokes and stories. Here, he recalls his personal experiences gained over some fifty-odd years I would guess, offers some wry political commentary, and waits for conditions to improve in the countryside.

I don't know what to say about myself exactly. I don't remember when I was born, of course, but who does? I was brought up by my grandparents in El Sauce. They took me in when I was little. My mother was very poor; she would take me to my grandparents' house when she went to work, and pick me up afterwards. After a while, my grandfather told my mother just to leave me there with them, and they would take care of me. She did, until I was about ten. We went to mass a lot, prayed to the images in the house, the saints, you know. When I grew up this practice ended; hardly anybody has even one *santito* now. I don't know why; people used to be so Catholic and all that. And people used to go to church more too. Now we go sometimes, when we need special help with something. But I listen to the voice of God on the radio every day, also to the Voice of Nicaragua and Radio Católica, which was closed for a long time like *La Prensa*, but not anymore. I sit here in my hammock and listen to the radio; one can hear the word of God everywhere, not only in church. Anyway, one day my father came and took me away with him to live on a farm that he had. I stayed with him until I was about fifteen, and then I left to be on my own. I never went to school. My father didn't send me because we lived so far out of town. When I was very little my grandparents sent me, but just for a few days, because it was too much trouble. I didn't understand about school.

On the farm, I milked the cows, and worked in the field where we had corn, plantains, and bananas. We had plenty to eat; in those days there was food left over and you gave it away to people; you didn't sell it. People didn't start selling their extra food until the railroad came to Río Grande, and there they began selling. I remember fish went for one and a half pesos for a hundred, and one hundred bananas was about the same, maybe two pesos. Can you believe that? Now it's eight hundred; that's nearly a thousand pesos for one banana! My father inherited his plot of land; his father had worked for a lady named Irene Uriarte, and she divided it four ways and my grandfather was one of the four people. It was big, about three hundred *manzanas* and we worked there together.

I had no other brothers and only one sister, who was born when I was already big, about eight or nine years old. She still lives in the place where

I was born, near El Sauce. She works on a farm. She has cattle, coffee. We hardly ever visit them. But they came here two weeks ago because my father just died, and they came for the novena they pray for the dead. He died here, he was living with us. He died of old age, but first he suffered for two years.

Like I say, I left home when I was fifteen. I don't know why, but I no longer felt content there; I guess I was restless. I started working in that same area, but on my own, cutting wood out there in the mountains, and selling it in places like Managua and León, also Chichigalpa and Chinandega. I carried the wood by truck; I would borrow a truck and pay rent for it. Now there's hardly any wood left to cut. It's a recent problem. When Somoza was around, it was also true that if you didn't have a permit you couldn't take out wood. But now, it's prohibited; they hardly give any permits at all. Possibly because there are fewer trees, but maybe too because they're depriving the little people, because I think there's still a lot of wood around here. Before it was free; now you have to get a forestry permit and cut where they say, and they have to show you the site.

I was a woodcutter for fifteen years or more. I met many people that way. I traveled all around, also to Matagalpa; I sold wood everywhere. We were rich with wood in those days; there was so much of it. *Pochote*, bombax, is the one we cut most; but now it's scarce. It was perfect because it was not a hard or a soft wood, but in between, so you could use it for a lot of things. We also cut hard woods like ash and *guanacaste*, conacaste, and mahogany as well, but it's not as hard. On a typical day I would get up at dawn, about 3:00 or 4:00 a. m., because I had to travel a long way to work. Sometimes I had ten or twelve people cutting wood for me. We would have two, three, or four oxcarts, and each oxcart had two people, not counting the laborers, who were separate. I hired them on a per day basis. It was a fabulous, fabulous job because it was something I knew how to do. I also liked being in *el monte*.

When that job finished, I went for two or three years to a place called San Juan de Limay to cut pine trees, again on my own. I like being on my own. I took the wood and sold it in what is now Ciudad Sandino; I also took it to some factories that used wood to make furniture and things. I brought it by train or by truck. I caught the train at Río Grande and came here to sell. I also sold pine in Chichigalpa. I would sell to the one who gave me the best price, but that's all over now. There's no more, no more wood except if you work for a company or for a cooperative like they have in the north, in Cerrillo for example. I've thought about it, because I'm bored here in the city with nothing to do; but it's not my way, it's not for me. And I think it would cost a lot because they use tractors, they don't use oxen or carts, so you have to have machines. A long time ago there were private tractors and I worked for two years with tractors, for

Estanislao Zavala in Chinandega; he had a tractor he rented about fifteen years ago or so.

I also lived in the Department of León in a place called Monte Frío. We left there in '71 for Managua, and then came the earthquake the next year! We lived in another neighborhood, but we left it. We came to Managua because of a circumstance that came up so that I couldn't stay in Monte Frío any more. What happened was this: I had a few cows, and then some rustlers came and stole them from me. The guardia got them back for me, and then the thieves were angry and came to kill me. Alfredo Sánchez was after me; there were three of them, but he was the worst. So I had to sell my little farm and get out of there. We lived pretty well too, and we had work.

After the earthquake of '72, we got out of here and went back to the country where we bought another little farm, a *finquita,* in Villa Nueva, in Chinandega, about 180 kilometers from here by truck. The road was good then; it's the one to Honduras. It was paved too; it was a real highway, and we were only about one or two leagues off the road. We went there because, well, I don't know why really, but we liked it and stayed six years. Then we went to a place near Guinea, on the coast, where we stayed three more years. My wife knows the dates better than I; let's see, this is '87, well, I can't remember when it was. I can tell you this though, if it hadn't been for the war, we wouldn't have come back here. That's for sure.

That was the best place we ever lived in. It was called the Carlos Fonseca Amador colony, and it was about 30 kilometers outside Nueva Guinea. The land was so fertile there that everything you planted grew, and the beans were wonderful. During the time of Somoza, I used to plant quite a bit, and there was a company that bought from me. But with the contra war, I lost my crop two years running, what with the trouble and all. Nobody bought *anything* from me then, nothing, or from anyone else either. Let's see, I've been here three years, and I was there three years; that would make it about '81, '82, '83, '84 or '85, right? That place was marvelous, green and fertile. It was a beautiful place to work. Many journalists and foreigners came there too, collecting information for different things; I guess because of the war. But mostly it was full of army people, because the contra were usually in the montaña.

Anyway, I built a pretty house there; it was huge. Why, this house here is small and ugly by comparison. I spent about 100,000 pesos building it, and had to sell it for 41,000! What a joke, but that's the breaks. It was made of *tambo;* everybody there made their houses from *tambo* and wood planks. It had one large room, one "free" room for eight people, and a separate kitchen, a little house set apart a bit, because when you have a kitchen in the house you get too much smoke and you can get burned too. I don't like these kitchens they have now, inside the house.

Like I said, we were there three years, and I kept hearing about the contra but I never saw one. The one time they entered our village, I was away in Managua, so I never saw one, and still haven't. My family didn't see them either because they were hiding under the bed or else were flat on the floor because of all the bullets flying around. I imagine that the whole village was like that, on the ground, and nobody saw anything. Maybe *no* one looked up and saw a contra, but they were there for about four hours, shooting things up, throwing bombs, starting fires, and people were killed. The army was nearby and came later; nobody was afraid of the soldiers, just of the contra. Because of that we sold our house and came here, bought this *ranchito;* we all came together.

We found this place because, you know how it is, poor people always have to keep looking until they find the cheapest place to buy. We bought a *ranchito* on this site for 50,000 pesos, but it wasn't this nice house you see here, no. No sir! It was a crummy little wooden shack which I tore down. Then I built this, which is much bigger and nicer, and has concrete blocks. It's very difficult to find construction materials, but we went a little at a time. I finished this place about three months ago, and it took about two months to build. The problem is that you can't just go to a store and find the things you need, either because they don't have them or because they don't sell them to just anybody. They have some stock in the hardware stores for example, but they may or may not sell it to a person like me.

I like building houses. Wherever we've gone, I've built us a house. Many places, many houses. Except for here, they've always been in the country. It's not the same, life here and life in the country. I don't like it here. The difference is that in the country, everything is more favorable, easier, and if a person wants to plant, well, he just plants, and that's that. It's up to him. Also, in the country you don't have to buy water, you don't have to buy wood, and so on. Where we were in Fonseca we did buy firewood, but we got it cheap from a friend in the neighborhood who was a woodcutter. But here you work and work, you work more and don't have any money or anything else to show when you're through. Here, if you want a job, you can get something, but not my kind of work. What I mean is that I don't want a *job,* to go out and get a job. I like to work, but not at a job. I just can't get used to it. We simply work here at the house ourselves, to keep going. When there are any, I butcher hogs for a few people here in the neighborhood, and my wife makes tortillas and *nacatamales* and sells them to our neighbors.

I don't know the neighbors very well, people come and go a lot here.

I have a few relatives here that I see from time to time. But we really don't get out much; we hardly leave our house. I greet people in the street, and occasionally we take the bus to the *Mercado Oriental,* the Eastern Market, but that's our main outing. We also take the bus to the hospital and to the clinic. Like when we just buried my brother last Friday. You see, he came here for my father's novena and funeral. But he drank too much, so we took him to the hospital, Manolo Morales. He was beyond help by then and he died there. They tried very hard and were very good at the hospital. They worked on him a long time, but it was no use. Then we took him by truck to Chinandega to bury him, because his family is there. All our barrio goes to a nearby health clinic that's good, but they don't have enough medicine and by 4:00 a.m. the lines are already long. They're not too many campesinos in this barrio; I think I'm the only one. There are mostly people who lost their homes because of the earthquake. But there's a newer barrio a little ways up, where my friend Domingo lives and where everyone is from the campo.

Things have gotten worse because now we have less. Our way of living has gone down. Before, we had more resources, we had cattle, pigs, chickens; we used to live better. Now life is very hard. Whose fault is it? There's no one to blame, because neither government has helped, neither the one that left or the one that's here now. Nobody gives away anything to anyone. Although, during the Somoza years, I had quite a bit of work. The bank helped me, gave me loans and credit so I could buy seeds and grain. Whenever I asked for credit at the bank, they would give it. Now, the government doesn't do that because we don't even have any work to ask credit *for;* we are living just to eat. But if I was out in the country again, I could get credit. They would give it to me because in the past I always paid back my loans. If we went back, they'd help us again. Now, here, if my wife or I have to buy anything, we have to have our children help us, because we don't have any money of our own. Four of them are working, one does housecleaning; one does bookkeeping; one works in a cloth factory; and one, my only son, works where they make feed for animals. He's nineteen years old.

I don't know if I'll stay here or not. If things get better, I'll go back to the country, because there I can *do* something, and here I can't do *anything.* But my children like it better here because they have a way to make their living; they're employed and what would they do if we returned to el monte? If things get better out there, I'll go back by myself. Yes, that's what I'll do. My wife, she'll stay here, not because she likes it, she likes the country more, but because everyone is working and she has to take care of them and the house. But *yo sí puedo salir,* I sure can go, and I can go alone, because *hay que trabajar uno siempre; del trabajo vive uno,* one must work always; one lives from one's work.

Yes, my family would stay here. My kids can all read and write some. And I'm proud of them. I can only write a few letters of my name. That reading, I tell you, reading is the future, and they're ready for it. I never was involved in anything political, never had any contact at all either with Somocismo or the revolution, except, well, yes, except for the Literacy Crusade. They sent to our area those who were going to teach and we helped them. We gave them food, animals to carry them, we did everything but take lessons. I didn't want to learn; I went to a class for a few days in Villa Nueva but, bah, it was too late for me, and nothing stuck. Many others went though. In some parts the *brigadistas,* the teachers, were well-received by the campesinos, but in others the contra was after them; they were also after the campesinos who went to classes. Where we were no, but not far away they killed one youngster who was teaching. A few of my friends went to classes during the crusade and then afterwards did the follow-up courses for a little while, but that's all over now. That was just for a certain time. But they did learn something. As for me, I'm the last illiterate left in Nicaragua!

Before, things were better. There was more freedom in the countryside. You didn't have to worry about the contra, about having enough, or about the government taking things away from you. For example, I used to like to buy cows and pigs, but now with this MICOIN business (Ministerio de Comercio Interior, Ministry of Internal Commerce), these government people rationing things, you can't even bring *frijoles,* beans, back from the country. That MICOIN institution says they're the only ones who can buy grain; it's the government you know. If I take a *quintal,* a hundred pounds, of beans on the bus with me, they'll take it away because it's prohibited. They just come on the bus and inspect and take it away. I think that they keep it and take it to their house, or they sell it. Yes, it's bad; it's not right. If I go to Esteli to buy a *quintal* of corn or beans, on the highway, MICOIN will take it away from me.

Last year I lost a lot of corn that way, in Juigalpa. They stopped the bus, MICOIN did, and took it away, just like that. They say it's because that way they're protecting the consumer. They say they don't want the consumer to get cheated, so instead of someone else cheating you, *they* do it. Ha! Lately though, I went to Chichigalpa and they let me back in with no hassle. I think it's worst in the north, not because of the war, but because it's a better business for them there. For them, maybe, but for the rest of us, *se ha quebrado la vida al mundo entero;* we are broke, really bad off. I wish things would get better. We have to keep on hoping.

18   Guilhermina Fiedler (b. 1910)

". . . we did not let things get the best of us, because we always looked for a way to survive, we have always had that custom."

"I can get along with this government. They leave me alone and I leave them alone."

Doña Guilhermina was seated in her favorite spot, the secluded patio at the back of her small guest house, amidst the luxuriant, carefully tended plants still dripping from their thorough late-afternoon watering. As the steam began to rise from the tiles, the dignified, silver-haired grandmother began to recount her singular past, conversing with me while mending by hand the worn but spotless pillowcases for her guests' use.

Doña Guilhermina's faultless memory endows her narrative with a fluid coherence and vividness, whether she is recalling her earliest memory as a refugee at age two, seeking sanctuary in a church in León; her family's deportation by Anastasio (Tacho) Somoza during World War II because of their German birth; her eyewitness account of the bombing of Dresden; or her more recent experiences as owner of a private business in revolutionary Nicaragua. Here we see one who has learned, practically from the cradle, what it means to be a survivor.

I am from León, where my father was a doctor. He was German and my mother was Nicaraguan. When I was a little girl in León there were no paved streets or any electric lights. When my father took me to Germany in 1922, I had never seen electricity and to me that's what Europe was, electricity! Of course, I was eleven years old then. We were five children, I had four younger brothers. My parents took the three oldest of us to Europe after the First World War.

My earliest childhood memories, they are not of games or play, but of revolutions. Remember, we are in Nicaragua! I recall vividly something that happened when I was *two* years old! My father had been here in Nicaragua for a number of years, when he had to go back to Germany for a while because his mother had died. What I remember is that my mama was afraid to be by herself and she was afraid that something would happen to us, because there was so much shooting and also random violence at that time. Mama had an *empleada,* she was the one who took care of us, take us to La Recolección church, where many people had fled for shelter and safety. Normally, at La Recolección, they took in young girls who were like orphans and had no home or parents. But now there were many more people than usual and there was not enough room for everyone. We slept in the crowded corridors on *petates,* straw mats. I was afraid of the gunfire and the bats at night, especially the bats because they would fly about the corridors and doorways. I couldn't see them but I could hear the noise they made when they flew around.

I am five and one half years older than my oldest brother. He lives in Germany. My family is small now, because only my brother is there now. The other three fell in the Second World War. I have two cousins and two nephews, children of my dead brother, and my brother who is still alive, he has two married daughters, that brother is also a doctor like our papa.

My father came to Nicaragua because he wanted to experience something new and different. He met a German doctor by the name of Rochu back home in Dresden one day. That doctor had lived here in Nicaragua, and he was of the same student association as my father. He told my father all about Nicaragua, where he worked with another German, named Gibler, who had a pharmacy. Those two friends worked together as a pharmacist and a doctor. My father came over to join them, but he didn't stay in Managua where the other two were. Instead, he struck out on his own to León. He was about twenty-eight at the time. It was a great adventure in those days. Just imagine, he traveled by steamship both to get here and then to get from place to place within Nicaragua.

My three brothers who are dead, well, World War II came and they served Germany and were killed. Guillermo, all our family is named Guillermo, but I'm talking about the one following me. Do you know that I have my family tree from my father's side that goes back for hundreds of years, I will show it to you. Well, my papa took my brothers and myself over there to Germany to go to school. We were staying with my grandfather, and an unmarried sister of my father took care of us. My brothers, well Guillermo is still a doctor there, and another was an engineer, and the other two who fell were just students. One studied engineering, and the other medicine.

I went first to a public school there because none of us knew German; we had always spoken Spanish at home because mama didn't speak German, so we knew only Spanish. We could say "good morning" and "good evening" in German, and that was all. You can't imagine two more different languages or cultures either, completely different. We would enter a room and leave the door open. They would ask us, "Don't you have doors in your houses in Nicaragua?" We would say, "Yes, but we don't close them because of the heat." We only closed the door at night. And over there it was just the opposite, you had to close the doors because of the cold.

Another thing I remember was that I had never seen a gas stove; I was familiar only with a wood fire, because that's how we did all our cooking. I had watched our cook put the milk on the fire back home, and what she did was heat it until it boiled over, remove it from the fire, return it to the fire, and repeat that process twice more, so that it boiled over three times in all. When my aunt in Germany asked me to fix the milk one morning, I followed the exact procedure that I had observed at home, because I thought that was the proper way to do it. I still remember the scolding she gave me for making such a mess in the kitchen.

School there was hard for me; I spoke with almost no one outside the house, and only with the teacher in school. I felt very self-conscious trying to speak in my bad German. This teacher made me go around and observe other classes, and be with other children when they were playing so that I would become more familiar with the language and customs. I stayed in that school for the six years of primary school. After that, they put me as an internal student in a colegio, a secondary school. After that comes the *gimnasio,* and then the university. But I just attended secondary school. Maybe I wasn't a good student, but I was much more interested in practice than in theory, which is what they taught us.

Afterwards, I returned home to Nicaragua because my mama was saying that she had five children and not one of them was with her. My mama arrived in Germany after we had been there for four years to leave my two youngest brothers. My papa was here in Nicaragua the whole time. We all missed each other a lot. At first I was so lonely that all I could think of was coming back to Nicaragua, but then I made friends and I got used to the customs. However, it was difficult, and when I got married, I told my husband that I didn't want our children to go to Germany to study when they were young, only when they were older. I wanted them to finish secondary school here and to know how we live, do things, and earn a living in this country before going away to study.

I was in Germany until 1931, when I came back to León to be with my mama. Since I was the only daughter, I was the one who came back. That's when I met my husband in León. He had a contract to work with a German mercantile house. He was German too; when he finished his contract with that firm, we got married and he went into business for himself. At the beginning, he had a store where he sold household articles. He also exported and imported cowhides, which they put in frames in order to dry and stretch. He also exported to Germany cotton and raw rubber, which was brought down from Las Segovias. These were very small businesses at the beginning, but they grew so that he even had a branch office in Managua. I helped him when he was just getting started.

But when the Second World War came, and they put my husband on the blacklist, he could no longer work here in Nicaragua. They took him prisoner, and my father too, for being German, and my father was quite elderly at that time. Then, they sent them to the U.S. They sent my husband with a group that went to a place called Segoville, I think that's correct, it is near Dallas. Later, I joined him there. Then we were taken to Crystal City. That's how my daughter came to be an American citizen; she was born in Texas, in 1943.

Segoville was at that time a girls' reformatory school from which they dislodged the young women in order to make room for us, the deportees from Nicaragua. We were deported because we were German; well I wasn't, I was a Nicaraguan citizen, but since my husband and my father were German that's all that mattered to the authorities. We were treated very well there, we just couldn't leave the premises, which were enclosed by a fence and which had guard towers. Somoza was pressured by the U.S. government to send all people of German descent to the U.S. It was against our will that we went, but they treated us well there.

In the meantime, my father and my husband had to abandon their professions, although my father was just about retired. At first we were in different places, my husband was in Camp Kennedy. When I came, they took my group to Segoville. After I had been there a while, a group of men arrived which included my husband. You see, at first they separated the men and the women. First, they took my husband away from Nicaragua. Then he wrote me from Camp Kennedy saying that it would be good if I could leave too because we didn't know how long the war would last and how long we would be apart, so the best thing would be to try to get together now, and with our children, that was in 1942.

There were Japanese, Italians, and Germans there in the same encampment. Practically all the Germans were married to *latinas*. There were

German women too, but the majority of Germans were men. They were sent there from Costa Rica, Peru, all Latin America, because of U.S. pressure, no? *Toda la vida ha sido así, ¿no?* It's always been that way, right? The worst problem for us was that my husband was in deep despair from having nothing to do. He was young and active, about forty-three years old, and all he was allowed to do was play soccer. And once a week, they took him to work a construction shift on a swimming pool that someone was building in the countryside.

We were more than 2,000 souls there in that camp, and my husband and I were among the lucky ones, we had a bungalow. That's when I fell in love with bungalows; they are precious and so comfortable. I always thought that when we returned to Nicaragua, if I could just have a bungalow, I would be happy. I don't want anything more than a bungalow, I would tell my husband. But I had a great need to work and work hard after my husband died. I will tell you about that later.

What happened was that we were in Texas for two years, until 1944, and then we were sent to Germany. We were exchanged on a one-to-one basis. That means that for every German that was sent back to Germany, a North American who was in a concentration camp was returned to the U.S. We were taken in Red Cross steamships to Lisbon, and then we went by train to Austria *en plena guerra,* in the middle of the war. There, in Austria, was a *lager,* a camp, where people like us who were coming from outside would arrive. They had told us that by going to one of these places, one of these *lagers,* we would have a better chance of finding lodging or maybe an apartment. But it was not true, for everything was in chaos because of the war, there was no system or organization for us.

Through much searching and inquiring, my husband and I finally got an apartment through a friend in Dresden, that's where my husband was from originally. That friend didn't need the apartment for himself because he was free and could go. My husband had made a little money in *acciones,* in stocks and investments, before the war, later we lost every penny, because he was always looking for a way to secure the future of our children, since everything around us was so insecure. His plan was that the interest on the money we had in Nicaragua would pay for the childrens' education, and that the day they wished to establish themselves they would have the savings to divide among themselves. We then began to work just for ourselves, my husband and I, for our future, but the war came at that time, and we were deported. Anyway, once we were deported to Germany we had no money for ourselves, so my husband had to work very hard. He tried to work in stocks there in Dresden, but that was a complete disaster; there was no normal business activity then, and we were totally without money. Fortunately, my husband was able to get a job in a grocery store, so we had enough to eat from then on.

We were there during the bombing of Dresden. It was terrible! We didn't live in the downtown area, thank God, but about 7 kilometers outside. We lived on the middle floor of a three-story flat. At night, we always listened to the radio, and we rolled down these heavy dark shades so that no light could be seen. It was practically pitch black inside our flat. When the bombardment began, it was as if we were standing out in the patio in the noonday sun. It was brilliant with light, incandescent like Christmas lights, that's the way they described it at the time, like a Christmas tree. Everything was illuminated with such intensity that it was blinding. What we did was to run out to the patio to see what was happening, and then we went back inside and woke our three children up and took them down to the basement. Later, we felt the fear.

I will never forget it, but we did not let things get the best of us, because we always looked for a way to survive, we have always had that custom. Then came the Russian occupation, and I had nothing to do with them. To tell the truth, I thought that they were *en cierto modo brutos,* brutish and rude. I heard how the women in the neighborhood, see, we had the last house on the street, and immediately beyond it there was a little forest, and the Russians would drag the women out there and we could hear the screams. I never went outside, I just stayed in the house. We were three years in Dresden; we spent a year in Berlin too.

In Berlin, there was a North American refugee camp. The people arrived there, refugees I guess you would say they were, and since we were Central Americans and two of my children had been born in Nicaragua and I had too, and my daughter was an American citizen, we had the right to go there. They took us in and we stayed for six months. Then they threw us out because we had no papers. All our papers had been taken away from us when we left the U.S. so we were unable to identify ourselves. We had nothing but our word to tell them about our nationality and identity. Through the Red Cross we wrote my mother, who had stayed here in Nicaragua, but since you were allowed only twenty-five words, she never understood what we wanted. She remembered that we had left Nicaragua with papers, right, and she didn't understand that we wanted more papers in order to return. Of course, there were no diplomatic representatives or anything at all like that, just the opposite. In France I heard that there was someone, but we had no idea who it was or how to find that person. Besides, we could not travel to France because we had no papers.

Later, President Román y Reyes was installed here in Nicaragua, and through him my mama was able to arrange that our papers be sent to us and for my husband to be given a safe conduct. Then we could begin the process of applying for permission to leave Germany. The war had been over for about a year by then. Like I said, we were a year in Berlin, six months in the refugee center, and six months outside. We already had permission to enter Nicaragua, all of us, but not to leave Germany, that is what we were waiting for. Finally, we all received permission to leave except for my husband, whose visa was denied. So what could he do but *salirse negro,* leave clandestinely.

I left with the children for France, Paris, and there we met up with my husband, who had traveled hidden on the train. When they would arrive at a *control,* a checkpoint, or a guard would come by, he would sit very calmly and read the newspaper. And it worked! They didn't pay him any attention. The trains were very crowded and that helped too. Also, earlier, in order to leave Dresden, we had to pass through Russian *control.* We had travel permission for only one person, but there were five of us. Again, we were lucky, because we all went together on the train and no one investigated us. We had luck and maybe a little courage, at least my husband did; he was very brave.

I waited in Paris for two weeks for my husband; he had told me that he would be arriving around such and such a date and to wait for him. So, I waited for him, and he arrived. He then tried to figure out how we should make the trip to Nicaragua. If we went by ship it was a lot cheaper, but very difficult. We knew many people who were waiting for boat passage for a long time, but they were paying in hotel fees what they were saving in fares. So my husband said, "We have to go by plane," and that's how we did it. That was the first time I had ever flown across the Atlantic Ocean; it was on KLM. We went from Paris to Amsterdam, where we changed to KLM. Then we went to Iceland, and from there to New York. From New York to Curacao, then to Panama, to San Jose, and finally to Managua. The day we arrived in Nicaragua, we celebrated my oldest son's twelveth birthday. We just missed having to pay adult passage for him! And that would've been impossible since we had spent everything for the tickets.

Returning to Nicaragua after six years absence we went straight to León where my mother had a large house and we lived with her while my husband began to see how he could reestablish himself. He soon decided that he couldn't get the kind of work that he wanted in León because before, when there were no highways to Managua, all the commerce that came from Las Segovias would go to León along *caminos de carrete, por mulas,* paths traveled by mule-drawn carts.

My husband decided to move to Managua because that's where business opportunities now were. But he had no funds; the money we had left in the bank here when we were first deported to the U.S. had been frozen. When we returned here it was the same thing as having no money at all, because the funds remained frozen and my husband remained on the blacklist. So, I was always going to the U.S. embassy begging them to remove my husband from the blacklist, that we had to eat. My mama had already mortgaged the finca so that we could eat. My father was still in Germany, unable to return. My husband could not get a job while he was still blacklisted. Finally, they took his name off and he began to look for a job.

My husband began with *representaciones,* that is, representing foreign houses, U.S. and foreign firms doing business here. Later, when Germany was on its feet again, he began doing business with German firms. It helped a lot that my husband could read, write, and speak English and German as well as Spanish. That's what he worked in from then on, but he no longer exported, he just worked as a representative.

My husband died in a terrible accident. He went to the Atlantic Coast, and the plane that he was returning home on crashed into a volcano. It was an Aeronica plane with sixteen people aboard, and everyone was killed immediately. It will be thirty years ago in January. The crash occurred on the island of Ometepe in Lake Nicaragua; the plane crashed into Concepción volcano. At that time our oldest son was in Germany studying, but I was no longer able to support him there. He had finished his degree in Germany, where he had studied commerce, but we wanted to send him to England to study further. After the accident, I had to bring him home.

My son returned to Nicaragua to work after the death of my husband. My other son, in those days, was finishing his secondary degree, and my daughter was thirteen and was going to the American school here. At that time, my brother, the one who is now back in Germany, was here in Nicaragua, because he too had returned here after the war. He worked in León as a doctor, of course, right!

I didn't have time to grieve after my husband's death. I had to learn quickly how to make a living for myself and my two younger children. But I had no trade, no degree of any kind, and I had never worked at all except for helping my husband when we were first married, which by then was many years ago. The only thing I knew how to do was to cook a *little* and run a household. So, I thought that I should try to run a small guest house, because that would be like a house, only slightly larger. That way I could always stay at home, because I prefer not to go out, but to come out here to the patio when I need peace and quiet and fresh air. I had this house built here, because we had lived downtown until shortly before the earthquake.

I was very nervous when I opened up the guest house, not knowing if I could make a go of it or not. To tell the truth, I knew very little about cooking, and I didn't think that people would like the meals that I prepared. However, I had very good fortune, because the first people to arrive were a couple, an Italian husband and a Spanish wife, and an old man who was

Italian too. Those three were so friendly and appreciative that they gave me great encouragement. I really needed that because I was timid and uncertain of myself. After they left, two Germans came, and they too were good people and gave me more encouragement to continue.

My son Federico, not the oldest who studied commerce, but the other one who is an engineer, drew up the plans for this house. My mother gave me my inheritance, because I certainly needed it at that time, and since she was very old she offered it to me. She told me, "Why not? Just give me the interest that the bank gives you, because I have to eat too." And that's what I did. I bought this plot of land and began to build the first floor. Where the bar is now was a patio. I rented five rooms because Federico was unmarried at the time and he lived here with me. I gave three meals a day to the clients at that time. *Mucho trabajo*. I did all the cooking. By 5:00 a.m. I was already in the kitchen, because the guests took their breakfast at 6:00 a.m. In those days, everyone started their work day very early, so I had to give people their breakfast early.

Federico worked and studied at the same time, and my daughter was still in secondary school. My daughter never did live in this house. Almost exactly when I opened up here, it was in September, she went to the U.S. to study. I don't remember the year, but I was here before the Intercontinental Hotel opened. Later, my other son, Jorge Guillermo, named after my husband, separated from his wife and came back here with his four children. They were very small then.

After I had been here for three years and I saw that I could make a go of it, and I had saved a little money, we added the second floor so that I could accommodate more guests. I took out a second mortgage on the house, and had this built. I worried that I was taking on too much responsibility and risk, because I had no idea if I could fill the rooms, but I have been fortunate. That second floor we put on before the earthquake, and it withstood it just fine. You see all these are support columns, it is very strong because my son designed it.

By the way, my daughter decided to stay in the U.S. She and her husband have been there for nineteen years. They decided at the beginning not to have any children, but I don't know why. Her husband is Cuban, and he has been in the U.S. for many years. They met because my daughter had a Cuban roommate when she was studying in Denver, and one day the young man came to visit his compatriot and met my daughter. They fell in love on the spot and got married shortly after they met. He is a dear person, poor, but very good. He works for some company in Fort Worth, I don't know the name, and she works for American Airlines. They live near Dallas.

In a certain way, it was easier to do business under Somoza, because there wasn't as much bureaucratic paperwork as there is now. And I could go out and buy whatever I wanted as long as I had the money, because there was plenty of everything. I went to the market twice a week and I would buy all the vegetables and fruit you can imagine. I would order meat by the boxful and they would deliver it here, but now we can't even buy meat for ourselves. Eggs, everything, was plentiful and I would take a taxi and shop without a thought about whether they would have something or not. Everything is harder now, because there is nothing. I could go to the *tienda diplomática,* the so-called "diplomatic" store, where there are things to buy, but you have to have dollars to go there and I have none. Here I receive dollars in payment from the guests, but I have to deliver them to the government bank and they give me back córdobas. The *tienda diplomática* is for foreigners who have dollars.

As for my guest house, under Somoza I had almost all businessmen who came here, but now those who come are here to give help to the government. They come from all parts of the world. Did you see the Hindu that was here? He left yesterday; he was here working with CEPAD, he said, on a development project. I try not to get involved with the clients and what they do or say, or to overhear their conversations, even when they have to shout over the phone in the dining room. I never got involved in anything under Somoza either. So I have never been afraid under either government. I can get along with this government. They leave me alone and I leave them alone. Same with my children, only it's a very, very bad climate for commerce. Jorge has a plant, a bottling plant outside the city but there are no *divisas,* or dollars, and so the raw material to go in the bottles no longer is piped to him. According to *La Prensa* it's because of all the money that they spend on arms, and there is none left over for the people.

There's no feed for the chickens now, and so there are no chickens to buy. Up until the beginning of this year, people would come to the house to sell chicken and eggs. But no longer, I have to buy everything on the black market, and it is *carísimo,* very expensive. If I were a government-owned business, then I would have access to more things, but this business is private, it's my own, therefore I have no access. They won't take advice or suggestions either. The only advice they take comes from Cuba and Russia. I can only make comparisons with Germany, and there too they help the poor, but the other people can still go to the market too and buy things.

Many businesspeople have left, and others keep leaving. My daughter keeps telling me to leave, but I am not leaving. This is my home, and I can still get along here with the new system. No one is bothering me. I don't want to leave unless things get much worse. Who knows if they will or not? I stayed here during the earthquake, during the revolution, and I will stay now. The only time I left was during the war, and that was not my decision.

The people here are suffering; they are beyond the limit. Before, the poor could make a good pot of soup with a little meat, a soupbone, and plenty of vegetables. Today, no. It's too expensive. And the poor are the ones with so many children to feed. They are suffering, but I am too, and I am not even poor. I've been on a diet since January because of problems with cholesterol, uric acid, and arthritis. You go to the doctor, and he examines you and gives you three or four things, saying if you do not find this, buy this, this, or this. So you go to the pharmacy, and they have none of those things. You go to another pharmacy, and it's the same thing. Now, *no hay nada de nada,* there is nothing at all. Many say that it is the U.S. embargo, but I don't know. Mexico used to sell us oil, but since we didn't pay them, they cut us off.

La Prensa says we owe eleven billon, and most all of it has been spent in arms. Anyone who can is taking their children out of school before they are seventeen, and sending them out of the country, to Costa Rica, so they will not have to go to the mountains. My grandson was studying medicine here, and he had only one year of service to do in the hospital to complete his training, but he was called up for his military service. He left Nicaragua with his papers in order, not secretly, and he went first to the U.S. There, he was not able to study, I don't know why, but they let him enter the country since he has a double citizenship. My other grandson, the one who is in Bluefields, has been there for years. But the one who was studying medicine here, went to Jacksonville to study. He spoke English, but very badly. He went to the university there only as an *oyente,* an auditor, sitting in on classes to hear the language like I did when I was a girl in Germany.

Then he returned to Costa Rica and took up his studies again. But he had to go one year longer, because he lost a year's study in all the moving around. My son paid for him and for his other two sons, all three studied abroad. The one in Costa Rica is now established and on his own, he has married too. His idea was always to specialize in the U S., and with the diploma from Costa Rica, he will be better able to do that. Plus they have always had a German passport. Did I tell you about Jorge, when he was studying in Buffalo, that they gave him a position as assistant to the professor? We'll see how he does, because my son can't support him any longer. My daughter is in Germany. She wants to return to the U.S. too. She studied in Miami.

We have a long history in our family of leaving and returning. We never dreamed that our grandchildren would leave here to study and not return. Let me show you the family tree now. I have brought it out and dusted it off. You are the first person I have showed it to in years. This story of my life, it is mine. I don't know if anyone will be interested, but these are the things and the times that I have lived through.

19 María Morgan (b. 1947) and Marlene Rocha (b. 1950)

"As for this government, they haven't made my life better that I can see, maybe life is better for them now, I don't know, but not for me."

"I think that if President Ortega really cared about us, we would not be in this situation; things would've changed for the better."
María

"I think the Sandinista government has helped my husband some in his work. I think it has helped me a little bit too, because with the job I have now, I have some more time to be with the children."

"At the hotel, we all are paid for overtime and get vacation time now. . . ."
Marlene

The gentle tapping at the window told me that María and Marlene were now off duty and ready for our bus ride to the Mercado Oriental, *the Eastern Market. When we arrived at the stop where dozens of people were already waiting, my heart sank as I realized that the overcrowded, dilapidated excuse for a bus that was chugging tentatively to the stop and listing precariously to one side was in fact ours. Packed like just another sardine with sweaty people sitting on my head and shoulders, I smiled wanly at my friends as they began to relate their stories, unique for the particular details of their lives, but representative as well of the lives of the working poor.*

So eager were they to talk and so pleased was I to listen and learn, that our conversation stretched into the evening hours and over the next several days, during which time María and Marlene invited me to meet their friends and families, to visit their homes, and to share meals with them. I was again struck by the innate hospitality and generosity of the Nicaraguan people, who give willingly of what little they have.

Good friends and employees at the same hotel in Managua, these two domestic workers recount their family histories; numerous migrations from city to country and back again; typical work days; concern for the health and education of their children; the vicissitudes of living with husbands who are alcohol abusers; and describe their life and work both before and after the Revolution.

María

My life has been one of suffering since I was a child. I was born on the island of Ometepe. I grew up there and I consider it my home still; I used to return every six months for a visit, but now I can only get back once a year because it is too expensive. I have three children there on the island, and one, a daughter, here with me; their ages range from twenty-three to thirteen. Danelia, the one who is here with me, is twenty-one. I had six children but two died, one at birth and the other when he was six months old. He was sick with colic and I brought him to the hospital, but then they told me to take him home that there was nothing they could do. I was only about fourteen at the time. And the father didn't help me at all; *no servía para nada,* he was good for nothing, I was all on my own. That's the big lesson to learn, that you are on your own.

My father died young and my mama and three sisters and I got along the best we could there on the island. My parents were campesinos, they planted beans, corn, rice, tobacco. We still have their little plot and that's how the family maintains themselves. They used to have enough to eat and to buy shoes, but not now, now *está duro*, it is difficult. Mama does not work, and we help her out. We are ten children, but only four of us can help because the others have too many mouths to feed themselves. Three of us are living here in Managua, one is in Costa Rica, and the others still live in Ometepe. The sister in Costa Rica has been there for many years; one day when she was very young, about eleven, she just picked up and left.

When I go to see my family in Ometepe I usually stay a week or two, but no longer because although it is very beautiful there, there are no opportunities or conveniences. For example, there is absolutely no work except in the fields. That is a hard life, and I remember it well. We were ten children in a middle-sized house; it had one large room that we all lived in, and we were very poor. Daily life for us consisted of working from about the age of seven when we learned to use a machete, to cut tobacco, and to plant rice, beans, corn. We would get up around 1:00 a.m. to make breakfast and do the houshold chores, and at 5:00 we would go out to the campo, the fields, and return to the house at 10:00 am. Then we would go back to the fields from 1:00 p.m. until 4:00 p.m., all the children. We would sleep a little at midday; for lunch we had *pinol*, made from ground corn, water, and sugar, or *pinolillo*, the same thing but with cinnamon or cocoa added, and maybe we also had a little beans and rice. In the evening, coffee, *gallo pinto con cuajada*, that is beans and rice, tortillas, and a kind of cream cheese.

We did not have much entertainment, we did not dance or sing or play the guitar, and we rarely went to parties, but we did go to mass regularly because it was a very important part of our life. We are very Catholic. In school on Saturdays, they taught us doctrine, and we prayed at home too. On the island I went to a primary school, that's all they had there. They would just put you in any grade; now you have to pass first grade and then go on to second, and so forth. But then they put you all together, and if you passed or failed it didn't make any difference.

The school was just one room but it was private, my parents made a big sacrifice to pay for it because they didn't want me to grow up *tan burro*, too ignorant. Just two of the ten of us, myself and a brother, went to school because we were the only ones who were interested; my brother knows even more than I do. We had good teachers, but they punished us, I mean physically, when we were lazy. I went to school in the afternoons, and worked in the fields in the mornings. I had a very normal childhood in that the way I lived was the way everyone else lived too, except that I finished elementary school.

I came to Managua when I was fifteen, having finished school when I was about thirteen. I came by myself because I wanted to get away from the island. I cried when I couldn't find work, but I didn't return home. It was difficult to get a job, but at last I found work with a Mexican couple, cleaning for them. They loved me and treated me like a daughter, and I was very fond of them too. But then she left with another man after she and her husband had a fight. I worked for them for two and a half years, I was about seventeen by then. It was great working for them because Mexicans are so kind, they are good people.

I have a niece who is living in Chicago now, working for an American family; she left here in December and is very happy there. She left because the Nicaraguan woman she had been working for since she was ten years old decided to go to the States; since she was very affectionate toward my niece, she took her along. The lady was a nurse here, and now she is studying to become a doctor in the U.S.; she has two more years of schooling to go. What happened was that she was studying here during Somoza's time, and she had a lot of trouble with the dictatorship. She went to Mexico to study medicine for three years, but then Somoza cut off her scholarship funds and she had to come back here. Anyway, now they are in Chicago and my niece is there too.

I have been going back and forth between Managua and Ometepe since I was fifteen, like a jumping bean. After the Mexican couple broke up, I found work with a North American couple, and we were very fond of each other. That family was very good to me; they traveled a lot, and they would leave their baby in my care when they went away. They wanted me to return to the States with them, but I didn't want to go then. Now, I would like to go but no one offers! Then came a series of Nicaraguan families that I worked for, also a Costa Rican family.

When I was about eighteen I had a child, but you can't be a live-in cleaning lady and have a baby. So I had to go back to the island and stay with the baby for one year; then I left him there and returned. I would go and see him every two or three months; it wasn't as expensive then.

I was married for a long time, but I am now divorced; we didn't do either one legally, of course, it is too expensive, just by personal decision. The thing is that my husband dedicated himself to one thing only, drinking. He wouldn't work and he spent all my money on alcohol. He would beat the children, and he would beat me too; I nearly went crazy. But I stayed with him for twenty years. I didn't want to leave my kids, you see I didn't throw *him* out, *I* was the one who had to leave because we were living with his mother, and I didn't want to find another compañero either. Also, I was afraid of him.

I finally got the courage to leave when I came home one day and he had sold everything, the dishes, my clothes, even my underwear, the room was absolutely empty. When I saw all that, that all the things that my hard work had bought were now gone, I became so angry that I left. *Hasta aquí no más,* I've had it, I said, even though that meant that I was out on the street. The children stayed with him and I live alone now. They all wanted to stay with their *abuela*, their grandmother, because she had been taking care of them. For a while, I was distraught and very lonely; I cried all the time. Now, I am resigned to it and I pray to God that he give me a hard heart so that I can stand it. I take them money and go to see them, but it's not the same.

There is much to worry about. For example, I have a seventeen-year-old son, Elías, and he has not done his military service yet. His father is totally useless, but I took him out of school so they would not come and draft him. To go into the army is to get killed. He's back on the island, maybe they won't find him there as easily. He wants to continue studying, but it's impossible now because they would grab him. My other son is younger, only thirteen, and he can stay in school for several more years.

He has dedicated his life to liquor, my ex-husband has. I tried and tried to get help for him, vitamins, doctors, Alcoholics Anonymous, good food to the point where I wouldn't have enough money to buy food for myself. But he wouldn't make any effort, and only continued drinking my paycheck. Now, he doesn't even eat; if you could see the way he lives, it would make you sick. He always drank, but at least in the early years he worked some too, and I guess I kept hoping that he would get a job again, but this has gone on for many years now, and it's hopeless. So, I am left alone, trying to support my children and my mama while I rent a small room at the end of the bus line. The problem is that they don't want to rent to one person only, because there is such a housing shortage, but for now at least I have a room.

It seems as if everything got worse after the earthquake. Actually, it's more since the revolution than since the earthquake that things have become so difficult. Now, cleaning at the hotel I earn 66,000 córdobas a month, but a new dress costs 80,000. If I go to the market with my paycheck, I can't buy a pair of shoes, which now costs more than 100,000, and you know how much a nice dress costs. Same for food. Plus you have to stand in line all afternoon, from two until five o'clock for food, rice, sugar and soap, which they distribute every two weeks. They give it out to heads of families according to the number in their family. It's fair in that everyone shows their card and you get rations according to your card, but no one gets enough. Now, there's hardly anything to buy even if you had the money because everything is scarce, including food.

I don't know why things are so difficult now except that before you didn't have to buy a license to work or have your own stall, and now, they have to buy all these permissions. Even if you wanted to set up an ice water stand, you'd have to have a permit! Another reason things are bad is that there is more violence now than before. There were robbers before, but now there are more and several youths will go together and rob women as we get off the bus to go home; I've had my purse stolen twice on the bus. Maybe there is more frustration lately, especially in the city. The *pueblos* are still more tranquil. As for this government, they haven't made my life better that I can see; maybe life is better for them now, I don't know, but not for me.

I don't see much future for my twelve-year-old either. I talk with my friends in the Eastern Market and we all feel the same way. I think that if President Ortega really cared about us, we would not be in this situation; things would have changed for the better. They blame everything on the U.S.; that's their defense. They also say that all the money has to go to the army, but they give them very bad food.

My friend's brother is in the reserve now, so he goes every three months, but he says that the soldiers are hungry, they sleep on the ground, and they are always sick. It's hard to be in the reserve and have a career, because Dionisio, her brother, tried studying twice, but each time he had to stop because they called him up and it was for more than forty days too. Dionisio is twenty now and wants more education, he was in the first year of secondary school, but how can you go to school like that? So he just continues working at the aspirin factory.

Marlene

The biggest thing on my mind is my children and how to keep them out of trouble while I am working. Fortunately, I've now got my oldest son Alexis in school from 7:00 a.m. until 5:00 p.m., and his brother Henry goes in the afternoon. Yes, I had to do this, because at the school he was going to before, Alexis would come home in the afternoon, throw his books down, and go out and play baseball with his friends the entire afternoon. He wouldn't fix lunch for the baby or for his little sister; he wouldn't eat lunch either, the milk would spoil, and I would have to throw food out. This would happen every single day, and I would spank him for it every day too but it didn't make any difference. With his playing baseball all the time with those other lazy boys, his grades began to slip; the teacher began to call me, and then he failed the year. At the end of the following year, he failed that too. Things were going from bad to worse.

Alexis is at a difficult age now, fourteen, and his father died several years ago; he and Henry call the father of my daughters papa. When I started living with the girls' father, Henry was only three years old and Alexis was about five, so he calls Rafael papa. I had stopped living with Alexis's father a while before he died, but what happened is that he was killed in an automobile accident; he had been drinking. But, I will tell you about that in a little while.

I was born in Managua, and I am the oldest child in my family but I am so skinny that I always looked like the youngest one, and everyone thought that my younger sisters were older than me. I always told people, yes, she's the oldest and she's responsible for me. We are seven, four girls and three boys, all here in the city. I went to primary and secondary school both. My mother looks young but she is sixty now; she has never worked because there were so many of us to take care of. My father has been dead for four years now; he died from too much drinking and smoking, and from all the dust on the highway. He helped build the road to the Atlantic Coast, and worked for a long time around Rama and Batea. There is a lot of dust out there, and that was a bad combination with his drinking and smoking.

I went to elementary school at night, because, well, my mother had given me to a lady as a sort of *hija de casa,* a house child to do light work, a little cooking and washing dishes, so I went at night. I also gathered the eggs from the chickens, things like that. My mother's husband was not my father, though he recognized me as his daughter; however, as I said, he drank a lot when we were little and he beat us severely. My mother had to look for someone to keep us since he would beat us so badly for the slightest little thing. *Nos castigaba salvaje,pues,* I mean he punished us fiercely. I was about eleven years old when my mother gave me to the lady, and she's the one who put me in school at night. All the other students were adults.

My sixth and last year in elementary school, I moved back home and continued through the third year of secondary school. We paid tuition but it was very little, it was a state school. I just had two years to go before finishing but I got married to Alexis's and Henry's father. After Alexis was born, I went back to school and began the fourth year. I tried, but I couldn't because Alexis was born with kidney trouble, and he was in treatment for eight years straight. Twice he had to be catheterized for about three months; the defect is that the urethra is very narrow.

It was during the change of government that I went, Alexis was about seven or eight, and the doctor said to me, when the child is ten years old bring him back; he's fourteen now and still has a problem. When Johana was born, I took Alexis back because he was sick again and the doctor took an x-ray. Then he wanted to take another one because it looked like Alexis needed an operation and he wanted to be sure. All this was during the current government. I got the slip of paper and went to have Alexis x-rayed but the machines were broken because they needed parts from the U.S. I returned later, and the machines were still broken. I returned a third time and the machines were working but there was no liquid and the director of the hospital de-authorized the order because x-rays now could only be for those who were already hospitalized.

I still have the prescription in case Alexis gets sick again and I have to take him for an x-ray. He suffers a lot from pain on urination, so I still am in doubt as to whether he is well or not and what his problem actually is. I don't know what hospital to take him to now anyway, because they have changed everything. For example, where I took him before, Berta Calderón Hospital, is all maternity and another, well, I don't know where it is.

At any rate, I was unable to continue studying. Then came Henry, and I enrolled in an accounting class for a year, but that was when Alexis was hospitalized for the second time, and I didn't finish. I was living back home by then; I had left my first husband before Henry was born because he drank all the time. He was very handsome, tall, strong and had green eyes. He also had a job driving trucks for the army. That's how he died, in a truck accident when he was drunk. That was about a year ago, but we had separated when I was pregnant with Henry. He drank too much and had too many women. They would come to the house looking for him, and that made me feel very bad, humiliated.

When Henry was born, my father took care of him and he became the spoiled child. No one could touch or scold Henry, he could do whatever he wanted, turn the table upside down, throw food. If I would get after him, he would run to my father and claim that I was hitting him. One of those times, my father gave me such a slap that it knocked me across the room. I told my father, "If I beat him, it's because he's mine, and I am the one paying for him." And it was true, not that I hit Henry, but that I paid for him, because my father contributed not a penny to his keep; I was the one working and paying for his food and clothes.

When I was in the fourth year of secondary school I left home for the Literacy Crusade, in '80. They sent me to Jinotega and that's where I met the father of my girls. I was so happy because I got to leave my father, I got to take the bus to a place I had never been before, and I got to meet new people. I went to Rafael's parents' house, but I was not supposed to teach there because that was destined for some male teachers, they had separate teams of boys and girls, I was assigned to a house further into the countryside.

But the lady of the house where I was supposed to live changed her mind at the last moment, and decided she didn't want us; that's how I came to stay at Rafael's family's house with my two other female companions. The old man wouldn't let us lift a finger both because he said that is what he paid his help for, and because we were city girls and surely couldn't do anything anyway. So, we sat there idle, but we slept well and ate well, good tortillas, beans, and fresh cheese.

I was giving classes in a hacienda and it was a long way away from where we were housed. I taught children in the morning and adults in the evening after they had finished their workday. Sometimes I would cry, because when Rafael's grandmother rode the horse, I had to walk. It was a long way, and I would arrive exhausted and with sticky mud up to my calves. But all in all, I loved it and was happier than ever before, because I learned things that I had never known before, and I met interesting people from other places. For example, I always thought that country people were dumb, and I found out that they were sharper than we were. Of course, now no one has that idea, but before, that's what we thought.

The best thing is that was how I met Rafael. I told him that I had these two sons, that I lived in my father's house, that I had not lived with the father of the boys for years, and that if he was really interested he could come to my house when he was ready. He already knew Managua because he had run away from home at twelve and had been living and working here off and on; in fact, he had just returned to his grandparents' home in Jinotega when we came with the crusade.

Rafael's grandfather had a fair amount of land that he had inherited, enough to live on. But even though he was familiar with Managua, Rafael spent one entire day trying to find my neighborhood because the city is so crazy, what with the strange directions and addresses we have had since the earthquake. Anyway, one day he showed up and asked me to go back to Jinotega with him. My father gave his permission, although he did not want me to take Henry.

I took the two boys and we went to Jinotega for about a year because Rafael's father had built us a little house on the farm. But my father was complaining the whole time and sending word that he was sure that Henry was not eating, that he must be thin and miserable by now. After a while my brother came to get me to come back home and bring Henry, which I did. I left him with my father for a few months while I went back to Jinotega where Alexis had started first grade. I don't need to tell you that Henry had been just fine the whole time there in Jinotega with me, very chubby and healthy; it was my father who had the problem.

This was about '82 when Alexis started school there, but that same year we moved back to Managua so that we could all be together, and Rafael found work here. Since then we go back to visit when we can, but it is very dangerous, the contra are there, and my father-in-law's farm is in the red, or danger, zone. The family had to leave the farm, but it is fortunate that my father-in-law died first, because he would've hated to be uprooted. He didn't want me to come back here to Managua; as soon as I left, he got sick. We were very close and I think he became ill from sadness, but he died soon after.

The others in the family are now in the *guardaraya*, right on the dividing line of the safe zone, so I don't know how secure it is. Rafael goes to visit his mother and grandmother there; it's very near Pantasma, and he hitchikes because he can't afford a ticket. He has done this a number of times now, even though I tell him that it's dangerous. But he says he wouldn't get to see his family otherwise, and that the contra know him now so they don't bother him.

Here Rafael works in a cardboard box factory; he cuts the cardboard and the women put the boxes together. He learned the job just by watching, and now they have sent him to take courses because he is curious and wants to learn more. His course and the factory both are in Tipitapa, where the Somocista guardias are in jail. The factory has been there for a long time; it was there under Somoza too. That's where they make uniforms, suits, and that's where they sent him to take the course in the afternoons; he works the morning shift.

I think the Sandinista government has helped my husband some in his work. I think it has helped me a little bit too, because with the job I have now, I have some more time to be with the children. In a factory, I would be working much longer hours; however, here sometimes the other staff don't show up and I'm stuck doing their work until nine or ten at night. For example, I don't think that Claudia is coming today to relieve me; she says that it is because she is sick, but I think she has had too much to drink again.

Claudia is one who has been helped by this government; I have been helped slightly as I said, but my friend María has not had any improvements in her life; she has a very hard time. Now Claudia is another matter. Before, she was even poorer than we were, and the man she had been living with had deserted her. When that happened she hit bottom and drank all the time, went to bars and stayed out late at night. After the revolution they gave her training and a good job, and now she belongs to the union. In a way, she has started life all over again, taking care of her teen-age son, her mother, and her new husband Salvador, he does wrought iron repair work and often has no job, but he is a good man. We all are paid for overtime and get vacation time now, not just Claudia.

Claudia is one who has benefited. She has a more responsible job than María or I do here; for example, she gets to place phone calls for the customers and to unlock the refrigerator, which is a special privilege the owner gives her. I don't think that the owner likes the government very much, because now we have to be paid more. Claudia is having troubles again though, because her mother doesn't like Salvador, and they are having arguments. I hope that she doesn't start drinking like before. She has brought herself up so much now, she even goes to labor union meetings, it would be a shame to throw all that away.

I'm glad that Alexis was telling you about his school and that he likes it. They arrive at 7:00 a. m. and leave at 5:00 p. m.; this is his second year there. I enrolled him when he was in the fourth grade; he had previously failed two grades at the other school, and now he is in fifth. Would you believe that last year he was third best student in his class, and this year I have noticed even more of a change; this year he is also one of the best. One day the teacher didn't come to class and they put him in charge as a substitute.

Day before yesterday they gave him a certificate for having done so well in the sex education class. He says that he would like to give the class himself now! They teach them all about pregnancy, birth control, venereal diseases, and so on. This is a new program of this government, because when I was in school we didn't have anything like it. Some parents are scandalized but I think it is very important that they know, and I am relieved that I don't have to teach him. The other day he did an interview with the neighbors, which was part of the assignment, and he asked my sister, "How do you know that you are pregnant?" "What do you mean I'm pregnant? Get out of here; I'm not pregnant," she responded.

It's hard to get into that school. I got Alexis in through a friend, the director's brother works with my sister, and she talked to her friend and asked him to ask the director to admit Alexis, which he did. This year I enrolled Henry too; he doesn't know how to read. Henry has been in school for five years but can't seem to learn how; it appears to be impossible for him. He's ten years old now; he spent two years in first grade, and then three years in the second grade because he can't pass. He just can't catch on; I think he has a general problem because he has always been very slow, even when he was a baby, with turning over, sitting up, crawling, walking, talking. For several years we thought that he was going to be crippled and never walk. I hope the teachers at Rodolfo Rodríguez pay attention to him and can tell us what is wrong.

This school was founded especially for working children, those who sell newspapers, chewing gum, fruit, for those whose parents can't really take care of, or control, them. But there are other children who have gotten in too, like mine, and now I hear that there are 100 youngsters who are going to be taken out and put in another school because they don't need to be there. But they haven't given me a slip because when I went in to talk to them, I told them that I cook, clean, and wash dishes all day and that there is no one at home to take care of the boys, so they let them stay. They give Alexis and Henry lunch at school and don't charge us anything.

Johana and Elizabeth stay with my mama now that Henry is back in school, and Johana has just started school herself. I pick the girls up from my mother's on my way home from work. They just play there, because I bathe and feed them before I take them to my mother's. Before, when Elizabeth was tiny, I paid a neighbor girl to look after her, I took her to the girl's house. Four children is enough, especially since I have now had three Cesarians. I have hopes for my children, especially for Alexis; he says that he would like to win a scholarship. The only problem is that practically all the scholarships are to Cuba, East Germany, the Soviet Union, and Bulgaria, but mostly to Cuba.

I was very enthusiastic about the revolution when I was a *brigadista,* a volunteer teacher in the crusade, and afterwards I worked for quite a while very actively in the CDS, the neighborhood defense committees. I participated in their vaccination program for undernourished children, things like that. During that time, Elizabeth became very ill from drinking spoiled milk and I took her to the doctor. He said there was nothing he could do, so I took her to a folk doctor, you know, where they give herbs and potions, and they cured her. The woman gave her a purgative of salad oil, magnesia, and lime juice. Elizabeth nearly died and was nothing but skin and bones for a long while. I have had a hard time trying to keep my children healthy. The milk is often spoiled and they get diarrhea frequently, but I've found that Pepto Bismol works well too when I can get it.

Recently, Alexis, Henry, and Johana have all been ill, but thank heavens Elizabeth has not. They had very high fevers, and I even had to take Johana to La Mascota, the children's hospital, where we spent the entire day waiting to see a doctor. They must've helped her, because she is all right now. Even though they are often sick, and we have hardly anything to speak of, at least I can give the children enough to eat, and that is the main thing.

20 Ariel Durán Mondragón (b.1944)

"I had no problem with the revolutionary changes, which basically involved trying to see how the majority of people could enjoy a better standard of living, especially with regard to health care. That was a very different ethic from trying to see how much money one could amass."

"The state pays us medical workers, but since one of the fundamental principles of the Revolution is pluralism, we also practice private medicine."

It was well over 100 degrees in the sweltering, overcrowded corridor where old men and mothers with children waited interminably to see a doctor. When my turn finally came and I was escorted into Dr. Durán's air-conditioned office, I breathed a deep sigh of gratitude. Relief was short-lived however, for the power supply was so low that it was hotter in the airless office than outside, but at least it was quiet. My preoccupation with my own discomfort soon dissipated as the easy-going and expansive Dr. Durán began to relate his absorbing story, highlighting with good humor the contrasts in his life before and since the revolution.

Dr. Durán was studying in Uruguay at the time of the revolution. When he returned in 1980, he first experienced "shock and confusion" on seeing the revolution regarded by many people as a piñata filled with treats for those who got there first. Gradually, things settled down and a new concept of medical care emerged, one in which the goal of health care for all stands in sharp juxtaposition to the shocking lack of even the most basic requirements, such as hygenic facilities and sufficient supplies of water.

As assistant director of medical services and coordinator of teaching at Manolo Morales hospital in Managua, Dr. Durán is intimately acquainted with both the noble objectives and the stark realities of health care in Nicaragua today, as well as with the type of training that medical students are currently receiving. However, it is not in his nature to be depressed by these contradictions. Rather, he enriches his own life, and those of his patients, coworkers, and students, by his jovial personality and cheerful acceptance of the challenges that life offers.

My father is Dr. Julio Durán Zamora, and my mother is María Elena Deuda. I have two brothers and three sisters; I am the oldest. One brother graduated in chemistry; the youngest brother studied business administration in Mexico, but he had to come back before he finished, because of the war here in Nicaragua. He finished his studies here in agricultural administration, which is the field he is working in now. As for my sisters, at that time women really didn't go to secondary school or to study for a career except as a secretary. My three sisters studied secretarial sciences; there wasn't much freedom for them to choose differently.

Yes, I am a second cousin of Msgr. Oswaldo Mondragón, on my mother's side; my mother is from Granada like Oswaldo's family. Do we look alike? Ah, yes the same smile and eyes. My father was a doctor, educated here in Nicaragua, at the medical school in León. Afterwards, he was an itinerant doctor for a while, going from town to town looking for a way to make a decent living. It was very difficult to earn one's living as a doctor because, first, there were very few doctors, with only five or six graduated every year. At first you would think that it would be easier with so few doctors; but it was very difficult because you had to go to a town where the people could support you, not just pay you with promises, and you would be the only doctor there. What this meant in practice is that you had to keep moving on until you found what my father called the ideal town, in the economic sense.

They found the ideal town in Chichigalpa, where I spent my early childhood. My first six years of schooling were in the public primary school for boys there. I remember it well. We had a very strict teacher. Whew, was he strict! Extremely disciplined, and he made us keep rigorous discipline inside the classroom and outside as well. If he ever saw any one of the students misbehaving anywhere, in the street, wherever, the next day he would punish them. He was very fond of the military style and way of life, although he was a civilian. How about this, he even had uniforms, including helmets made from calabash gourds. He would use any excuse to dress us up in uniform and march us down the street with stick rifles!

Despite such foolishness, the primary education I received there was much better than what they receive now. For example, as of about three or four years ago, the books that I read in elementary school are now assigned at the secondary level. I think it was better then. I don't know why education isn't as good today; maybe it has to do with a different pedagogy, another way of teaching. They would give us three or four pages and we had to memorize them, right? That way, one remembers things. The same with our mathematical tables. We memorized information and then we could use it. Boy, did we read! But now they seem to be learning more by doing things, whereas we learned it all by memory. Of course, we had no understanding of what four times four was, of what it meant, but we could compute it. Now, they know what four times four means, they understand the concept, but they can't figure out the problems! It was better, more demanding then.

There was no secondary school in Chichigalpa, a town of about 20,000, so I came to León to study. It's not far from Chichigalpa, about 30 kilometers. I was an internal student at a private Catholic school. There was a public institution too, but they did not have internal students, and I had to stay at the school because the distance was too far for me to travel each day. I was eleven when I started there in León, but after a while my mother decided that I was too far away from home, so we moved to Granada where I could continue my schooling. My father had to stay in Chichigalpa because that's where he had work, and he had to pay to keep us in school. But every vacation we were on the road, coming and going, always on the move; it was a very enjoyable way to live, especially for a youngster.

My brothers and I went to the Colegio Centro América in Granada, a Jesuit school. It no longer exists, having been donated by the Fathers as a vocational school to train technicians, mechanics, and the like. It was one of the best secondary schools in all of Central America. Well-to-do people from Salvador, Costa Rica, from all over Central America, would send their kids there as internal students. By that time our status had improved enough for my father to send us there.

The educational program was excellent. I think the education at the secondary level was better then than now too. I loved math, literature, history, theology, but I tell you, they really pounded it into us, and it stuck, history and literature particularly stayed with me. What beautiful subjects! Take history for example. You think you are in a unique situation, with unique challenges and so forth, and then you study history and you see that it's all really happened before. Who knows, maybe we're just going around in circles, and we think we're so smart! As a student, I also wrote whenever I could, poetry, stories; nothing ever saw the light of day, I just circulated it among my friends. There was a group of us who would get together to talk about everything, including poetry. This was before 1961, because that's the year that I graduated. I tell you, it's a good thing that I wrote then, because I surely don't have the time now.

During the latter part of the '50s, that's when the riots began, including the student uprising in Granada in '56 in which four students were killed and many were wounded. You see, after Somoza was assassinated in 1956, things started to heat up and the guardia went around rounding up large groups of people. I was still in primary school in Chichigalpa when Somoza was killed, but I remember it well because they came and arrested my father since he was one of the founders of the opposition party PLI (Partido Liberal Independiente, Independent Liberal Party). My father was involved in local politics; however, since most of those involved in politics at that time were professional people, lawyers, engineers, doctors, and since he was known at the university, he was drawn into things, such as being one of the founders of PLI, without having the same level of belligerence of others in the PLI.

The guardia came at dawn and took my father away, just like that. I was maybe ten years old, and the others were all younger. The neighbors helped my mother take care of us, donating rice and beans, helping us out for the two months that my father was in jail. They treated him very badly, and that was just there in Chichigalpa. They kept threatening to take him to Chinandega or Managua, but they finally figured out that he wasn't one of the ones that they were after. Rigoberto López, the poet who assassinated Somoza, was a member of the PLI, and that's why they rounded up my father. Would you believe that the person who carried out the arrest was his first cousin, a lieutenant for Somoza! That's life, isn't it!

My mother had a great influence on me as I was growing up. She was the one who pushed me to go after things, to set goals. She still is an influence. They both are, but especially my mama. She taught me how to want something and to go after it, how to be decisive, and to keep on achieving. I'm sure that her inspiration has much to do with where I am today. My papa also influenced me in that he was a doctor and his clinic was at home, so I saw medicine practiced and I learned about it. All kinds of people would come to our house to be treated. This was, as you say in the U.S., like a wild west town, especially on weekends. My father would get patients with gunshot and knife wounds from fights. Many of my father's political friends would come and hold PLI meetings in secret; it had to be in secret because they were the opposition.

I started at the Universidad Nacional in León in 1961 or '62. At that time, student ideologies were becoming more pluralistic than before, The opposition was beginning to grow, and more groups were tolerated, such as Christian action groups, Marxists, and liberals. I participated in two groups. One that was completely independent, not Marxist or social

Christian. In the School of Medicine, we won the right to compete for the student leadership of the entire university, because after the run-offs there were just two candidates left, one from the Social Christians, and then us, the Independents. But we lost; actually, we were trounced, probably because we were badly organized. The Social Christians already had their party organization, their system, and we were a ragtag, motley bunch.

At that time we were a lot more dedicated to our studies than to politics. For example, it wasn't until after I had been studying medicine for about three years that I became involved in politics at the university, about 1965. Let me tell you a little about what medical school was like. First, one had to take an entrance exam. Two, three hundred students would come to take the exam, and of these, forty-five would be accepted to study medicine. After I received my secondary diploma, I knew that I wanted to study medicine. So I went and took that entrance exam, and I passed. The first year of study for these people, including myself, was called *el año de pregrado,* a year of background preparation, during which we studied math, chemistry, biology, and physics. Perhaps it's like what you have in in the U.S. for those who want to study medicine, two years or so of biological sciences, after which the students go on to study medicine proper. But here it was just for one year. After that first year, we went directly on to a more specialized study of medicine, histology, anatomy, etc., for the next five years. Then we had to spend one year working as an intern in a hospital. In all, it took seven years, followed by six months of social service, often in some remote town with no medical services. Medical students enjoyed tremendous status; the public looked up to them as the highest of the high, because they had such a rigorous program of study and they were so carefully selected. People looked at you as if you were really something terrific. Of course, we didn't deserve that reputation.

Later, the university began to change, admitting sixty rather than forty-five students a year; five years later, they were admitting ninety students, because there were more *bachilleres* coming out of high school. Compare this to my time, when I entered medical school, I was the only high school graduate from the town of Chichigalpa. What was happening was that the number of *bachilleres* was increasing and, therefore, the pressure on the university to accept more people was also increasing.

My classes were quite good. In general physics, the teacher was an engineer and he tried to do practical things, not just theory. In biology, we had laboratory work. In anatomy too, because we had cadavers. In histology we had lab materials, as well as in parasitology and general chemistry. But for biochemistry, we had no lab; it was a very new field and it was all theory. We trained the professor for that one; he made his debut with us. We had a good amount of hands-on experience. I almost forgot, we had one course in sociology, in the third year, just stuck in there like that as an anomaly. In those days, remember that I am talking about the 1960s, the medical student lived a hermetically sealed existence. You dedicated yourself to your specialty, and to nothing else. No political science, history, literature; you had to take those somewhere else. I think our course of study was very sound though, because the basis that I acquired there, in the Facultad de Medicina de León, continues to serve me and to help me develop as a doctor. My professors were Nicaraguans, but almost all of them had studied abroad, especially at the Sorbonne.

It was quite difficult to pay tuition and fees for medical school in those days, because in medicine you had to be full time. This meant that you had to be supported by your family. In other faculties, students did not have to be full time and they could work to maintain themselves. You can see what a limitation that requirement was; it meant that not just anybody could become a doctor. The books and other materials also were very expensive and we had to buy them. Our texts were in English, French, and Spanish. And of course, we had to try to figure out on our own how to read English and French, because they were not taught at the Faculty of Medicine. Your class was your dictionary, period. But by the time we did our residency, we could at least read French and English, and many people found tutors to give them English classes.

I went to the U.S. to study English, at the University of Mississippi in Hattiesburg. The situation was this: when you finished medical school in Nicaragua, you had to go abroad for further studies, because you could not learn much more in the hospitals of Nicaragua. Every single person in my group felt that way, and the big question was *how* to get a position abroad.

There was a related problem which had to do with our social service. We had to try to find a pueblo where we could make a living, and *even* put a little aside, so that we could continue our studies later. I understood then what my father meant when he talked about the search for the ideal town. I did my social service before going to the U.S., because otherwise they wouldn't have given me my doctor's title, since the service was part of the program. The government paid you a little during your social service and during the internship, but you couldn't live on it, maybe you could eat a small meal, that's all. A big help, right? But at least you could work in the morning, for example from 8:00 until noon, and then in the afternoon, you could practice private medicine at your house. That's how you could make enough money to continue studying afterwards, to go to the U.S. for example, which is where I wanted to go.

There were some towns in the north where you could make more money, to such an extent that the doctors who went there were assured that they could pay their way to study abroad later. I had the darndest luck though.

My problem was that I got sent to a town that couldn't pay for *anything*, Waspán, on the shores of the Río Coco along the Honduran border. Not only were the people *unable* to pay for anything, but, what's worse, they were *unwilling* to pay. What timing! It turns out that President Kennedy's Alliance for Progress had sent tons of medicines and instruments by ship to this town, and had kept the people well supplied and healthy.

By the time I arrived, that policy was all over with, but the people were still left with the impression that everything was a present and that I should shower them with free medicine. "Oh, that's medicine," they would say. "What a nice gift!" The people in that area also have the reputation of being lazy; they don't like to work, and the more things that are given to them, the better. Further, the Alliance for Progress had given contraceptives to the women, which caused serious problems among the villagers, and I was left to deal with the aftermath of that situation as well. That was quite an assignment! When it was finally over, I left to do my residency in a hospital in Managua.

I got married when I was a medical student in León. I met my wife, Marina Ternura, in Granada, her hometown; we met before I went off to study in León. Our courtship was a long distance one by telephone and letters. We went together to Waspán. After I finished the six years in León, the last year could either be in the hospital in León or the one in Managua. I chose Managua, because supposedly there were better materials here. The hospital was called El Retiro, but the earthquake destroyed it. In truth, it really was better, because here we had doctors who had graduated from schools in the U.S., and there were simply more possibilities being here in the capital city.

Many of my friends already had their plans made to go study abroad because they had done their service in towns where they were able to make some money. They went to Miami to take an exam that you had to pass in order to be able to study in a hospital in the U.S. Just think of the avalanche that the U.S. would've had if it hadn't been for that exam. I couldn't go to Miami; funds were always short, but I presented myself here in Nicaragua to the American embassy for the exam, and I passed it on the first try! The medical parts, that is, but the English part, I flunked completely. Plok! So, I kept studying English on my own, and the second time I took it I passed.

But I realized that I didn't know English well at all, so I used the little bit that I'd saved during my residency and I went to the University of Mississippi to study English. It was peaceful and beautiful there. I loved it. I just picked it out of the newspaper; I saw an ad saying they were accepting students and to write for more information. There was another in Louisiana, in Baton Rouge, but the one in Mississippi was a little cheaper, so I decided to try for it. What a peaceful life! I lived in a house, because there they have a different conception of a doctor, of one who has graduated from medical school, so the university thought I should live in a house instead of a dorm. I was there for six months only, taking intensive English classses. Of course it was ridiculous to think that I knew anything about English, but here in Nicaragua I was in a course at the twelfth level, and since there are only sixteen levels, I was considered advanced. When I took the exam there in Mississippi, they made you take an exam at the beginning, I found out that I knew nothing! Later, about halfway through the course, I had to take another exam. Then I could see a big difference in my performance.

After that experience, I started writing letters to the different hospitals in the U.S., trying to obtain a position in internal medicine. The problem was that it was necessary to go back to the U.S. to have an interview, and to do that, you had to have money. That was ruled out for me. Then someone told me to apply for what was called a matching program, where you match your hospital with one in the U.S. Well, I got into that program, and one of those doctors who came here, a neurosurgeon who during the time of the Revolution had a certain militancy, I don't remember his last name, anyway, he advised me to apply to the best hospitals in the U.S. According to his thinking, most U.S. doctors would be in Vietnam, and hospitals in the States would welcome my assistance and invite me to come up there. Guess what? It didn't turn out to be the case! I wrote all these letters, and the U.S. hospitals answered saying that they chose from their own graduates, don't call us, we'll call you. Then, someone suggested that I lower my sights a little, and write to second level hospitals in the U.S. and other places, which I did. I was accepted by the Hospital de Clínica in Montevideo, Uruguay.

In Nicaragua I had studied internal medicine for about four years. In Montevideo, I studied rheumatology as my subspecialty. I was there for two years with my wife and daughter, after which I was certified as a specialist in rheumatology. In Uruguay, they gave me a scholarship which covered my board and studies. But for my wife and my daughter they provided nothing, and living was very expensive. What most people had were supplementary scholarships from the government of Nicaragua. But these were all given to Somocistas or people who were friends with government officials. Since I did not fit in those categories, I was turned down for a scholarship. Pow! Just like that! I felt totally rejected about that time, the U.S. didn't want me, the Somocistas didn't want me; it seemed that nobody wanted me. I didn't give up though.

I finally remembered that I had a first cousin who was a big shot in the government. He was a doctor of economics; he had studied in the U.S. and France and he was second in command at the Banco Central. I went to visit him, explained the problem, and jokingly told him that they're not calling me to tell me that I've won a scholarship, and I wondered if he could facilitate that phone call. Facilitate is an understatement, because I was supposed to be in Montevideo three days later to begin work there. Yet the scholarship, assuming I were to receive one, would take two months to be approved. Nevertheless, my cousin got it for me in *one* day! That's the way things were then; if you had influence, you had everything, and if you did not, you had nothing.

The program in Montevideo was good; it was very selective and they took people from many other countries. There were also many positions that were filled by the Organización Panamericana de Salud (Pan American Health Organization). There was a three-story building just for rheumatology, and I was able to do much practical work. While I was down there, the war broke out here. I went down there in '78, and in '79 the war broke out. I returned here in '80 to work. Even during the revolution they kept sending me money to continue studying. I had been afraid that my funds would be interrupted or cut off, but no. They kept sending me money so that I could finish, which I did, and then I returned home.

This is the interesting part, how I felt when I came back. Up to this point, my life, as I have been relating it to you, has taken place in a period of capitalism, when one thinks of oneself, of one's own future. That's the atmosphere I grew up in. But on returning here, at first I experienced shock and confusion. For example, some of the people I had known and worked with before were acting like this was a piñata and not a revolution; they were greedily dividing up the positions. I think that 1980 was a year of confusion, certainly it was for me personally. It really got me, seeing people who I had never thought of as politically inclined or socially interested, now claiming always to have been in favor of the revolution, blah, blah, just in order to get in on the spoils.

Later I saw that things began to settle down, and the atmosphere was gradually changing. I had no problem with the revolutionary changes, which basically involved trying to see how the majority of people could enjoy a better standard of living, especially with regard to health care. That was a very different ethic from trying to see how much money one could amass. That individualistic conception has changed; now, you no longer feel that you should offer your service in a given situation only if you are going to be remunerated, or advanced in your position because of it. Currently, the idea is to find a way for medical care to reach everyone. We still have some privileged ones who have the greater share of medical help, and we are trying to make things more fair.

On arriving home in 1980, I was assigned to be a staff doctor at this hospital, Manolo Morales, where I also served as an internal medicine doctor and rheumatologist. By '81 and '82, I was in charge of teaching internal medicine to the residents; my own colleagues named me to that position. Until recently, internal medicine was taught only in León, but they have since moved that faculty to Managua, and I have had some of the first students here. I was in charge of coordinating their studies within the hospital, both for beginning and more advanced students. They study medicine at the national university in Managua, UNAN. I coordinated at both places, UNAN and the hospital. Later, they put me in charge of *all* the teaching that is done at the hospital. After I carried out those duties for a while, they assigned me to the medical attention area, which is where I am now. My title is Subdirector de la Atención Médica (Assistant Director in Charge of Medical Care).

That title means that I am in charge of medical attention. I coordinate the different chiefs of services; I am over the other chiefs of medicine, surgery, orthopedics, but only in order to coordinate services, to see that the surgery is done, that the attention is adequate, that treatment is given, that misinformation or confusion is cleared up, that the patient understands what is going on. It is a large administrative job.

But I also have my little internal medicine cubicle, and I practice rheumatology too. Of course, I continue to teach internal medicine to those who come here from UNAN, at both the *pregrado* and the *posgrado* level. From 7:00 to 8:00 a.m., I go around questioning, inspecting, asking how the medical attention has been for the patient; from 8:00 to 8:30, I do paperwork; from 8:30 to 10:00, I do my work as a doctor in internal medicine and rheumatology, seeing hospitalized patients; from 10:00 on, more administrative work here at the hospital. One morning per week, Friday, from 7:00 to 10:00, I see outpatients, only in rheumatology, who come here just for the consultation. And of course, I also have to give classes to the medical students and to those who are doing their specializations in internal medicine and rheumatology. These are formal classes. But from 8:30 to 10:00 in the mornings, when I go from patient to patient, they go with me on these rounds. The group consists of myself, a resident, an intern, and the students. Later on in the day is a formal class with twenty or thirty students. I get here at 7:00 a.m., and before I know it, it's 1:00 p.m. You don't get bored here!

The greatest problems we have are lack of machinery and medicine. The equipment we lack we need to get from the U.S. in order to do various kinds of routine examinations, or to be able to care for certain kinds of patients. For example, in the intensive care unit, we lack respirators; a patient comes in with lung problems and we don't have the capability to save his life. We have just one respirator and when we have two who need it, we have to choose who gets to use it. This is not a hypothetical situation. It is often the case because of lack of technical equipment. We are not God, but we have to act as if we were. We usually choose in favor of the younger person, if that is an option. And also according to the prognosis.

We give treatment to the one who has a better chance of recovery. What are we to do?

In the lab, there are countless items that are lacking that keep us from making more accurate diagnostic tests. We also need the liquid for myleograms, so we cannot do myleograms at all. In the Lenín Fonseca hospital they can do them, so we send patients there, but then there is a long wait because that is where everybody goes. We need machines to carry out all of our laboratory procedures. We need microscopes, for example. Sometimes we have only one functional microscope to use for a huge number of examinations. The result is that we often do not do exams that require lab work, since there is just one microscope. This is the daily anguish that I live with. We also have no replacement parts for the machines that we do have. The x-ray machines do not work either; they are too old, having come from the Retiro Hospital after the earthquake in 1972, and who knows how long they had been in use before that time. Everything that had been in that hospital was brought here, including the surgical instruments. They are old and worn out. Many times the surgical scissors are missing screws, and we have to put clips on them.

Another problem is that it is extremely difficult to maintain adequate hygiene in the hospital, especially on Wednesdays and Saturdays, because that's when the water is shut off everywhere in our zone because of the shortage, and those days we have no water in the hospital. What does the patient do who needs to bathe? Or the doctor who needs to wash up before surgery? They have to try to save water from the day before. There is a tank kept in strategic places, such as the operating and emergency rooms, from the day before, to wash the instruments, and hands, that's all. They're digging a well out there now, but they haven't hit water yet, and they've gone a long way. Whenever they do hit water, we're ready!

We have sufficient beds usually; sometimes people have to wait, but this is not our big problem. We lack machinery, equipment, materials for examinations, precise diagnoses and treatment. All these things slow us down, slow down treatment, delay us, but we try to give the best service possible. I plan to stay here in this hospital, where I've been since 1980. If the Ministry of Health wants me somewhere else, okay, but I like it here because I have grown in my experience as a doctor and I have perhaps brought a little prestige to the hospital.

The patients do not have to pay for their hospitalization; it is all free. The medicines for one who is hospitalized are free as well. For outpatients, there is a charge, but for the medicine only ; they do not pay for the consultation. The state pays us medical workers, but since one of the fundamental principles of the revolution is pluralism, we also practice private medicine in the afternoon, not in the hospital of course. I, for example, have a private clinic too, on the weekends. That's the only time that I'm not working here at the hospital. Saturdays I'm at the hospital until noon. Then I spent the afternoon, from 3:00 on, and all Sunday at the clinic that several of us have together. And the patients pay.

It's almost a necessity to have a practice on the side in order to make a living for one's family. You already know from your work here that the salaries of workers in Nicaragua are insufficient to live on, just a pair of shoes costs a month's salary for most people. Part of the problem is the lack of control over prices. For example, if you ask four people how much something costs, you will get four different answers, ranging from one hundred to one million córdobas. Prices have gone crazy around here, and it is very frustrating. So, salaries are nothing, and people have to go around being businessmen. Everybody is a businessman here, because you have to find out how much things are at one place as compared to another, what you have to sell, how much you can get for it, and so forth. It takes all your time and energy just getting enough to scrape by on. If it weren't for private medicine we doctors couldn't make it; that is how we get by. The ideal thing would be for doctors to make a good salary; then we could be devoted totally to medicine, and that would take away the terrible pressure of having the private practice and wondering if I'm going to make it or not this month. I suppose that with these peace talks, Esquipulas II [the Arias Plan], stability will be achieved, and perhaps we can get up off the floor where we've been for about ten years, and that health care will be available for all.

In the meantime, it is difficult to make ends meet. My wife does not work. She used to work as a secretary when we were first married. But they made her work extra hours, and we liked being together a lot then, so she quit, and did not return to work. Would that she had extra hours now! We have a fourteen-year-old daughter and a seven-year-old son. We get along with the larger family quite well, in spite of economic privations and political differences. I am not an enemy of anyone, especially of my family. I can sit down and chat pleasantly with my cousin Oswaldo, but we don't talk about politics. I also have an aunt who is a nun, Mercedes Marina is her name. She is of the María Auxiliadora order, and she is the secretary of Cardinal Obando y Bravo! But we get along just fine, because mostly we talk about family things. I am open and I like everyone; Mondragón is that way too.

Perhaps religion has had some influence on me, for better or worse. In the Colegio Centro América there was an apostolic section where they gave you more religion classes with the intention of making you a Jesuit. I was in that group because I had recently arrived in Granada. My cousin Mondragón was in the seminary and we lived nearby, and my girl cousins there were very religious. They belonged to the Legión de María, where they talked a lot about the life of the Virgin and they also did social work, such as volunteering at hospitals and schools. All this was when I was in secondary school. But I had so much of that atmosphere, that by the time I got to the university I was ready for a different image. That's when I stopped going to mass! And now, I don't really have the time.

21 Nubia Gómez (b. 1961)

"In the classroom we always have to be comparing then and now, then was bad, now is good. I really think that it is vice versa."

". . . the biggest limitation is the scarcity of things, starting with texts. It is really pathetic."

The chubby, young woman with the short, dark hair gave me a tired smile and invited me inside her very simple home. It was situated on a large mound of dirt heaved up by the earthquake in 1972 and surrounded by broken remnants of what was once a street or sidewalk. As I maneuvered my way past the large pig that guarded the door, I was reminded again of the bizarre nature of this capital city, in which a jeep and the ability to interpret directions such as "three blocks to the left and one alley down from where the statue used to be" are basic requirements and vivid reminders that the earthquake is a continuing presence.

Nubia Gómez and her husband are both educators. They, like many other Nicaraguans, each hold down two jobs in an attempt to make ends meet. They are overworked and stressed, for which they hold the government responsible. They also blame the Sandinistas for the extreme scarcity of educational materials, and they flatly oppose the ideological content of the new curriculum. Still, they are surviving within a system that is not of their choosing.

Currently working as principal of a private elementary school in the mornings, and as teacher in a public elementary school in the afternoons, this experienced educator offers some interesting observations on the two types of schools. Further, she has taught in both the old and the new systems, and is well-qualified to make comparisons between the past and the present. At home on maternity leave, Nubia Gómez welcomed the opportunity to share her views on education in the revolution and on the frantic pace of life for working families clinging tightly to the lower rungs of the middle class.

I was born in Tipitapa of lower middle-class parents. My mother worked at home, while my father was a small farmer and a carpenter. My mother works now because both people have to work in order just to scrape by. We are four children, two girls and two boys, and I am the youngest. The two oldest live in Chontales now and the other, a brother, lives in Miami; he left shortly after the insurrection, looking for a better standard of living.

I went to elementary school in many different places, all six grades, part in Chontales, part in Nandaime, part in Managua, because my family was always looking for a way to make a living. Then I went to secondary school, and I wanted to go to university, but I had to stop studying because of all the political problems in the country. The guardia would come to the university and randomly spray everyone with their machine guns, attacking students, professors, bystanders.

I entered the normal school instead, and graduated as a teacher. I received my high school degree from the Instituto Maestro Gabriel, and then went to the normal school for my teacher training. I have eleven years of teaching service now. There were public primary and secondary schools all over the country before the revolution. Whoever says that there weren't schools available just didn't want to go to school, because they were in every corner of the country. They had to have double shifts at many places because the student population was growing, but there used to be schools everywhere.

I have two jobs, I am an elementary school principal at a private Baptist school in the mornings, and a teacher in a public elementary school in the afternoons. My husband has two teaching jobs too; if we didn't, we couldn't subsist. A big problem is that we work so much, but we don't like leaving our children here alone. My son is in sixth grade, my daughter is in third, she is in a nun's school nearby, and then we have a newborn baby who is only forty-five days old. That's why I am home now, because I have a three-month maternity leave.

The baby was born at seven months; they sprayed an insecticide at the school and I slipped down and hurt myself. They took me to the hospital but everything was normal, and the baby was born early. I have to find someone to care for the baby when I go back to work, so far I have no one. My parents live in Chontales with my older brother and sister, I am the only one married with children.

When I was in school the program was better; I graduated from the Instituto in '75 with my elementary certificate, having finished high school in '72, and at the time the academic level was still very high. The normal school was all teaching courses, methods, curriculum, also child psychology. My classes were very good because everyone in my group had already graduated from high school, although other classes were mixed with students from the first through the fifth year of high school. The normal has three kinds of teachers that they graduate now: in basic or general education, in secondary, and in complete, that is those who can teach at any level. When I graduated they only had one kind. But now, they have several, and they also have twelve normal schools now, where there used to be only two. But those two turned out *good* teachers! You can tell the difference when the teachers present themselves at our school to observe classes. There are more normals now, but the quality is much lower.

The educational structure is as follows: first the Ministry of Education, the next level are the zone offices, then the directors and the teachers within the zones. Things go from the top down, and if you want to change a teacher, or criticize a policy, for example, you have to work through the whole structure and it takes forever, so usually you don't do anything.

They now have adult education, which began with the Cruzada, in '80, the Literacy Crusade. Since the Cruzada, the whole educational system has been transformed. In '81 and '82 they began the transitional programs, everything was "under construction" as they said, as if they were repairing the walls. When '83 arrived, the educational system really was transformed, beginning with the first grade. We had new texts and a new teaching agenda. In '84 the second grade was transformed, with a new program and texts. In '85, the third grade was transformed, and so on successively until now they are starting with the secondary. From first through fourth, they call fundamental education; from first through ninth, basic general education; after that comes the pre-university, which we did not have before.

In their first four years students learn how to read and write well; they learn the basics in the first grade. When they arrive at fifth or sixth now instead of graduating from primary school, they have to continue until the ninth grade before they complete their basic general education. Then come two years of pre-university education, and then the university. The first nine years are required; it sounds better than before, what with the different texts, and the new methodology, it seems like the students are getting more schooling, but that is just the way it sounds.

What we teach has to be in agreement with the educational philosophy of the current regime. This government's philosophy is plastered all over the new textbooks. For example, in mathematics, you say x number of soldiers went away to fight, x number were killed, how many were left? Instead of apples they are soldiers. The first grade books talk about the soldiers, national defense, and so forth, since '83 when they changed the system. In the first grade they teach all this with a uniform method, so that a student in Managua is learning the same thing in the same way as a student in another part of the country.

Before, we had various books which we consulted and could choose from. But from '83, they abolished those books and supplied the new approved ones. So you have one method and one book now. The method is called "FAS", Phonic, Analytic, Synthetic. It is based on the phonemes, on analysis, and on putting together what you learn in order to read. It is a good method, but it is the only one that you are allowed to teach here. Little by little everything is being changed over to their [the government's] system; as I said, they are now revising the secondary curriculum. Soon everything will be sequential and one will pick up where the other left off.

Here is a first grade reader, *Carlitos I*; in the second grade they have *Carlitos II*, and so on. Some tell about Carlos Fonseca and others about other things such as how happy you would be to join the Association of Sandinista Children. Anyway, here is how we teach reading in the first grade. First we do the vowels. Then we teach the phoneme m, which when we join it to vowels, we can begin to form words. Then we do p, connect it with vowels and form words, and then brief sentences. Then the b, capital and small, and the V and v, so students learn four things at once here. They learn to make cursive letters, they do not print their letters.

Then comes the u, and the i which they put with the dipthongs, and then comes the s sound, all of them, s, c, z for example. It's a good way to present all this. Then they do the c; they study the s and the c together because they have the same phoneme. This makes very good sense pedagogically.

It's when we get to the readings that things get heavy. Let's take a look at the first grade reader. Here's one, "La Plaza" : "We go to the Plaza, we hear applause and 'vivas' for the FSLN." Here you see a picture of the family, and of food, and of the "brave soldiers on parade in the plaza . . . the soldiers defend the country, long live the soldiers." Here's one about David and Delia, two children who are happy because "they study and they belong to ANS [Sandinista Childrens' Association]. Their neighbors respect them, and they respect their neighbors. Both are good students." If a child does not join, they do not pressure them, but indirectly you are left out of a lot of activities. The same is true for us teachers; it's okay if we do not join things, but we miss a lot if we do not. Some of the readings are very good; they teach the children about the different regions of Nicaragua, about which we knew very little before.

I will say that with this method the children learn to read very quickly. Here is Carlos Fonseca, who "showed us the way," they have a little biography of him; here is the flag of the Frente Sandinista, we have both in the school, this one and the national flag. This is all still a first grade text. For the sound of *gu*, we have *guerrilleros* (in this context, Sandinista soldiers), *guardafronteras* (border guards), and *vanguardia* (vanguard). Listen to this: "Guillermo y Miguel are border guards. Border guards are defenders of the country. They are very brave. . . . The FSLN representatives are in the vanguard and they listen to the people. We are winning the battle of health, education and production. Long live the Revolution."

Here is one about Germán Pomares, who was one of the principal combatants who fell. They have a picture of an army to teach the sound of the *j*, for "ejército" (army). Here is *la gigantona*, the giant, a lovely folk tradition of the people of León. During Holy Week celebrations they make these huge papier-mâché masks and heads for their parades. Here is another one in which they speak of Jinotega; these are very nice readings. Here is another about Wiwilí, which was a zone of heavy combat, along with Waslala. Here they tell about *wawul*, a typical meal from the Atlantic Coast. This is good. Here is something on José Martí; yes, this is good too, some things are fine. After they learn all the phonemes, they basically know how to read, and then come the readings.

Since at the end of the first year students can read, ANDEN, the National Educators' Association of Nicaragua, the teacher's union, has a letter in here for the students: "Dear little friends, You should feel very happy because you are studying. You and we teachers work together. We are compañeros. Our Revolution allows all Nicaraguan children to study and to be happy. You are the future of our country. You should always go forward in your studies and in your work. Unified and hard-working, we can construct the new society that Sandino and Fonseca dreamed of. Success in your studies. Fraternally, ANDEN." Then, *"La niñéz es alegría; alegría es la Revolución"*. That is a slogan; it says, "Childhood is happiness; happiness is the Revolution."

Here is a cradle song; here is a reading about our body; one about the children in the Revolution; here is one about cleaning up the city through the CDS; one on our daily chores; the tropics, animals. Here are longer readings. "We are Nicaraguans." In it, the symbols of the country and of the revolution appear together as if they were the same thing. "For this flag, Fonseca and Sandino gave their life. The good children of Nicaragua respect, love and understand the symbols of the country and of the Revolution." Here is one on the "Héroe de las Segovias" (The Hero of las Segovias); it's about Sandino. Las Segovias is a town in Nicaragua where Sandino fought for a long time. Here is Carlos Fonseca's biography. We've about come to the end of the book, and then they go on with *Carlitos II*.

Carlitos II is more advanced, but always with the same message. Here is a reading about Pochomil, a beach nearby; here is one about the Atlantic Coast under the topic of we are Nicaraguans; here's one on ANS, trying to get students to join. What they do is go camping, take excursions, like the Scouts, except that they have another line. This is the second grade, they don't have as many loaded readings as in the first year book, but it is always the same line. Here is *Carlitos III*. The fourth year book has another name because it has more advanced readings. Here in *Carlitos III* it tells how Fonseca went to the Soviet Union and met with schoolchildren there and told them about Nicaragua. Here is a song about Monimbó, and here appears Camilo Ortega, the brother of Daniel; Camilo fell in the battle of Monimbó, before the insurrection. Monimbó is a barrio in Masaya. And so on.

Each reader has its workbook to accompany it. These have been edited with the pedagogical assistance of educators who have come to Nicaragua to help. They've given *un montón*, a huge number, of seminars to orient the teachers, to teach them so that they can master this new methodology. It's been difficult because everything is new. The advisors visit at a higher level than the local school. They visit with the Ministry of Education. They don't visit us. Who visits us are zone technicians; here everything comes from the top down.

When they wrote the objectives and principles of the new education, they took into account the organizations, and invited one representative from each organization, Sandinista Youth, the parents' organization; the teachers' union; the workers, etc. This was the the Great National Consultation, the Gran Consulta Nacional. Very representative, if you belonged to some organization, and the document now is our bible, because that is what we have to comply with. Approximately 50,000 people participated through thirty organizations, and were given a fifty-five item questionnaire proposed by the Ministry. The document was revised in fifteen meetings of the Consulta Nacional.

I belong to ANDEN because it's easier, you really are supposed to join, and it's the only way to get information that we need. My diploma serves me as a protection, but you need the other too. In the classroom we always have to be comparing then and now, then was bad, now is good. I really think that it is vice versa. I used to be able to choose any readings I wanted. I direct a Baptist school, but we too are part of the system. The inspectors come to check to see if we are following their plan. If there is a problem, then we have a big meeting of the directors, the teachers, and the inspectors to discuss it. They say that the new education will produce "liberating self-criticism," but that seems an ironic statement to me.

A typical day for me begins at 7:00 when I go to the office; I return home at noon to fix lunch for the kids. From there I leave for my afternoon job; I return at 5:00 to work at home, and the next day the same thing. We have Saturday and Sunday to get our clothes ready and do the other chores, because we have no one to help us. Before, no one had to do this. And to tell the truth, by the afternoon, I am beat, and I am much less effective. Before I had one job, and it was hard to get. Now, I have two, and it is easy to find teaching jobs because there are not enough teachers. The salary of an elementary teacher is 200,000 per month; it's ridiculous. We at least have a car although it has been broken for a while because of lack of parts, and the parts that you can get are sky high. So I walk as much as possible because the buses are impossible.

My son is almost twelve; he goes to school where I teach in the afternoons, and he stays here in the morning to look after the house. And my daughter goes to school in the mornings, and in the afternoon when I leave, I take them both. But with the baby now, I will have to look for someone to take care of them here. It will be difficult to find someone, because our salaries are so small. A principal earns about 5,000 córdobas more than a teacher, the difference is very small. Teachers have always been poorly paid, but this is ridiculous.

The problem is that we are not in the productive sector, you can't see the results of our work. It takes a long time to know what kind of person you are helping to educate. It's not like making a pair of shoes, where you produce a thing and you can see your product right away. They want you to go to help with the coffee harvest during vacations because that's productive; but they can't make you, and of course, it's volunteer work, and during that time you are leaving your house and children unattended, so I don't do it.

As I said, my son is twelve now, and before he is seventeen and they take him for military service, I am going to send him to Miami with my brother. It takes a ton of dollars, and this is so difficult for us, but we have been saving a little bit each month for years now. If he leaves before he turns seventeen, he can go legally; the problem is paying for the ticket, and every day prices go up and what we have is worth less. Many send their sons secretly, illegally, but we intend to do it legally; we'll see.

As far as education goes, I think the biggest limitation is the scarcity of things, starting with texts. It is really pathetic. This year they had to use the books that the children used the year before, because the Ministry simply does not have the funds. It seems that last year Germany donated funds for texts, but this year, with the war and everything, there are none.

We can't even give the children the most absolutely fundamental things because of the lack of texts. Paper and pencils are scarce too. They are sold each semester by the Ministry, very cheaply. But if a student uses up his notebook too soon, then that's too bad; he has to wait until the next semester. There are children who sit on the floor because we lack desks. So we cannot require correct posture and penmanship for example, when the kids don't even have desks; that would be ludicrous. Everything is blamed on the war of aggression.

The children, many of them work in the morning in order to be able to go to the afternoon shift, and others work in the afternoon and attend in the morning. Those who attend in the afternoon often arrive late because of transportation problems, they sell tortillas, newspapers, or keep care of the house while their mother works. They don't have the life of a child, but that of a working adult. Those students do not produce good work, we can't require much of them. They arrive poorly nourished, usually without having had lunch, tired from work, and they fall asleep in class.

The teachers as well, especially if they have worked a morning shift. We teachers hardly ever have what you could call a vacation. When we are not teaching, we have much preparation, many meetings to attend, and innumerable seminars given by the Ministry. The academic year begins in February and ends in November. December and January we are not with students, but we are working on the educational programs and going to those endless seminars.

It's true that it is hard for husbands and wives and children to see each other. But at night, and on the weekends we try to catch up. My situation is difficult because we are both teachers, and we seem always to be crossing paths going somewhere different. Our great satisfaction is our children who love and appreciate us. In a way, I wish that I could do more in the community, but I am too tired and have too little time. I don't belong to our CDS, for example, because I can't go to meetings at night; it's too hard to try to do it all, and I have my preparation to do. They understand and don't pressure you; I don't feel like I have to join. But they do good work in the community in addition to their clean-up campaigns. When they take a census for the purposes of distributing food, I try to help out then. Their tasks, such as the clean-ups, really are *para el bien de todos,* for the good of all, like the Sandinista police say.

We have religion classes at the elementary level, but only in the religious schools, because the nuns are autonomous in their own schools. But the rest of the education, the curriculum, the texts, everything is the same whether it is a state or a religious school, and there are supervisors and everything, just the same. The private schools still are in better condition than the public schools, which have very little in the way of facilities, as I was describing. Also, the type of child is different, because the students in the private schools, their parents are able to afford the tuition. The fees go to pay the expenses of the school, its administration, and the salaries of the staff. Private teachers receive only what the parents pay in fees; they do not receive a salary from the state. The children of these parents are better dressed, better fed, and they perform better in school. Those in the public schools come from poorer families, the children work, are poorly dressed, and so forth, although you will always find some who do well in spite of these things because they are intelligent and want to learn.

I have already said that I think the major problem we face in education is the lack of everything, materials, resources, funds. Another serious obstacle is the imposition of the government's ideology and methodology, something that is obvious in the materials that you have seen, and with which I disagree totally.

22   Mauricio Rocha Ruedas (b. 1949) and Carmen Blandón (b.192?)

"This is the worst crisis that we have ever suffered, and there have been many that have hit Nicaragua, but the food crisis is the worst, it could be our downfall."

". . . who knows, maybe the government has wanted to do things differently, has wanted things to be better, but it has been a struggle for them because our debt is so huge."
Mauricio

"If I could, I would live in Costa Rica. . . . I felt more content there because they have plenty of everything; you don't have to go around looking for necessities all day like you do here because of the war."

"If the whole family could go somewhere . . . we would all go to Costa Rica or the United States, especially the U.S., directly, nonstop! Most people who leave go to those places."
Carmen

After lunch, of which I ate every last morsel while doña Carmen stood watchfully beside my chair, I took the family's photograph in front of the plastic-covered picture of the Last Supper. I also snapped Oscar and his pet duck, which he clasped proudly and tightly under his arm. The adults in this warm, hospitable family of campesino background have had no formal education and have had to struggle to make a living for themselves and their children.

Son-in-law Mauricio, a former bartender and now a sometime mixer of drinks for neighborhood parties, and mother-in-law doña Carmen, who takes in washing and ironing for a living, share with seven other family members a modest two-room house on the outskirts of Managua at the end of the bus line.

Here, Mauricio and doña Carmen relate life experiences as varied as Mauricio's long battle against an alcohol dependency, a common problem in Nicaragua today, and doña Carmen's appearance before President Daniel Ortega at a De Cara al Pueblo, *or Face the People, forum, to request a medical discharge from the army for her son Oscar. In the course of their narratives, these two verbal campesinos offer some valuable and perceptive insights on life before and since the Revolution.*

Mauricio:

I was born into a very poor campesino family, and most of my relatives still live in the country. My father is dead; a boy killed him in a freak accident. He used to love to play with children; there were always neighbor kids around our house. One day a youngster started playing around with him while my father was peeling an orange; he fell on the knife and it killed him. He was just about thirty years old and we were young, but we remember the tragedy perfectly clearly. Suddenly, we were left without a father and I was the oldest of the boys, myself and my twin. I thought it best for me to leave as soon as I had any chance of making it on my own, because we had almost no resources, and there were so many mouths to feed, we were eight children. About two years after my father's death, I left home.

I thought that if I went to the city to seek my fortune, I would find a good job and help my brothers and sisters come here to look for a better life. Four of them eventually followed, while the others stayed in the country. I was just about fourteen when I left home, but my age wasn't the worst problem. The difficult part was coming to the city without any education. I never went to school at all back home; I had no idea how to read and write, or how to do sums, nothing. I was a complete burro, and

I tried to learn everything here all at once. My "school" was the street, and I took many hard blows just trying to get along from day to day in such a strange environment. I lived on my own in the street, sleeping on the steps. I came here with nothing, absolutely nothing. Finally, there was a lady who felt sorry for me and helped me; I owe her a lot.

I worked in factories, mostly where they make *aguardiente,* or cheap whiskey. My job was to mix the syrup and extract the liquor from it. I was called a "mixer" because what I did all day was to mix and test to see if it was the right strength, and then mix and test some more. In that job I really became corrupted; I drank too much, way too much. I was still just a kid, but I suppose that was the beginning of a long battle with alcohol. After that, I worked in bars at restaurants, mixing drinks, and later as a waiter.

Carmen:

Before the revolution, everything was calmer and easier. I remember that I would go to the market with ten pesos, and do you know what that would buy today? A busfare! Yet, back then I bought all my food with those ten pesos. And that was for a family of three children. I could buy cheese, beans, meat, rice, and bananas. Now a liter of milk costs one thousand pesos. You know what a *plátano,* or plantain, costs? Eight hundred pesos. A banana costs 600. People at times buy them, but for me it is not so easy because I also have to buy firewood and other things as well. I wanted to buy a *plátano* yesterday so that I could make *tostones,* fried plantain slices, for you, but the ones they had were too small and very expensive.

We all cooperate in this family; we all pool our resources. My son-in-law Mauricio contributes from his work as a barman at parties. My daughter, Nila, Mauricio's wife, contributes from her earnings as a seam-stress and a masseuse, but she also has the four children to care for. My son Oscar helps out with his job as a waiter; that boy has been working at one job or another since he was thirteen. My daughter Nancy works as a secretary and studies at night. As for me, I take in washing and ironing as my job. A big problem was when my iron broke and it took so long to get it fixed because there are no parts, and I lost a lot of income just because of that.

I have a son older than Oscar who is in Masaya, and another one in Costa Rica, but I really don't know exactly where he is over there. He has been in Costa Rica for eight years now. I went with him at first and spent two years there, but then I came back here because Nila was very ill in the hospital. Afterwards, I couldn't go back because I didn't have the money. I worked in Costa Rica at a soda fountain; I was a short-order cook, preparing the meat and the chicken dishes. I went back when they told me that my daughter was ill; she had had a Cesarian, and was hemorraging two months after the birth of Mauricito. Now I don't have any news of my son Danilo over there. Although I always call a lady I know there by phone, I never learn anything because we can only talk briefly.

I took Oscar with me before he went to do his military service, and he stayed for a month, but he got it into his head to come back here. He was still very young, and he cried and put up such a fuss that I brought him home. And now we can't return. This was in 1982, when things were beginning to get bad here. We should have stayed, because they got Oscar and sent him to do his service right after we returned to Nicaragua.

Danilo, my oldest son, did not go to Costa Rica in order to avoid his service; he had been one of the literacy workers in the mountains, and I went to visit him various places in the interior. Then Danilo came back and looked for work but couldn't find anything; military service was all that was available, and he told me that he didn't want to go, but that there was nothing else. So he went to do his basic training. Well, I don't like army things any more than Danilo does, and I think that I can still be in favor of the government and everything, but not like military life. So I took Danilo out of there; I just took him away from where he was doing his training exercises. I told myself that if someone comes to get me, fine, but I'm not going to make him stay there if he doesn't want to. I was lucky that no one came to take him back. The only person who came to see me was a man who asked me if I wanted Danilo to go to Costa Rica with him. "Of course. Take him away then!" I responded. A month later I followed. Danilo was seventeen years old at the time.

In Costa Rica he washed dishes and cleaned and they paid him 100 colones plus his meals. Then they gave him a little raise. He liked working there and so did I. If I could, I would live in Costa Rica; you feel right at home there, and it is easy to adapt to their customs. We were in Esparta, in the Punto Arenas mountain range area. I loved it. I felt more content there because they have plenty of everything; you don't have to go around looking for necessities all day like you do here because of the war.

Before, when Danilo was still able to send me a few colones, I wanted my daughter Nila and son-in-law Mauricio to go to Costa Rica, and I would stay here to take care of their children as if they were mine. But they didn't want to leave their kids. Now, I'm trying to tell my younger daughter to go while she is single, go and learn about another people, go somewhere where she will have some opportunity to find a good job and get ahead. If the whole family could go somewhere, and we wouldn't have to leave someone behind, or split up, we would all go to Costa Rica or the United States, especially the U.S., directly, nonstop! Most people who leave go to those places.

Mauricio:

Here, parents who have lost a son in the service are doing everything possible to try to have their second sons leave the country while they are about fifteen, before they are in danger of being taken to do their service, which is when they turn seventeen. Let me tell you, it is awful to be wandering around in the mountains as a soldier. You are sad, afraid, and sick all the time. They take you right out of high school, if you have made it that far, to do your two years. The problem is, of course, that they don't let you leave for the U.S. You have to have papers, but they won't give them to you. We have been going round and round trying to decide what to do and how to do it, because we have our children to think of.

Carmen:

I used to be fat and healthy, but now I am thin and I have trouble digesting almost everything. This all happened to me from following after Oscar in the mountains. I went to see him every eight days, going from place to place, visiting him and bringing him food.

Mauricio:

Yes, I often went with my mother-in-law. When we were in Jinotega we had a place to stay, because they were doing some basic training. It was terrible to have to argue with the officers as we tried to find Oscar; they would always say that he was not there, that he had been sent somewhere else, and so on. They were always giving problems to the mothers, and I went with doña Carmen as often as I could to try to help, but I don't think it made any difference. At least in Jinotega, where we went first, we found a room to stay in, since they were doing training there. After that though, they sent us to the battlefields.

Carmen:

Sometimes, I would arrive at the place where they said that Oscar and his group would be, and of course, they were not there, they had already gone somewhere else, or they had never arrived there in the first place, but had been ordered somewhere else without our knowing. When things like this would happen, I would fight with the chiefs, the lieutenants, because I am *mal geniada,* bad humored about such things. I was just getting the run around from all of them. Think of it: my son was there in the jungle without water, electricity, food, just the wilderness and the contra and here I was getting this nonsense! If you are lucky, the people will give you some food in their house, or you can buy a little when you go down to a town. I went everywhere by bus and on foot; so did Mauricio when he could accompany me. But often he had to stay here taking care of the children.

I insisted on going, and I risked my life because I knew that Oscar needed me. I was never mistaken for a contra though, thank goodness, nor vice versa. I wanted to make sure that Oscar was well trained, and well taken care of, but of course he was not. It really cost me a lot to get to see him, and they never let him come here to visit. I followed him many places: Jalapa, Bocay, Jinotega, all along the Honduran border, everywhere. Oscar did not complete his two years; they finally gave him a discharge after a year and a half. I say finally because it was a struggle. His hearing went bad; something in his ears broke because of the bombs and he became deaf for a while. Then, with the filthy water in the rivers, he got an infection and there was pus and blood coming out of his ears.

Would anyone believe us though? No sir! I had to insist, to push; I even had to go to a *De Cara al Pueblo,* or Face the People, session where I talked to Daniel [Ortega] himself, right in front of the crowd, and I let him know how we were being treated and what our problem was. He told me to give all the information to his secretary right there, and that she would give me an appointment to come to his office. I repeated everything to her, and she took it all down and made the appointment.

The next day I showed up at Daniel's office like they told me to do. I talked to that same secretary herself, she was very affectionate and warm, and she took some more information. She told me to write a letter containing all the medical history. Then I got some people to help me write a letter, and I took it back to Daniel's office, along with the medical records. Two weeks later, I called her as she had instructed me to do. She told me that she had talked to Daniel and that he had authorized Oscar's discharge on medical grounds.

I was greatly relieved at first, but then there was a big delay, much hassle and stalling on the part of the military because no one really believed that I had permission even though they read the paper with Daniel's own signature. I had to begin my rounds all over again. I went to a hospital to talk to another *jefe,* or chief, there. Next, I had to go to the Casa de los Combatientes, the Serviceman's Office (General Headquarters) to talk with all the secretaries and chiefs there. Then they sent me to Apanás in Jinotega to talk to those authorities. I went to all these places by bus. In

Jinotega they read the paper that Mauricio and I carried, the authorization from Daniel, after which they sent us to Wiwilí.

There, a Cuban doctor examined Oscar's ears, and I asked her if they could care for him in the hospital in Apanás. See, the chiefs had not wanted to allow me to take Oscar to a hospital in Managua, because they wanted to keep him there at Apanás. But I knew that the one in Managua would be better, and I also knew that I couldn't afford to keep going back and forth like that. So I told the doctor that I was very poor, that I wash and iron for a living, and could she please recommend that they transfer Oscar to a hospital in Managua. Every day that I am here, I am not washing and ironing and I am losing money, plus I have to spend money on the bus and on food. None of my children were working then and it was too hard.

Fortunately, they transfered Oscar to the Dávila Bolaños hospital here in Managua. They gave him all the ear exams there are because they did not believe us, even though we carried the *constancias,* the proof, and everything. They said they wanted to find out what was wrong with him, but really, they didn't believe us. Oscar had had an ear problem since he was little, and years ago, when I did the washing and ironing for a doctor who was very nice to me, he had taken a look at Oscar's ears. So I went back to him to see if he could help me out again. He studied all the evidence, and he wrote a note saying that all those papers were true. Even so, they *still* wouldn't believe it or accept his signature. So I asked the doctor please to go to the hospital to state in person what he had written, and that was how they finally demobilized Oscar.

First, however, they did additional tests, but I got photocopies of those exams, and I sent them to the government so Daniel would know. Let me tell you, photocopies are very expensive, and I had to send another whole set to Matagalpa. They said it was because that's where Oscar had his identification. They told me that nothing would be final until he showed up there in person. Now that's a long way away, even farther than Jinotega, and they were going to make him go there again. I thought, oh no, here we go again. I couldn't sleep; it was a nightmare, and I kept asking God what I was to do. Then Oscar said, "They can put me in jail if they want to, but I'm not going."

We decided to go to the local army headquarters because it's the place that I had been to before. So we did, and I started talking to the chief, and everyone there knew me by now. So I asked him "Look, since you mobilize people from here, can't you also demobilize them from here?" "Of course, ma'm, no problem." "Good," I replied, "look at this order," and I showed him the order with Daniel's signature, because by then I took it with me everywhere I went. However, there they asked me to get still more papers, can you believe it? So I went to get more papers, and about a month after I had begun with this latest request for papers, I went back and they said yes, they were going to give the demobilization. Two months later they processed it and they gave it to Oscar. *All* that time I was holding the authorization right there in my hand, but they did not believe me!

And do you know how much photocopies cost? Transportation? Meals? Being on the road, and not working? All we ate was rice and beans, because we were always dealing with this issue and we had practically no income. By then, my daughter Nila could work as a seamstress, so that's what got us by.

Nila also does embroidery and gives massages to take away wrinkles and to provide relaxation, in addition to caring for four children. People bring their clothes here to the house; Nila has an old machine but it still works. She has very few clients, just people in the neighborhood who come by to have her repair something, put in a zipper or a pocket. She just has Sundays free to to this kind of work, because that's the only day that she is at home.

The other days she works giving massages. She started out taking a class given by a doctor; in fact, she learned massage from an American. Then she worked in a doctor's office, giving head and neck massages to help people to relax. Afterwards, she worked in a barber shop, but she didn't like that because the men wanted more than a massage. You know what I mean? She doesn't like to give massages to men, although *they* like it, so now she is working in a beauty shop. There she gives feet and hand massages and does karate on the shoulders, but for other compañeras, women, only. There is a big need for people to give massages here because there is so much tension and stress. Are there many tense people in the U.S. too? Nila just saw that massage course advertised in the paper and signed up a little more than a year ago; now she earns much more than she did as a full-time seamstress.

Mauricio:

Nila is a hard worker, and we share all the household and work duties among all of us. Everyone helps out with everything. I met Nila five years after I came here, and then we got married almost right away. We had a civil ceremony, you know with a lawyer, where you sign the papers to make it official. We didn't have a church wedding because it takes too long and we wanted to get married right away; it's also cheaper that way. It's cheaper because if you have a church wedding you have to have fancy clothes, give a big party, serve lots of food, buy many things. It's true that you can just appear before the padre and ask him to marry you, but no one does it that way.

Most people who are officially married have a civil ceremony only, because the reason to get married is to have the law protect and support the children. Without the law, then the children and the wife may not have any support if the husband goes away, and many husbands just pick up and leave when it suits them. But I tell you, it's not hard for the authorities to find the husband and to make him take care of his kids. They may find him at work, through social security, and then they make him pay for his kids. But some men will even quit their jobs so that they will not be discovered and have to come back home and be responsible. This happens when the man is unstable emotionally or always going from woman to woman. There is much abandonment here. Fewer than half of the people are legally married, and fewer still marry in the church. People just get together and then leave when they want, especially the men.

The best protection for a woman, or for anyone for that matter, is to get an education. Take my sister-in-law Nancy; she works as a secretary during the day and studies at the high school level at night. She wants to make something of herself, and after high school she wants to go to a university and learn more about secretarial work and even learn English. Nancy says that if you know English, you have it made, plus there are so many people who come here from abroad and they all speak English.

She is not studying English yet, but there are Saturday classes at the university that anyone can sign up for. She says that she's afraid because everyone will know more than her. I keep telling her to stop talking about it and go do it, because you have to depend on yourself in this world, and she should be as prepared as possible. She is pretty and smart and will probably meet a good husband. But even so, you are always really on your own. I keep telling her, so what if other people know more; you have to go through difficulties in order to accumulate experiences and learning. The thing is that she doesn't know that yet; she is just seventeen. Her generation has not moved around very much like mine; they have just stayed here in one place.

My life has been an adventure. You could call it an adventure that I came to the city so young, and that I worked in the *aguardiente* factory, and then in bars and as a waiter in restaurants. I can mix any drink. As a waiter, I served all kinds of customers, and I met people from all over the world. I worked at El Alamo, a very picturesque place on the road to Masaya; it's now called Guayacán Número Uno. Their *lomito de costilla*, pork loin, was a famous dish when I was there. I worked there for eleven years, a long time. I had already married and needed a steady job. They provided my transportation, which was a big help, but not very long ago, this restaurant was taken over by the state. It had been privately owned, and the owner was ruined, poor guy. Then the state gave him back part of his money and he left for another place, I don't know where.

We never arrived at any agreement with the new administration of the restaurant because they wanted to put us on a kind of trial for a month or two to see how we would do, and to see if they wanted to keep us on as employees with the state as owner. They had their own personnel really, and I had put in so many years working at that restaurant that I didn't think I should have to pass any more tests. Maybe in some new place, yes, but where I had already worked for eleven years, ridiculous! They already knew that I was a capable and honorable person. Sixty days on a trial basis is the usual, and I think it is a good idea generally, but not for me at that job. So I quit.

I work now as a drink mixer for neighborhood parties. They come to the house and ask for me because they know that I am an expert mixer. For all occasions, a party, a *quinceañera* or fifteenth birthday, a baptism, wedding, funeral, whatever. Just a few days ago, I went with Oscar to do a farewell party for a señor who was going to the U.S., and we were paid 20,000 córdobas per hour! We make good money when we work, but it's not steady. At least working in a restaurant you get a regular salary. You see, restaurants are according to a scale, and the finest restaurants pay the best salaries to their waiters. At category A restaurants like Los Ranchos, Los Gauchos, El Camino Real, El Inter, you have to be a very attentive waiter and give excellent service, so in such places you earn more salary.

We have to pay about 5 percent of our salary in income taxes; I think that's the right amount but I'm not sure. Anyway, the officials say that the tax is for our social services, and so forth, that's what they say. But we haven't advanced any at all since the revolution; we just keep waiting, and that's many years now. You just have to wait, wait, wait for everything, and it is frustrating. However, Nicaragua has been hit by many blows. First the earthquake; I was working in a bar at the time, and it was completely destroyed. But Nicaragua tried to get up on its feet again, and then the war came, the war for liberation, and *nos vuelve a hacer leña,* that is, we get hit again hard, in the economic aspect. They liberated Nicaragua, and then the counterrevolution came, and what has happened is that we have suffered a terrible fall, a crisis. This is the worst crisis that we have ever suffered, and there have been many that have hit Nicaragua, but the food crisis is the worst; it could be our downfall.

I don't know who to blame, because we produce everything here. All that we need in order to live and eat we grow ourselves, cotton, corn, coffee. But we also know that the government of the U. S. finances this war so that the things that we produce here we have to export. We are forced to export all our products abroad in order to pay our debts; we owe a huge quantity of money and we must pay it because you have to pay your debts. The result is that we are in a crisis because we are exporting our food to pay our bills. I don't blame the U.S., but I don't think that Reagan's administration has been very good; in fact, it has been *bastante guerrerista*, quite warlike. To be sincere, I have never seen a contra, and I am a campesino from the mountains, from the *mero monte*, the heart of the interior. I went recently with the kids to visit my mama who was sick, and even then I didn't see a contra.

Oscar was on the battlefield with the contra, but me, no. He says that they are all peasants from the countryside, that no one is from the city. There may be some mercenaries from other countries that help Ronald Reagan, but the ones who fight are all Nicaraguans, as far as we know. The contra fight because they say they want a democratic state, like Costa Rica for example. They say that if they win, that we will not need to have a ration card anymore, a card that you have to present in order to buy things, which is what we have now. They say we will not have to buy sugar, or oil or soap on the black market at a high price because they are out of it at the government store.

But who knows, maybe the government has wanted to do things differently, has wanted things to be better, but it has been a struggle for them because our debt is so huge. We're stuck; the government has no other alternative. Because of the economy, we don't have spare parts or replacements either, and this just makes things worse. For example, just now a whole harvest of rice was ruined because a threshing machine was broken. The buses break down all the time because we have no parts, and the lines are huge at the stops. It's horrible at the bus stops. So, here we are.

I was born in Chontales, the same area that the Saavedra's are from, Daniel's mother's family. I think Daniel is a good person. In fact, we waited on him and the entire *estado mayor*, or military staff, Daniel, Humberto, and those who have left, such as Edén Pastora. He is still a hero here, Pastora is; I guess he is living now in Costa Rica.

I remember that occasion very well, because I was also battling with my alcohol problem at the same time. I had just come back on the job and wanted to do everything perfectly, and who should come in but Daniel and his group. It was a real shame what happened to me around that time, and a pure coincidence. I was arrested because I was drunk. The terrible part was that I got drunk every day; I couldn't seem to get control of my problem. The police picked me up and I had to stay at the jail. I don't recommend it to anyone, not my worst enemy; it's terrible, they don't even have any hygienic services. Three days was enough for a lifetime because it is so *feo*, or awful, there, and everyone looks down on you if you have been thrown in jail as a drunk. Even though I was from good, decent people, and I had a respectable job working in a restaurant, still I was behaving like a nobody, and I was treated that way.

Then I went back to work. When the government came to dinner, I had two feelings: I felt very important attending to the leaders, even though it was mandatory for us, I still considered this something really special; but I also was very tense and uncomfortable because I wanted to do everything just right, especially considering my own personal struggle that was going on. And you know, not just anyone can be a good waiter; it is very delicate job. At any rate, I took the orders of every one of them. The one who was the calmest and kindest was Daniel. He stopped to chat with us; he came in to the kitchen to talk, and we all loved him. He liked us and I, personally, liked serving him. I was both proud and uncomfortable. The thing was that I really felt the pressure to show them that I could do a good job, but the government people kept moving around, visiting the kitchen, talking with the staff, and I had to keep track of where they were and make sure they were served properly.

I don't want to work for the government; since the revolution, I have only worked for private institutions. I like the little extra independence you have, and maybe more flexible hours. I like that freedom. Our union, of hotel and restaurant employees, is associated with the government though. It's good because it offers us protection. We always have had unions, but before it was different, the owner could run you off whenever he wanted because he had the power. Now, things like that are discussed by the union, which will want to know why the owner wants to fire that employee. Before, you didn't have any security. Now, since I am no longer working in restaurants or bars, I don't have too much to do with the union. I'm just working at my home and at parties at other people's homes. I think that my new work has helped me deal with my alcohol problem.

I work very hard for my four kids. The best thing I can do for them is see that they are educated *para que lleguen a ser algo,* so that they can make something of themselves. What is important to Nila is that our children not be workers, so they won't be treated badly. She wants them to be professionals.

I think the most important thing is their education. With their studies behind them, they can find a good career, whatever it may be, and later they will say, *"Mi padre me dejó esto,"* that is, "My father left me this", because it shows great pride to speak that way of one's father. I wasn't able to say that about my father who died when I was so young, and my family was dirt poor with no means to keep us all there at home, much less to educate any of us. There are opportunities now that were not available then, and as long as I am alive, I want to work so that my children can improve themselves.

23 Adán Torres (b. 1919 ?)

". . . I am a repair artist. You name it, I fix it. I am one of the very few people these days who can do expert repairs."

"Now though, I prefer being in the U.S., things are too bad here. There is plenty of everything there, and nothing of anything here."

Don Adán greeted me at the doorway to his spacious concrete block and corrugated tin repair shop. Inside stood large piles of what looked like old junk, but what I soon learned were very valuable, carefully-sorted spare parts, the best ones dating from the 1972 earthquake. Don Adán proudly took me around the premises, lovingly explaining the history behind everything in his shop, from bailing wire to an enormous vintage juke box that he is still trying to fix. After the tour, he pulled up two heavy wrought iron chairs that he had made himself, and we sat in the doorway to catch the cross breeze while he began to relate his many adventures, including his work in the gold mines and in the lumber industry along the Atlantic Coast.

It was clear from the number of people who stopped by to chat, that don Adán is a beloved figure in the neighborhood. Sought after for his wonderful stories and jokes, repected for his honesty, fine craftsmanship, and his philosophy of life, don Adán is an institution in his barrio. The neighbors will miss him when he and his wife leave for the U.S. to join their children and grandchildren already there.

I was born in Managua, but I have lived all over the country. From the time I was very young, I would go to the fields by myself every day to work and would return home in the evenings. I worked in the gold mines also, in both the Limón mine and the La India mine, as fire stoker, mechanic, blacksmith, and as a driver as well. I did all these things because I was always willing to observe and to learn. I learned everything I know by watching others and picking up on what they do. I hardly went to school at all, not even long enough to learn to read, but I learned mechanics as an apprentice for three years. There they gave me three pesos a month, and if there was enough for food, I ate, if not, I didn't. I just had to stick it out until my next pay.

I washed my clothes myself, because my mama, Juana Torres, was very poor. We were three brothers and two sisters. We grew up with my mama, she took care of us, my papa never lived with us and we hardly ever saw him. Mama sold meat in what was many years ago called the Central Market. She also took in laundry, and that's how she kept us. We began to work very young to help her.

The work in the mines is *bien duro,* really tough. About 70 to 80 kilometers from Managua is where I worked. I was married by then. We were married here in Managua, by both the law and the church. After the mines, I came back here for a while, and then I went to the Atlantic Coast. There I worked transporting lumber with Charlie Freeman, a North American who was just crazy about me. He even wanted to take me to Belize with him because I helped him work the chain saw for cutting trees and preparing them for the trucks. I worked for the tractor operators, I worked loading wood, I also worked on those huge trucks, hauling timber.

I didn't want to go to Belize, but he sure wanted to take me with him. His business was to cut wood for North American companies and for other foreign companies too, but I don't know which ones. The kind of wood we cut for him was mahogany. It grows all along the coast and it is very beautiful. I was in Curinguá, Laguna de Perlas, in El Tablazo. There they had to *presupuestarme,* to "budget" me, the North Americans did, because I was earning too much. I was costing the company too much, because I was such a worker. I was here, there, everywhere working. They'd turn around and they'd see me taking on another task. A job would need doing, and there I would be ready to do it. So they had to set a ceiling and say "You can't earn more than this," but they let me stay there and all. I was an excellent tractor driver, and that was very difficult work too, because along the coast it rains nearly all the time, and it is very muddy. But even though that was the case and lots of the time I couldn't work because of it, they *still* had to *presupuestarme,* because I was such a eager worker.

But then my wife got sick with the flu, and I had to return to Managua. But before I did, I built a landing strip out there on the coast, with the tractor, that's how skilled I was. Yes sir! Before, planes couldn't land, and we would put out large containers for when the mail deliveries would come. The planes would come in as low as they could and throw the mail out the hold. Some of it would land in the containers, but much of it would blow away, or get wet. It was a big improvement having the strip.

I also panned for gold in the rivers there in my free time. We used bamboo poles in which we cut different sized notches. We would drag the sticks in the river, and then beat them against each other so that the water would run out and the little nuggets of gold would lodge in the notches or fall out on the ground. We would gather them up, polish them with quicksilver until they were very shiny, and take them to the market to sell. That kind of gold was excellent and you could use it for many different things, but we sold it for jewelry.

Did you know that I also was a jewelry salesman? Yep, I tell you right now, I've done a little bit of everthing in my time. I also had a salt mine, along the Pacific here, taking salt from the sea. I was in the fishing business too, in Granada, fishing and selling the catch to maintain my children. Six mouths to feed plus my wife and myself. But I worked freely at whatever I wanted to do. I would come and go as I wished and start or quit whatever kind of job I wished.

On the Atlantic Coast, I guess I worked for about eight months, maybe more, it's hard to remember. I earned a very good salary there with the American companies. The jewelry business, well, the way I did that was to make my things here in Nicaragua with a friend, and then take them and sell them just over the border in Honduras. There they bought the medallion necklaces for a store called Maxim's in Honduras. I decided to go to Honduras to sell gold jewelry because, well, one day I went to Honduras just to have a look at what kind of businesses one could carry on there. I bought some fabric to bring back to my family to sell, and I went to the markets there asking about gold and so forth. I noticed that the people in the marketplaces there like to wear gold chains a lot, you know the kind with religious medallions, and I decided, well, I'm going to take advantage of that. I set myself the task of making religious jewelry out of gold to take there and sell to those Hondurans. And that fancy store bought them too. How about that! Ha ha ha!

I took my wares overland via El Paraíso. We would cross over at midnight, but we would get lost in the jungle. It was pitch black, you couldn't see your hand in front of your face. The first time we crossed over, on foot of course, walking all night long, we got lost because we kept following a river. When it turned, we just kept following it, until our feet were killing us and we had to stop; then we realized we had taken a wrong turn. Ufh, we had to cross mountains and mountains and more mountains. It was freezing cold like it can be only in the mountains at night, and I was sweating with the effort, and then I would get chilled, and I was so thirsty. That was too hard a way to make a living, even though those Hondurans loved my gold medallions.

At that time we were living in the north in Ocotal, right there on the Honduran border. Once when we crossed back from one of our night trips, we found our youngest boy badly burned. He had been scalded by a pot of boiling lard that had fallen over on him. Fortunately, I had helped the nuns there at the hospital, because I always do Christian works. I'm always available to help out, and I had repaired many items for the sisters, and helped them build things too. We had no money to pay for hospital care for my son, but the nuns took care of him anyway and he got well. You do something for somebody and they will do something for you, I always say. You're wondering why I go so much from place to place? Well, it's to work, looking for a way to make a living; you have to move around to go where the work is. We were in Ocotal for about four years.

I left Ocotal because the Somocista comandante there had it in for me. I never did anything to him, but I didn't like the regime. I did not like Tacho Somoza one bit, and that Somocista colonel was always trying to get me to say "uncle." Know what I mean? *Me quiso mandar, y a mí no me manda nadie*. He wanted to boss me around, and nobody tells me what to do. So, I said adiós to Colonel Florencio Sevilla, rented a truck, and came back to the capital. My older kids were in Managua with some relatives and compadres, while the youngest ones had been up in Ocotal with my wife and myself.

All our six kids studied here in the Instituto Pedagógico in Managua. They *all* have their secondary school degrees. I am very proud of that. My wife did cooking for other people and I worked so we could have food, clothing and pay tuition. The oldest got a scholarship to Germany, a half scholarship and he went to Frankfurt to study engineering. He's in the U.S. now, in San Bernadino. He's only been there for about three months but he already has a house. He left with his family; the American embassy gave him a visa. He was a Mercedes Benz mechanic here for many years. He never did his military service ; he didn't like the revolution at all. He just didn't like life here anymore after the revolution. He earned very little and was always asking me, *"Papá préstame, préstame,"* "Dad, lend me some money." I don't know if he has found work in the U.S. yet or not. I have a house there in San Bernadino too you know, for when I leave here.

To return to where I left off, from Ocotal I came back to Managua, and worked briefly for a company that sent me to a lot of different places. Then I decided that I didn't want to work for anyone else any more. So I started working as a *bloquero,* making those cement blocks you see all around here. Then I bought a little truck, which even today I use for delivering the blocks. I still do that job; it's been thirty years now, but of course, I leave from time to time for other parts.

For much of the time when our kids were growing up we lived in a tiny house in Nazaret that we rented. We were spending every penny we could earn on our kids' education so we couldn't buy a house or anything like that. Those were lean years, but it was worth the sacrifice. Fortunately, I have a compadre who helped us out when we were out of luck. Of course, I helped him too. Maybe he would give us a little loan, but then I would do favors for him too. That's the only way. I made a little extra money hiring myself out as a driver, using my truck for that as well as for making deliveries of the blocks. I did soldering too because I have a soldering iron, which I found and repaired. That's how we got by.

The children, I made them work as soon as they came home from school. They helped me, working, learning; all the boys worked. They learned how to repair motors like experts. At that time I had in my workshop three old trucks and two broken-down vans which they learned on. But they always wanted to go to the U.S., those boys did. I have a daughter who is a teacher in the States, she's in California too. One son, Ronald, works as a police mechanic in San Bernadino. Another son, Fernando, earns one hundred dollars a day working in a garage! Can you believe that? They are all mechanics; it's a good profession because things always need fixing. But the important thing is that they *all* got their secondary school degrees!

Why and when did they leave? They didn't like the revolution. Well, actually, what they didn't like was the military service. They were afraid they would be called up to service, or that they would be killed in the war, and they emigrated. They lived here with me at the back of my workshop; I feel very separated from them now. I put this house up all by myself; it's a work of art, isn't it? One becomes more ingenious the more one works. Do you like the wrought iron decoration I made?

My clients come, well I'll tell you why they come, it's because I have a system. I never work for just anyone. I only work for big houses, and for people I can trust. They come here to pick me up and take me to look at what needs doing. I always tell them an estimate of what it is going to cost; I do the work, and then they pay me. I never ask for an advance from my clients, and I always charge a fair price. It's important to tell people what you think the repair will cost beforehand. I think honor is an important part of one's work. Because if you work honorably, you have nothing to worry about. Nothing will be poorly done, shoddy, people won't be upset with you, and you will be happy with your product. I've had the same clients for many, many years, they stay with me. They are nearly all private houses, also a few businesses, but almost no passers-by.

Changing the subject, there are about eight or ten persons in wheelchairs that I help take care of. My wife and I make dinner and take it to them. The way I figure it, *Dios me da más para dar,* God gives me more so that I can give. You've got to remember that God is the basis of everything you have, and so you have to give some back for others who aren't as fortunate. These wheelchair people are not friends or clients of mine, no. They are very, very poor people who God has brought into my life to help. They are so poor that sometimes their families can't even afford to bring water to them. So I bring them lunch and a little gift if I can, such as a piece of a bar of soap, but if I can't, I don't. They are so happy with me there, they can hardly wait for my visits. I repair cars, fixtures, appliances for the people in that barrio. I'm trying to see if I can't find an old bus to fix up for them now.

One of the ladies in the wheelchair group, she's dead now although she was young, but one day she was listening to a guy sing some songs on the guitar. She saw that I was enjoying the music, and she said that she was going to learn songs from my era, I'm almost seventy, to sing them for me. This lady weighed a tremendous amount, and it was really hard to lift her into a jeep or van for an outing. Once I hurt myself pretty bad trying to help her into the vehicle, and I got a hernia.

I do all kinds of mechanical work; I've had experience with just about everything in my time. First, I was an apprentice for three years in a repair shop. Then I learned shoemaking in another apprenticeship, although that was tough because the shoemaker also insisted that I be his driver even though I had not yet learned how to drive, but I did it anyway because I needed the work. But before that, I had learned at the hand of a tailor, so I knew about fabrics, patterns, and how to make things so they would fit. Later, I was taught how to drive a tractor, and I also learned the correct way how to be a good chauffeur. Then I went to the mines where I worked in various things because I had so many skills. I was very valuable to the company because I knew how to do so many different jobs.

In order to have a successful workshop like I have here, you have to know your business. You have to know how to repair many different kinds of things, how they work, what their parts are, what they need to be fixed, and how to substitute parts. That's very important nowadays, knowing how to substitute parts, and I have the best selection around. Look at all those toilet bowls, sinks, porcelain fixtures, wires, bolts, nuts, screws, girders, iron frames, bits of scrap metal. The reason I have so much is that I salvaged many excellent things from the earthquake. I took only from the best-constructed buildings because I knew that those items would be valuable later on. That's right, I went around just after the tremors stopped and before the looting started, and I found wonderful hardware, plumbing, appliances, and machine parts, almost all of it American-made.

Now, of course, there are no parts for such things, and people come to me from all over because I have such a good selection. Maybe things are fifteen or twenty years old, or even older, because I don't know how long the businesses and hospitals and other places had these items before the earthquake, but, with a little finagling and ingenuity, we can usually get them to work. People are very fond of me because they are grateful; I have helped them restore something that is very precious to them, maybe for sentimental reasons, but it is very practical too, because there is no way that they can buy a new lamp, say, so they are very thankful that I can fix the wire or repair the connection.

Excuse me just a minute please, here comes a friend. He's going to get me soap at the market so I can wash my clothes, and I will find a nut or a bolt for him. You help me, I help you, that's how it works. But we always pay each other; things work better that way, especially between friends. That friend works in the leather goods store, La Francesa. They have good quality cowhides which they actually work there at the shop, you know. He is a good craftsman, and he knows his trade. But, as for me, I am a repair artist. You name it, I fix it. I am one of very few people these days who can do expert repairs. I am well-known for that, at least that's what people tell me.

They also like the fact that if I can't fix it, I don't charge them for it. I don't believe in telling people that they have to pay for my time. No. If I fix it they pay, if I can't they don't. Of course, that hardly ever happens because I can fix almost anything. The only thing that still has me stumped is that old juke box over there. It's a big, beautiful old thing, look at the bright blue and red colors and the handsome wood trim, but so far, I can't get it to work. It's American you know, and of course we can't get parts for it, plus it is so old that they probably don't make the parts anymore anyway. But I keep the machine right there in full view, as a constant reminder of life's challenges. Would you take my picture standing beside the juke box, so people can see what a fine machine it is? I would give a lot to get it going again.

A long time ago, in 1942 it was, I worked for the highway department driving a tractor to construct the highway. There was lots of other heavy equipment all around, cranes, bulldozers, steamrollers, big dump trucks, that was very valuable. The boss ordered work to start when I arrived and to stop when I left for the day because he knew that he could trust me. He said, "No machine even moves until don Adán gets here." See, the thing was that all that machinery used lots of gasoline and oil, and the workers would come up and steal those things, remove seats, steering wheels, strip the vehicles of whatever pieces they could carry and go sell them. Then work would be halted because the machines wouldn't run. And he knew that I would never allow theft. I tell you, people who steal, they "eat it all up," and then they come back for more; they are never "full," do you understand? They just keep on stealing.

Life under the Somozas for us, well, I already mentioned that I didn't like the regime of Tacho at all, because they would just take people prisoner for no reason at all, just like that! They thought that they could do whatever they wanted to us, and they did. Once they even took me prisoner in Ocotal, remember that colonel I told you about? Well, he put me under house arrest, just because he had it in for me. I couldn't even leave my own house. All I said was that it was wrong to *matar a la gente por puro gusto,* to kill people just for the fun of it. At least that's how I came to learn to read a little, being stuck there in the house with nothing to do and no place to go.

Then I went to Costa Rica, Honduras, Guatemala, in order to stay out of the way of the guardia. I managed to scrape together the two hundred dollars they required for the deposit that you had to make in order to leave the country, and I hightailed it to Costa Rica, where I stayed for a while. Later on, I had to pay a *montón de reales,* a pile of money, in Honduras in order to cross over to Guatemala. I worked here and there as a mechanic, and since *no me meto con nadie,* I don't go looking for trouble, nobody bothered me. I just did my work and left politics alone. It's bad to get involved in politics because it's so up and down, one day these people are in power, and another day another group. If you stay with one group, you may get killed and all for nothing, because the next day some other bunch is in charge. It doesn't make any sense to me.

I have had very nice things happen to me, though. People are basically good. Once I had a beautiful vegetable garden in a valley with a river nearby. I grew beautiful crops, big, red tomatoes, sweet onions, everything. I would go to the highway to sell my produce and make a few extra *reales.* Once, I had a fever, and I was tired and weak, so I lay down to sleep along the side of the highway. It was about 6:00 p. m., and then this guy passed by in his jeep. He saw that I was sick and he took me to Managua to see a doctor.

Another time I wasn't so lucky though. You know, I've told you how I move around a lot, and how I like to go places. Well, one time I was coming back from Masaya about 2:00 a. m., and I saw some guys, turns out they were millionaires, lying there on the bridge, all beaten up. At that particular time, I had a big old Buick and a driver; I was doing pretty well for myself during that brief period. Anyway, I told the driver to stop because I saw a guy lying there unconscious. Then I saw two revolvers, another guy out cold, a bag of money, and then another guy who was knocked out. Three men in all. One of the people with me, when he saw the situation, he said, "Let's kill them, because I owe a lot of money and this would help me out of it." "No, hombre," I told him. I stopped and put those men in the car and told the driver to take them to the hospital. When we got there, I told the driver to guard the car while I went inside, and that if the guardia came to steal the car, just to do the best he could to convince them not to take it.

The three guys who had been beaten up recovered. I turned over the money and the revolvers about 3:00 a.m. Shortly after, the family of the injured men came to my house to ask me who I was; it turns out one of the victims was some kind of government minister real high up. The family told me that there aren't many people around like me, and that anyone else would've taken the money. But they didn't offer me any reward or even a thanks either. It was like I was kind of stupid for not having taken the money and left the men there beaten up on the bridge. But, what's the point? You can't take it with you; the gold dust slips through your fingers when you die.

My work and Julio Martínez have been the most important influences in my life. Julio is an entrepreneur from here. He started out as a coachman; then he opened a small spare parts shop. It grew into a bigger shop, and pretty soon he had the biggest parts and repair place in Nicaragua. I mean, he had everything, every spare part you could even imagine. It was unbelievable! He was very intelligent. Do you know he even had a representative in the U.S.! Who knows what all else he had. One day he says to me, "Adán," he says, "this is your house, and you have unlimited credit here." That was a big break for me, because then I started buying tons of things on credit from him. I would just sign my name, and then I would sell those items when I just didn't have any cash. He extended his hand to me a number of times when I needed help for my family.

He was very elegant too, and dressed beautifully. I could tell how fine his suits were because I learned how to spot good fabrics and high quality clothing when I worked for that tailor. And don Julio owned some repair shops that were *grandisisisisimos*, huge, enormous, bigger than you can imagine! What a successful man! And he did it by being a good person and not cheating anyone. Do you know he even worked together with his workers in partnership? That means that if something costs ten dollars, then five are for him and five for his worker, split fifty-fifty.

Another great influence was in the mines, the people there helped me a whole lot. The thing is that they could see how dedicated I was to working, and that made a big difference. Once, my boss, that was Charlie Freeman, gave me more money than he should have because I was such a good worker. The work in the mines was very difficult; it's the hardest work I have ever done. Sometimes I had to work in the wells repairing the water pumps. The mines were so deep that they had to have pumps to get the water out. Since the wells were down incredibly far underground, repairs were very costly.

What they did was to put long air hoses down under the ground so that you could spend more time down there in the hole, the well, but it was asphyxiating work because there was almost no air down there. And it was hot as a blast furnace. Outside, you would think it was so hot that you couldn't stand it; then you would descend into the blazing hole. When you finally came up to the outside again, it felt freezing cold to you. Yes, it was very hard. That was an eight-hour a day job, but you couldn't stay down there eight hours or you would suffocate, and also you sweat so much, it just pours off you. They had it so that you were three hours in the mine, and three hours out, and so forth. But that was a real experience, going down so deep. You think that each time will be your last because the hoist will break, or the earth will cave in, or the floor will flood.

You know, there's another thing I would like to tell you about; it happened to me in Curinguá, on the coast. I was there alone, and in the late afternoons after work in the mines, I was accustomed to pray the Our Father. Every evening, I would pray with a small group, and then we would each go to our little encampment. But one day, doña Nachita, a lady who was always at the meetings with us, did not show up. She had gone to the mountains to attend to someone who was about to have a baby. So I stayed there waiting for doña Nachita, until she was so late that I knew something had happened to her. So, I went to the mountains to look for her. I told everyone where I was going so they would know in case anything happened to me. There was a landing strip there that I had helped build, like I mentioned earlier, and I went over there to where my friend Charlie was. "Charlie," I said, "there's a lady who is lost. Will you lend me your truck so that I can go find her?" "Sure," he said, so I went round and round the countryside looking for her, to the center of the mountain, to the top of the mountain. I even went walking to places where the truck wouldn't go.

Then I came across another guy driving a truck, and he had just found doña Nachita. We knew that it was a miracle that a mountain lion didn't eat her up, because there she was out there in the *mera montaña*, the very wilderness. We took her back, and she was trembling and all from cold and from fright, and we asked her what had happened. She said that she was on her way down from the mountain after assisting her friend, when three men started coming after her. She ran and ran but they caught up with her, grabbed her and dragged her back into the jungle. She managed to free herself and run away, all the while begging to God to help her, before they caught her again. And that's when this other guy and myself showed up.

It's because she prayed that I went in search of her, I'm convinced, and it's because she prayed that the other driver and I found her. That's why I believe that Christ can do anything and everything. Faith is what matters in this life. Now, I don't go to hear mass that much. What I do is I go to church, give my offering, pray to God, and then leave. Every morning when I get up, I pray to God that he give me the day that He wishes. I don't leave the house until I have commended myself to His care for the day. If it's a good day, I pray that I will accept it thankfully; if it's a bad day, likewise.

My children were all brought up to believe that way too. One is an Protestant pastor, the one who is still here. He has many congregations and goes from one to the other making sure that they are running all right. He also repairs televisions. Another good skill he has is that he knows how to repair churches. When they are falling down, he comes in and fixes them like magic. Those monks from Spain would always come and ask him to fix their churches. His denomination is a North American evangelical one, I don't know its name, oh yes, Baptist. I tell you what I really like to listen to is the "700 Club." Wow, what a great program! And Jimmy Swaggart, I like him a lot too, but my favorite is the "700 Club." Those people *tienen una fe bárbara en Dios,* they have a fantastic faith in God. It's very inspirational. Here we don't get the show, but when I was in the U.S. I would get up early every morning to watch it, like I say, especially the "700 Club." I was always disappointed when it wasn't on, because I really liked that program. I asked my kids in the U.S. to send me a magazine or something from the program, so I can keep up with it a little because we don't get it here.

I go to the Catholic church, but it doesn't matter, all Christian churches lead us to Jesus Christ. I used to help the church of San Francisco a lot, the one over there in Bolonia. When I had the concrete block factory, I still make concrete blocks some, but then it used to be my main business, and some Catholics arrived, and they asked me if I would help the church with some blocks. And I did. Then some Protestants came and asked for blocks to build their church with too. And I helped them too. That's because all roads lead to Jesus Christ.

Once I was walking down the highway on my way to a little house I had by the sea at that time, and there was a river I had to cross. It was the rainy season and the river was swollen. I looked closer and I saw that at the place where people always forded, there was a body blocking the way. "This is no good," I said to myself, because I knew the reason that that body was there. So I went over to don David's place, he was a young man who had a lot of money, and I said, "don David, please give me a little money so that I may buy a small plot of land to make a little cemetery here."

You see, there was no place nearby for the people to bury their dead. They had to walk a long way carrying the body and go down to the cemetery by the sea. But in the rainy season it would flood and they couldn't cross the river on the way. So, they would have to wait until the rains stopped before continuing their procession. It was clear to me that these people needed a convenient place to be buried, so that's why I asked don David for the money. He gave it to me, and now there is a nice cemetery with a large statue of Christ.

I have seen so many things in my life, and now we are preparing to leave for the U.S., going to start a new life there as an old man. I will miss everyone and everything here, but we are just too far away from our family and from our grandchildren. What if we get sick, or they get sick, with some of us here, some of us there? Distance causes a lot of problems. A united family is a very important thing, and we are spread all over the place. *No sirve,* it's no good, we should be together. That's why we are going.

Once we visited for seven months. That's when I discovered the 700 Club. We are waiting for my wife to get her residency now, I just got mine. That means that I can go and come when I want, though this is a permanent move for us. I already feel a little like a North American you know, because I respect the law, and North Americans are very law-abiding. Also, I am a hard worker, and North Americans are hard workers too. So, I figure that a hard-working person who respects the law won't have too much trouble getting along in the U. S., right?

I feel pain, of course, on leaving, but I know that it's the right thing to do. I will really miss a young man here that I helped educate; he is a doctor now, and he has been almost like another son to me, treating me so well. I say, what you sow, you shall reap. Now though, I prefer being in the U.S., things are too bad here. There is plenty of everything there and nothing of anything here. We just have to wait for my wife to get her residency and then we're gone for good.

24 Aída Gutiérrez (b. 1969)

". . . I cannot be a Sandinista; that requires a level of commitment that I do not feel. . . . It doesn't take away from the good things that the revolution has done to recognize that it has also failed in many areas."

"I would not say that I am a typical Nicaraguan because I am a very dedicated student; I am burning to learn, and I am very independent in my life and in my thinking."

Her petite frame, tiny hands, and luminous brown eyes make this lovely high school senior appear delicate and vulnerable. That, however, is an erroneous first impression, for Aída is extremely strong and single-minded in her determination to study and make something of herself, come what may. This unusually articulate young woman offers us a student's perspective on secondary education today, on how she and her peers feel about the revolution, and on the values, goals and leisure activities of middle-class youth in Nicaragua. Ms. Gutiérrez's seriousness about the importance of learning and career preparation inform her remarkably coherent and mature testimony.

I am eighteen years old, and I have always lived here in Managua, except for right after the earthquake when we moved to the province of Boaco for a few months. We lived in a few other places around Managua for a while, and then we bought this lot. With the help of my mother's brothers, we put up a house and moved in when I was about seven years old. I like this neighborhood because it is very friendly; I like the atmosphere.

I have six brothers and sisters. My father was married and divorced before he married my mother, and I am from the second marriage. I have a twenty-four-year-old stepsister who works for the government, and a stepbrother who is a military man, a lieutenant. The oldest is working and studying physics at the university, UNAN. My father is an electrical repairman. He learned that trade as an apprentice. Once, he got a job with one of the television stations, and he had the opportunity to travel to the U.S., to Ohio, to take a technical course of some kind.

I have a sixteen-year-old brother, but he is in Cuba now studying. He is in secondary school there, and hopes to be able to stay there to go to the university. He's been there for about three years. But we write and send photographs, and he comes back for vacations. He does get homesick though; for example, after last summer when he came home and visited with friends and family, he did not want to return to Cuba. But we all told him to go back; otherwise, he would have to do his military service and besides, this is his last year of high school.

He is a very good student. Over there they are internal students; they all eat, sleep, and live at the school. I think this is good because it establishes an atmosphere for studying, and it is also good for those who study hard but who maybe don't catch on as quickly as the others. They can get help more easily if they are all living together. It also is a lot more fun. For example, he says that on Sundays they all pool their change together and hop on a bus to the beach, or go visit friends, or go out to eat, or just do whatever they want. But when it's study time they have to study, and he gets grades above 80 all the time. I think that way of doing things is the best way to raise the general level of the student. I never thought much about studying there myself; the idea of studying in Cuba doesn't appeal to me. Going to Cuba was not a goal that my brother had either; it's just that the opportunity for the scholarship came up, and he thought he'd give it a try.

I want to study nursing or odontology, I don't know which yet. There is a big need for people with technical skills. I would study at the polytechnic, as a day student, not an internal student; that's the way it is here. I wish it were internal; I think that has such a big influence on the quality of the student's work. Well, other countries like the U.S. are extremely wealthy and well-provisioned, and here we are working just to brush the dirt off ourselves and get back up.

Plus, another problem here is that they [the Ministry of Education] give students assignments with a political end. For example, they asked us to go to a business and ask questions about the workforce, the kind of capital investment, if it is private, who owns it, what are the means of production, and so on. Then the student adds a preamble, a table of contents, an introduction, a conclusion, and an appendix, and maybe sticks on an index. And that's how we're being prepared to succeed at the university and in life! Big deal! Here we are at the second semester of senior year, and they throw this at us! I would love to do a research paper; I need to learn how to take an issue or a problem, analyze it, gather information, and use my own head to come to my own conclusion. But they want to inculcate the conclusion in us. The assignment is set up so that we verify what they already have in mind.

Don't get me wrong; I believe that the intention is very valid, because we need to learn much more about social and economic issues, about the past and present of our country in order to get ourselves off zero, and even specific topics like the one they assigned are a good idea. But we need to do the actual problem-solving and research work ourselves, and to reason our way to our own conclusions. How will we ever do well in college or in a technical profession where you have to think? And how will we ever help our country progress that way? Students need to learn how to do these things, because, I will tell you something, except for about 20 percent, the students are all mediocre or worse. So I protested, and I told my teacher the reason for my criticism. She agreed, but said that there was nothing that she could do about it, as the program was set by the Ministry of Education. It is part of their plan to develop the student, but it needs revision. What the student needs are guidelines with regard to the process of researching and writing a paper, not having the thinking done for them.

I feel very strongly about this because what we need is *quality;* it is really depressing to see what poor students most of my classmates are. I am an extremely serious student, and it bothers and angers me for the Ministry to give counterproductive assignments like that when the quality of our students is so low. I don't know why the level is so low except for the poor, in many cases desperate, economic conditions that the students live in, and also because of the kinds of families that they come from. For some, education has never been a part of their lives, and for others, they are just too poor to give it much thought. All these things have their influence. There are many factors that build up and close you off from learning; there is not just one isolated reason.

With regard to the quality of the teachers, well, the salary is pathetic in comparison to the work that they do. But there are other problems as well, more from a student's point of view. I was trying to explain to my papa that I've got a big problem in chemistry; I haven't even mastered all the symbols, and I've studied chemistry for one year. I can't really say that I know chemistry because of the turnover of teachers. The first one left to have a baby; they they sent us a substitute from the social sciences. And they want quality! Well I want quality too! Then we called the university to see if they could send someone to help those of us who are serious students, because I really want to learn. I have learned a few chemical formulas, that's all. Our teacher did not come back after her three months pregnancy leave because she got a better paying job in business, and she already had another child to support. I don't blame her. There are also problems with the check, sometimes it is delayed or stolen, and teachers have a hard enough time as it is without those added aggravations.

I don't know exactly where teachers are on the pay scale, but I can tell you how the pay system works for some of my teachers, such as my biology teacher. She is department chair of biological sciences, including botany and chemistry. She puts in forty hours a week, a large percentage of which she is in class. She has told us that she earns 260,000 córdobas a month, for coordinating all five years of biology, and the two years of natural sciences! A normal size family can not even eat on that salary.

To give you a comparison, my mother says that the four of us now living at home often spend fifty thousand in three days, just on simple food, nothing fancy. We manage on what we have, but there is nothing left over; I think we are about middle class or so. Of course, we have no car. And you all have cars in the U.S.? Even if teachers there have old cars, at least there are cars available according to one's ability to buy. Here everything is sky high. Listen, a pair of pants, Lee's for example, costs 320,000 córdobas, and that's just Lee's, which is not one of the most expensive, while you have to pay about 250,000 for a pair of shoes.

How do we do it? How do young people try to dress, if not stylishly, at least to have a few nice things? Well, I for example, if I want a new pair of shoes, I tell my papa, and somehow he gets them. I have to get one pair that goes with everything. It's not as if I have the luxury of buying a pair of shoes just to match a dress or a purse. For example, I have these tennis shoes, which I wear practically all the time, even if they are extremely expensive, because they are so comfortable, and I have a pair of good shoes. Same with my clothes, nothing elegant, but sensible. For example, a blouse costs about 150 or 180,000 córdobas, so I just have a few things that I mix and match. If I am going to a ballet or a concert, then I borrow one of my friend's dresses. And for our neighborhood parties, we also borrow each other's clothes. My friends' families are like mine; we are much better off than most people, because we have enough to eat and to wear. I have two outfits, but others do not even have one.

I go to a Franciscan high school, called Madre del Divino Pastor (Mother of the Divine Shepherd). The sisters' building belongs to their order, but the teachers are paid by the state. The nuns have a contract with the Ministry in which the state rents the facilities and pays the employees. Almost all the teachers are lay people; only the director and a few others are nuns. At the elementary level there are more nuns.

The school is about twelve blocks from my house, but I go by bus around 6:30. It's more sociable that way, because I meet my friends and we chat on the way; sometimes I get a ride too. But I never walk because it's too hot. I start classes at 7:00 a.m. and leave at noon; classes are forty-five minutes long. We have eight subjects, but we don't have them all every day. Those we have every day in the fifth, or senior, year are math, biology, and physics. Then we have English, Spanish, physical education, political economy, Nicaraguan history, and religion. Most classes we have three or four times a week.

English class is pretty boring; we are just conjugating verbs and memorizing grammar. Now we are doing the verb "to have"; we are also doing "who," "what," "where," "when." The teacher is pretty good, better than others I have had. For example, the first year I began I had a nun just for the first semester, and then she had to leave to do something for her order, because the congregation was constantly calling on her for renewal and I don't know what else. Then another came and she was a total waste of time for everyone, but we had her for the rest of the first, and all of the second and third years. The teachers are all Nicaraguans. Once last year we had an English teacher from the Atlantic Coast, a good teacher, but he gave us these impossible translations to do, and none of us had any idea even of how to pronounce English sounds because we had always written everything. Our English instruction was very mechanical and monotonous, and the translations were impossible besides. It's not our fault that the teaching is so deficient. We need a different method where the student can ask what things mean and how to say things, so that you can use the language.

We have religion class just once a week. We learn about the history of the order, the founding of the school, about the poor, helping the poor, we learn about the books of the Bible, the Jews, the Protestants, and we read Bible verses.

I don't have many textbooks; I usually work in my own notebook. The only textbook as such that I have now is in political economy. It is by a Russian author, and it is really well done; it tells about all economic systems, including capitalism. It just cost 300 córdobas, which is very cheap. The Spanish and biology texts are pretty good too, and they are written here. I have to say that the books put out by the Ministry of Education are generally quite good and affordable.

This year the Ministry of Education implemented a new plan to encourage technical secondary education from the seventh grade through the eleventh, beginning in the seventh with general notions of mass and volume, the movements of the body, repose, kinesis, in an attempt to overcome our lack of habit, of familiarity, with technical, scientific knowledge. The idea is to unite theory and practice from the beginning, and I see in books that they do this in other countries. We are so underdeveloped that we have not been able to do these things before; but now we are all trying to get up from the bottom where we have been for so long. For the current group of students, this is a big adjustment, for which most are not prepared. But little by little, we will see results.

We have one laboratory now, but it would make you cry. I still haven't looked through a microscope; there is one, but it is so rudimentary that it does not amplify. Nor have I used acid or magnesium in chemistry, or done *any* experiments in chemistry in fact. Our school has very limited funds, and we have nothing that we need in order to carry out lab work in the sciences. There are a few schools that have equipment; the difference is that our high school is not totally a state school because our building belongs to the order, and the private schools have better facilities. For example, they can afford to have laboratories and persons to attend them to take care of the equipment. But I like my school, and I have been going there since the fourth grade.

I would like to study to be a doctor, but the medical program of study is eight years in all, all day long, full time, no outings, no friends; it is such an intensive career, so many years, and you have to pay for books, transportation. The real problem though is my papa: he is already sixty-five years old and he has glaucoma, and already some days he is too tired to work. What if I was halfway through the course and had to stop to go to work because something happened to papa? And I probably wouldn't get a scholarship because, although I need it, there are others who need it more.

I thought that nursing would be a good compromise, because it still would have to do with medicine, but it would be a shorter course of study, and I could be earning a salary before long for when the time comes for me to help out. I really want to do something in the health area, because I see such a great need, and there are such abuses by medical personnel. For example, when a nurse arrives at the school to vaccinate us and she treats us badly, rudely. If she would just say a kind word, that would make everyone feel so much better; that's especially important for a nurse because they are supposed to try to make people feel more comfortable.

In my spare time I just fool around with my friends. We play games such as volleyball, or go to the movies, especially action movies from the U.S. I have a friend who has a BetaMax, and that is a wonderful form of entertainment, because we get together and have a good time without having to spend any money, and we can stay right here in our own homes. But I also go out to parties; we go in groups to fundraisers at school, for example. Sometimes we also have a raffle to raise funds, or to help people with the tuition, which costs 1,000 córdobas a month, very minimal.

Many more girls than boys go to my school, partly because it is a religious school, and partly because of the military service. For example, this year in my section there are only five boys, and there are only seven in the whole graduating class, as compared to forty-nine girls. Some friends' parents take them out of school their senior year in order to avoid the military service, and they leave the country. But the majority stay here and do their service. You're not safe even if you are already at the university. Say you are in the first year; they still take you. But they try not to take you if you are in the third or fourth year, so that you can finish.

We don't actually have any clubs as such at school. We have a volleyball team, which I am on, and we train and go to matches together. But athletic, interest, or political clubs like you have in the U.S., we do not have here. That would be very nice. We have our groups, but that's just friends who get together and say let's go to the movies, or let's go out to eat, but that is different. We have participated in community activities, such as neighborhood watches, collecting funds for the poor, and humanitarian activities, but that is different also.

We are not that interested in politics, either. Sure, we talk about what is happening, look how ridiculous, what a shame, and so on, but usually in broad strokes, not in detailed discussions. We don't sit down to discuss political issues and concepts, no. Maybe it is because we basically share the same ideas. But if someone comes up and says "I am a Sandinista," that suggests a whole world of things, a big commitment and a level of political seriousness. It means that that person is, or is trying to be, for the revolution, trying to help the trajectory of the revolution. My friends and I, we talk about the government's political measures; we discuss them; we want to know a lot more about economic questions and why there is so much inflation, and why there is so much money and none of it worth anything; about why milk, fuel,everything basic is out of reach. We want to know why the government exports rice and buys cheaper rice to sell to us.

I really cannot define myself as a Sandinista person, but rather as a humanistic one. I can't say that I am apolitical, because that's impossible, nobody is that. But what I do is accept and reject as I see fit. For example, I accept and applaud the good things the revolution has done, especially for the campesinos, the hospitals, recreation centers, housing, almost infinite things that the revolution has done to improve our lot. Nevertheless, it has failed too, and those are the things that I reject. But to say that I'm a Sandinista, not really. Being a Sandinista, that requires a level of commitment that I do not feel. I recognize so many good things, but I am just not convinced; maybe when I am older, who knows? It doesn't take away from the good things that the revolution has done to recognize that it has also failed in many areas.

I would not say that I am a typical Nicaraguan because I am a very dedicated student; I am burning to learn, and I am very independent in my life and in my thinking. Maybe I'm not brilliant, but I am able. These things do make me atypical because the majority, I see them and I say, "I am different from them." I see the good and the bad in things and try to improve them, and that is different too. Where does it come from? I don't see this in either my mother or my father alone, but in the way the whole environment in which I live affects me, the home, the neighborhood, the school, friends, all those things that inform our temperament.

Right now the future is very much on my mind because I am graduating in just two months, God willing. I only have my exams left, and everyone is asking me what am I going to do? If I could study abroad, I would jump at the chance. It's that Nicaragua is so poor; we just don't have the basic things here that everyone else seems to have. And there is so much illness that medical teams have to try to deal with diseases that they are not prepared to treat. I want to continue my studies, become a nurse, have a family, and try to help others as much as possible. I read a book once about Florence Nightingale, who was one of the most exemplary nurses in the world, and I would love to be like her.

Afterword

These life stories speak for themselves, eloquent testimony of what life has been like during an unprecedented time of political and social upheaval and economic stress. Each life is unique; each autobiography, a unique crossing of individual lives with historic forces. But what can we say of the whole? What themes emerge from the mosaic of human lives in revolutionary Nicaragua?

Two things are perfectly clear: 1) the current situation cannot be reduced to easy or comforting black and white absolutes; and 2) the themes all are sobering reminders of the great impact that U. S. policy has had on the course of the revolution and on the lives of ordinary people.

Beyond these broad generalizations, we see a pattern of interwoven motifs. The first is the nature of the Somoza dictatorship, a strange mixture of arbitrariness, cruelty, brutality, corruption, and unpredictability. It was not an impersonal, efficient totalitarian state like that depicted in George Orwell's *1984,* but rather a personal, sometimes inefficient Mafia-like gangster regime in which family, friends, and those who cooperated and kept quiet got along just fine. Indeed, many businessmen, such as engineer Gilberto Cuadra, who received government contracts to help modernize the country, remember the Somoza years as the good old days. By the same token, many working people, such as don Adán Torres or María Morgan, remember wistfully that under Somoza at least they had enough to eat and they could buy shoes for their children.

For those interested in democracy, justice, or social progress however, the dynasty was intolerable, and they ran afoul of the gangsters' rule time and again. Reinaldo Téfel, for example, began participating actively in street demonstrations against Somoza García from the age of twelve, precocious even for a Nicaraguan, and later, in high school, organizing an opposition group that included classmates Ernesto Cardenal, Arturo Cruz, Rafael Córdova Rivas, and Pedro Joaquín Chamorro, among others.

Opposition took other forms as well. Doris María Tijerino, whose political awareness was also unusually precocious, recalls accepting a scholarship to study in the Soviet Union principally because to do so was to reject the fiercely anti-communist Somozas: "If Somoza doesn't like it, I have to believe in it." Others defied the dictatorship by tuning in to communist radio stations, a tactic perhaps initially disconcerting to North American readers, but quite reasonable given the Nicaraguan context. Doña Lidia Saavedra, for example, remembers with pride her husband's defiant act of turning up the volume on the Radio Havana broadcast whenever guardia patrols passed in front of their house. People such as these simply could not play ball with the dictatorship. It is well to remember that there were others, such as doña Guilhermina Fiedler and her family, who were apolitical, yet who were used as innocent pawns, in this case in Somoza García's cynical ploys to curry favor with the U.S. during World War II.

We saw that the paths that brought people to the revolution were very varied, their common denominator being opposition to Somoza and to Somocismo. The most important paths were democratic, socialist, Marxist, nationalist, and Christian. Perhaps the most surprising is the central role that Christians have played in the revolution and in the government itself, with individuals such as Reinaldo Téfel, Miriam Lazo, and Vidaluz Meneses standing out as obvious examples. What makes the Sandinista Revolution different from all others in the twentieth century is its Christian roots. In fact, it is the dual nature, political and religious, of this revolution that is difficult for most North Americans to grasp. The Sandinistas obviously reject the Marxist notion that religion is the opiate of the people. Politics and religion, historically so scrupulously separated in North America, are inextricably entwined in Nicaragua.

In the past, perhaps we could have said, along with the famed Colombian novelist Gabriel García Márquez, that the only difference between liberals and conservatives was the hour they attended mass. However, in Nicaragua today, the differences between the popular church and the traditional church are by no means trivial. Rather, they are so profound as to be unbridgeable at present. The religious schism within the hierarchy has further polarized the political climate as opponents of the Sandinistas tend to embrace the traditional Catholicism of Cardinal Obando y Bravo, while supporters of the government tend to rally around the liberation theology of the Antonio Valdivieso Ecumenical Center and its leading light, Father Uriel Molina.

For some, the popular church represents the coming of the kingdom; people like Sr. Luz Beatriz Arellano feel that they must apply the Gospel to their own social context to bring about social justice. For others, such as Msgr. Mondragón, the new church is the work of the Antichrist, for it undermines the discipline of the church and the authority of the Pope. This split is by no means limited to the Catholic church; it has affected Protestant denominations from mainline to fundamentalist, and it has reached even into the culturally separate Atlantic Coast population.

It is no surprise that in such a profoundly religious culture the seismic jolts from this rupture should reach far and wide. While the majority of Nicaraguans may continue to follow their usual practices, exemplified by doña Lidia Saavedra's worship of her favorite saints, and their centuries-old syncretic folk beliefs, and while others may be seduced by the rapidly growing fundamentalist sects, still the rift is a deep and extremely significant theme of these stories. Two things at least are clear from these autobiographies: 1) the fire-and-brimstone approach of the old Catholic church, with its emphasis on sin and fear, alienated many individuals, including, for example, don César Gómez and Comandante Manuel Calderón; and 2) as Sr. Luz Beatriz pointed out, the message of Christianity can be subversive. Those dictators who wish to remain in power should not allow the Bible to be interpreted by ordinary people, such as the young campesino Juvencio Salgado. That is the lesson of the base communities and, to a large extent, of the delegates of the word of the 1970s, a lesson that Somoza failed to heed when he dismissed Christian study groups as unimportant.

A related theme is the importance of ideas, something also consistently belittled by the Somozas, who thought only in terms of the carrot, promises or favors to quieten or buy off the opposition, and the stick, exile or torture by their goon squads. They never regarded ideas as having any power of their own. Thus, they were unprepared for the powerful effects of the Catholic social thinkers on Téfel's generation; of the works of Marx and Lenin read by the revolutionaries like Maribel Duriez in exile in Mexico; of the Brazilian pacifist priest Dom Helder Câmara, read by Sr. Luz Beatriz at the Sorbonne; of the radical equality espoused by educator Paulo Freire, whose works were read clandestinely by youths like Verónica Cáceres at her conservative high school in Granada; and of the wide-ranging reading of intellectually curious campesinos such as don César. Then there are isolated works that had particular meaning to certain individuals because their reading coincided with critical moments of self and/or social awareness: Miriam Lazo's consciousness-raising treatment of the poem of the gaucho outlaw *Martín Fierro;* Luz Beatriz's timely reading of the book *Rabonni;* and Doris María Tijerino's gift from her mother of Gorki's *La madre,* for example. Thus, books, ranging from the Bible to the *Communist Manifesto,* and ideas, from Christianity to Marxism, have had much to do with the way people in Nicaragua have lived over the past several decades, and, more recently, have tried to shape their social institutions.

These autobiographies have also given us insight into the nature of the Sandinista regime. By nearly all accounts, it is not cruel or brutal; it is not totalitarian, Violeta Chamorro's understandable claims to the contrary notwithstanding; it is not communist ; it is not even very collectivist. It is not Russian; it is not Cuban, but consciously Nicaraguan. It is not even anti-American. In fact, North Americans are generally regarded with great fondness as we have seen, though there is also anger expressed at the U.S. government. One wonders what will become of the friendly attitude toward North Americans a generation from now, when students have graduated from universities in the Soviet Union or Cuba, for everyone it seems has a relative studying in some Soviet bloc country. Perhaps the best thing the United States could do would be to give 1,000 scholarships a year for Nicaraguan youths to come and study here. At this point at least, they would still much rather come to the U.S. than go to the Soviet Union.

The Sandinista government is a mixture of Christianity, nationalism and Marxism tempered by pragmatism. People are free to speak and move about, to organize opposition parties, and to complain loudly about the government. Although there are considerable limitations on civil liberties, and some instances in which the Sandinistas have equated opposition with treason, as Lino Hernández maintains, the extent and accuracy of his claims have been questioned by other human rights groups. However, the two complaints that kept recurring were not about restrictions on individual freedoms; rather, they were about dire economic hardships and compulsory military service. These were by far the two most unpopular features of the government. In the economic realm, pluralism is vitiated by the fact that government marketing boards buy crops for sale and distribution to the people. By the same token, the government is the sole supplier of raw materials to most manufacturers, providing a disincentive to individual enterprise whether by coffee growers or coffee pickers. It is not clear how far the government's rationing scheme is the result of wartime necessities or of marxist policies, but the fact is that the people do not like it at all. In truth, we don't know what the Sandinistas would be like if they had their way, because so far they have not.

Hardship was not at first a main experience of the revolution, though Nicaragua has always been dirt poor. It is impossible to assign blame for the current situation with complete accuracy; certainly, in many areas the Sandinistas have been inept managers and ineffective bureaucrats. However, in all fairness it should be pointed out that their ability to govern under relatively normal conditions is untested. First, the massive exodus of the educated middle class has left a near complete vacuum of talent at the lower and middle managerial levels, to the extent that frustration and incompetence are the norm in what has grown to be an unwieldy state bureaucracy, despite the administrative reorganization of 1988.

Further, much to the Sandinistas' consternation, the great fact of their period in office has been a war that to them, though not to the U. S., is a total war. It has come to consume more than 50 percent of the national budget, and the army of about 40,000 regular troops and 20,000 active militia members drains away individuals sorely needed for economic production. When one adds the extremely effective U.S. policies of trade embargo and of "low intensity warfare," it is easy to see how the economic situation has plummeted to the desperate level. The war has frustrated the Sandinistas' social programs, and it has wrecked their plans for economic growth. It is hard to imagine how, in these circumstances, even experienced and expert managers could have coped.

Whether one faults the U. S. or the Sandinista government, or both, the plain truth is that the shortage of basic foodstuffs, medicines, and spare parts is so severe as to be literally inconceivable to most North Americans. If you have an aspirin in your pocket, you are hailed as a doctor, and if you have the simple ten-cent spring or bolt required to repair the aged printing machine, you are a hero to the press. Meanwhile, the hope of buying a pair of shoes becomes a bizarre fantasy, a hallucination brought on by hunger. Scarcity is an overwhelming theme of the autobiographies we have read.

We can say that the Sandinista government has an egalitarian ideal, in that they have tried to bring about social progress and equality to those most marginalized during the Somoza years, especially the campesino majority. We can also say that they have tried in the areas of cultural development, health, education, social security, and welfare. Indeed, the fact that they are still struggling and achieving in these areas shows that they are priorities in the revolutionary program. As we have seen in various INSSBI programs, such as those for orphans, the elderly, and for the disabled, and in initiatives promoted by the Ministry of Culture, in poetry workshops and folkloric dance for example, the idea is to value that which has been heretofore denigrated, the campesino, the poor, and native culture, and to strengthen a sense of individual identity and of national cultural autonomy.

The generation gap and the government's unsuccessful efforts to close it provide yet another theme. Despite recruitment for the Sandinista Youth, professional Sandinistas such as Maribel Duriez express concern that adolescents now entering the university, and who were only nine or ten years old during the revolution, have only vague memories of the sacrifices made for them and their generation. High school senior Aída Gutiérrez illustrates the validity of this concern. She is dutifully appreciative of the gains brought about by the revolution, though they seem distant to her; however, she, like many others, is sharply critical of the government's heavy-handed attempts to implant ideology through the educational system. Mostly, Aída wants to be able to plan for her future. The government is important only insofar as it is able to deliver the goods for her, jobs, training, services, necessities, but the fact that it is a *Sandinista* government is of little consequence to her.

The theme of family disruption runs through every autobiography. For many reasons, mostly economic necessity, family separation has long been a fact of life in Nicaragua. Childhood is short in poor countries, and fourteen-and fifteen-year-old campesinos have always gone out to find work, for in a premodern world every family member must contribute. Failing that, youths have struck out on their own, like Mauricio Rocha did, even if it has meant sleeping in doorways in the city. Transient fathers too, have always left their families behind, whether to go in search of a living or of the macho ideal of freedom. Even so, the family has always remained as the country's most basic and cohesive social unit.

The new disruption that rends the family fabric is ideological. Brother is separated from brother, wife from husband, child from parents. Never before have families been so bitterly divided over the direction the nation should take, to the extent that the painful split within, say, the Chamorro family, or the Meneses family, is by no means an isolated extreme. Rather, it serves as a representative example of the deep ideological divisions that have occurred within the traditionally close-knit Nicaraguan family at all social levels and in all parts of the country.

Meanwhile, the age-old phenomenon of geographical dislocation continues unabated. Beset by civil wars, foreign invasions, and natural disasters, including the great earthquake of 1972 and the devastating Hurricane Joan in 1988, the Nicaraguan people have had to pull up stakes throughout their history. Now, however, with the massive relocations caused by the contra war and by government policy, the number of wooden shacks of refugee families increases daily. Whether they are campesinos, such as don Ernesto, who have been pushed off their land by the war and are only marking time until the day they can return, or representatives of the distinct Caribbean culture of Bluefields on the Atlantic Coast, completely destroyed by the recent hurricane, they are all suffering the economic and psychological effects of dislocation and loss on a large scale.

Family divisions and geographical uprooting are made more stressful by the fact that in Nicaragua today, almost everyone works nearly all the time. That certainly emerged as a clear, significant theme and complaint. Partly because there is so much to be done and so few trained people to do it, and partly because economic necessity often requires two jobs each for many couples, the workday has stretched to consume virtually all waking hours, leaving little time for oneself or one's family. This observation is true whether we are talking of comandantes like Leticia Herrera, domestic workers like Marlene Rocha, professors like Verónica Cáceres, elementary schoolteachers like Nubia Gómez, government officials like Vidaluz Meneses, or medical workers like Dr. Ariel Durán. Grandmothers and older siblings play an extremely important role today, for now, more than ever, they are the ones caring for the children while parents put in long hours at work, supporting or opposing the revolution, or simply trying to get by.

The revolution has been hard on families but it has played an important role in heightening the consciousness of Nicaraguan women generally, and in bringing concrete gains in their status. The Nicaraguan woman has always been strong and independent in certain circumstances. Clearly, in most of these stories it is the mother who has formed these individuals, instructed them about the world, and helped shape their values and goals. Dr. Ariel Durán credits his mother with being his greatest influence in becoming a doctor; Doris María Tijerino admired her mother's reading, incipient feminism, and advanced political ideas; Manuel Calderón, who refers affectionately to his mother as *mita,* praises her for pushing him to excel and for giving him his strong sense of right and wrong. Doña Lidia, in her role as mother, fought tenaciously and fearlessly for improved conditions for her sons when they were prisoners, and she traveled faithfully to visit and to protest under all circumstances. Then there is the illiterate campesina doña Carmen. Who can fail to be impressed at her courage in traveling around the interior, oblivious to the dangers, in search of her son Oscar; her blunt face-to-face complaint to President Ortega; and her dogged persistence in obtaining a medical discharge for her son despite shocking bureaucratic obstinance and incompetence?

These are examples of the strength and the power of mothers in Hispanic, Catholic countries like Nicaragua. It is nearly impossible to refuse a mother's request, especially if she is determined not to give up! However, not all mothers are as stalwart as those described here, and, besides, women have various roles in addition to that of mother. These have been inscribed within a traditional, machista, conservative, Catholic cultural context. The Revolution has called this context into question and opened the opportunity for women to be authors of their own identity. Until recently, women like María Morgan endured beatings from alcoholic husbands because they could not summon the courage to leave. One hopes that María's daughters will not wait twenty years as she did before making such a decision; even better, one hopes that by that time the situation will be much less likely to arise.

The visibly altered situation of women in Nicaragua today has often been measured by the number of feminists in the revolution, such as Doris María Tijerino, or by the growing membership of AMNLAE (the Nicaraguan Women's Association), or by the number of women holding important governmental posts, and these are indeed all significant measures and revolutionary changes. But the subtler, more subversive changes are taking place within the home, where slowly, husbands and wives, like Maribel Duriez and her husband, or Mauricio Rocha and his wife, are creating a partnership based on equality. The woman's growing awareness of her own capabilities is, as Miriam Lazo has pointed out, one of the themes of the revolution, and one whose impact will be felt in future generations.

The growing self-confidence that Nicaraguan women are experiencing is part of the overall gain in self-confidence that I observed in collecting these autobiographies. It is one of the contradictions of complex social movements that positive and negative cross-currents comingle and occasionally cast up some new creation. Whether it is the result of the revolution itself, the hardships that have been borne, or the resilience of the human spirit, the Nicaraguans with whom I have spoken without exception regard themselves very positively, as the equals of anyone, anywhere.

Whether they are disputing another new regulation with some impassive bureaucrat, arguing over a traffic ticket, or waiting in an interminable line for rationed goods, they stand up for themselves. This strong sense of individual identity and self-awareness is an extremely valuable building block for the future.

Closely associated with this clear sense of identity and reinforcing it daily is the extremely *vocal* quality of the Nicaraguan people today. As Reinaldo Téfel has said, "the greatest accomplishment of the revolution is that the people have found their voice." Indeed, the theme that has struck me above all others is the people's articulate, forthright, coherent, and animated self-expression on virtually any and every subject. Whatever the limitations on individual freedoms, this is no police state, and the voices of Violeta Chamorro, Lino Hernández, Gilberto Cuadra, Oswaldo Mondragón, María Morgan, Nubia Gómez, and Adán Torres can be heard along with those of comandantes and boosters for the Sandinistas. However staggering the obstacles, failures, and contradictions of the revolution, there is much hope for a people who have found their voice after so many years of officially imposed silence during the Somoza era. Though it is certainly possible for voices to deteriorate into nothing more than unintelligible babble, or meaningless parroting of a party line, it is also possible for them to join together in constructive conversation. The hope is that both internal and external powers will encourage the latter; the fear is that they will not. In the meantime, the lives of the people we have come to know hang in the precarious balance between hope and fear.

Index